EXTRAORDINARY TENURE

MASSACHUSETTS AND THE MAKING OF THE NATION:

from President Adams to Speaker O'Neill

EXTRAORDINARY TENURE

MASSACHUSETTS AND THE MAKING OF THE NATION:

from President Adams to Speaker O'Neill

NEIL J. SAVAGE

Ambassador Books, Inc.
Worcester • Massachusetts

Visit the author's website at:
www.masspoliticalhistory.com

The Publisher wishes to thank the following organizations for permission to use the images on the cover:

American Antiquarian Society: Map of the Colony of Massachusetts Bay, 1780.
Boston College: Thomas P. O'Neill, Jr.
Massachusetts Historical Society: John Adams (1735-1826). Pastel on paper by Benjamin Blyth, ca. 1766. Dimensions 57.3 x 44.8 cm

Copyright © 2004 Neil J. Savage

Library of Congress Cataloging-in-Publication Data

Savage, Neil J., 1929-
  Extraordinary tenure : Massachusetts and the making of the nation : from President Adams to Speaker O'Neill / by Neil J. Savage.
     p. cm.
  Includes index.
  ISBN 1-929039-25-5 (pbk.)
  1. Politicians--Massachusetts--Biography. 2. Massachusetts--Politics and government. 3. Massachusetts--Biography. 4. United States--Politics and government. I. Title.

  F63.S28 2004
  974.4'009'9--dc22

                                    2004012931

Published in the United States by Ambassador Books, Inc.
91 Prescott Street, Worcester, Massachusetts 01605
(800) 577-0909

Printed in the United States.
For current information about all titles from Ambassador Books, Inc.,
visit our website at: www.ambassadorbooks.com.

To the Peg of my heart

Gratitude

It is my pleasure to thank those people who gave me their time and expertise in the completion of this book.

William Frohlich, former publisher of Northeastern University Press, who first encouraged me to undertake the project. Those who edited and fact checked the manuscript in its various stages: Tom Mulvoy, who added his professionalism as former managing editor of the *Boston Globe*, Bill Hennessey, Barbara Rappaport and Timothy Savage. The staff of the Massachusetts State Library, the staff of the reference desk, Social Sciences, Boston Public Library, the staff of the office of the Clerk of the Massachusetts Senate, in particular Paul Coughlin and Bob Yeager. Representative Michael Rush and his administrative assistant, Michael Pastore, and especially, James Horrigan who has been for many years the very knowledgeable if unofficial historian of the Massachusetts Legislature. Jonathan Cullen who created the book's web-site www.masspoliticalhistory.com. And Claire Campbell, who miraculously transcribed much edited drafts to readable text.

Neil J. Savage
Boston, Massachusetts
July 2004
www.masspoliticalhistory.com

Contents

PREFACE

WHILE IN THE PROCESS OF RESEARCHING THE HISTORY OF THE Massachusetts Legislature, I became increasingly aware of the unusual number of its members who went on to high federal office, elected or appointed. When I more closely examined that aspect of the political history of Massachusetts, I realized that not only from its legislative but also from its educational, business, and literary world, Massachusetts has made a unique contribution to the governance of the United States of America. It has been an extraordinary presence that may be measured as much in the shortness of any gap as in the length of its continuity.

In the near two hundred years from April 30, 1789, when John Adams became the first vice president of the United States, to January 03, 1987, when Thomas P. O'Neill, Jr., laid down the gavel as Speaker of the United States House of Representatives, there have been only nine years when a Massachusetts man or women has not held high federal office. Even during those years the Commonwealth was represented in the United States Senate by men of national repute and influence such as Daniel Webster and Charles Sumner.

Why has that been? Why has a state set at the edge of the continent, lacking in substantial natural resources, small in size and rendered ever less electorally influential as the political and demographic center of the nation moved westward, produced so many of the nation's leaders? Other states have provided more incumbents in specific federal offices—Virginia: presidents and New York: justices of the Supreme Court—but none in more variety or with greater consistency than has the Commonwealth of Massachusetts.

From Adams to O'Neill, four presidents and an equal number of vice presidents have been Massachusetts men, as have eight justices of the Supreme Court. The gavel of the speakership of the U.S. House of Representatives has eight times been in the hands of a son of the Commonwealth—twice as many speakers as from any other state in the Union. In forty presidential administrations, thirty-eight Massachusetts men and two women have fifty times served as cabinet secretaries, and eighty-seven have represented the United States in various diplomatic positions in foreign capitols.

Their politics have been diverse: Federalist and Anti-Federalist, Whig, Democrat-Republican, Free-Soiler, Know-Nothing, Republican and Democrat, liberal and conservative. Their backgrounds have been disparate: theocratic Puritans, aristocratic Yankees, and the progeny of impoverished immigrants. Their motivations varied: Puritan leaders believed they were the Elect of God chosen by Him to see to the welfare, temporal as well as spiritual, of those He had given to their care. Public office was to the Brahmin Yankee an acceptable way to discharge the obligation to public service placed on him by social standing and financial security. To the Irish and the other immigrant groups that rose with them, to seek and serve in public office was to claim a participation in their own governing denied them in the land whence they or their forebears came.

Where, then, lies the common thread that has allowed Massachusetts to weave such influence into the fabric of the nation's political history? My conclusion is that it is the culture: There exists in Massachusetts a political culture that, although certainly present in other states, manifests itself in the Commonwealth to a unique degree. A heritage of political participation inherent in the circumstances of the birth of the Bay Colony, boldly extended by town folk who met in democratic assemblies to see to the governance of local affairs, and nurtured by the early establishment of public grammar schools and a college to train men for service to God and the Commonweal.

It must not be thought that the actions of the progeny of that culture were universally noble or that their accomplishments were always in the best interest of the people's common good. There have also been the cheats and trimmers, the power grabbers and the self-serving. The Puritans were intolerant, the Yankees haughty, and the Irish sometimes naughty.

Yet there can be no question of the truth in the ringing words of Daniel Webster when he defended Massachusetts against its political detractors: "There she is. Behold her, and judge for yourselves. There is her history; the world knows it by heart. The past, at least, is secure."

This book follows the path of the Commonwealth's extraordinary historical influence on the government of the United States by recounting the public lives of those who contributed to it. It makes no judgments, nor does it dwell on private lives except to the extent they may have influenced the public careers of its subjects.

The book is not an academic treatise, nor is it meant to be. Rather, it is written for, and dedicated to, those foot soldiers of participatory democracy who slogged through colonial mud to the meeting house, who distributed broadsheets against whatever they were denouncing on the streets of Boston; to the stamp lickers, envelope stuffers, sign holders, canvassers, poll watchers, and coffee makers who won and lost with the candidate of their choice; political reporters and media commentators; to anyone who ever ran for public office, be he or she winner or loser; and, of course, to the political aficionado—junkies of the culture—of which this Commonwealth can boast a large number.

Neil J. Savage

A Long Journey
the Short Distance

*Puritanism, believing itself quick with the
seed of religious liberty, laid, without knowing
it, the egg of democracy.*
— *James Russell Lowell*

ON THE 29TH OF AUGUST 1629, A GROUP OF 27 MEN OF THE SAME
blood and belief met in a large room of a London town house. The
decision they would be asked to make was so fraught with danger that
at the conclusion of their previous meeting, on July 28, they had been
cautioned to keep it secret lest it be discovered and stopped. At the
conclusion of the August meeting, having duly considered and debated the report of the committee for and the committee against, the
clerk put this proposition to a vote: "As many of yow as desire to haue
the pattent and government of the plantacion to bee transferred to
New England, soe it be done legally, hold vp yor hands. Soe many as
will not, hold vp your hands. Where, by erection of hands, it appears
by general consent . . . that the government & pattent should be settled in New England."

Some months earlier their king, Charles I, had granted these religious dissenters—so called Puritans—a royal charter styled: "The
Governor and Company of the Massachusetts Bay in New England."
It was this document that the Puritan leaders of the venture had voted
to take with them over the vast and often turbulent sea to a land they
did not know. Their decision was a bold one, for royal charters were
supposed to remain in England, available to the king's men for inspection and enforcement of its terms. The Puritans' transporting of their
purloined "patent" to the new world was to have a profound effect on

their posterity, much to do with the fate of English America, and by extension, the history of the world.

Royal charters created commercial companies managed by entrepreneurs who had been given the right to settle lands, to fish and mine, to harvest timber, and to engage in trade. The proprietors of the enterprise were given powers of government sufficient to see to the peace and good order of the settlers. In the case of the Massachusetts Bay Charter, the powers granted were broad indeed.

The basic governing body was made up of the "freemen" of the Company, those who owned stock in it or provided some needed skill, such as a carpenter or stave maker. From their number the freemen would elect 18 "assistants," and from the assistants, a governor and deputy governor. The executive, judicial, and legislative powers rested in these three groups. When sitting together as the "Great and General Court" they were empowered to "make all laws and issue all orders." Two restrictions were written into the charter to maintain control of the colonial government in the hands of the king and his Privy Council. Any law passed by the colonial legislature had to be, within three years of its enactment, sent to the Privy Council for acceptance or rejection, and all Englishmen in Massachusetts were to have the same right of appeal to the king from decisions of the colonial courts as did their brothers from courts in England.

There had been opposition on the part of some of King Charles's advisers to the granting of such a charter to the Puritans, born of an apprehension that the brethren were more intent on setting up a sovereignty of their own where they could worship their God as they believed He wished them to, than they were in catching fish and growing corn.

Time proved the doubters right. For the next half century, until their charter was taken from them in 1684, and through the ensuing years as a royal province, those who governed Massachusetts by guile and boldness, temporary retreat and cautious advance, sworn affection for their royal liege and abuse of his minister, stood their ground. Even in the years of great royal pressure, Massachusetts became as sovereign a government as existed in the royal realm. And never once of its own volition did the new government send to England a law to be approved or a legal action to be appealed.

While the General Court was waging its protracted war against the king and Parliament, it was itself beset by those whom it governed. The people defeated attempts to weaken the power of the freemen, saw to the extension of the franchise, and refused to pay for a fort, the cost of which had not been voted on by their freemen on grounds of the nullity of taxation without representation. Much to the consternation of their leaders, the colonists began to meet among themselves to decide issues of local importance and to elect minor officials. While a republic, for which they could find biblical justification, was desirable in the eyes of the Puritan leaders, a democracy, with its elements of divisiveness and individualism, was surely the work of the devil.

The people's move toward democracy and the government's toward republic had, in the words of Edmund Burke, created in Massachusetts a place where "the greater part of the people is composed of a substantial yeomanry, who cultivate their own freeholds, without a dependence upon any but providence and their own industry. . . . The people by their being generally freeholders, and by their form of government, have a very free, bold, and republican spirit. In no part of the world are the ordinary sort so independent. . . ."

The attitude of the people toward both English authority and their own government was succinctly summed up by one (perhaps the best) royal governor, Thomas Pownall, when he was departing the colony in 1760. The citizens of the Bay Colony, Pownall wrote a friend in England, were "light, mobile, [of an] unstable turn of mind [that] caused them to turn against the legislature and easily against me. If . . . any troublesome demagogue in their town meeting should oppose it [legislation] the representative will almost fear to say that his soul is his own."

That vexatious trend of independent thinking was, almost from the beginning days of the Colony, fomented by education. On October 28, 1636, the General Court agreed to give 400 pounds "towards a schoale or colledge," subsequently named for one of its early benefactors, John Harvard. The purpose of the institution was to train young men for service "to God and Commonwealth."

In 1647, the General Court took a further step that was to greatly influence Massachusetts political culture by leavening the mix of independent spirit in the legislature and participatory politics in the town meeting with the potent yeast of a literate citizenship. The order stated that "every towneship having 50 householders" was to appoint a schoolmaster "to teach all such children as shall resort to him to write & reade," and if there are "100 families or householders, they shall set up a grammer schoole."

The State of Massachusetts Bay

On September 17, 1776, eighteen months after the first volley of the American Revolution had been let loose at Lexington and Concord, the General Court passed a resolution decreeing that the next elected House of Deputies (Representatives) be empowered to adopt a form of government "for the State of Massachusetts Bay." A committee to see to the task, consisting of members of the Governor's Council and House of Deputies, was appointed the following May. The draft was submitted to the voters on February 28, 1778, and in March it was soundly rejected.

For too many years and at too great a cost, in their town meetings and legislatures, against kings and crown governors, the people of Massachusetts had sought the rights and liberties they considered their due: too many years and too many struggles to now accept a government not of their own making. Chastened by the overwhelming rejection of the constitution it had drafted, the House, on February 20, 1779, passed and sent off to the clerks of the towns a two-part inquiry to be put to the people: Do they choose to have a constitution or new form of government created? And would they empower their representatives to call a State Convention for that purpose? To both questions the response was emphatically yes.

Thus instructed by the people, the House of Deputies passed a resolve on June 17 summoning them to meet in their various towns and elect delegates to a constitutional convention to be convened in Cambridge on September 1. On March 2, 1780, having worked on it for six months, the convention issued a proposed constitution and submitted it to the voters. The document was debated in minute detail and at great length, with some town meeting members going over each section clause by clause. Never before, and seldom since, have a people been so thoroughly consulted on just how and by whom they were to be governed.

The counting of the returns from the several towns on the question of adoption began in the Brattle Street Church in Boston on June 7. On the 14th, the committee appointed for that purpose reported: "The people of the State of Massachusetts Bay have accepted the Constitution as it stands, in printed form submitted to the people for their revisions."

On October 25, 1780, in the State House, the Honorable John Hancock having been sworn as governor, the Messenger to the General Court, William Baker, in the stentorian voice reserved for such solemn moments, shouted out for the first time: *God save the Commonwealth!*

The Massachusetts General Court which had first assembled at the hastily built house of Governor John Winthrop on King (now State) Street on October 19, 1630, as the governing body of a royal colony, 150 years later almost to the day, just a few score steps up the street, convened as the government of a constitutional republic—the independent Commonwealth of Massachusetts. The traverse the people of Massachusetts had taken from being subjects of a king to being citizens of a republic took them along a road little traveled and scarcely marked. In their town meetings and in their legislature, in the autonomy of the government they had fashioned from a purloined charter, in their defiance, under their God, with their blood, they gave birth to and nurtured not only a government but a culture: a political culture that held the doing of the people's business—the public life—in high esteem, and that called upon the governed for a vigilant participation in their own governance.

PART I

Beyond Revolution

*Our new Constitution is now established, and has
an appearance that promises permanency.*
   — *Benjamin Franklin, November 11, 1789*

IN HIS *OXFORD HISTORY OF THE UNITED STATES*, SAMUEL ELIOT
Morison quotes from an interview by Judge Mellen Champerlain conducted in 1842 with an 89-year-old veteran of the battle of Concord.
After exhausting all possible reasons why the old man had taken up
arms against the mother country, in defiance of the Stamp Act and the
philosophical ruminations of John Locke concerning the eternal principles of liberty, the judge had his curiosity satisfied by the old farmer:
"Young man, what we meant in going for those Redcoats was this: *We
always had governed ourselves, and we always meant to. They didn't mean
we should.*"

Raising a rebellion is one thing, launching a nation quite another,
and many have faltered between gun and government. The daunting
task of nurturing the embryonic American republic began on April 30,
1789, on the balcony of Federal Hall at the corner of Broad and Wall
Streets, New York City, when Mr. George Washington of Virginia,
dressed in a plain brown suit of American cloth, was sworn in as
President of the United States.

The uniqueness of Washington's initial term as president was not
only that he was the first to hold the office, but in the office itself. There
existed, after all, models for the new nation's judiciary in the English and
colonial courts, and its legislature was, to a great extent, modeled after

the Massachusetts Great and General Court. For the nation's chief executive there was no model, for he was neither prime minister chosen by his party, nor hereditary king. The President of the United States was both head of state and head of government elected, albeit indirectly, by the people. Adding to the uniqueness of the position was George Washington the person. The esteem the people held for him was demonstrated on the journey of the savior of the Revolution from his home at Mount Vernon, Virginia, to New York City for his inauguration. More the stuff of the return of a conquering Caesar or the coronation of a king than that of the chief executive of a republic, Washington traveled over beds of strewn roses, under triumphal arches, past maidens dressed all in white singing songs of adulation. Yet, in many ways, no matter how grand and sharp the image George Washington would stamp on the coin of office, its tender among the people and foreign nations would depend on the character and ability of those whom he chose to work with him in his pioneering administration.

In the first 40 years of the Republic, from 1789 to 1829, the executive branch of the government was dominated by the Commonwealths of Massachusetts and Virginia. Four presidents—Washington, Jefferson, Madison and Monroe were from the Old Dominion State and two—the Adams's father and son were from the Bay State. As John Adams had looked south to Virginia to recommend Washington to command the Revolutionary army, the Virginians looked north to Massachusetts for men to help administer the new government.

During his eight years in office, President Washington appointed several Massachusetts men to high office, including William Cushing, the first associate justice of the Supreme Court; Henry Knox, secretary of war; Samuel Osgood, postmaster general; and Timothy Pickering, postmaster general, secretary of war and secretary of state. In the diplomatic field, the president chose Rufus King, minister to the United Kingdom, and John Quincy Adams, in turn minister to the Netherlands, Portugal, and Germany.

In the Congress, Samuel Otis would begin long years of service as Secretary to the Senate, and Theodore Sedgwick, before he played a more significant role as Speaker of the House, would be President Pro Tempore of the U. S. Senate.

CHAPTER I

A Government Functioning

WHEN THE CONGRESS WISHED TO INFORM GEORGE WASHINGTON OF his election as president, they dispatched Charles Thomson of Pennsylvania to the president-elect's home at Mount Vernon. Thomson had been secretary of the Continental Congress from its inception. A noted patriot and in the words of John Adams, "the Sam Adams of Pennsylvania," all of which came to naught in Thomson's campaign to be selected as secretary of the newly convened U.S. Senate. On April 8, 1789, one day after it had selected a doorkeeper and two days after it had achieved its first quorum, the Senate, on the recommendation of Thomson's great admirer, Vice President John Adams, chose Samuel Allyne Otis of Massachusetts to be its secretary.

Samuel Otis was born at Barnstable, Massachusetts, on November 24, 1740, the tenth child of James and Mercy Otis. Among his siblings, Samuel could count James Otis, who had so brilliantly argued against the Writs of Assistance before the Superior Court of Judicature of the Province of Massachusetts Bay in 1761, and Mary Otis Warren, a poet and chronicler of the American Revolution. One of Samuel Otis's children, Harrison Gray Otis, was a leader of the Massachusetts Federalists and the third mayor of Boston (1829-1831) after the town became a city.

Samuel Otis was elected to the Massachusetts House of Representatives in 1776 and busied himself on the committee formed to supply the Continental Army. During the Revolutionary War, he was deputy quartermaster in Washington's Army and as such was heavily criticized for providing inferior clothing to the troops. At the conclusion of the hostilities, Otis again was elected to the Massachusetts House and served as its Speaker in 1784 (as did his son, Harrison Gray Otis, from 1803 to 1805). Samuel Otis was an active member of the historic convention that produced the oldest written constitution still in existence in the world, the Massachusetts state constitution.

Otis served for a quarter of a century as secretary of the U.S. Senate. He was a courtly, urbane man, an unabashed Federalist even as that party began its decline as a national entity during and after the War of 1812. The defeat of John Adams in the election of 1800 saw control of the Senate pass from the Federalists to the Democratic-Republicans. Despite his inability, or lack of desire, to moderate his life-long Federalist convictions, Samuel Otis was retained as secretary and continued in the position during the six succeeding congresses in which the Democratic-Republicans controlled the body.

As the years went by and advancing age took its toll, Otis was subjected to increasing criticism for his handling of his duties. Yet, he remained scrupulous in his tasks, and continued in attendance as he had every day the Senate was in session during his twenty-five year tenure. When Samuel Allyne Otis died on April 22, 1814, at age 73, the government he had so faithfully served for so many years went into a month of mourning, with every member of the Senate, Democratic-Republican and Federalist, wearing a black armband in tribute.

Mr. Justice Cushing

Samuel Adams was once asked how much support existed among the people for the Revolution. He responded, "One third supported it, one third was in opposition and the other third didn't care one way or the other." Unlike Samuel Adams, who rushed at full fury, many prominent Massachusetts men came to the insurrection against their king and Parliament with greater reflection. Of all such men in the pre-Revolutionary province of New England there lived no man with a more impressive pedigree than William Cushing. He was the great-great-grandson of John Cotton, first Unitarian minister at Boston, and William's grandfather and father both served as members of the

Governor's Council and the highest court of the province, the Superior Court of Judicature.

Young William Cushing took his A.B. at Harvard, Class of 1751, taught for a year at the Roxbury Latin School, received an M.A. from Yale in 1753, and a second M.A. at Harvard in 1754. Cushing read the law in the Boston office of the renowned provincial lawyer, Jeremiah Gridley. For a dozen years, Cushing was a probate judge and registrar of deeds in Lincoln County, Maine, where he was often associated with lawyer John Adams as the latter traveled in the Northern Circuit, which was then a part of Massachusetts. In 1772, Cushing succeeded his father as a judge of the Massachusetts Superior Court. He was, as one contemporary put it, "remarkable for the secrecy of his opinions" about the rising tumult about him. In 1774, Judge Cushing was faced with what would be a revealing, if cautious, choice. The General Court decreed that judges of the Superior Court would be paid from the provincial treasury and ordered them not to accept a salary from the Crown. Chief Justice Peter Oliver refused, was impeached and removed. Judge Cushing assented, but with a "reluctance that his taciturnity could not conceal." Cushing's silence concerning things political allowed him to retain the confidence of King George's loyalists without any diminution of his standing among the rebels. Although removed, along with Justices Hutchinson and Browne, from the existing Superior Court by the Revolutionary Council of State in 1775, Cushing was appointed to the new post-Revolution Superior Court at its creation the same year and in 1777 was elevated to chief justice succeeding John Adams, who, being busy elsewhere, never took his place on the bench.

In 1783, in a criminal action at Worcester against a man accused of assault while attempting to repossess a runaway slave, Justice Cushing ruled that the bill of rights in the Massachusetts Constitution of 1780 abolished slavery in the Commonwealth. In that case there existed no conflict between the law and Justice Cushing's personal abhorrence of slavery, a comfortable situation afforded a Massachusetts judge but not the federal judiciary.

In 1789, President Washington called Justice Cushing to New York to sit on the first Supreme Court of the United States as its first associate justice. Cautious, straightforward, and brief, Justice Cushing joined the majority in their important decisions that citizens of one state could bring suit in the Supreme Court against citizens of another and that a duly executed and confirmed treaty with a foreign government became the law of the land.

When the Senate refused to confirm President Washington's appointment of John Rutledge of South Carolina as chief justice of the Supreme Court in 1795, the president substituted the name of Associate Justice Cushing. The following week, in January 1796, before the Senate could act on the nomination, the 64-year-old Cushing, after agonizing over his potential new role, decided his health precluded taking on the additional burden of supervising the Court and declined the appointment. Despite his concern about his health, he continued to serve on the Court until his death 14 years later. William Cushing, the longest serving of President Washington's appointments to the Court, died on September 13, 1810 at age 78 with the dilemma that had always haunted him—how to reconcile the moral evil of the institution of slavery with the tacit sanction given it by the Constitution—remaining as yet unsettled.

Books and Bullets

Profane, expansive, generous and rotund (over 300 pounds) and aided by his stout, interfering and jovial wife Lucy, Henry Knox was said to keep the best table in the Capital during President Washington's Administration. His parents, William Knox and Mary Campbell, were Northern Ireland Scotch-Irish who landed in Boston in 1729. The couple had ten children, all boys, of whom Henry, the seventh, was born in 1750. Mr. Knox was a shipmaster who died in the West Indies in 1762, leaving the 12-year-old Henry as a major supporter of his mother. Young master Knox found work in the bookstore of Wharton and Bowes in Cornhill in Boston town and on his twenty-first birthday opened his own store, The London Book Store.

The success of Knox's store depended greatly on the patronage of English officers stationed in Boston. That economic fact and his marriage in 1774 to Lucy Flucher, daughter of the Royal Secretary of the Province, Thomas Flucher, would seem enough to have precluded any involvement on the part of Knox in the rebel cause, but it did not.

A witness to the Boston Massacre, where he attempted to restrain Captain Preston from firing on the mob, Knox showed an interest in things military that led him to aggressively study military science and engineering. At the outbreak of war, Knox offered his expertise to General Artemas Ward. By November of 1775, he had been commissioned a colonel and put in charge of the Revolutionary Army's artillery.

In May of that year, Ethan Allen defeated the enemy's garrison at Fort Ticonderoga and seized a number of British cannons. With General Washington's encouragement and the help of one of his brothers and other volunteers, Knox managed to drag the ordnance to Boston, where Washington ordered it assembled on Dorchester Heights overlooking the town. British General Gage, fearing siege by the imposing artillery, abandoned Boston, taking with him many of the Anglo-American aristocrats, including Henry Knox's in-laws.

There were few significant battles of the Revolution in which Henry Knox, eventually promoted to the rank of general, did not take part. He was at New York, at Princeton, at Monmouth, and with Washington at Valley Forge. It was Knox who directed Washington's troops in their crossing of the Delaware to Trenton. Washington considered Knox the most valuable man on his staff, and when Ducoudray, a French artillery officer, arrived in 1777 expecting to be commander-in-chief of American artillery, Washington would not have it. General Washington informed Congress that Knox was "a man of great military reading, sound judgment, and clear conceptions." In his appraisal of the successful siege of Yorktown, Washington concluded that Knox had so strategically placed the American cannon that "the resources of his genius supplied the deficit of [our] means."

The rough and tumble General Knox and the much more refined General Washington were close friends as were their wives, despite Lucy Knox's notoriety for making social faux pas. An early advocate of the establishment of a military academy, Knox was appointed secretary of war by the Congress in 1785, and continued in the post under appointment of Washington in 1789, thus becoming the first Cabinet secretary in the nation's history. Henry Knox died at age 56, on October 25, 1806, not inappropriately for a man of his appetite, as the result of a chicken bone lodged in his intestines.

Delivering the Mail

After the successful Revolution, a number of patriots who had opposed the governing of the American colonies by King George and the English Parliament, transferred their abhorrence of strong central government to the newly established Republic. Among those who currently and those who eventually served in the federal government was Samuel Osgood, the nation's first postmaster general, confirmed by the first Senate on September 26, 1789.

Osgood, born on February 3, 1744, in Andover, Massachusetts, was of the fifth generation of Osgoods who settled in that town in about 1645. Samuel graduated from Harvard College in 1770, but his ambition to enter the ministry was thwarted by ill health. The young man joined a business with his brother Peter and developed a financial acumen that would in time be of great value to his country.

Samuel Osgood was a captain in the militia at the outbreak of hostilities and eventually rose to the rank of major as aide-de-camp to General Artemas Ward. He was a delegate to the Essex Convention in 1774, to the provincial Congress in 1775, and to the Constitutional Convention in 1779. He was elected to the state Senate in 1780 and took his seat in the Continental Congress in June of 1781. In December of that year, the Congress appointed Osgood a director of the Bank of North America.

Osgood's concern—obsession some of his contemporaries called it—with the evils of centralized power in government and of a ruling aristocracy was manifested in his bitter opposition to the adoption of the proposed federal Constitution. Robert Morris, who individually held so much financial power over the country, was a prime target of Samuel Osgood's democratic wrath. When, much through his own efforts, the U.S. Treasury was reconstituted into a three-man commission in 1784, Osgood, with some helpful machinations of his friend Elbridge Gerry, was appointed one of the commissioners.

By 1789, Osgood was sufficiently reconciled with the new government to solicit President Washington for a Cabinet appointment, and was awarded the postmaster generalship. Recognizing the importance of connecting the Capitol with all parts of the country, Osgood drew up plans for a network of post offices. Congress, however, failed to act on his proposals. When the Capitol was moved from New York City to Philadelphia, Osgood chose to remain with his New York-born wife. Osgood subsequently was elected to the New York Assembly and in 1800 was elevated to Speaker. A founder of the Society for the Establishment of a Free School for the Education of Poor Children, the Public School Society, and a founder of the American Academy of Fine Arts, Samuel Osgood died on August 12, 1813.

Mr. King—of Massachusetts and Other Parts

Men will differ and find comfort in the companionship of those whose differences they share. Almost as soon as the Congress of the United States was confirmed in its right to make law by the ratification of the Constitution, the dream of the more idealistic founding fathers of a republic governed by selfless men with no partisan agenda other than that thought best for the people gave way to reality. In its stead two factions formed, not parties as yet, but groups of representatives and senators whose aspirations for the new nation were alike and whose political philosophies coincided. On the one hand there were the Federalists to whom so much credit for the stability of the new republic must be given. Believers in a strong central government and distrustful of democracy, the Federalists generally supported commercial and financial interests. The lineage of the many and powerful Massachusetts Federalists, transformed by the events of history, might be traced back to the Puritans' idea of hierarchical governance by the Elect of God.

The Democratic-Republicans were the champions of the artisan, of the mechanic, of the farmer, and sometimes but not always, of the immigrant. Alexander Hamilton personified the Federalist; Thomas Jefferson, the Democratic-Republican. The Federalists were strong in the North, the Democratic-Republicans in the South. The Federalists were anglophiles who abhorred the French Revolution. The Democratic-Republicans considered that struggle, at least before its excesses, an extension of America's Revolution.

By the time the 18th century was becoming the 19th, Democratic-Republicanism was on the rise; Federalism was in decline. John Adams was to be the last Federalist president, Theodore Sedgwick its last Speaker of the House. When John Quincy Adams was sworn in in 1824 to the office his father had occupied almost three decades before, it was as a Democratic-Republican, not as a Federalist. The last candidate for president offered by the Federalists was Rufus King, in 1816. Born at Scarboro, Maine (part of Massachusetts) in 1755, Rufus King was educated at Harvard and began the practice of law at Newburyport. A member of the Massachusetts General Court (1783-1785), King, as a delegate to the Continental Congress sitting at Trenton (1784-1787), introduced a resolution forbidding "slavery and involuntary servitude" in the Northwest Territories, a stipulation later incorporated in the Ordinance of 1787.

A great orator in the glory days of the art, Rufus King was an active and influential delegate to the Constitutional Convention, and he signed the Constitution on behalf of Massachusetts. He was quite instrumental in having the Commonwealth ratify the federal constitution at a time when the result of its doing so was by no means certain. On March 30, 1786, King married May Alsop, the only daughter of a wealthy New York merchant, and moved to that city, where he was active with Alexander Hamilton in building the Federalist movement. As a U.S. Senator from New York, King took the lead in 1820 in opposing the Missouri Compromise. In 1826, ill health forced him to leave the post of minister to Great Britain, to which President John Quincy Adams had appointed him the previous year. He died on April 29, 1827.

The First Vice President

Under the Constitution as it was originally written, no distinction was made on the ballots of the electoral college between president and vice president. The person whose name appeared on the greatest number of ballots would be president, the second highest would be vice president. In the new nation's first presidential election, that of 1788, George Washington's name appeared on all 69 ballots, that of John Adams of Massachusetts on 35, the rest were scattered among several candidates. Mr. Adams was thus elected the first vice president of the United States, an office he later disparaged in a letter to his wife Abigail (December 19,

1793), as "... the most insignificant office that ever the invention of man contrived or his imagination conceived. ...." President Washington declined to stand for reelection to a third term in 1796, and when the ballots were counted they showed 71 for John Adams of Massachusetts and 68 for Thomas Jefferson of Virginia. The Federalists had elected their candidate but the peculiarities of the election process thwarted the election of the man they wanted for vice president, Thomas Pinckney of South Carolina. A number of Federalists, especially New Englanders, did not cast their ballot for Pinckney, which resulted in the second highest number of votes going to the Democratic-Republican, Thomas Jefferson; a bit of a setback for President John Adams and a precursor of more serious problems his administration was to encounter.

Mr. Gerry and Mr. Pickering

Etymology has not been kind to the political memory of Elbridge Gerry. The man was much more than the governor of Massachusetts who redrew the lines of senatorial districts to favor his party. It was an effort only partly successful, for while the twisting borders that, or so the story goes, reminded the painter Gilbert Stuart of a salamander resulted in a majority of Democratic-Republican senators, Gerry himself lost the election and was entered forever into the lexicon of American politics the pejorative "gerrymandering."

Small in stature, personable and energetic, and throughout his life a favorite of the ladies, Elbridge Gerry was born in 1744, the third of twelve children of a ship's master sailing out of Marblehead with cargoes of dried cod and returning with Spanish goods and bills of exchange. Young Elbridge inherited and nurtured that fierce independence and stubbornness seemingly endemic to the natives of Marblehead. "Their town's name best describe the lot of them," lamented one Boston merchant. Graduating from Harvard College in 1762, Gerry soon came under the influence of the radical Samuel Adams. To the idealistic young Gerry, rule from England was as much a moral question as a political problem: the British system was corrupt and thus should not survive; America was pure, and must prevail.

An active revolutionary, Elbridge Gerry was among those the British hoped to arrest when they set out for Lexington and Concord from

Boston on April 18, 1775. Warned of their approach by one of the many patriot spies along the road, Gerry eluded capture by lying flat on his stomach amid the stubs of a cornfield.

One of only six given the opportunity to put his name to both the Declaration of Independence and the Constitution of the United States, Gerry signed the former but initially refused to subscribe the latter (although he eventually did) on the grounds that, as originally drawn, it failed to provide sufficient protection for the liberties of the people—a bill of rights.

Unlike Gerry, who embraced it enthusiastically, Timothy Pickering, his contemporary in neighboring Salem, came reluctantly to the Revolution. The son of an unremittingly intolerant, abrasive, crusading deacon, young Timothy absorbed the Calvinistic ideal of frugality and hard work. Shy and unsure of himself, Pickering nevertheless, perhaps as much for social acceptance as out of conviction, joined the loyalist Library Society of Salem in 1765, subscribed to its denunciation of the Boston radicals, and refused to oppose the Stamp Act. When Pickering did come to support the Revolutionary movement, he did so with enthusiasm but was severely criticized when, as commander of the Essex County militia, he failed to boldly pursue the retreating British in April of 1775, thus enabling them to escape destruction. It was a failure that weighed heavily during the public life of a man so much given to self-examination and introspection.

Whatever difficulty Pickering may have had in coming to terms with the actuality of armed rebellion, his devotion to the embryonic republic was reflected in a public life of extraordinary length and variety. In order of incumbencies, he was commanding officer of the Essex County Militia during the battles of Lexington and Concord, staff officer with General Washington at Valley Forge, adjutant-general and quarter-master general of the Colonial Army, postmaster-general and secretary of war in the Cabinet of President Washington, and secretary of state under both Washington and Adams.

Elbridge Gerry and Timothy Pickering, born a year apart in the neighboring towns of Marblehead and Salem, would each according to his own convictions render great service to the nation they helped found. And in doing so, become the most bitter of enemies.

Treachery Abounds

For whatever reason—a belief in the doctrine of Cotton Mather that, absent any evil in their public or private lives, officeholders were not subject to removal save for ill health or death; respect for the departing president; to placate those Federalists who did not like him; or just because there existed no precedent for it, President John Adams retained without change the Cabinet members who had served under President Washington. Along with the then secretary of state, Timothy Pickering, the new president also got both Oliver Wolcott, Secretary of the Treasury, James McHenry, who had succeeded Pickering as secretary of war, and three Cabinet members who looked not to the short and stout New Englander, President Adams, as the leader of party and country, but rather to the tall, elegant New Yorker, Alexander Hamilton.

From the day President Adams took office until near the end of his term, he was a victim of the divided loyalty of these three. Whatever was discussed in Cabinet, whatever the president's thoughts or plans, were reported to Hamilton. The seldom reticent Hamilton never failed to respond with his own ideas and directions. That they were often contrary to those of the president to whom the three owed their position and allegiance mattered not.

The major issue President Adams faced when he took office was an inherited one. In 1794, President Washington sent John Jay as a special envoy to Great Britain to try to resolve outstanding differences, among them the harassing of American vessels on the high seas by ships of the British Navy. Ratification of the treaty that bears John Jay's name was debated in secrecy by the U.S. Senate. When its terms finally became known, a public outcry ensued. Southern planters were especially critical because the treaty did not provide for compensation for runaway slaves impressed into the British Navy. Others lamented the lack of any commitment to pay pre-war debts. The French were furious not only because their former ally had not sufficiently consulted them in dealing with a country with which they were at war, but also because the terms would make their shipping more vulnerable to attacks from British men-of-war released from American duty. In retaliation, the French Directory (the coalition then in power in France) ordered the seizure of American ships carrying British goods.

Shortly after his inauguration, President Adams held an extraordinary meeting of his Cabinet to address the deteriorating relations with France. The meeting lasted two days and the proceedings were dutifully reported to Hamilton by Secretary of War McHenry. The president and his reluctant Cabinet agreed that war with America's revolutionary hero was to be avoided, so a peace mission was to be formed and sent to Paris.

Although apparently agreeing with the president in his desire to keep America from war with France and the resulting entanglement in the seemingly perpetual conflict between France and Great Britain, Pickering had another agenda. To him and to the anglophiles among the Massachusetts Federalists—a not insubstantial number—military intervention by America on the side of the English against the French was eminently supportable—and moral. To stand against the siege of the legitimate order in France, Church and Crown, by the ignorant peasantry was surely to do God's work. Pickering and his cohort in the Cabinet urged the president to request appropriations by Congress to raise a substantial army and navy. President Adams declined, promising reconsideration should negotiations fail.

The Senate assented to the president's call for a peace commission and stayed in session awaiting his nominations. Two of the names submitted were both known Federalists: Virginia lawyer John Marshall and Charles Pinckney of South Carolina. The French had previously rejected Pinckney as Washington's minister to France, but the two men were acceptable to the majority Federalist Party (58 to 48 Democratic-Republicans). The nomination of the third member, Elbridge Gerry, Adams's old friend and now also Jefferson's, was a strategy on the part of Adams not only to include a member with Republican leanings, but also to have a man in whom he could place his personal trust. Wolcott, McHenry and Pickering opposed Gerry on political grounds. Pickering also carried intense personal animosity toward Gerry.

In 1795, Wolcott had turned over to then Secretary of War Pickering a packet of correspondence captured by the British, the contents of which in the wrong hands had the potential for creating mischief in America's relations with the French. Some of the letters purported to be between the then secretary of state, Edmund Randolph, and a French diplomat, Joseph Fachet. Giving the broadest and most self-serving interpretation of betrayal on the part of Randolph, Pickering persuaded Washington to confront the secretary of state. Randolph, a distinguished Virginian, insulted that his patriotism should thus be put into question, resigned. After trying and failing to get his next choices to accept the post of secretary of state, the president reluctantly assigned it to Pickering.

To Elbridge Gerry, the perfidiousness of Pickering in the Randolph-Fachet affair was typical of the man: Pickering was an anglophile, an enemy of republican government—and thus of the people. Gerry had urged Adams to dismiss Pickering when Adams became president. Pickering was appalled at Gerry's appointment to the Peace Commission. Not only had Gerry refused to sign the Constitution as originally written, but he also had publicly vilified Pickering and had denigrated him for the service he had rendered his country.

Faced with solid opposition from his Cabinet, Adams withdrew Gerry's name and substituted for it that of the sitting chief justice of the Massachusetts Supreme Judicial Court, Francis Dana. Much to their chagrin, the enemies of the president realized too late that they had been out-maneuvered by a man they constantly scoffed at as politically inept.

At the time of his nomination, Francis Dana was 53 years old and very sickly. A journey to France and the ensuing tension of heady diplomacy was out of the question for Dana, and he declined the nomination. Taking advantage of the Senate's desire to see the peace mission on its way and then to quickly adjourn, Adams resubmitted Gerry's name. Gerry was promptly confirmed. In addition, in a move that was to prove crucial, the president dispatched the ever reliable William Vans Murray as minister to The Hague, a station the French were known to use as a channel of unofficial communication when it suited their purpose. Adams then reassigned his son, John Quincy, from his post as minister to the Netherlands and sent him to Germany, there to wait and listen and inform his father.

The year Elbridge Gerry was to spend in France proved more repugnant to Timothy Pickering and the increasingly strident "war hawks" in the Federalist Party than had Gerry's appointment to the Peace Commission in the first place. The three American commissioners, and Gerry, were early on introduced to the devious state of European diplomacy, or at least as that art was then practiced in France.

On October 18, 1797, while they were sitting together in Gerry's apartment, the commissioners were visited by three men, among them Hottenguer, who were representatives of Monsieur Talleyrand, minister of the French Directory. The Americans were informed that if their government were willing to hand over $250,000, to make a substantial loan to France at a favorable rate, and President Adams were to apologize for remarks in his inaugural address deemed insulting to their country, then negotiations for a settlement of their growing differences could commence.

While Marshall and Pinckney were trying their best to absorb the ramifications of Talleyrand's demeaning proposal, Hottenguer, whom Gerry had met in Boston where the Frenchman had fled to escape a slave uprising in Santo Domingo, managed to get Gerry alone. Monsieur Talleyrand, Hottenguer told Gerry, would be pleased to meet with him, but with him alone, not with the other commissioners. Gerry took the bait and agreed to the clandestine meeting in direct violation of the instructions he had received from the president that the Peace Commission was to do nothing not agreed to by all three.

On October 28, after being stood up several times, Gerry finally met with Talleyrand, who repeated the French demands for a bribe and a loan. Gerry's response was the same as the commissioners had already given: they had not authority to do such things, to which Talleyrand's acerbic reply was: "then get it." Frustrated, Gerry abandoned his promise not to do so and informed Pinckney and Marshall of his meeting with Talleyrand. They were naturally upset at Gerry's betrayal.

At a subsequent meeting with Gerry, Talleyrand miscalculated and, temporarily at least, reunited the divided commission. If the American commissioners would not capitulate to his demands, Talleyrand assured them, then he would go over their heads. There was, he knew, a "French Party" in the United States, and he would set its adherents against the president and his policies. All three commissioners took the threat of a foreign power to interfere in the domestic affairs of their country as an insult to its sovereignty and to its elected leader.

On January 23, 1798, President Adams, foreseeing the possibility that his peace mission might fail and in the light of the increasing toll of French raids on American shipping, called his Cabinet into session to ask their counsel on the questions of preparations for war, an embargo against French shipping, and a possible alliance with Great Britain. McHenry, on behalf of Wolcott and Pickering, dispatched a copy of the Cabinet proceedings to Hamilton and asked his advice.

On March 4, in his capacity as secretary of state, Pickering received a packet of diplomatic dispatches that excited him as much as the Faucet-Randolph letters three years previously. Not only did the communication announce the failure of the Peace Commission, but they also recited the circumstances of the French demand for a bribe. The agitated Pickering, messages in hand, hurried directly to the president's home. War was on his mind when he burst in on Adams; war was what the French wanted, and war was what they shall have. No red-blooded Americans would shrink from their president's call to arms once they had learned of the contempt the French had for America. War it was to be, and an alliance with Great Britain.

In Philadelphia the Congress was in an uproar. Convinced that Adams's peace mission was but a ploy, doomed to failure and used as an excuse for a buildup to war, the Democratic-Republicans demanded release of the dispatches from France. When Adams complied and the extent of the French perfidy became known, the Democratic-Republicans were embarrassed and the Federalists elated, for surely now the people would rally to arms.

On March 19, Adams sent a short message to Congress announcing the failure of the peace mission, his intention to recall the commissioners, and urged passage of the moderate defense measures he had recommended earlier. In New York, Hamilton began to speak of a larger war than the one the president feared. America would seize not only the territories claimed by France in North America, but all colonial lands in South America as well. With their ten-vote majority in the House and eight-vote majority in the Senate, the Federalists removed an obstacle to the commencement of the conflict by declaring null and void America's 1778 Treaty of Cooperation with the French Republic. Both Hamilton and Pickering were, by that juncture, certain they would be able to use their party's congressional majority to place their own rather than Adams's choice as head of the resurgent U.S. Army.

Emboldened by the seeming inevitability of war and with it the downfall of Adams, Timothy Pickering went so far as to openly lobby against an Army commission for the president's son-in-law, William Smith. Smith was refused the commission, a stunning personal rebuke to the president of the United States at the hands of his own party, engineered by his secretary of state.

Believing Hamilton and his associates quite capable of insurrection, opposed by his own Cabinet and subject to the frustration of his foreign policy by Pickering, Adams set his face in Yankee flint. He used Vans Murray and others to let the French know the door to peace was still open. He was convinced that keeping the young nation from entanglement in European conflicts was necessary to its survival. The personal price he would have to pay was just as apparent. The enemies in his own party would destroy the public life he held so dear and had so long pursued.

On April 19, Charles Pinckney left Paris, first to visit his daughter elsewhere in France and then to continue on to America. On the 24th, hurried along by the winds of approaching armed conflict, John Marshall also set sail for home. Gerry, despairing of any further usefulness in Paris, wrote Adams, informing his old friend of the circumstances of his lone negotiations with Talleyrand and suggesting the president send new emissaries if he thought it would be useful. To Marshall and Pinckney the usefulness of their presence in France had ended, the mission terminated by their departure. Talleyrand evidently thought otherwise in the case of Elbridge Gerry.

When the sole remaining commissioner requested his passport he received instead a warning: should Gerry attempt to leave the country, his departure would be seen as breaking off relations between France and America, resulting in a declaration of a state of war between the two.

On May 12, Gerry received notice of his recall from Paris. Talleyrand's reaction to Gerry's latest request for his passport was to point out how wasteful his long months in Paris would be if he should leave without an agreement. It was a mild rebuke and fit in with the more conciliatory tone Gerry had been detecting in the last few of the minister's letters to him.

The truth was that the French had suffered a series of defeats at the hands of the British Navy, and American vessels were having more and more success against French marauders in the Caribbean. In The Hague, Vans Murray was given access to French diplomatic correspondence indicating that a war with America had become less attractive to the French, if indeed it ever had been. Thomas Boylston Adams, another of the president's sons, arrived in Boston—ironically on the *Alexander Hamilton*—carrying a packet of correspondence addressed to others but obviously meant for the eyes of the president. In one of them Talleyrand, using the very words previously used by Adams, gave his assurances that an American plenipotentiary sent to France would be received with all the "respect due the representative of a free, independent and powerful country."

On July 22, Commissioner Gerry was told by Talleyrand that it was not the policy of the French government to condone attacks by its ships on American vessels. A week later, Talleyrand sent word that the Directory would no longer require either a loan or an apology from the president before substantial negotiations leading to a peaceful settlement of outstanding differences could begin. To which the lone remaining commissioner replied that he now had no authority in the matter. In early August 1798, passport finally in hand, Elbridge Gerry left for Le Havre and America.

– ◆ –

On February 18, 1799, a messenger hurried into the chamber of the U.S. Senate, sought out the clerk, and handed him a communication from the president, which the clerk immediately passed to Thomas Jefferson, who was then presiding. Banging his gavel for attention, the bemused vice president read the communication to the body. The event of events [as Jefferson was to later describe it] announced in Adams's letter brought forth great whoops from the Democratic-Republicans and sullen silence from the Federalists.

In the House, the Congressman from Massachusetts, Harrison Gray Otis, among the highest of the high Federalists, was exhorting his fellow members to vote overwhelmingly for legislation to substantially increase the size of the American army in preparation for the coming war. Otis was interrupted by a shout from the door to the House. "The legislation is no longer necessary" declared a colleague as he rushed down the aisle to hand the Speaker a copy of the president's message. The visibly shaken Otis sat down. After the Speaker read the message, the Federalists were so palpably upset he thought it best to adjourn the House and so ordered.

The message was that after receiving reliable indications that he would be accepted by the French government, the president was pleased to nominate the Honorable William Vans Murray as minister of the United States of America to the Republic of France. In the desperation of imminent defeat, Timothy Pickering began systematically leaking to Federalist newspapers presidential documents he believed would embarrass Adams. On the 10th of May, a week after he had stunned McHenry with a vitriolic personal denunciation, and pronounced Wolcott and Pickering as arrogant saboteurs of the peace process and traitors subservient to that bastard and foreigner, Alexander Hamilton, Adams sent a messenger to fetch Pickering. The secretary of state refused to come, sending instead a letter expressing the certainty that Adams would not be reelected and that he, Pickering, felt it his duty to stay in office to salvage as much as he could of the true Federalist foreign policy. Uncertainty existed at the time as to whether or not a president could dismiss a Cabinet member without the consent of the Senate, the body that had confirmed the secretary of state in the first place. That question was forever settled when President Adams sent a message back to Pickering summarily firing him.

After President Adams accepted the resignation of McHenry, his perfidious secretary of war, he appointed one of the two sitting senators from Massachusetts, Samuel Dexter, to the post. When the president, despite the man's disloyalty, gave Secretary of the Treasury Oliver Wolcott a desirable federal post, Dexter succeeded him; and when John Marshall, Adams's choice to succeed Pickering as secretary of state, took his oath as chief justice of the Supreme Court of the United States, Samuel Dexter was made pro-tem secretary of state to see to the swearing in.

In the election of 1800 Adams received 65 electoral votes, his fellow Federalist Thomas Pinckney, 64, with the Democratic-Republicans Thomas Jefferson and Aaron Burr tied at 73. The election of the president devolved to the House of Representatives, which the Federalists still controlled until the seating of the newly elected Democratic-Republican majority. It took the House 36 ballots to decide that between Jefferson and Burr, the former was the lesser evil and would be the next president.

Timothy Pickering lost a bid for election to the House of Representatives but was subsequently elected to the Senate and served there until 1811. A formidable debater, he was the scourge of the Democratic-Republicans during the administrations of Jefferson and Madison. After the death of Hamilton, Pickering became a premier leader in the Federalist Party. Convinced that the interests of commercial states were being ignored, he urged on his fellows the desirability of a peaceful separation of a Northern Confederacy from the Southern states. Elected once again to the House in 1813, Pickering turned his increasingly venomous oratory on the supporters of the War of 1812. Retiring at the close of 14th Congress, Pickering sold his farm at Wenham, Massachusetts, and returned to his native Salem, where he died in 1829 at age 84.

A man of considerable literary talent, Timothy Pickering left an extensive body of insightful writing on the events and leaders of the early years of the United States. An agriculturist of note, he also did much pioneering work in crop rotation, soil fertility, and animal husbandry.

Elbridge Gerry, ostracized by Federalist friends in Boston for his work with Adams, became a perennial candidate of the Democratic-Republicans for governor of Massachusetts, and lost four times before finally being elected to the post in 1810. Although defeated for reelection in the contest that was to give partisan redistricting his name, Gerry was elected as James Madison's vice president. On the way to preside over the Senate on November 23, 1814, Gerry was stricken with hemorrhaging of the lungs and died within hours.

Mr. Speaker

Three times in the history of the United States, both the president and the Speaker of the House of Representatives have been Massachusetts men. The first time was 1799 to 1801 when John Adams was president and Theodore Sedgwick was Speaker of the

House. Despite their common home and political party, the two Bay Staters did not always see eye to eye.

Born in West Hartford, Connecticut on May 9, 1746, and fatherless from age ten, Sedgwick, through the financial sacrifice of an older brother, was sent to Yale in 1761 to prepare for the ministry, an ambition thwarted when young Theodore left the college before graduation for committing what was recorded as "infractions of college discipline." Whatever that was, it was not so bad as to prevent Sedgwick from being awarded his degree in 1772, as a member of the Class of 1765.

The pulpit's loss was the bar's gain. Sedgwick began his law practice in Berkshire County in 1766. It was lawyer Sedgwick, by that time carrying on one of the most lucrative practices in the province, who, without fee, successfully defended the negro slave Elizabeth Freeman Mumbert. Sedgwick argued before Justice William Cushing that slavery had been abolished in Massachusetts upon enactment of its Constitution.

Although active in support of the rights of the colonists, Sedgwick was, as late as May of 1776, wary about independence. A member of the State Senate and of the Massachusetts House, where he was Speaker from 1788 to 1790, Sedgwick was a delegate to the Continental Congress of 1785-1788. Elected to the first and three successive U.S. Congresses, Sedgwick turned down Washington's offer of Secretary of the Treasury after Alexander Hamilton's resignation from the post but did accept election by the Massachusetts Senate to an unexpired term in the U.S. Senate, where he served from 1796 to 1799 and as president pro tempore for a period in 1798.

When Sedgwick's term in the U.S. Senate expired, he returned to the House, where he was elected Speaker in the Sixth Congress (1799-1801). Sedgwick's election as Speaker made him the first of three Massachusetts men who accomplished a legislative distinction now virtually impossible: that of serving as both President Pro-Tempore of the U.S. Senate and Speaker of the House of Representatives.

Sedgwick was a physically imposing man who moved at a slow and considered pace, and thought himself the aristocratic better of most men. He brought to the Speakership a high degree of intelligence, a short temper, and little tolerance for obfuscation and delay. He also helped define an office created under the brief constitutional mandate that "The House of Representatives shall choose their speaker and other officers." The question arose as to whether the Speakership be modeled after that of the British Parliament—a nonpartisan presiding officer whose duty it was to interpret the rules and keep order in the House, or one more akin to that of the Massachusetts General Court, where the holder of the office was more often than not an advocate for his party's political agenda.

Few men in the nation's Capitol at the time of Sedgwick's elevation to the Speakership were more partisan than he. Sedgwick pushed the Federalist agenda with such uncompromising vigor that at the last session of his term as presiding officer, the then Democratic-Republican House refused to accord him the unanimous vote of thanks and commendation that was traditional in civilized legislative bodies. An enemy of Adams, as were many of the high Federalists of Massachusetts, Theodore Sedgwick went so far as to engage the president in a shouting match over the former's policy toward France at a presidential function, and to conspire with others of his convictions in denying the president a second term in office.

When Sedgwick returned to Massachusetts at the end of his congressional career, he was given a lifetime appointment to the Supreme Judicial Court, where he distinguished himself by introducing a new standard of courtesy and decorum.

A trustee of Williams College from its founding and a member of the American Academy of Arts and Sciences, Theodore Sedgwick died while on a visit to Boston on January 24, 1813.

Mr. Jefferson's Massachusetts Men

The election of Thomas Jefferson in 1800 was accompanied by a precipitous decline in the fortunes of the Federalist party. For the first time the Democratic-Republicans would not only hold the White House but control both branches of Congress. The party's control of the national legislature would continue for 24 years, and that of the presidency for 36 years. The fortunes of the Federalists were no less dire in Massachusetts than they were elsewhere, and from the growing ranks of Bay State Democratic-Republicans, Jefferson chose Levi

Lincoln as attorney general and Henry Dearborn to be secretary of war, and sent James Bowdoin off to Spain as U.S. minister.

Levi Lincoln

Born into modest circumstances in Hingham, Massachusetts, in May of 1749, Levi Lincoln was apprenticed as a young man to a local blacksmith. Although this arrangement satisfied Levi's father, other members of the family thought it a waste of potential for such an obviously intelligent boy. Lincoln was allowed to leave his apprenticeship and continue his schooling. He was awarded a degree by Harvard, in the class of 1772.

It was Lincoln, by that time a successful lawyer, who did much of the nitty-gritty and unpopular work of building the Democratic-Republican Party in Federalist Massachusetts. After election to one term in the state House of Representatives and to another in the state Senate, the rise of Lincoln's career on the federal level was meteoric. In less than three months—December 19, 1800, to March 5, 1801—Lincoln was elected to Congress twice and to the U.S. Senate once, and was appointed secretary of state and attorney general of the United States.

Under the terms of the Massachusetts Constitution at the time, if no candidate for state or federal office received a majority of the votes cast, the election would be thrown into the General Court, where the House would nominate and the Senate would elect the winner. Dwight Foster had resigned his seat in the Sixth Congress to serve out the unexpired Senate seat of Samuel Dexter, who left to become secretary of the treasury in the dying days of the Adams administration. Lincoln was chosen on December 19, 1800, to replace Foster, but only after three hotly contested ballots. In the meantime, Lincoln had won the regular election on November 3, 1800, as a Representative to the Seventh Congress. Before he could take his seat in the House, Lincoln was called to Washington to keep warm (for one day) the seat of the secretary of state until the late-arriving secretary designee, James Madison, showed up. That frenetic pace was slowed considerably when President Jefferson appointed Lincoln his attorney general, an office in which Levi Lincoln served for three years, from March 5, 1801 to December 31, 1804.

The office of Attorney General of the United States that Lincoln entered upon had neither the responsibility nor the prestige it enjoys today, and the ever political Lincoln spent much of his time in Washington the same way he had in Boston—building up the fortunes of his Democratic-Republican Party, a quite successful construction immeasurably aided by the judicious spreading of the mortar of federal patronage. So blatant was the dispensation of collectorships-of-the-ports, postmasterships, and judgeships by the nation's chief law enforcement officer, that the newspapers screamed and the (Federalist-leaning) clergy of the Commonwealth denounced Lincoln as a tool of the anticlerical, anarchistic, French bloody-revolution-supporting, slave-holding Jefferson. Levi struck back with an equally vehement denunciation of the interfering clergy, reducing them first to mumbling and eventually to silence.

President Jefferson reluctantly accepted his attorney general's resignation in 1804, and Lincoln returned to Massachusetts, there to see his efforts at party-building rewarded by the election of a Democratic-Republican governor and lieutenant governor (Lincoln himself) in 1807. On September 12, 1810, Justice William Cushing, the last of Washington's appointees to the Supreme Court, died. When he learned of it, Thomas Jefferson is said to have remarked that the death of the Federalist judge was "another circumstance of congratulation." President Madison, presented with the opportunity to have a Democratic-Republican majority on the Court, offered the appointment to Lincoln, who, citing his poor eyesight, declined and lived out the last ten years of his life on his farm in Worcester.

Secretary of War

Henry Dearborn, born in Hampton, New Hampshire, in 1751, was destined to have a military career that would begin in glory and end in disgrace. In April of l775, undeterred by the spring mud and flooded streams, a hard-riding messenger brought the awful and wondrous news of Lexington and Concord to the little town of Northingham Square, New Hampshire. Quickly assembling his troops, Henry Dearborn, town physician and captain of the militia, marched off with 60 troops for Cambridge to be mustered on the common into General

Washington's forming army. In the ensuing struggle, during which he would rise to the rank of major-general, Henry Dearborn fought at Bunker Hill, was taken a prisoner while with General Arnold at Quebec, saw action at Ticonderoga against General Burgoyne, endured the terrible winter at Valley Forge, fought alongside General Sullivan against the Six Nations, and witnessed the British surrender at Yorktown.

Appointed marshal for the District of Maine (now Massachusetts) after the war, Dearborn was elected to the third and fourth Congresses before being appointed by the new president, Jefferson, as secretary of war on March 5, 1801. Dearborn served in that capacity until February of 1809, when he resigned to accept the lucrative post as Collector of the Port of Boston, a political sinecure considered a just reward for such distinguished public service, one that would enable General Dearborn to live out his years without want and in dignity. Unfortunately for both his pocketbook and posterity, another war interfered.

A Most Unfortunate War

In the latter stages of the intermittent and seemingly interminable war with France, Great Britain used its superior navy to prevent American merchants from trading with the British enemy, France. American ports were blocked, ships were seized, and American sailors suspected of being deserters from the harsh discipline and horrid living conditions of the British Navy, were pressed into service. Some British captains were evoking the doctrine "once a subject of the King, always a subject of the King" and were seizing American civilians as well.

The United States adopted a series of counter measures: the Non-Intercourse, Embargo, and Non-Importation Acts. British actions at sea and the American boycott of British trade combined to do much economic harm to both countries, each being the other's major trading partner. By summer of 1811, it had become obvious to President Madison that a sovereign nation such as the United States could no longer tolerate the abuse being meted out by the British Navy. In November, the president called Congress into a special session for the purpose of considering a declaration of war against Great Britain. About the same time, in London, hordes of workmen who were jobless and hungry as the result of falling trade, took to the streets in protest, while merchants and manufacturers in much more orderly fashion petitioned their government for relief.

On June 18, 1812, by a vote of 79 to 40 in the U.S. House, and 19 to 13 in the Senate, Congress declared that a state of war existed between the United States and Great Britain. Congress was unaware at the time that two days previously, on the 16th, His Majesty's government, by Orders in Council, had decreed an end to the blockading of American ports, the seizing of its ships and impressment of its seamen. The daunting task of raising and supplying a military force to fight the coming battles would fall to the man whom President Madison had appointed secretary of war to succeed Henry Dearborn—William Eustis.

William Eustis

William Eustis was a physician by training, as had been his predecessor in the post of secretary of war. Born in Cambridge on June 10, 1753, young William prepared for Harvard at Boston Latin School, and after receiving his degree, studied medicine with Doctor (General) Joseph Warren, before opening a practice in Boston. Unlike Warren, who was fatally injured at Bunker Hill, William Eustis escaped from that battle unscathed. An Anti-Federalist politically and an early and enthusiastic supporter of Jefferson, Eustis served in the General Court for six years and in 1800, in an election indicative of the coming decline of the Massachusetts Federalists, defeated one of that party's most prominent members, Josiah Quincy, for a seat in Congress. Two years later, in a vigorously contested election, Eustis defeated young John Quincy Adams by 59 votes out of the 3,789 cast. ("I had a majority in Boston," Adams would later point out, "but two or three neighboring towns [lately] annexed to the Congressional district and a rainy day lost me the election . . .")

When Eustis arrived at the War Department, he found eight clerks and little else save a pitiful navy and a virtually nonexistent army. He tried his best to improve the situation in the years leading up to the War of 1812, during a time when such a military buildup faced potent political opposition. When the war did come, a great chorus of charges of incompetence, led by Henry Clay, forced Eustis from office, but not from public life. President Madison appointed Eustis minister to Holland, where he served four years.

This "amiable man and efficient politician," as he was described by Edward Channing, served once again in Congress (1820-1823) and again proved an electoral giant killer when he defeated the estimable Harrison Gray Otis (by 4,000 votes out of 65,000) in the gubernatorial contest of 1823. William Eustis died in Roxbury on February 6, 1825, in the former home of the Colonial Governor William Shirley, which Eustis purchased in 1819, and which still stands today.

Major General Henry Dearborn

The British blockade and American countermeasures leading up to the War of 1812 virtually destroyed the New England trading industry. Ships lay idle and rotting, seamen were land-bound, and ships' captains and merchants went bankrupt. The instant that word reached Boston of Congress's declaration of war, all hope for resumption of the lucrative trade with Europe was gone, as was that with the West Indies, both now at the mercy of the mightiest navy in the world.

In July of 1812, U.S. Senator Joseph Varnum and a group of supporters of President Madison and the war, were set upon and beaten as they left a rally in Boston.

Several New England militia confined themselves to guarding their own territory, refusing to join a national service. It was under such circumstances that the corpulent, slow-moving, 61-year-old collector of the Port of Boston, Henry Dearborn, was called back into service as senior Major General of the Army of the United States. Dearborn's assignment was command over the most important theater of war, the Northeast, specifically the territory running from the Niagara River, where it formed part of the Canadian border, to the New England coast.

The general drew up plans for simultaneous attacks against British forces at Montreal, Kingston, Niagara Falls, and Detroit. Militarily sound, the attacks, if successful, would not only give the Americans virtual control of the border between the United States and Canada, but would also negate as far as was possible the effectiveness of British naval forces in the Great Lakes. Delay, however, defeated the general's plan. Returning from his Albany headquarters to Boston, Henry Dearborn spent a great deal of time supervising the construction of coastal defense and recruiting the large force necessary for such an ambitious campaign. The British already had an army and wasted no time in using it to force the surrender of Detroit, and to defeat the Americans at Queenstown. The finally stirring Dearborn, with some six to eight thousand troops, mounted a march to the Canadian border. He got his troops 20 miles north of Plattsburg, New York, where they sat, unwilling to advance farther.

The fortunes of war seemed to turn in Dearborn's favor in the early months of 1813, but even then his victories proved pyrrhic. He captured Kingston (Toronto) but incurred heavy losses. (Dearborn burned the city, an act for which the British gained revenge by subsequently putting the torch to Washington). Dearborn also took Fort George, at the mouth of the Niagara, but in doing so left the American base at Sackett's Harbor so exposed that the British fleet had free rein in attacking it.

On July 6, 1813, in the face of mounting criticism, Secretary of War John Armstrong removed the general from his command. Dearborn's request for a court of inquiry into his actions was ignored by the War Department. Instead he was put in charge of the forces defending New York City. Yet his honorable discharge from the service in June 1815 did not end his public career, nor the controversy surrounding his military career. President Madison's seemingly inexplicable nomination of Henry Dearborn once again to be secretary of war was met with howls of outrage and prompt rejection by the Senate. Having succeeded in denying Dearborn his post, the Senate, in recognition of Dearborn's great service to his country, had the proceedings rejecting his nomination stricken from its records. President Monroe appointed Dearborn as American minister to Portugal in 1822. He served there for two years before returning to his home in Roxbury, where he died on June 6, 1829.

Americans Abroad

Francis Dana

Francis Dana, born in Charlestown in 1743, by the time the cauldron of Boston revolutionary fervor was heating to a boil, was one of the town's most successful lawyers, with a "competent" fortune in land. He was also the father of Richard Henry Dana. Francis Dana was one of those colonists whose grievances against the Crown, while real, were as yet insufficient to justify rebellion. Dana believed that if the patriots' position could be adequately presented and addressed in London, harmony might be restored. In 1774, carrying letters from Josiah Quincy, Dr. Joseph Warren and others, Dana sailed to England on such a mission. For eighteen months he gained access to the most influential men at the King's Court and in Parliament. After unsuccessfully toiling against British intransigence, Dana returned to America in April 1776 convinced that fighting for independence was the only course left to the colonies.

When John Adams was appointed minister plenipotentiary to negotiate peace with England in 1779, Dana accompanied him as the delegation's secretary, and in December of 1780, he was appointed by Congress as minister to Russia at the court of Empress Catherine in St. Petersburg.

Francis Dana's efforts in 1774 and 1775 on behalf of his sponsors to prevent an irreconcilable split between the United Kingdom and the Massachusetts Bay Colony were semi-official, yet they justify counting him as the first American diplomat and the first of an imposing number of Massachusetts men who were to represent their country in foreign lands.

In the Diplomatic Service

The end of the War of 1812 would extract America from military involvement with European nations for the better part of a hundred years, but not from the machinations of that continent's diplomacy. It was a diplomacy, as George William Erving and James Bowdoin were to learn, heavily influenced, even haunted, in the early years of the 19th century by the persona of Napoleon Bonaparte.

George William Erving and James Bowdoin were cousins, ardent Jeffersonians, and Oxford educated—Erving at Oriel College and Bowdoin at Christ Church. Erving, who spent a great many of his mature years in diplomacy, and Bowdoin to whom it was more of an avocation, came to the service of their country from different political inheritances. James Bowdoin was the son of a patriot leader and the second governor of the Commonwealth of Massachusetts, while the elder George Erving, a Tory, fled Boston with his family to Halifax, Nova Scotia, and eventually to England.

Bowdoin's life was that of a wealthy merchant whose conservative instincts proved quite successful in preserving his family's fortune, a significant portion of which benefited the college in Maine that bears his distinguished father's name. James served several terms in the state legislature and on the governor's council and was a delegate to the state convention that ratified the federal Constitution. In November 1804, Jefferson appointed Bowdoin as minister to Spain.

Meanwhile, at his father's urging, in 1790 George Erving returned to the United States where that son of a Tory was able to obtain an introduction to Thomas Jefferson from no less a patriot than Samuel Adams. Young Erving took enthusiastically to Jefferson and Jefferson to him. When the Virginian became president, he offered Erving the post of charge d'affaires in Portugal. Erving declined that post, as he did the position as consul at Tunis. Erving did go to London, however, as an agent looking after the claims and appeals of American sailors.

Despite chronic ill health, Bowdoin sailed for his assignment in Spain in the spring of 1805. At about the same time as Bowdoin was dispatched to Spain, the president transferred Erving from his post in London to the American legation in Madrid as charge d'affaires doing what he could to advance American interests until such time as the minister-designate, his cousin James Bowdoin, should arrive. Those interests consisted mainly in the possibility of the United States acquiring West Florida, the western boundaries of the Louisiana Purchase, and American claims against Spain. Erving did what he could, but relations with Spain had become so difficult that Bowdoin thought it best to delay his arrival in Madrid. Negotiation of the issues was transferred to Paris and thus came under the domination of Napoleon. "The wonder, the dread, and the admiration of Europe," was Bowdoin's evaluation of General Bonaparte in a letter to Jefferson.

James Bowdoin's stay in Paris was neither happy nor productive. He was unable to establish good working relations with his fellow negotiators, including the American ambassador to France, General Armstrong. But even a harmonious legation would not have been sufficient. Bonaparte's foresight, ruthlessness and deceit overwhelmed the baffled Americans. The mission failed, and Bowdoin returned to America in 1808. His cousin was to be more successful in Spain. In 1814, President Madison sent Erving from Copenhagen, where he was special minister dealing with spoliation claims, to Madrid to serve as minister. Erving, who had learned Spanish, waited for two years before he was received by the Spanish government court, but eventually succeeded in negotiating the Treaty of 1819.

James Bowdoin spent his remaining years in improving his estate at Buzzard's Bay, acquiring wealth in the burgeoning wool industry, and engaging in philanthropic activities. He died without issue in 1811, and the residue of his estate passed, after the death of his nephew, James Temple Bowdoin, to Bowdoin College.

Although President Madison stated that he had never had a minister more capable or faithful than Erving, the diplomat did not enjoy the full confidence of Secretary of State John Quincy Adams—not unusual in a relationship with the accomplished but acerbic Adams. For reasons of health and business, Erving resigned from the diplomatic service after completion of the Treaty of 1819. Never having married, he left copies in several places of a will written in his own hand but with no witnesses in attendance, resulting in his considerable wealth being distributed according to the laws of the State of New York, where he died on July 22, 1850.

Mr. Speaker Varnum

In the first two hundred years of the Republic, there have been seven Massachusetts men who traveled from Beacon Hill in Boston to Capitol Hill in Washington to wield the gavel as Speaker of the U.S. House of Representatives. (An eighth, Joseph Varnum, did it the other way around, first being Speaker of the House and then serving in the

Massachusetts House, where he was also Speaker.) Like his predecessor, Theodore Sedgwick, Joseph Varnum had the distinction of serving as President Pro-Tempore of the U.S. Senate. Mr. Varnum's journey to high federal office began on a trip to Boston in 1767, where, as a seventeen-year-old, he stood on the side of the Common watching in fascination as British soldiers drilled in various formations up and down the open field. This show of military discipline and precision inspired young Varnum to join his local militia and led to his presence at the Battle of Lexington eight years later.

Born in Dracut, Massachusetts, in 1750, Joseph Bradley Varnum was the son of a farmer and was a farmer himself. Self-effacing, rather shy, and largely self-taught (which later led to his enemies scoffing at him as illiterate, which he was not), Varnum and his wife Molly had a dozen children. He would be the last Speaker of the U.S. House of Representatives to have served in the Revolution. His road to the speaker's chair—indeed, the political career of this quiet man—would be anything but tranquil.

Varnum was a representative and senator from his hometown in the Massachusetts legislature and a lukewarm Anti-Federalist delegate to the Massachusetts convention held for the purpose of ratifying the federal Constitution (where he spoke strongly for the inclusion of a bill of rights). Varnum ran against the popular Federalist incumbent—Samuel Dexter—for the Second and Third Congresses, and lost both times, which so disappointed his fellow townsmen that they determined to do something about it should the opportunity ever again arise.

On Varnum's third try for Congress the officials of the town of Dracut waited until the returns from other parts of the congressional district were counted and found that Dexter was ahead, but not by much. Seeing their duty the townsmen proceeded to do it, by reporting a sufficient plurality for Varnum in Dracut to overcome Dexter's slim lead in the rest of the district, and to elect their favorite son to Congress by a 17-vote margin. Although the Dracut voters' enthusiasm for their native son may not be faulted, their arithmetic might. The total vote reported from the town was 60 more than the number of registered voters. Samuel Dexter howled in protest, but in such matters the House itself, not the circumstance of the representative-elect's arrival there, is the final arbiter of who will sit. After appropriate hearings, Varnum was seated and reelected by more unassailable margins to eight succeeding Congresses.

Aligning himself with Jefferson as a leader of the New England Democratic-Republicans, Joseph Varnum was against a standing army, the creation of a navy (particularly the proposed construction of the U.S.S. *Constitution*), and direct taxation. Early on, he spoke against slavery and the slave trade, and criticized President Adams for what he considered personal extravagance.

A feud, quite bitter at times, had erupted between Congressman John Randolph and his fellow Virginian, President Jefferson, over the latter's attempt to acquire Florida. When the Tenth Congress (1807-1809) assembled to select its speaker, Jefferson, smarting at incumbent speaker, Nathaniel Macon's support for Randolph, threw his backing to Varnum, who was elected the presiding officer by one vote. Varnum's speakership in the Tenth and Eleventh Congresses proved to be mediocre. Perhaps his most notable (or regrettable) accomplishment was adjusting the rules of the House that limited debate.

In 1809, while still serving in Congress, Varnum received the Democratic-Republican nomination for lieutenant governor of Massachusetts but lost to David Cobb. Although his support of the Embargo Act brought down upon his head the condemnation of the Massachusetts Federalists, the changing politics of the Commonwealth saw the Legislature, after several days of deadlock, elect Joseph Varnum to succeed Timothy Pickering in the U.S. Senate in 1811.

From June 29, 1811, to March 3, 1817, Varnum served as president-pro tempore of the U.S. Senate. On his retirement from that body, Varnum once again served in the Massachusetts Senate. A pioneer member of the American Peace Society, Varnum abandoned the established Congregational Church and converted to Baptist. He died in 1821 and is buried in the family plot in Dracut.

Brothers at Sea

In 1805, President Jefferson called upon Jacob Crowninshield of Salem to succeed Robert Smith as secretary of the navy. The nominee's respectful declining of the appointment did not sit well with the president, who sent the appointment to the Senate for confirmation anyway. Crowninshield's nomination was confirmed by the Senate and his name is listed in the official records as being secretary from March 3, 1805, to March 7, 1809. Mr. Crowninshield, however, never showed up to assume his duties, forcing Secretary Smith to stay for the remainder of Jefferson's term. It was not that Jacob was that far away, serving as he did in the Eighth and Ninth Congresses (1803-1807), and dying while serving in the Tenth on April 15, 1808.

President Madison for a brief time experienced the same Crowninshield reluctance to serve when he appointed Jacob's brother, Benjamin, to be Secretary of the Navy in 1814. Benjamin at first declined, thought it over for a few days, and accepted.

The Crowninshield brothers were the sons of George Crowninshield and Mary Derby Crowninshield, a marriage that united two prominent and wealthy merchant families of Salem. A common school education to age eleven or so, time in the family countinghouse and then to sea was the pattern laid out for all his sons by George Crowninshield. Both Benjamin and Jacob commanded their own ships before age twenty. The family, all enthusiastic Jeffersonians, was able, or so it was rumored, to compensate for large losses brought about by the Embargo Act through some profitable privateering.

Benjamin Crowninshield's tenure as Secretary of the Navy is not particularly noteworthy. An efficient enough administrator, he was handicapped by his wife's insistence he be in Washington only as long as Congress was in session. What was needed at the time was a Secretary of the Navy with a vision of what America's naval force should be—a prescience Benjamin Crowninshield lacked. President Monroe retained him in office, but, dissatisfied with the role he was playing, Crowninshield resigned his post on October 1, 1818.

A Federal Judiciary

It was generally agreed among the delegates to the Constitutional Convention in Philadelphia that the government they were creating would have to include a court or courts to be the arbiter and enforcer of the law as it was created by Congress and applied to the nation as a whole. Some delegates advocated a separate system of federal courts, while others felt that federal matters could be adequately handled by existing state courts. The Convention, not for the only time in the development of the Constitution, addressed the problem as architect, not builder. The delegates created a skeletal Supreme Court and left its fleshing out to the upcoming Congress. That first Congress (1789-1791), controlled by advocates of a strong federal government, passed a Judiciary Act creating a Supreme Court of six justices, federal district courts in each state, and circuit courts made up of a district judge and two justices of the Supreme Court. The "circuit" court was literally that, with the judge traveling from courthouse to courthouse in his district on horseback or by a carriage.

Originally distrusted by the people and generally ignored by the Congress that created it (the justices were not even assigned chambers and had to borrow a room from the Senate), the Court heard no cases for its first three years. The office of chief justice was hard to fill, and more than one prominent lawyer who was offered an associate justice-ship concluded that he would gain more prestige and earn more money in private practice.

The appointment by President John Adams in 1801 of the much respected John Marshall as chief justice did much to raise the Court in the estimation of both Congress and the people, but even then vacated seats were hard to fill. President Madison's first choice to replace Justice Cushing, who died in September of 1810, was Levi Lincoln of Massachusetts, who turned him down; the Senate refused to confirm Alexander Wolcott of Connecticut. The American minister to Russia, John Quincy Adams, when informed of his appointment to the Court, replied that he would really prefer to stay in St. Petersburg if the president didn't mind. With Cushing a year in his grave and after three rejections, the president sent the name of Joseph Story of Massachusetts to the Senate for confirmation. It was an appointment that brought an objection from Thomas Jefferson, who thought Story not enough the stalwart Republican to counter the rampant Federalism on the Marshall Court. Jefferson reminded the president of his nominee's failure to toe the party line in the matter of the Embargo Act.

Justice Story

Joseph Story was born in Marblehead in 1779, the son of Elisha and Mehitable Story. His father, a successful physician and surgeon, helped heave the British tea into Boston Harbor. Elisha Story was unusually fecund, siring 11 children by Joseph's mother and seven in a previous marriage. A self-admitted academic grind, Joseph Story was permitted to enter Harvard halfway through the freshman year and graduated at age 19, second in his class only to the great Protestant divine William Ellery Channing, who was an apostle of Unitarianism, a faith also embraced by Story.

A voluble man when he was not immersed in his books, Joseph Story was an early leader in the Democratic-Republican Party in the Commonwealth, a member of both the state House of Representatives (and Speaker in 1811) and the U.S. House of Representatives. Story suffered the same ostracism from Boston society for his politics as did the Adamses, Gerry, Lincoln, Varnum, and other defectors from orthodox Federalism.

As a Marbleheader, Joseph Story enlivened his interest in maritime law at a time when that branch of jurisprudence was neither well established nor commonly understood in America. By diligent study of the pertinent English law, Story made himself an expert in the field. Story was appointed to the Supreme Court of the United States by President Madison in 1811, and when the havoc to American shipping, privateering and piracy brought on by the War of 1812 resulted in a flood of maritime cases in his circuit court, the justice was well prepared. It was Story who firmly established the jurisdiction of the federal courts in such cases and put American admiralty law on a sound basis.

A prodigious author of legal treatises and publisher of new editions of the works of other prominent legal scholars, Joseph Story was called upon more and more often to write the opinions of the Marshall Court. Between 1832 and 1845, Justice Story published a 12-volume series of *Commentaries*. Written to encourage discussion, these treatments of aspects of the law replaced the existing practice of lectures only at Harvard Law School, where Story became the first Dane Professor of Law. So well thought of were his *Commentaries* on the

U.S. Constitution, that the series was translated into French, German and Spanish and brought Story international recognition as the first American legal scholar. Story's distaste for slavery did not extend to abolitionism, the stance held by many Massachusetts leaders of the day, including John Quincy Adams. The fact that the Constitution avoided dealing with the issue of slavery while affirming the concept of individual liberty was for a conscientious man like Justice Story a continuing vexation.

In January of 1841, a case came before the Supreme Court that would offer John Quincy Adams, as advocate, and Joseph Story, as judge, an opportunity to strike a blow against slavery: Adams with his blistering eloquence, and Story with his acute legal reasoning. On July 2, 1839, 53 Negroes being transported on the Spanish slave ship *Amistad* had risen up, killed the ship's officers (save one to navigate for the mutineers) and sailed for home—or so they thought. The rebellious slaves were captured at sea by an American vessel, and were eventually charged with murder and piracy. The Spanish owners of the *Amistad* claimed the slaves, the Spanish government claimed both the ship and its cargo under the Treaty of 1795 and the officers of the U.S. ship that captured the *Amistad* claimed salvage.

A federal court in Hartford, Connecticut, ruled that while slavery was legal in Cuba (the slaves were en route from Havana to Puerto Principe on that island) importation of slaves from Africa, where they had been enslaved, was not. Thus, the ruling went on, rather than being merchandise, the Africans were victims of kidnapping and had the right to escape. The federal government appealed to the U.S. Supreme Court. That the case involved maritime law made it ripe for Justice Story's unchallenged expertise in the field. For Adams, who had represented the former slaves in Court, it presented an opportunity both to strike at that immoral institution and to display his eloquence. By a most persuasive and narrow reading of the treaty with Spain, Justice Story succeeded in having the high Court declare the slaves free.

That blow against slavery, however, was in contrast to Justice Story's decision in another case. In that instance, his inability to reconcile his moral disdain for slavery with his duty to uphold the law as it then existed resulted in slavery gaining explicit constitutional standing. Justice Story felt compelled to rule that the personal freedom law of the state of Pennsylvania violated the federal law having to do with the return of runaway slaves. Perhaps to assuage his conscience, Story added that states were not legally required to participate in the rendition process if they chose not to.

When Joseph Story, fourth choice though he may have been, came to the Supreme Court, he brought with him preeminent scholarship and a legal mind of extraordinary depth and interests. Continuing and bitter personal attacks by the abolitionists, particularly after his decision in the Pennsylvania case, convinced Justice Story that it was time to retire. He wished to spend his remaining years in teaching and scholarship but died in September of 1845, before he could retire from the Court. When President Madison chose him to be an associate justice of the Supreme Court of the United States at age 32, the Massachusetts lawyer was the youngest appointee to the Court and remains so to this day.

CHAPTER II

Goodbye, Mr. Adams

SEVENTY YEARS HAD PASSED SINCE THE STIRRING WORDS OF THE Declaration of Independence had first been publicly read in Philadelphia. If one were compelled to sum up the totality of the contribution to the Republic by Massachusetts men during those formative years, it could be done in three words: John Quincy Adams.

On February 21, 1848, having just cast a resounding "No" to a resolution congratulating the generals who had taken part in the Mexican-American War, John Quincy Adams, the congressman representing the district in Massachusetts where the historic town of Plymouth lay, resumed his seat. As was his custom, he had been at his desk since early morning, and he would usually stay there until darkness engulfed the chamber. The old man, though often irascible, seemed quite cheerful that day, as he busied himself between roll calls writing poetry requested by a friend, reviewing his notes, and signing autographs for congressmen who would not be returning, as he expected to, for the next session of the House of Representatives when it assembled a month hence.

The opposition of Adams to heaping praise on the commanding generals was as futile as his opposition to the war itself. As the clerk commenced reading the tribute to the generals, Adams began to rise as if to address the Speaker, seemed to hesitate, then fell forward in a faint. Judging from the color of Adams's face and the limpness of his body, those close by knew the attack had been serious, perhaps mortal. "Stop, Mr. Speaker, stop! Mr. Adams has collapsed," the shout went up. One of the several doctors who were members of the House ran to his side and ordered Adams taken to a sofa in the Capitol Rotunda. In an attempt to get more air, the sofa was moved to a door opening off the east portico, but it was damp and chilly there.

Adams's inert figure was then carried into the Speaker's room. The Massachusetts representative seemed to be in no pain but was seldom alert. Once he called for his old friend Henry Clay but did not recognize Louisa Catherine Adams, his wife of half a century. The House adjourned, as did the Senate, deeming it inappropriate to continue. What was by then a deathwatch continued that day and the next. A steady stream of congressmen and senators, including the first-term lanky young representative from Illinois, Abraham Lincoln, came by to inquire of the old man's condition.

The President

In 1803, in an act that was the basis of future irony, the Massachusetts legislature sent both John Quincy Adams and Timothy Pickering to the U.S. Senate. When they arrived, the debate over President Jefferson's plan to acquire the Louisiana Territory by purchase from the French was in full swing. Adams immediately declared the manner of the acquisition a "flagrant violation of the Constitution," since the Congress had no right to give the president's appointees military, judicial and civil power over the inhabitants or to tax them without their consent. It was a position that delighted the anti-Jeffersonian Federalists. But that delight soon enough turned to chagrin when Adams voted to support the appropriation for the purchase. And chagrin turned to outrage when he endorsed Jefferson's actions in regard to British aggression on the high seas. Adams went so far as to support the Embargo Act of 1807, a piece of legislation that was sure to wreak havoc on New England shipping interests. It was the first time that an action of an Adams outraged his then fellow senator and deposed secretary of state, Timothy Pickering. In consequence, Pickering organized a movement in Massachusetts that in June 1808 forced Adams to resign his Senate seat.

Of the four presidents immediately succeeding George Washington, three of them—Jefferson, Madison, and Monroe—had previously served as secretaries of state, and by 1824 the office had become a stepping-stone to the presidency. The legislative caucus system was prevalent at the time for choosing presidential electors, which enabled both Jefferson and Madison to virtually hand pick their secretaries of state to succeed them, but by the elections of 1824 that system was breaking down. The same could be said of the previously well-ordered system of two major competing candidates, one from the Federalist Party and one from the Democratic-Republican Party. The Federalist Party was no more; the Whigs had not yet formed; and 18 out of the 24 existing states had adopted the procedure of choosing their electors by popular vote rather than by caucus of their legislature.

The chaos produced five presidential candidates, all under the banner of the Democratic-Republican Party (although Adams preferred the designation of "Independent Republican"). The candidates were William H. Crawford, Secretary of the Treasury, who was the party caucus's choice; Speaker of the House Henry Clay, supported by Westerners and Southerners; Secretary of War John C. Calhoun, who subsequently dropped out of the race; Andrew Jackson, the hero of the battle of New Orleans, who was nominated by the Tennessee legislature; and Secretary of State John Quincy Adams, the only Northerner in the contest. When the electoral votes were counted, Jackson led with 99 electoral votes, or 43.1 percent of the popular vote; Adams was second, with 84 electoral votes and 30.5 percent of the popular votes; Crawford had 41 votes and at 13.1 percent ran third; and Clay, with four fewer electoral votes and the same popular vote as Crawford, was last.

Because no candidate had received the requisite majority of electoral votes, the contest was thrown into the House of Representatives, where each state delegation had one vote. Crawford, who had had a stroke, was not seriously considered, and Clay, having received the least number of votes, was eliminated, whereupon he threw his support to Adams, allowing Adams to carry 13 out of the 24 state congressional delegations and be declared president-elect.

The fact that Adams, not Andrew Jackson, who had bested Adams in both the electoral and popular vote, would be sworn in as president infuriated the Jackson adherents, not only among the people but in

Congress, where the Jackson forces had considerable strength. When President Adams appointed Henry Clay secretary of state, the supporters of Jackson, who had previously suspected a deal between Adams and Clay for the latter's support, were convinced of the perfidy.

An activist during his entire public life, President John Quincy Adams pushed for improved internal infrastructure and a national observatory and university. He also supported a national bank and high tariffs. Such activity frightened the strict constitutionalists in the Southern states, who believed federal activism would eventually lead to interference in the institution of slavery. Ever a nonpartisan, Adams attempted to enlist his enemies in his administration and hesitated, as had his father, to remove political opponents from office.

For the first time in the nation's history, the mid-term congressional election of 1826 resulted in both the House and Senate containing a majority of members, in this instance supporters of Jackson, who stood in opposition to the president. In the 1828 presidential election, with no party to back him and still denounced by the Jacksonian Democrats as a thief of the office, President Adams was crushed by Andrew Jackson, 178 to 82 electoral votes. Like John Adams, when defeated for reelection to the presidency three decades earlier, John Quincy Adams took the long journey home to Massachusetts—home to Boston and the calculated coolness of a political aristocracy who believed his independence amounted to betrayal—home to his beloved Quincy, where he could find peace.

Retired now after so many years of service to his country, the 62-year-old Adams had much to occupy however many more days the good Lord would allow him. There was an autobiography to write, books long neglected to read, and essays and poems to compose. He would look to history, not his enemies, to judge his public life.

Hello, Mr. Adams

A former president of the United States has no upward mobility either socially or politically, having already been at the pinnacle of both realms. To a lesser man, or perhaps one who thought himself greater, the invitation of political leaders in the Plymouth District to John Quincy Adams to stand for election to Congress mere months after his presidential term would seem demeaning. Not to John Quincy. He accepted and was elected without party affiliation to the 22nd Congress. He was then reelected to the succeeding eight Congresses, and served almost 17 years. The aging freshman took his seat in the House of Representatives on March 4, 1832, and began the final chapter of his public life, one that would turn out to be in many ways the most important and productive.

John Quincy Adams arrived in the halls of Congress with an intimate and personal knowledge of the Republic from its birth that no other man living or dead could equal. With his unquestionable integrity and his skill in debating (as often with an axe as with a rapier), Adams instantly became a compelling force in the House, and held many important committee assignments. His advice was sought, his eloquence was admired, his independence was envied, his stubbornness was abhorred and his stands were reviled. All in all a dangerous man of principle.

Adams had not long been in his service in the House before he became the symbol, in the North and in the South and eventually in Europe, of the antislavery forces in Congress. It was not that Adams was an abolitionist—far from it. He was a gradualist in that he believed that slavery could be eradicated by the establishment of a date certain after which the importation of slaves would be prohibited and a date certain after which all the children of slaves would be born free citizens of this country. The principle he would use in his opposition to slavery, indeed the pinnacle from which he would thunder against it—unrelenting, unafraid, and assuredly ungentlemanly—was the people's right of petition.

In the 1640s, to some extent because of the rise in the power and influence of town meetings, the General Court of Massachusetts passed an order decreeing that any inhabitant of the Colony could present himself to the General Court in any matter over which the court had authority. This right of virtual unfettered citizen petition was reflective of the right of any Englishman to come before the king's Privy Council to appeal decisions of the courts or to seek justice in other matters. To Adams, the right of petition to the governing by the governed was fundamental, sacrosanct and divinely inspired; it was the core of the Bill of Rights, the very heart of democratic government.

"Let us not speak of them; but look, and pass on." —Dante Alighieri

It was in the interest of slaveholders and their supporters in Congress that that body and, by extension, the constituency of its members, not be continually roiled over the issue of slavery. They could not control the rantings of the radical abolitionists of the North, but they could deny them a national platform, at least in the House. Because they were in the majority at the time, the slaveholders managed to impose a gag rule decreeing that petitions against slavery, of which there were an ever growing number, would be automatically "put on the table," thus preventing debate on their merits. Efforts by Congressman Adams to eliminate the rule preventing action of such petitions continually failed to reach a majority, yet he would introduce them, dozens of them, year after year. In February of 1837, Adams rose to inquire of the chair if the gag rule applied to a petition Adams had received from 22 slaves. The pro-slavery members hooted and hollered in derision. When the din subsided and Adams spoke, he revealed that the petitioners were not against, but in favor of slavery, which further angered his opponents who realized they had been duped. Further, they resented any insinuation that slaves even had a right of petition.

In January 1842, the Southerners' bête noire seemed, even in the eyes of some of Adams's supporters, to have gone too far; far enough to invite his impeachment and removal from the House. To a chorus of moans and groans, John Quincy Adams rose that day, as he had for so many opening sessions of the House, to introduce a petition. This petition, surprisingly, was not about slavery; it was an appeal from some citizens of Georgia asking that Adams be removed from his chairmanship of the Foreign Relations Committee. The purpose of the ever parliamentarily adroit Adams's rising was not to advance the petition, about which he did not give a rat's tail, but to gain the floor of the House. Having been personally attacked in the petition, Adams invoked the rule of personal privilege to defend himself, to which the Speaker was forced to assent.

Instead of being compelled to listen to the former ambassador, secretary of state and president defend his expertise in the field of foreign affairs, the Southern slave supporters reeled under a verbal lash of vituperative abuse the depth and breadth of which had seldom before been heard in the chambers. "Sit down," came the shouts, "Be quiet. Shut up." No, he would not. They would not succeed in stilling his opposition to the extension of slavery and to the admittance of Texas into the Union as a slave state. Then, as if not satisfied with the tumult he had created, Adams pulled out another petition. This one was from the citizens of Haverhill, Massachusetts, praying for the dissolution of the Union on the grounds that so much of the federal government's money was being spent on sustaining the South that it had become an unbearable burden on the free states. Adams coyly added that although the time for such dissolution was not yet at hand, if a civil war should come, "the war powers of Congress would extend to interference with the institution of slavery in every way by which it can."

The utterance of those words and their implication by a man of the stature of Adams—"dissolution," "war," "emancipation"—set the place ablaze. Soon enough a proposal for reprimand had escalated to one of censure for the "crime of high treason." The more moderate of the Southern members recognized too late the trap that Adams had set for them. They attempted to shelve the charge of treason, but Adams had the votes to defeat it. Now, said Adams, he was on trial, a trial in which the liberties of the country were "enduring in my person." Good lawyer that he was, Adams's defense was to try his accusers. Relentlessly, through uncompromising point and unbending principle, Adams tore into the befoulers of his country, the prostitutors of its liberties. He calculated that his censure was doubtful. If it should succeed he reasoned, his constituents would promptly return him to the House. Adams reveled in his role as defendant, thrilled by the acclaim it gained him not only in antislavery America but in Europe as well. On February 4th, Adams allowed the censure motion to come to a vote and saw it defeated 106 to 93. Yet the nays over the yeas was not where his victory lay. His victory was in the realization by supporters of slavery that he, John Quincy Adams, was, in the words of the congressman from Virginia, Henry A. Wise, "the acutest, the astutest, the archest enemy of Southern slavery that ever existed."

Despite the enmity he engendered and that he delighted in fueling whenever the occasion arose, Adams was often called upon by fellow Representatives, friend and foe, for advice and guidance. As it attempted to organize in 1839, the House found itself closely divided between Democrats and Whigs. The question of which party would control the speakership and committee assignments hung on whether a contested delegation from New Jersey would be seated. The clerk of the House, a holdover from the previous Congress whose main duty before the organization of the new Congress was to list the members presenting valid credentials, was subsequently dependent on the composition of the House for his own reelection and refused to certify the contested seats. For three days the House wrangled, unable to organize. Time enough for Congressman Adams to run out of patience and announce his intention to put the question of ordering the clerk to read the names of those holding the New Jersey governor's certification of their election. At that point, both sides, neither of them sure they would prevail, turned to the nonpartisan and astute Adams. For 11 noisy days he presided over the divided House, skillfully controlling the rambunctious factions until he thought the time was ripe to have the clerk read the names of those members certified by the New Jersey governor.

If we count, as well we should, when at age eleven he accompanied his father, John Adams, on the latter's diplomatic mission to France; through John Quincy Adams's service at age fourteen, as secretary and translator for Francis Dana, the American minister to Russia and Great Britain; as U.S. Senator, secretary of state, president, and his service of nine terms in the U.S. House of Representatives—it can be said that the public life of John Quincy Adams was a metaphor for the death of colonialism and the birth of an enduring republic.

On the evening of the 23rd of February, 1848, John Quincy Adams, age 81, born a British subject in one of 13 colonies hugging the east coast of English America with a population of not more than three million, died. He died a citizen of a republic of 29 states stretching as far west as Texas with a population of over 20 million, while, as an observant fate would have it, doing what he had done for so long: attending to the people's business.

In the Diplomatic Service

From the administration of John Quincy Adams to that of Andrew Johnson, the United States was actively engaged in diplomacy on several fronts. In the Orient it was the American government's policy to attempt to extend its commerce and influence. In South America, in the face of insurrection and revolution against colonial rule, the United States was insisting that the European powers take seriously its self-declared supremacy in the affairs of the Americas. In the escalating polemic between the federal government and the Southern states, it became important for the former that the latter not gain European capitals. It was a time of turbulence and promise and of the need for effective diplomacy. In those years, a significant number of Massachusetts men would serve as American ambassadors, ministers or commissioners to foreign nations; three of them would become secretaries of state, and the brother of one of those would serve as chief clerk of the state department. The first of these diplomats was Alexander Hill Everett.

Alexander Hill Everett was the brother of Edward Everett, the famous orator and abolitionist. After serving in the state legislature for several terms as a Whig, Alexander Everett abandoned that party to join the Democrats. Worse than the political embarrassment Alexander's politics caused his brother Edward, a leader of the Whigs, was the disgrace brought on the family by the financial losses Alexander suffered after acquiring a controlling interest in the *North American Review*. The disgrace was monetary rather than literary, as the articles Alexander Everett wrote about his diplomatic experiences attracted considerable favorable attention and were translated into several languages.

Born in Boston in 1790, Alexander Everett graduated from Harvard in 1806, both the youngest and the highest-standing graduate in his class. Three years later, 19-year-old Everett accompanied the newly appointed minister to St. Petersburg, John Quincy Adams, as his secretary.

It was essential to American foreign policy and to the preeminence of the Monroe Doctrine that the European powers, in this case Spain, recognize the revolutionary governments of those South American colonies desirous of independence. Appointed minister to Spain by President Adams in 1825 (he had previously been secretary and charge d'affaires at The Hague), Alexander Everett was instructed by Secretary of State Henry Clay not only to effect Spanish recognition of the legitimacy of the revolutionary governments of South America, but to deal with the question of Spain's ability to hold onto the islands of Cuba and Porto Rico (Puerto Rico). Everett's suggestion that the United States loan cash-starved Spain large sums of money, with the United States taking Cuba as collateral, was never acted on.

Alexander Everett's service as minister to Spain ended in 1829, and after a brief period as confidential agent to the government of Cuba, he took the position as president of Jefferson College in Louisiana. In 1845, President James Polk recalled Everett to the diplomatic service as Commissioner to China, the first American representative in that post under a recently negotiated treaty. Unable to complete the long journey because of ill health, Everett was forced to turn back. When he thought himself fit enough, he set out once again, only to die in Canton, China, on June 29, 1847.

Mr. Adams's Agent

The policy of the American government to support revolution against colonial rule in South America was selective rather than universal. It did not follow that the success of the Americans in ridding themselves of foreign rule predisposed their government to support all subsequent revolutions having the same goal, especially those in its own backyard. Toward the end of the Monroe administration, Secretary of State John Quincy Adams expressed concern about uprisings in Chile and Argentina. While he wished the new governments well, the Secretary saw in Argentina "no prospect that [it] would establish free or liberal institutions of government" but rather would be a government of "arbitrary power, military and ecclesiastical."

Adams wished to wait and see how things would go, but was hampered in the effort by the American agent in Buenos Aires, J.B. Provost. Adams thought Provost, who also represented the United States in Chile, too enthusiastic for the rebel cause. Adams was limited in what he could do, however, since Provost was a particular friend and protégé of President Monroe.

Adams set out to undermine Provost's influence by pointing out to the diplomat that the two posts he served, Chile and Argentina, were one too many for any man, and he ought to choose one or the other. Provost chose Chile, and Adams immediately dispatched a long-time friend and most trusted ally, John Murray Forbes, to Buenos Aires and gave him the designation of Agent for Commerce and Seamen.

Forbes was born in 1771 in St. Augustine, Florida, to the minister of the church there, Reverend John Forbes and his wife, Dorothy Murray Forbes. John was only two when his Milton, Massachusetts-born mother took him North with plans to have him educated in her native state. Forbes responded by completing his formal education at age 16 as the youngest graduate of the class of 1787 at Harvard. Forbes then took up the study of law with his fellow Harvard classmate and good friend, John Quincy Adams.

For the sometimes dour and always serious Adams, his choice to send his uncommonly witty and constantly jolly friend Forbes to Argentina proved a canny one. A diplomat of a foreign nation takes sides in the domestic quarrels of his host country at his own peril. Provost had done just that in Argentina, and by the time Forbes arrived in Buenos Aires, he had run afoul of the side having the upper hand at the time and had been ordered out of the city. Forbes's impartiality between the competing forces in Argentina was just what Adams wanted, and Forbes's diplomacy served the policy of the United States well. When Caesar Rodney was appointed minister in Buenos Aires, Forbes was made Secretary of Legation in January 1823. When Rodney died in 1824, Forbes was appointed charge d'affaires, a post he held until his death in 1831.

A Consequential Vote

The U.S. Constitution requires that the president be chosen by the House of Representatives should no candidate receive the requisite majority of the votes of the Electoral College. Each state's congressional delegation, not each congressman himself, has one vote. It was no surprise when the clerk of the House called the roll in the 1824 election that the Massachusetts delegation delivered a resounding vote for John Quincy Adams. What was surprising was that the vote was not unanimous. Congressman Francis Baylies had voted for Andrew Jackson, explaining that he considered Adams "morally unfit" to be president of the United States. This vote was not without its political consequence, as Mr. Baylies found out when he was soundly defeated for reelection. In casting such an unpopular vote, Francis Baylies showed the same courage of his convictions as had his grandfather, an iron master, who sacrificed profit to his Quaker pacifism by refusing to make cannonballs for the Louisburg Expedition of 1745. (Pacifism over profit and patriotism was lost on his descendants, however, who made iron from bog ore for the cannonballs of Washington's Army.)

Such political sacrifice as Francis Baylies made deserved political reward from its beneficiary. When Andrew Jackson became president in 1829, Baylies's friends tried mightily, albeit unsuccessfully, to secure Baylies an appointment to the president's cabinet, which is not to say that President Jackson did not have something in mind for his Massachusetts supporter.

In the year of President Jackson's inauguration, the de facto and somewhat piratical governor of the Falkland Islands banned pelagic fishing (fishing on the surface of the open sea as opposed to in coastal waters). New England fishermen, who had long and successfully labored in the now proscribed waters, defied the decree, citing the doctrine of long and continued usage. The governor had the Falkland Islands fishermen's vessels seized and held for condemnation. President Jackson, eschewing diplomacy at least for the time being, dispatched the sloop of war *Lexington* to protect the fishing rights of the Americans. The governor and his associates were themselves seized and deported from the Falkland Islands to stand trial.

In 1832, President Jackson sent Baylies to Buenos Aires with credentials as acting minister with full authority to settle the matter. The government of Argentina refused to negotiate until it received apologies and reparations for what it considered the kidnapping of Falkland Islands officials. Baylies would not yield. Subject to harassment and personal indignities, the minister requested his passport and sailed for home on September 8, 1832, three months to the day after his arrival. Convinced that war between the United States and Argentina was imminent, the departing minister took all of the American legation papers with him. Although war never came about, it was not until 1844 that full diplomatic relations between the two countries were resumed.

A historical scholar of note, Baylies wrote *An Historic Memoir of the Colony of New Plymouth*, which was published in four parts. But the author was hampered by the absence of Governor Bradford's chronicles, which had gone missing. Francis Baylies died in 1852. Three years later Bradford's chronicles were discovered by Samuel T. Armstrong hidden in the belfry of the Old South Church.

China Hands

For many a man and boy, landlubber or old salt, who sailed out of New Bedford or Boston or Salem or Marblehead in the early decades of the nineteenth century, the voyage around South America and on to the vast Pacific Ocean, through one horizon then the next, to the Sandwich Islands, Formosa, and Macao ended at the entrance to the inscrutable empire of China at the port of Canton. While they still had the ability to do so, the Chinese, ever suspicious of the "foreign devils," restricted trade to the South China city of Canton and subjected foreign traders to regulation by the Chinese government. The Portuguese had been there, and the Spanish, and the English with their powerful East India Company: now the Americans were playing catch up.

The trade monopoly previously held by the East India Company was abolished in 1834, and British traders, chafing under the restrictions imposed by the Chinese, pressured the British government to intervene. Much of the British purchase of tea and silk at the time was being paid for by the sale of opium from India, and Chinese efforts to end that evil resulted in their defeat at the hands of the British in the Opium War of 1839-1842. The Cantonese system of controlling foreign trade was replaced by a series of five port "treaties" under the terms of which foreigners were allowed to live and work beyond Chinese jurisdiction. It was after those events that the United States made a concentrated effort to establish diplomatic relations with the Ching Dynasty.

In 1843 Congress appropriated the sum of $40,000 to send a mission to China. The position was first offered to the then-sitting American minister to Great Britain, Edward Everett. Everett declined the appointment, citing the possibility the mission would fail and the inadequacy of the appropriation. (The political talk in Boston and Washington, however, was that Everett felt he was being eased out of his post in England to make room for Secretary of State Daniel

Webster, who wanted out of the Tyler administration.) The task of representing the United States in the Celestial Kingdom then fell to Caleb Cushing—a heaven-sent choice as things turned out.

In the decades before the Civil War, Essex County, Massachusetts, could boast of having produced men of distinction and accomplishment such as Rufus Choate, Nathaniel Hawthorne, John Greenleaf Whittier, William Lloyd Garrison and, not the least of them, Caleb Cushing. Cushing was born on the seventeenth day of the first month of the first year of the nineteenth century to a prosperous Salisbury, Massachusetts, merchant ship owner. The son of Joseph Cushing and Lydia Dow Cushing, young Caleb was handsome and precocious. He was a freshman at Harvard at age 13, a student of government and law, and was proficient in French, Spanish and Italian and able to read other modern European languages. In 1858 Cushing had the honor of introducing his friend and the future president of the Confederacy, Jefferson Davis, when the latter gave an address at Faneuil Hall in Boston. A quarter of a century later, Cushing was honored by the man who brought down President Davis and his Confederacy, Ulysses Grant, when President Grant nominated Cushing to be chief justice of the U.S. Supreme Court.

Like his political contemporaries, Edward Everett and Daniel Webster, Cushing was both beneficiary and victim of his obeisance to the Constitution, his reverence for the Union, and his moral outrage at the institution of slavery. To this increasingly untenable position, Cushing added a strong pro-Southern bias. He practiced his politics as a manly art: always tough, sometimes ferocious. A hint of the drama that was to be the hallmark of his public life came when Cushing, then a state senator, was attempting with the blessings of both Everett and Webster, to defeat John Varnum in the congressional election of 1826. An enthusiastic rally of his supporters was broken up in a near riot when the fiery and fearless abolitionist, William Lloyd Garrison, stormed into the hall and soundly denounced the candidate for his stand on slavery. The attack, both bitter and personal from a man who had been the beneficiary of Cushing's legal advice and financial assistance, proved fatal to Cushing's candidacy. However, with the enthusiastic support of John Greenleaf Whittier, Cushing was elected to the U.S. House in 1834 as one of the 98 representatives of the newly formed Whig Party.

Cushing served four consecutive terms in Congress, all with distinction. Few men in America could show such promise of local and national leadership as did Cushing by the time he reached his fortieth birthday in 1840. Both Webster and Everett had given tacit approval to Cushing to be their successor in the leadership of the Whigs. The election that year of the party's first president, William Henry Harrison, for whom Cushing had written a campaign biography, seemed to assure Cushing national prominence. That promise became a might-have-been when the new president, coatless at his inaugural on March 4, caught pneumonia and died only a month later. As a consequence Cushing would be caught up in a power struggle for control of the Whig Party, and the political agenda for the nation, between the senator from Kentucky, Henry Clay, and the new president, John Tyler. It was a vicious contest that would lead to the decline of many political careers and one that would haunt Caleb Cushing for the rest of his political life.

Even before the death of President Harrison, Henry Clay had assumed the leadership of the Whig Party. Tyler, who had previously been a Democrat and still adhered to some of that party's philosophy, vetoed two bank bills that Clay had sponsored. In the resulting uproar, Tyler's entire cabinet resigned, with the exception of Secretary of State Daniel Webster, who was at the time negotiating a treaty with Great Britain. Senator Clay had the president of the United States expelled from the Whig Party. Cushing, who had previously been the most orthodox and constant supporter of the Whigs, now joined a small band of Whig congressmen who supported the beleaguered president. With equal consistency Cushing endorsed the president's principles and legislation, now more Democratic than Whig. Such a course was a matter of principle for Caleb Cushing, who believed Senator Clay's attempt to dictate national policy was an intrusion into the power and responsibilities of the presidency.

Congressman Cushing was to leave the House in March 1843 at the expiration of his term. On the evening of March 3rd, the day Cushing gave his parting address, President Tyler sent over to the Senate his nomination of Cushing to be secretary of the treasury: Cushing was nominated not once but three times, only to be defeated by the vengeful Whigs with increasing majorities. Having been denied his choice of

Cushing for the Secretary of the Treasury and faced with Edward Everett's refusal to go to China, the president waited for Congress to adjourn and then appointed Caleb Cushing U.S. Commissioner to China.

It was an extraordinary mission undertaken by an extraordinary man. During the long voyage to the Orient, sailing not on one vessel but on a considerable fleet, Cushing mastered the Manchu language to the extent that no interpreter was required in his dealings with the Chinese. The resulting Treaty of Wang Hiay, approved by the Senate on January 16, 1845, opened five Chinese ports to American shipping, settled disputes over tariffs and trade regulations, and established the principle of exclusive jurisdiction of American laws and officials over its citizens living in China.

Cushing's domestic political career was revived by his appointment in 1853 as attorney general in President Franklin Pierce's cabinet, where Cushing served with his friend, Secretary of War Jefferson Davis. The diplomatic skills that Cushing had displayed in his triumphant mission to China were put to the test when he was elected permanent chairman of the national Democratic Party's nominating convention in Charleston, South Carolina, in April of 1860. The party was split between those supporting Stephen Douglas and the party's radical slavery element. Douglas led, but did not prevail for 55 ballots. Unable to break the deadlock, the convention adjourned in chaos and reassembled in June with Cushing in the chair. When it became apparent that Douglas would be nominated, the radicals marched out, calling for a breakup of the Union. When Democrat Douglas was subsequently beaten by Republican Lincoln in the election of 1860, Cushing declared that if the new president and the incoming Republican administration could not make concessions to them, the Southern states should be allowed to secede in peace.

In December of 1856, before his new administration took office, President James Buchanan had sent Cushing to Charleston to try to prevent the passage of an ordinance of secession. Cushing arrived too late; the ordinance had passed, but he would be most welcome to attend the signing ceremony, his Southern friends assured him. Indignant that he should be invited to witness a document of unilateral dissolution of the Union, Cushing left and forever abandoned his association with the South. Cushing's consorting with Southern politicians and his defection from the Whig Party was fresh enough in the minds of many in Massachusetts that its wartime governor, John A. Andrew, judiciously declined Cushing's offer to serve in the Civil War. The new Republican president had no such reservations, however. Lincoln accepted Cushing's legal assistance while entrusting him with several important government tasks.

Later, in December 1873, President Grant appointed Cushing minister to Spain. Just as the 73-year-old Cushing was about to set sail, word reached him that the president had submitted Cushing's name to the Senate for confirmation as chief justice of the Supreme Court. Political memories often live beyond the generation of their gestation, and thus would it be in the case of the nomination of Caleb Cushing. In their opposition to his confirmation, the Republican Senate, with a majority of 30 votes, resurrected the fact of Cushing's friendship with Jefferson Davis, his sympathy with the South, his support of President Tyler and his injudicious condemnation of the abolitionists. The proceedings became so acrimonious and personal that Cushing, acknowledged even by his enemies to be a worthy successor to the likes of chief justices Taney and Marshall, requested that his name be withdrawn.

Cushing served extraordinarily well as the U.S. minister to Spain from 1874 to 1877 and died among his books at his home on High Street in Newburyport on January 2, 1879. He was a man whose intelligence, scholarship, versatility and devotion to his country made him one of the nation's most outstanding public servants of the nineteenth century.

The Flag and the Cross

Nial Ferguson, in his book *Empire*, traces the evolution of the British Empire from commerce to Christianity to conquest. It was certainly the belief of many pious New Englanders that the Christian Cross of conversion would soon enough follow the American flag of commerce to China. In the case of Peter Parker, the U.S. Commissioner to China from 1855 to 1857, that order was reversed. A medical missionary and diplomat, Parker was born in Framingham, Massachusetts, in June 1804 to a farmer and a farmer's daughter of orthodox Congregational faith.

Parker's teenage despondency followed by a joyful religious conversion was a sign to both his parents and their families, and soon enough to Peter himself, that the ministry was to be his life.

In 1827, his formal education having been delayed by his parents' need for his help on the farm, Peter entered Amherst College. The college was founded in 1821 by Noah Webster and others to train indigent young men for the ministry. The meager resources at the fledgling institution so frustrated the eager student that he transferred to Yale College, where he received his undergraduate degree in 1831 and completed his studies in theology and medicine in 1834. Parker was ordained a Presbyterian minister in Philadelphia in May of that year and in June sailed for Canton, the first American Protestant medical missionary to China. The ever wary Chinese authorities restricted Parker's practice and preaching to Macao and the foreign enclaves of Canton. Parker removed himself to Singapore, where Christian proselytizing was more acceptable and spent several months there studying the language.

On his return to Canton, Parker, with the help of British and American merchants, opened a hospital specializing in diseases of the eye and the removal of tumors. Parker also instructed several Chinese students in the arts of Western medicine. It was mostly through his initiative that the Medical Missionary Society in China was founded. The society was soon in a position to give substantial aid to Parker's hospital in Canton and to make it possible for him to open another hospital in Macao.

The outbreak of hostilities between Great Britain and China in 1840 gave Parker reason to return to the United States, where, at the behest of Secretary of State Daniel Webster, he gave several lectures imparting his knowledge of China to members of the Harrison and Tyler administrations. In May of 1841, Parker married a relative of Daniel Webster, Harriet Colby Webster. In June of the following year, Parker again sailed for China to resume his medical practice, but the lure of involvement in the exciting drama of American-Chinese relations was turning his head from the ministry to diplomacy. Parker served as one of Caleb Cushing's secretaries in the minister's successful negotiation of the Wang Hiay Treaty. In 1855 President Polk appointed Parker the American commissioner/minister to China. The two

years during which Parker served in that post were particularly difficult due to the resumption of Anglo-Chinese hostilities.

The Reverend Parker returned to Washington after the end of his
diplomatic service in China. By that time he had added commercial
jingoism to his missionary zeal. Parker's advocacy of the military occupation of Formosa in furthering foreign claims was more aggressive
than the decision makers in Washington were willing to pursue. Peter
Parker died in Washington on January 10, 1888, at age 80.

The Reluctant Duelist

On May 22, 1856, in a bloody prelude to the carnage that was to
come in the approaching Civil War, Preston S. Brooks, a congressman
from South Carolina, beat the junior senator from Massachusetts,
Charles Sumner, to near insensibility on the floor of the U.S. Senate.
The provocation for Brooks's attack, which the assailant believed justified its viciousness, was an antislavery speech Sumner had delivered
during debate on the deteriorating situation in Kansas. To Sumner's
supporters, among them the *New York Tribune* and Henry Wadsworth
Longfellow, it was brilliant oratory. Some of his fellow Republicans,
however, feared that he had gone over the line and had put himself in
personal danger. Congressman Anson Burlingame of Massachusetts
and two of his colleagues offered to escort Sumner to and from his
duties to protect him from further attack, but the senator declined.

In the heated debate over what action, if any, the House should take
in disciplining Brooks, Burlingame denounced his fellow congressman
in stinging words, comparing the South Carolinian's stealthy attack on
Sumner with Cain's on his brother Abel. The response of the hot-tem-
pered Brooks was to challenge Burlingame to a duel. Burlingame
accepted and, as the challenged, exercised his right to designate the
place of combat by choosing a site on the Canadian side of Niagara
Falls. Brooks, facing an arduous trip through the hostile territory of
Pennsylvania and New York, declined.

Anson Burlingame was born at New Berlin, Chenango County, New
York, on November 14, 1820. His father was a Methodist exhorter and
lay preacher married to a woman with the incongruous name for the
spouse of a man of the cloth: Freelove Angell. Early in life Anson had

moved with his parents to Seneca County, Ohio, and later to Detroit. At age 23, educated at the embryonic state college at Ann Arbor (later named the University of Michigan), Burlingame moved east to attend Harvard Law School and eventually to make his home in Massachusetts.

Like his friend Charles Sumner, Anson Burlingame had a gift for oratory. He was elected to the Massachusetts Senate in 1852 and served in the U.S. Congress from 1855 to 1861. In recognition of his unstinting service in the Republican cause during the 1860 national campaign, Burlingame was appointed by President Lincoln as minister to Vienna. Austrian authorities, however, were aware of Burlingame's support of independence for Sardinia and refused to accept him, so he was posted instead to Peking. This turned out to be a fortuitous turn of events both for Mr. Burlingame's historic reputation and for the furtherance of Chinese international interests.

Burlingame reached Peking at a troubling time in a land where such a state of affairs, at least to foreign diplomats, seemed perpetual. Because of the degree of autonomy enjoyed by local authorities, the imperial government was having difficulty implementing the treaties of 1848. The often greedy European merchants were putting pressure on their governments for military intervention. The threat of invasion, foreign penetration into the provinces and even partition of China was real. If force came to be used, the U. S. government would be at a disadvantage because its naval forces had been recalled from the area to serve in the Civil War.

Burlingame brought with him to China instructions from Secretary of State William Seward to cooperate closely with the treaty powers. Burlingame possessed a singular lack of racial prejudice and an aura of superiority that was characteristic of the European diplomats. He also brought an urbanity, intelligence and charm that soon made him the leader of even the more experienced China diplomats. The American minister forged an agreement among his fellow ministers to resist the pressure of their merchants and to adopt a more tolerant attitude toward the Chinese. Burlingame's success so pleased the imperial government that it sought his advice on a variety of problems.

As minister, Charles Burlingame promoted the practice of placing American technical advisors in the employ of the Chinese government and urged Peking to emulate the Japanese by sending diplomatic representatives to the Western powers. When Burlingame announced his retirement in 1867, the Chinese government offered him the post as head, with two Chinese colleagues, of an official delegation to the West intended to observe European culture and to attempt to renegotiate existing treaties that the government felt were inimical to Chinese interests. (One of the provisions of the convention Burlingame fashioned between the United States and China was a bilateral immigration clause primarily designed to bring Chinese laborers to America to work on the transcontinental railroad.)

Anson Burlingame's extraordinary mission on behalf of China met with great success in America and a more limited gain in England. In general, he failed on the continent. His efforts on the part of the government of a people he had come to know, respect and love took him to London, Paris, Berlin, and lesser European capitals. Unfortunately, when he arrived in St. Petersburg in February 1870, he caught pneumonia and died.

CHAPTER III

To Her Majesty the Queen (and the Odd King)

THE PREMIER POSTING IN THE AMERICAN FOREIGN SERVICE FOR most of the history of the United States has been to the Court of St. James in London, especially in the embryonic years of the Republic. Equitable relations with the nation from which America sprang and with which it had fought two wars were essential. England remained America's most valuable trading partner and continued to be one of the dominant powers of the world. Maintaining a friendship with England was essential to the maturity of America both domestically and internationally.

Diplomacy with the mother country also provided the added benefit of an occupation for several generations of the Adams family. The first American Adams presented his credentials to King George III in 1785; his son, John Quincy Adams, offered the same to that aging monarch in 1815; and his grandson, Charles Francis Adams, presented his credentials to Queen Victoria in 1861. All in all, in the years between the epochal presidencies of George Washington and Abraham Lincoln, seven Massachusetts men would at eight different times represent the interest of their country at the Court of St. James. All three of the American ministers who served there between 1841 and 1852 hailed from Her Majesty's former colony.

Your Vote Counts

Marcus Morton had 12 children and was a candidate for governor of Massachusetts 16 times. History does not score the successes of his children but it does his own campaigns for governor: 14 losses, 2 wins, the most significant of the latter being his defeat of the incumbent governor, Edward Everett, in the election of 1839. A giant among orators in a day when public speaking was both art and entertainment, Edward Everett had the singular honor (and oratorical anonymity) of having given a brilliant two-hour address at the dedication of the battlefield at Gettysburg immediately preceding President Lincoln's three paragraphs.

Edward Everett was born in 1794, the son of the Reverend Oliver and Lucy Everett. Edward showed the same precociousness in his youth as that of his contemporary, Caleb Cushing: he was the youngest member of his college class and the one achieving the highest honors. After graduating from Harvard in 1811 and receiving his M.A. in divinity studies three years later, Edward, not yet 20 years old, was installed as pastor of Boston's most fashionable and largest Unitarian congregation, the Brattle Street Church. In 1812 he took the newly established chair of Greek literature at his alma mater. Traveling to Europe in 1815 for further study, Everett was awarded the first Ph.D. ever given an American by the University at Gottingen, Germany.

Everett's gifts of musical voice, sense of drama, and grace of words led him away from the ministry and academia to the public life. Chosen to give the Phi Beta Kappa oration at Harvard in 1824, he enthralled his listeners with a brilliant address, concluding with a moving tribute to the Marquis de Lafayette, who was present. Everett's spellbound audience sat in silence for a long moment before bursting into sustained applause. His memorable speech so impressed a number of influential listeners that they saw to his nomination and election to a seat in Congress.

Politically conservative and fearing that continuing agitation for the abolition of slavery was threatening the stability of the Union, Everett showed deference to Southern feelings on the subject. In 1835 he was elected to the Massachusetts governorship with the vigorous support of Caleb Cushing and a Whig Anti-Mason coalition. The two political parties in the Commonwealth at the time were easily distinguishable along social and economic lines. The Whigs were the party of the conservative, wealthy and aristocratic: ship owners, manufacturers and bankers. The Democratic Party was that of the workingmen, farmers and immigrants. The divisive question of slavery, always in the wings but now entering center stage, was an agitation to both parties. To the "Conscience" Whigs it was a moral question; for the so-called "Cotton" Whigs, dependent as their mills were on cheap Southern cotton, it was economic.

Nor was there unanimity for the abolition of slavery among the adherents of the more liberal Democrat Party. To many, free slaves meant competition for often scarce jobs. (In 1835, a Boston mob seized the virulent abolitionist William Lloyd Garrison, and dragged him through the streets with a rope around his neck. They may well have hanged him if not for the intervention of the city's mayor, Theodore Lyman.)

In 1839, Governor Edward Everett, the putative leader of the Massachusetts Whigs, decided to seek reelection to a fifth term. The Democratic convention once again nominated Marcus Morton, at that time a sitting justice on the Superior Court for Suffolk County. The convention then issued a public declaration opposing the reelection of Everett and pledging to work against him and to vote for Morton. Among the names appearing on the manifesto was that of the convention chairman, Everett's brother, Alexander Hill Everett. Complacency had settled over the long-governing Whigs, and the Democrats were faced with a rote vote for their consistent loser, until the abolitionists set fire to the campaign.

In an open letter appearing in the Boston press, Nathaniel Borden, an abolitionist leader, asked Governor Everett, "Are you in favor of the immediate abolition of slavery in the District of Columbia . . . and opposed to the admission into the Union of any new" slave states? To which Everett answered a week later: "I respond to both of your enquiries in the affirmative" upon which Garrison's paper, *The Liberator*, endorsed Everett.

When Everett carried the city of Boston on election day by less than half the votes of his previous election, he knew he was in trouble. There were reports of irregularities as the unofficial tallies flowed in, a not unusual circumstance then as it is now in close elections. Under the terms of the state constitution at the time, a successful candidate had to garner a clear majority of the votes cast, not a plurality, as is the case now. With no definitive winner, the voters would have to await the official tally by the appropriate committee of the Massachusetts legislature. If neither Morton nor Everett had a clear majority, the House would nominate two candidates and from them the Senate would elect the governor. The committee reported that the total number of valid ballots cast was 102,066. Some votes were scattered among other candidates, but of the 51,034 needed for election, Mr. Everett had 50,725 and Mr. Morton 51,034, the required number. Had just one more vote been cast for Everett—his brother's or that of his friend Secretary of State John Bigelow, who did not vote at all—Morton would not have had the required majority, and the election would have devolved to the legislature, where Everett may well have prevailed.

Gentlemen of that day with the means to do so took their disappointments on a European tour. Soon after his defeat, Edward Everett sailed to assuage his wounded pride and to allow his consumptive wife some relief in the warmth of southern Italy. In August of 1841, while in Florence, Everett read a report in recently arrived American papers that President Tyler had sent several diplomatic nominations up to the Senate, among which was Everett's to be U.S. minister to the United Kingdom. If slavery had been a subliminal issue in Everett's defeat for governor of Massachusetts, it would be an open one in the struggle for his confirmation by the U. S. Senate. All the deference he had shown his Southern colleagues on the issue when he had been a member of Congress would go unrequited. The advanced thinkers of the Southern cause fully realized that the attitude of the American minister at the Court of St. James was of vital interest to slaveholders.

Britain was already seizing American vessels engaged in the slave trade. The American minister would be expected to protest such action and seek damages. The South was attempting to build up a party of supporters in England, so surely the minister should be a Southerner or someone sympathetic to their cause. Southern senators suggested that Everett's name be withdrawn. President Tyler, through Secretary of State Webster, refused, and the nomination became both symbol and substance of the growing national divide.

The debate began amid a flood of letters from the North demanding confirmation and from the South warnings of dire consequences should that happen. Immediately the choice of Edward Everett for nomination became both personal and vindictive. Senator King of Alabama, leading the opposition, concluded a bitter and abusive attack on Everett by shouting that if a man who held such views on slavery as did the nominee was confirmed, the Union itself would be dissolved. Whereupon Henry Clay sprang to his feet, pointed a trembling finger at the Alabama senator and declared: "If a man so preeminently qualified for the position of minister should be rejected by this Senate and for the reasons given by the Senator from Alabama, the Union is dissolved already."

The vote was cast on September 13, with the Whigs in control of the Senate, 28 to 22. Everett prevailed 23 to 19. Every Democrat who voted, along with two Southern Whigs, voted nay. Several Northern Democrats took a walk.

It had been the recommendation of Secretary of State Daniel Webster to President Harrison that his successor, President Tyler, choose Everett for the post to the Court of St. James. There the new minister would prove invaluable in the secretary's coming attempt to settle long-standing and dangerous disputes between the United States and Great Britain. The English aristocracy was quite appreciative that a man of such grace and charm, education and oratorical ability should be sent from what some still considered a rather pedestrian former colony. When Tyler succeeded to the presidency, Everett was criticized by some of his fellow luminaries in the Whig Party for staying on in England. He was, in the words of Ralph Waldo Emerson, too much "attracted to the vulgar prizes of politics." Everett's election as president of Harvard in 1846 gave him the opportunity to leave public life. There he found the duties of administration not to his liking and resigned the Harvard presidency in 1849.

Edward Everett succeeded the late Daniel Webster as secretary of state from November 1852 to March 1853, in the dying days of President Millard Fillmore's administration. During his tenure in office, Everett rejected in very vigorous terms a French/English proposal that the United States join them in guaranteeing Spain's continued possession of Cuba and that the United States forbear from any attempt to acquire it. Everett replied that the proximity of Cuba to the United States and the fact that the United States had already purchased Louisiana and Florida precluded it from being forever bound not to make a similar acquisition of the island.

Everett resigned as secretary of state in March of 1853 to take the seat in the U. S. Senate to which he had been elected by the Massachusetts legislature. Daniel Webster had died the previous October, and Caleb Cushing was serving as Attorney General of the United States, so the mantle of political leadership in the Commonwealth, with its potential for a national role, fell to Everett. It was not to be, for just as it had so adversely affected the political fortunes of Caleb Cushing and so vexed the public life of Daniel Webster, the problem that the Founding Fathers had dared not face—the antislavery question—would end the political career of another Massachusetts titan.

Antislavery agitation was on the rise in the nation, markedly so in the Commonwealth. By temperament and ties a supporter of the Bay State's moderate, Union-defending Whigs, Everett saw his political demise engendered by his stand on the Kansas-Nebraska Act in 1854. The opponents of that bill believed its enactment would nullify the provision of the Compromise of 1850, which forbade the introduction of slavery in new territories of the Louisiana Purchase that lay north of longitude-latitude 36/30. Everett spoke against the bill but without the malice and denunciation the Massachusetts radical antislavers thought he should have. Everett was ill and unable to be in the Senate when the final vote on the measure was taken, and his political fate was sealed. To the abolitionists the Senator's absence appeared a cowardly ruse, and they heaped such scorn and denunciation on him that he resigned his seat at the end of the session.

In the election of 1860, Edward Everett with little enthusiasm agreed to be the vice presidential nominee of the Constitutional Union Party, with John Bell of Tennessee the choice for president. A remnant of old-line Whigs, the newly formed party was dedicated to preserving the union of sovereign states by then hell-bent for dissolution. Bell and Everett finished last among the four contending sets of candidates, with under 13 percent of the votes cast.

The attack on Fort Sumter brought to Everett the harsh realization that he must abandon any hope of maintaining both peace and the Union. Despite his age, 67, the greatest orator of his time used that gift to travel extensively throughout the North exhorting all within hearing range to ever greater effort to defeat those who had torn asunder the United States of America. Summoned to Faneuil Hall on the night prior to the reelection of Abraham Lincoln, Everett, who had a surfeit of appreciative audiences during his public life, was so overcome by the tumultuous applause that he wept. Charles Francis Adams (who was married to Everett's sister), with that uncompromising frankness so marked in the Adams character, had said of his brother-in-law after the Kansas-Nebraska affair that Everett's character was "stuff not good enough in rainy weather, though bright enough in sunshine." Of his service to his country during the Civil War, Adams was later to write that Everett had come: "to a point where his fears no longer checked him . . . his interests run on all fours with his conscience. He spoke at last with all the power he really felt. To me his four last years appear worth more than all the rest of his life, including the whole series of his rhetorical triumphs."

Edward Everett died on January 15, 1865. Earlier he had written President Lincoln that "I would be glad if I could flatter myself that I came as near the central idea of the occasion [the dedication of the battlefield at Gettysburg] in two hours as you did in two minutes." To which the president replied that he took pleasure in Everett's conviction that what little he, Lincoln, had said "was not entirely a failure."

The Literary Ministers

While a student himself at Harvard Divinity School, Everett had supplemented his income by tutoring Harvard freshmen in Latin. Of all the scholars who passed through his life none had, according to Everett, "a more teachable temper" than George Bancroft. Born in Worcester in October of 1800, Bancroft was the eighth of thirteen children of Aaron Bancroft and Lucretia Chandler Bancroft. His father was a leader in the Unitarian schism among the Massachusetts clergy and first president of the American Unitarian Association.

At age 11, having completed his early schooling at Worcester, young George attended Phillips Exeter Academy, and studied there for two years before entering the freshman class at Harvard. After graduating at age 17 in the class of 1817, he spent a year at the divinity school.

Encouraged by Harvard's President Kirkland and funded with a scholarship from the university, Bancroft sailed to Europe in 1818 to further his studies at Gottingen, Germany.

Bancroft did not travel directly home when he completed his courses in Oriental languages and biblical studies at Gottingen; rather he took a leisurely sojourn on the continent, where he was able to meet and spend time with such luminaries as Hegel, Curlier, Gallatin, Lafayette and Lord Byron—an education in itself. From Germany he had written President Kirkland that "the plan of life, which I have adopted, indicates clearly that I must become, either an instructor at the University, or a clergyman, or set up a high school."

Bancroft tried all three and at all three he failed. As a clergyman he lasted only a year, his preaching failing to impress either his minister father or the suffering congregation. Before his first year as an instructor at Harvard had run its course, Bancroft was lamenting: "I have found college a sickening and wearisome place." After eight years of effort, the school he and J.G. Cogswell founded—Round Hill in Northampton—based on the model of the kind he so admired in Germany, also failed. Even in the profession in which he was to become nationally renowned, that of an author, his first effort was unsuccessful. In 1832 Bancroft published a book of poems so bad that in later years he was to disclaim it as but a "youthful indiscretion." But even though poetry was not the gift of George Bancroft, prose was.

His first long piece of prose was the text of an oration he delivered in Springfield, Massachusetts, July 4, 1826, commemorating the fiftieth anniversary of the Declaration of Independence. From that time on he was a prolific contributor to the *North American Review* and other periodicals. The first volume of Bancroft's epic ten-volume *History of the United States*, the work that was to gain him the accolade "Father of American History," was published in 1834 to much acclaim—and some criticism. No one could find fault with the depth of research or the quality of Bancroft's writing, but not a few critics thought that he had passed over the line from nonpartisan historian to ideologue defender of democracy.

In the days of Bancroft's ascendancy as a major American writer and historian, a good number of Massachusetts gentlemen of education and erudition could be found in the Whig Party, but few among

Democrats. Bancroft, a Democrat, put his pen at the disposal of the party but hesitated to stand for election himself lest it offend his Whig in-laws. When he did run for the Massachusetts General Court in 1834 he was unsuccessful, but his service to the national Democratic Party called for reward. Bancroft's was that of an appointment by President Van Buren to be collector of the Port of Boston. (In that post, Bancroft found sinecures at the Custom House for two needy fellow men of letters: Nathaniel Hawthorne and Orestes A. Brownson.)

In the election of 1843, the Democratic Party ticket featured James K. Polk for president of the United States and George Bancroft for governor of Massachusetts. Polk won; Bancroft lost. The new president from Tennessee, however, had not forgotten the distinguished author from Massachusetts. Bancroft had done yeoman work for Polk at the Democratic nominating convention and was rewarded with an appointment as Secretary of the Navy. It was during Bancroft's relatively short term in office (18 months) that the United States Naval Academy was founded.

A cabinet post was not what Bancroft really wanted from the president. He longed, rather, for a diplomatic posting in Europe, where he could use both his personal reputation and the prestige of his office to gain easier access to the records he needed for the completion of the research for his *History of the United States*. In September 1846 Polk appointed him minister to the United Kingdom. While as minister, Bancroft was able to successfully pursue his research, his diplomatic tenure was uneventful. His most important accomplishments were the conclusions of postal and commercial agreements between Great Britain and the United States.

When George Bancroft returned from England in 1849, by this time a citizen of the world, he settled in New York, summered at Newport, rode horses and grew roses, enjoyed the company of high society, and devoted himself to completion of his massive treatise. Yet as a political man, historian, and opponent of slavery, Bancroft could not ignore the turmoil building in the land. As the crisis grew, he abandoned the Democrats and threw his support to the new Republican Party. Like many other well-educated and accomplished political men of the day, Bancroft had little faith that the tall, gangling man from Illinois, Abraham Lincoln, possessed anywhere near the capacities to successfully lead the Union through its looming troubles. To his credit, however, and long before others, George Bancroft realized he had made a mistake in judgment about Abraham Lincoln, and lent the support of both his pen and his voice to the beleaguered president.

In 1867, President Andrew Johnson offered Bancroft the post as U.S. minister to Germany. He accepted, was continued in that office by President Grant and spent seven happy and productive years in the country where he had received his doctorate a half century earlier.

George Bancroft, author, historian and public servant, died in Washington, D.C. on January 17, 1891, nine months before his ninety-first birthday. As he wished, Bancroft was buried in his native Worcester. Not for the first time, nor for the last, a president of the United States ordered the lowering of flags as the bier of a distinguished American passed by on its way from the nation's capital to the welcoming soil of the old colony at Massachusetts Bay.

The Industrial Diplomats

The War of 1812 dealt a severe blow to the merchant traders of New England. In its aftermath the more astute of them, in conjunction with investors and bankers, turned from the sea to industry. They were to build new cities with giant mills where men, women and children would produce cotton and woolen goods, machine tools, shoes, and clothing. Great fortunes were to be made, and the industrialists and their progeny would become the backbone of a political party that would dominate the Commonwealth's government and contribute much to the nation's for a century and more. Among the first of these merchant traders was Abbott Lawrence who was born in 1792 on a farm in Grafton, Massachusetts.

Abbott Lawrence's brother Amos had established a business in Boston. When he was 16, Abbott was sent to Amos to be an apprentice. In 1814, having come of age, Abbott Lawrence was admitted to the partnership in A. & A. Lawrence, a merchant firm that for a half century was a stalwart of the city's commerce. In 1815, with the ink on the treaty that officially ended the War of 1812 hardly dry, Abbott, always energetic and aware, hastened to England while his company's competitors still slept, and returned with a supply of goods that had been unavailable during the war.

Ill health forced Amos Lawrence to retire in 1830 just about the time Abbott and other entrepreneurs—the Lowells, Appletons, and Jacksons—began the building of the industrial infrastructure that rose along the rivers of Massachusetts. The Lowells had established the mill city of that name in 1825, and a quarter century later Abbott Lawrence built a great mill town bearing his family name on the banks of the Merrimack. Buoyant, quick to decision, full of energy and of a sanguine disposition, Lawrence was often called upon by his fellow merchants to represent their interests in dealings with the political establishment. Characteristic of his class and wealth, Lawrence had a sense of public obligation that was, and would continue to be, part of his nature. Lawrence devoted much time and talent to public improvements in his adopted city. When Boston was building the works to bring in a fresh and healthy supply of water, it was Lawrence's opposition to private exploitation that resulted in the water sewer system being publicly owned.

A leader at the 1827 Harrisburg, Pennsylvania Convention held to discuss the promotion of domestic manufacturing, Lawrence was elected to the U.S. Congress from Boston in 1834. As an ardent Whig, he was active in the party's nominating convention of 1844, and four years later was a leading but unsuccessful contender for the vice presidential nomination to run with Zachary Taylor. President Taylor offered Lawrence first the post of Secretary of the Navy and then that of Commerce, both of which he declined. He did, however, accept the president's appointment to be American minister to the Court of St. James and served there with dignity and distinction from August 1849 to October 1852.

Abbott Lawrence engaged in many acts of philanthropy during his lifetime. He was a generous benefactor of the academy at Groton, Massachusetts, where he received his early education. He supported the work of Louis Agassiz, and, in what may have been his most enduring charitable legacy, created an endowment for the establishment of the Lawrence Scientific School. When he died in 1855, Lawrence bequeathed $50,000 to construct model lodging houses for the working men and women of Boston—an act of ironic generosity from a man who was Yankee in origin, Protestant in faith, and Republican in politics. His legacy was to provide proper housing for laborers who were increasingly Irish, Catholic, and Democrat, and whose sons and grandsons would eventually oust Lawrence's own descendants from political power in the Commonwealth.

Black Dan Webster

It was a fully produced drama, with a cast of real estate hucksters, British lords, American statesmen, openhanded politicians and the king of the Netherlands. The props included erroneous surveys, mysterious maps, secret government funds, generous bribes, winks and nods, and conflicts of interest so blatant as to define the term. The script was propelled along by the threat of war and enriched with subplots of piracy, ships' seizures and suppression of the slave trade. When the curtain came down, what had been produced was the Webster-Ashburton Treaty, a document that went beyond its expressed purpose of settling the Canadian-American border dispute between the United States and Great Britain to create the diplomatic threshold of a "special relationship." There would be one or two other stumbles over that threshold before the cementing of the amicable and productive relationship between the two great English-speaking nations that endures to this day.

The American signatory to the treaty, Secretary of State Daniel Webster, was born on a farm in Salisbury (Franklin), New Hampshire on the 18th of January, 1782, and died in Marshfield, Massachusetts, on October 24, 1852. Webster's delicate health had the positive result of substituting the hard labor of farm work for, as his father put it, "the advantage of learning." Webster's path to learning took him from Phillips Andover Academy at Andover to Dartmouth College, where he received his degree in 1801.

The swarthy complexioned Webster (hence the sobriquet "Black Dan" given him by contemporaries in his youth) began the study of law in his hometown before taking a position teaching at an academy in Fryeburg, Maine. It was not instructing the locals that lit a fire in the breast of young Dan Webster; it was the opportunity of going to Boston. When the choice of a permanent teaching position at a generous salary (and the use of a house) or joining his brother in the "Capital of New England" presented itself to Webster, he unhesitatingly chose the latter. In short order Webster secured a clerkship in the office of distinguished lawyer Christopher Gore. The New Hampshire farm boy's association with Gore permitted him entry into the city's leading legal and political circles as well as its social whirl. From the former Webster gained a salutary intellectual stimulus, and from the latter a not-so-healthy life-long taste for good food and fine wine.

The illness of his father required Webster to return to the farm, forcing him, as he lamented, "to drop from the firmament of Boston gayety and pleasure, to the level of a rustic village, of silence and obscurity." But not for long. After his father's death, Webster took up the practice of law in Portsmouth, New Hampshire, built up a lucrative practice and married Grace Fletcher.

In his politics, Daniel Webster was the quintessential Federalist: conservative, nationalistic, elitist. He once observed that "more than two-thirds of the talent, the character, and the property of the nation" were combined in that party. Elected to the Thirteenth Congress (1813), and reelected to the Fourteenth, Webster came back to Boston halfway through the second term to open a law office. Eschewing politics, at least for a while, the gentleman from New Hampshire was soon earning $15,000 a year in the capital of New England.

Webster's reentry into politics was marked by uninterrupted success. He served in the U.S. House of Representatives from March 1823 to May 1827, when he was elected to the U. S. Senate. Reelected as a Whig in 1833 and 1839, Senator Webster resigned in 1841 to take up his duties as President Harrison's secretary of state.

The newly elected president was convinced that the senator from Massachusetts should hold high office in his new administration, and felt the same about the senator from Kentucky, Henry Clay. The problem posed by the fact that the two often clashed was solved by Clay himself when he informed President Harrison that he would not resign his seat in the Senate to accept a presidential appointment and added that he thought Webster the ideal choice as secretary of state.

The new secretary arrived in Washington with a new chief clerk of the department, his son, Daniel Fletcher Webster. Like many sons of gifted fathers, Fletcher suffered from undue comparisons and self-doubts. Yet he performed most capably as a key figure in a department whose responsibilities far outnumbered both personnel and resources; and in his father's absence, he was de facto secretary of the department.

The circumstances under which the new secretary was to assume his duties were not benign. The Whigs had tut-tutted at the Democratic Party's patronage during the presidential campaign, but much of Webster's first weeks in office were taken up dispensing the same to worthy Whigs. War between the United States and Great Britain could not be entirely ruled out if long-festering disputes over the border between Maine and Canada and other issues were not settled. The House Foreign Relations Committee would be chaired by a man who was not an admirer of Webster and who had more expertise in the nation's diplomatic affairs than the new secretary of state—or anyone else for that matter: John Quincy Adams. Then there was Henry Clay, a force unto himself to be reckoned with. To further complicate matters, the unexpected death of President Harrison elevated the politically suspect John Tyler to the presidency.

On Saturday, September 11, 1841, a letter was delivered to President Tyler at the White House announcing the resignation of the full cabinet he had inherited from his deceased predecessor. What President Tyler had done to precipitate the unprecedented action was to veto two pieces of legislation sponsored by Henry Clay reestablishing the Bank of the United States. It was as if the Democrat-leaning Virginian Tyler, nominated only to balance the ticket and surely not to govern, was trying to sabotage the first-ever Whig government. Clay, who was attempting to run that government from the Senate, had the sitting president expelled from the Whig Party. The only cabinet secretary's resignation missing during the mass exodus was that of Daniel Webster. After consulting with other Whig leaders of Massachusetts who wished him to stay in office, and with the belief that a properly drawn bank bill would later pass, Webster followed his own inclination against resignation.

Now that he had decided to stay on, there were several points of contention between the United States and Great Britain that Webster as the secretary of state had to face. The friction centering around the still disputed border between the northeastern United States and Canada was aggravated in 1837 during an uprising against British rule in Canada led by William Lyon Mackenzie. The rebel forces had engaged the American steamboat the *Caroline* to fetch them supplies. A British-Canadian force crossed the border into the United States and seized and burned the ship. The question of an apology and reparations, if any, remained unsettled.

On February 12, 1839, Rufus McIntire, a United States land agent, was sent into the Aroostock region (between New Brunswick and Maine) to chase out Canadian lumberjacks. McIntire was arrested, and in the ensuing uproar, militias were called out, the Nova Scotia legislature appropriated war funds, and the U. S. Congress authorized the conscription of 50,000 men and the expenditure of $10 million for military action.

In November 1841, 19 African slaves being transported on the American vessel *Creole* seized the ship, wounding several and killing one of the crew. The American consul to the British Bahamas, where the ship had been taken, vainly implored Her Majesty's authorities to help him to return the vessel and its cargo to the rightful owners. Instead, the slaves, by that time in British territory, were declared free under the authority of the Parliamentary Acts of 1833.

The British navy, in its ongoing effort to suppress the slave trade, routinely boarded and searched suspicious American vessels off the west coast of Africa. Such actions left open the possibility of British impressments of American sailors under the "once an Englishman, always an Englishman" doctrine. The Treaty of Paris that had ended the Revolutionary War had not settled the border dispute. Nor were the parties to the Treaty of Ghent, which ended the War of 1812, able to come to terms about the dispute. Finally, the contending parties turned to the king of the Netherlands to arbitrate the question.

Handicapped by a faulty map drawn by colonial surveyors, which placed the forty-fifth parallel somewhat north of its true position, and unable to pinpoint some of the land in dispute, the Dutch government put forth a "split-the-difference" compromise. United States senators from the North, however, urged on by their stubborn brothers from Maine, blocked its acceptance. There the matter lay, a clear and persistent danger, ignored by both presidents and prime ministers until the rise to power in England of Sir Robert Peel and the commencement of the Harrison-Tyler administration in America.

Anxious to have all outstanding matters between the two countries amicably settled, Peel appointed a commission with the authority to do so. Alexander Baring (Lord Ashburton), whose family had grown its modest London bank into a leader in international finance, was appointed to head the British delegation. Lord Ashburton was married to an American woman and had extensive land holdings in New England, and the Baring Bank had overseen the financing of the Louisiana Purchase. If that constituted a conflict of interest on Lord Ashburton's part, it was offset by the one apparent in the financial dealings of his American counterpart, Secretary of State Webster. Like many other prominent public men of the day, Webster had invested heavily in the Western land boom. When things went bust, Webster was bailed out by his banking friends, including the Biddles of Philadelphia and the Barings of London. (And by Abbott Lawrence and other industrialists whose interests Webster had assiduously supported while he served in the U.S. Senate.)

The Americans were handicapped in the negotiations over the United States-Canadian border by the existence of two maps. One had been purchased by Webster from the estate of Friedich Von Steuben, which the Revolutionary War general had purportedly received from John Jay. The other, recently discovered by Harvard historian Jared Sparks, was folded in a letter written by Benjamin Franklin. Since both Jay and Franklin had been members of the Paris peace commission, their idea of where the true border lay was crucial. On both maps, the line drawn supported the British rather than the American position. For his part, Lord Ashburton's flexibility as to what he could negotiate away in return for American concessions was hampered by Lord Wellington's insistence that almost all of the disputed land was needed for England's defense.

Webster realized early on that acceptance by the state of Maine of any compromise he and Ashburton might agree to was crucial. To that end, he hired as his agent Francis O. J. (Fog) Smith, a mover and shaker in real estate and politics in Maine. Smith was compensated from secret State Department funds. If money was to be a factor in bringing the stubborn Maine leaders along, Ashburton was pleased to make his contribution. The sum of $14,000 was made available to convince reluctant state lawmakers that they ought to see to the passage of legislation establishing a commission, with full authority and without further reference to the legislature, to settle. Webster and Ashburton, the former giving up claim to the Madawaska settlement and the latter allowing the Americans to have Rouse's Point and navigation on the St. John's River, came to a settlement—to which the gentlemen from Maine gave a resounding "Never!" Webster, after several days of despairing that a settlement would ever be reached, turned up the heat on the delegates from Maine, pointing out that of the 12,000 square miles in dispute, the 5,000 going to Britain was only 500 more than proposed by the Dutch king. There would also be, for the sake of justice, a cash settlement for Maine in the sum of $125,000 from the American Treasury. (And an equal settlement for Massachusetts, of which Maine had been a part prior to its elevation to statehood on March 15, 1820. It was a princely sum for the Bay State Yankees, who had done nothing more substantial than look on.) The Maine delegation relented and agreed to Webster and Ashburton's terms.

On the question of the boarding of American vessels by the British Navy in the suppression of the slave trade, it was agreed that each country would be allowed cruisers off the African coast with total armament of at least 80 guns. These ships would cooperate in the antislavery effort, with each boarding and searching the other country's vessels. Outside the treaty, in an exchange of letters, the British would not abandon their position that America-bound slaves who managed to reach Her Majesty's territory were free men. As to an apology for the seizure of the *Caroline*, Ashburton may or may not have provided one. The thriving practice of criminals of both nationalities using the joint border to escape the law was addressed in an extradition treaty that did not include runaway slaves.

In retrospect, Daniel Webster's conclusion of the treaty with Great Britain may be considered the most significant accomplishment of his public life. Having achieved that, and unable to arrange his diplomatic appointment to the Court of St. James, Webster resigned his post on May 9, 1843. Heavily in debt, the now-corpulent lawyer resumed his law practice in Boston. Webster and old associates in the leadership of the Whig Party of Massachusetts were soon reconciled; in 1844 Webster enthusiastically supported the unsuccessful candidacy of Henry Clay.

That year the Massachusetts legislature once again sent Webster to the U.S. Senate. In him the Commonwealth's industrialists had more an indentured servant than a friend. Dependent as he was on their generosity to stay financially afloat and in line with his own beliefs, Senator Webster declared it his "especial business" to work for the preservation of the great industrial interests of the country against Democratic free-trade propensities. Webster opposed the war with Mexico and the acquisition of Texas, with its potential for the expansion of slavery. He also paid a great personal price during that conflict when his son, Major Edward Webster, died of exposure near Mexico City.

On the issue of slavery, Webster held that institution to be "a great moral and political evil." Yet, like many of his Northern contemporaries, the senator conceded that in the Southern states it was a matter of domestic policy and within their exclusive control. Daniel Webster's dream of the presidency still haunted him, and in the spring of 1847, he toured the South to test the waters. Too much fine wine and rich food and the realization that he would never be president of the United States sent him home to Marshfield suffering from ill health and depression. The death of his daughter, Julia Appleton, depressed him further.

Much to his frustration, Webster could not get his fellow senators in Washington to address the issue of a protective tariff that was so dear to his heart. Slavery, its extension to the newly acquired Southwest territories and the increasingly open talk of Southern nationality and succession filled the chamber. In a speech from the floor of the Senate in support of the Compromise of 1850, which would maintain the balance between free and slave states, Webster attempted to pour oil on the troubled waters of sectional enmity.

Speaking "not as a Massachusetts man, nor as a Northern man, but as an American," Webster decried slavery as an evil, but not as much an evil as disunion. Turning to his Southern colleagues, he warned them that they could not peacefully secede. He chided the Northern abolitionists for their extremism and the North in general for failing its obligation to return runaway slaves. Webster's conservative supporters thought the speech "Godlike." The antislavery element in his own party saw him as a portly, heavy-drinking old man in office well beyond the days of his usefulness.

After President Taylor's death in 1850, Webster once again became secretary of state, this time in the administration of Millard Fillmore. Webster fell gravely ill in July of that year. By fall it was apparent he would not live much longer. Those standing vigil by his beside on October 24, 1852, heard Webster whisper, as if to respond to an inquiry: "I still live." Those were the last words from the mouth of a giant of pre-Civil War American politics.

CHAPTER IV

The End of Illusion

THE LAND THAT BLACK DAN WEBSTER DEPARTED FROM WAS A WONDROUS place. Not yet a century old, a measure of time hardly worth the calculation, the United States of America had become a union of 31 states with a population of 23 million. A vast half-continent spread east to west from the Atlantic to the Pacific and north to south from Canada to Mexico. It was a huffing, puffing place where steamboats plied mighty rivers and man-made canals, and great engines chugged trains of people and commerce to and fro. Factories and mills harnessed the power of New England rivers and the rich soil of the South produced great fields of cotton. Bankers in Philadelphia, New York and Boston supplied the capital, and immigrants—2.5 million of them in the decade between 1851 and 1860—the labor. Who could argue that divine Providence was not manifesting the nation's destiny to "overspread the continent for the development of our yearly multiplying millions."

A land wondrous and troubled. The pursuit of the white man's destiny seemed to require the conquest of the lands and dismissal of the culture of the native people. To many, the rising tide of immigration had become a frightening flood. "Boom" and "bust" were the operative words of the nation's economy. By 1857 financial panic had once again set in. The relatively orderly metamorphoses of the America political party system, Federalist to Whig and Democrat-Republican to Democrat, was in chaos. The Whigs were divided North and South and in the North further between the "Conscience" Whigs, who deplored slavery, and the "Cotton" Whigs, whose factories depended on the product of slave labor. The Liberty Party, an attempt to unite antislavery forces, was formed in 1844, nominated James Birney for president, got 62,000 votes and disappeared. The Free-Soil Party, a coalition of former Liberty Party members, antislavery Whigs, and hybrid New York Democrats, with their slogan of "Free soil, free speech, free labor and free men," was formed to oppose the extension of slave labor into territories acquired from Mexico.

By the mid-1850s, the American Party, which espoused a platform of extending the waiting period for citizenship from 5 to 21 years and banning the foreign-born from holding public office, came out into the open from its mysterious lodges and clandestine meetings. The party's candidate for president, Millard Fillmore, received 21 percent of the popular and 8 percent of the electoral vote in 1856. Four years later, the Democrats, hopelessly fragmented among its Unionists, States Righters, Abolitionists, and Slavers, nominated two candidates for president: Stephen A. Douglas from its Northern wing, and John C. Breckinridge from its Southern.

The American political system, indeed the nation itself, was beset by the imbedded thunder and crackling lightening of a fast-approaching storm—a hurricane of disunion and death gathering force ever since, in the words of Thomas Jefferson, "The clause . . . reprobating enslaving inhabitants of Africa," was struck from the language of the Declaration of Independence.

"I will vote," Robert Charles Winthrop, the Whig candidate for the U. S. Senate from Massachusetts in 1851, declared "for [a] just, practicable, and constitutional mode of diminishing or mitigating so great an evil as slavery." Three years later the president of the United States felt it necessary to order U. S. Marines and soldiers into Boston to escort a fugitive slave, Anthony Burns, out of the city. The prisoner and his escort marched passed sullen crowds and American flags at half staff, while church bells tolled a mournful tune to mark the black man's departure from freedom in Massachusetts to human bondage in Virginia. By then it was too late for "practicable and constitutional" means to diminish or mitigate such an evil as slavery. "We went to bed one night old fashioned, conservative, Compromise Union Whigs &

waked up stark mad Abolitionists," Amos Lawrence wrote about Anthony Burns's "abduction" by the force of the federal government. Lawrence backed up his words by supplying arms to the antislavery forces in the bloody battle for Kansas.

At 4:30 A.M. on April 12, 1861, a battery of the Confederate States of America opened fire on the United States of America's Fort Sumter at Charleston, South Carolina.

In the years preceding that military action, the question of America, half slave and half free, had been fought in Congress and in the courts. In those legislative skirmishes, Massachusetts men, as they had even before the birth of the nation, played a vital if sometimes ambivalent role.

The Dandy and the Bobbin Boy

Robert Charles Winthrop was not so much born to the social and political aristocracy of Massachusetts as he was a continuation of it. A descendant of John Winthrop, the first governor of the Massachusetts Bay Colony when it settled in Boston in 1630, Robert Charles Winthrop was born on May 12, 1809, in the house of his late granduncle, James Bowdoin, the second governor of the Commonwealth. His father, Thomas Lindall Winthrop, served as lieutenant governor of Massachusetts from 1826 to 1833. The years during which the pedigreed Winthrop would grow to maturity and seek and find public office, were a time when "Our beloved Commonwealth" John G. Palfrey, a dissident Whig, lamented, "is at present governed by a perfect aristocracy as ever existed."

As would be expected of one of his station and expectation, Robert Charles Winthrop prepared for Harvard, where he completed his studies in three years, graduating in 1828. The law, of course, was the profession for such as he, and he began his law studies in the office of Daniel Webster.

Nathaniel Prentiss (sometimes Prentice) Banks was born, quite literally, into the Boston Manufacturing Company. Nathaniel's father was a foreman at the pioneering Waltham mill, and his family lived in a company house. Young Nathaniel was taken from school at age 14 and set to work removing empty bobbins and replacing them with ones filled with thread.

The paternalism of the Boston Manufacturing Company allowed Nathaniel Banks to attend lectures at the Rumford Institute. There, the "Bobbin Boy" was exposed to instructions and oratory from such as Daniel Webster, Caleb Cushing and Charles Sumner. Banks was convinced that escape from the drudgery of factory work that seemingly was to be his lot in life lay in learning, and set out to educate himself. On his days off, when other boys were playing, Banks and his friend from the mill, Charlie Nelson, walked the ten miles to Boston, where the librarian at the Athenaeum would let them read to their hearts' content. From bits and pieces of spare wood, young Banks built a space in the attic of his house for a library. The first book he purchased was John Locke's *Essay Concerning Human Understanding*.

Intelligent and voluble, Nathaniel Banks always seemed able to maneuver himself into the center of attention. While working at the mill, he organized dances for the young men and women. (The management, however, frowned upon the late hours their young workers were keeping on dance nights and decreed that if they attended, they would be fired.)

Robert Charles Winthrop was tall, good looking, and personable. A bit of a dandy who in later life took to walking about Boston wearing a wide-brim hat, broadcloth coat, velvet collar, and cape. In his youth he was a frequent subscriber to the festive dances of his social set. Born a Whig, lived as a Whig and died as a Whig, Winthrop held himself aloof when most of his political fellows abandoned that dying party to join the newly founded Republicans.

Banks, on the other hand, would be elected or defeated for Congress carrying the banners of six different political parties. "An ideological stalwart" Winthrop's friends would say of him. "A political whore" was the judgment of Banks by his enemies. Banks would serve as governor of Massachusetts and Winthrop as U.S. Senator, and both of them, at most crucial times, were Speakers of the U. S. House of Representatives.

Disorder in the House

Robert Winthrop had been elected as a Whig to the 26th Congress (1839-1841) in 1840 to fill the unexpired term of Abbott Lawrence, who had resigned. Reelected to the 27th Congress, Winthrop left the House in May 1842 to return to Boston to attend to his dying wife.

After Mrs. Winthrop died, Nathan Appleton, who had been elected to fill the vacancy caused by Winthrop's resignation, also resigned, and Winthrop returned to Washington and to the House. The 28th and 29th terms of Congress, to which Winthrop was reelected, were firmly in control of the Democrats and generally served the purposes of that party's pro-slavery element. In the 30th Congress (1847-1849), the Whigs took control with 115 to 108 Democrats, with four adherents of other parties. In what in the near future would be considered a relatively mild contest which went to only three ballots, Robert Charles Winthrop was elected Speaker of the House. His attempt at reelection two years later was a far different matter.

Despite the efforts of both the Whig and Democratic presidential candidates in the 1848 election to suppress it, the central issue of the campaign was whether slave-holding states had the power to extend the institution of slavery to the new territories acquired in the Mexican-American War. Winthrop, who had come to Congress with the reputation as a brilliant Speaker in the Massachusetts House, had presided over its national counterpart with fairness and decorum—too much fairness, in the opinion of Whig abolitionists and representatives of the newly-founded Free-Soilers Party, especially in the makeup of those congressional committees dealing with matters affecting the slavery issues. In the 31st Congress (1849-1851) the House was divided into 112 Democrats, 109 Whigs and 9 "others." If party loyalty prevailed, the Democrats would have an excellent chance of electing one of their own to replace Winthrop, who stood for reelection to the chair. Party unity, however, was becoming a rare commodity in those tumultuous day in Congress. The House rules at the time required the Speaker to be elected by a clear majority, not a mere plurality.

The Democrats and Free-Soilers formed a coalition strong enough, should it hold together, to withhold a majority from any candidate it opposed. Election of the Speaker commenced in confusion, with no fewer than 11 candidates at one point, eventually devolving into a contest between the sitting Speaker, Robert Winthrop of Massachusetts and his challenger, Howell Cobb of Georgia. For 59 ballots, an unprecedented number in the history of the House, the increasingly wearing battle continued between one candidate who was still in search of a "just and practicable" way to mitigate the evils of slavery and an unabashed proponent of the constitutionally conferred and biblically condoned right to practice it.

The Free-Soilers were adamant that the new Speaker be someone who would appoint to such congressional committees a majority opposed to the expansion of slavery such as the District of Columbia and the territories. They could not support Cobb, and they withheld their support from Winthrop because they were not sure he could be trusted to do their bidding. As the balloting went on, motions were made that the Speaker be divested of his power to appoint committees; that he be chosen by lottery; and that members receive no salary until a Speaker was chosen, all of which went down to defeat. After the 59th ballot, a motion that the Speaker be elected by a mere plurality, provided it was a majority of a quorum, was introduced and passed. On the 60th vote, Cobb led, but there was no quorum. On the 61st, it was Winthrop, but again no quorum. The mathematical maneuvering by the managers of both candidates was intense. On the 62nd ballot a quorum was present, but the vote was tied. On the 63rd with a quorum present, Cobb led by two. The House then took the unusual step of confirming Cobb's election by resolution.

Through all of this the Free-Soilers stuck with the often self-defeating political strategy of "our way or no way." If they had set aside their misgivings and supported Winthrop, the coming of the Civil War might have been delayed or the terms of the Compromise of 1850 significantly different because the power of the Speaker was no longer in control of the characteristically even-handed Mr. Winthrop, rather the ideologically pro-slavery Howell Cobb held the power.

As improbable as it seems, the contest to elect a Speaker in the 34th Congress (1855-1857) was to last longer and be more intense than that of the 31st. The bitter contest was made all the worse by a physical danger never before present in the lower branch of the national legislature: the loaded pistols. One knowledgeable observer estimated that between those on the floor and those in the gallery, upwards of 200 such weapons could be counted in the House on any given day. If blood were to be spilled over the questions of slavery, states' rights and the inviolability of the Union, there was a good chance it would run first on the floor of the U.S. House of Representatives. Violence had already erupted on the streets of Washington: Horace Greeley, covering the proceedings for the *New York Daily Tribune*, had been set upon and beaten by a congressman from Arkansas.

On May 30, 1854, just a few days after he had ordered federal troops to Boston to effect the return of the run-away slave Anthony Burns, President Pierce signed into law the Kansas-Nebraska Act. Its provision that "all questions pertaining to slavery in the Territories [would be left] to the people residing therein" effectively nullified existing compromises on the extension of slave power in the United States. The previous February and again in March, a group of Free-Soilers, antislavery Democrats, and so-called "Conscience" as opposed to "Cotton" Whigs met in Ripon, Wisconsin. Certain there was no way to effectively contest the growing influence of slave power as long as its political opposition remained divided, the delegates formed a new party. The founders decided to call the party Republican, ironic as it now seems, in honor of the man they considered their philosophical sire, the Demoncratic-Republican slaveholder Thomas Jefferson.

The success of the new party was immediate and spectacular. In the very next Congress—the 34th—between those elected in the party's name and defections to it among incumbents, the Republicans held 108 seats in the House and 15 in the Senate. There was no hope of control of the upper house because 40 of the 60 senators were Democrats, with five scattered. The House, however, was another matter. Of the 234 members, the 108 Republicans constituted the largest bloc, the Democrats were second with 83 and the remaining 43 were scattered among Free-Soilers, Know-Nothings and various others along the political spectrum. If the Republicans could unite behind one candidate and attract others in opposition to the extension of slavery, they might elect the Speaker. A daunting obstacle to electing the presiding officer of the House was its rule, reinstated after the Winthrop-Cobb contest, that required a majority, not just a plurality, for election. That number would be 118 if all 234 members were present and voting. As hard as they tried, it was a number the Republicans and their allies would never attain.

The first of what would eventually number 133 ballots was cast on December 3, 1855; the last on February 2, 1856. The early ballots attracted 21 candidates, many of them frivolous. William A. Richardson of Illinois was the most formidable of the serious contest-

THE END OF ILLUSION • 109

ants, with 74 votes. Among the others was Nathaniel Banks, the second-year congressman from Massachusetts. If the goal of the Republicans was to attract enough votes from other parties to best the Democrats, the candidacy of Banks, who had been elected to Congress with the endorsement of the Free-Soil, Democrat and Know-Nothing parties of his district, might be the one to do it. It was soon obvious that Richardson could not win, so the antislavery forces turned to Lewis Campbell of Ohio. Campbell was thought by some (but not all) to have the best record on the slavery question. The balloting went on, tedious day after tedious day. Partisan crowds, itching for trouble, confronted each other on the streets of the capital.

Eventually Campbell's support began to evaporate, as much because of his abrasive personality as his suspect political philosophy. Banks, on the other hand, cool and cooperative, seemed to be gaining favor and scattered votes. A proposal was put forth to drop the candidate with the lowest number until there were only two, but it did not carry. Banks was the beneficiary of Campbell's decline. By December 10th he had 107 votes—enough to lead but 11 short of victory. As the balloting continued and more and more antislavery representatives became convinced that Banks could not move beyond his 107 solid votes, a caucus was called to find a candidate to break the deadlock. The name of A. M. C. Pennington was proposed. A number of members of the House asked Charles Sumner about the advisability of endorsing Pennington. "My counsel," he reported to friends, "has been to stick with Banks and leave the future to take care of itself." Pennington went unendorsed and the balloting went on.

Nathaniel Banks held on with cement-like support from the Know-Nothings, who considered him their champion, and from the Free-Soilers, who thought of him as "the very bone and sinew of Free-soil-ism." Others were not so sure. There was nothing wrong with Banks personally, charming and persuasive as he was. If the House was looking for a parliamentary leader to get them through the rest of the term without blood on the floor, Banks was their man. Had he not skillfully presided over the 1853 Massachusetts Constitutional Convention "the ablest body that ever met in Massachusetts." It was the depth of Banks's convictions—indeed if he had any—that remained in question. Banks had opposed antislavery agitation in Boston, all the while maintaining contact with Free-Soilers and the city's abolitionists. His supporters could point to but a single act of political courage—when Banks became one of the few Democrats to vote against the Kansas-Nebraska Act in the previous Congress, a vote that forced his departure from the Democratic Party. It was an expedient vote, his enemies explained, made only to placate the growing antislavery forces in his district. Banks courted the newly enfranchised immigrants in his district, yet when nativism became a political force, he hurried himself off to join and eventually take control of the Waltham, Massachusetts, Lodge of Know-Nothings.

The House had reached a stalemate and was unable to organize for the people's business. December had passed; January was nearly gone; February was at hand. Through it all Nathaniel Banks was the picture of coolness and dignity. When supporters came under fire, he was quick to defend them. When reminded of a speech he had given in Maine the previous summer that called for the dissolution of the Union if slavery were allowed to survive, he now declared for the "Union as it is. . . . I will meet its enemies in the field for the Union . . . fight for the Union . . . and trust that its existence will be perpetual." When the candidate made a statement that seemed to favor racial intermarriage, Southern congressmen flew into a frenzy and demanded that Banks's name be withdrawn. Banks responded by "utterly" disclaiming any support of miscegenation, adding that he "felt that there was an inequality of capacity and the condition of the races," and reminding his listeners that he had "never asserted their equality."

The incumbent clerk of the House, John Forney, had planned to retire as soon as he was able to announce the election of the Speaker. He was beginning to despair that he would ever have the opportunity. By the first day of February, the situation had become intolerable for both sides. The Democrats could not maintain control of the House; the Republicans could not seize it; and the rest had no leadership to offer. A motion was made to change the rules of the House to those existing in 1849, which allowed choice of the Speaker by plurality. The motion passed, and the die-hard slave power advocates and their friends rushed to fend off what they feared was impending defeat by solidly backing Representative William Aiken of South Carolina. The outcome was far from certain. The Aiken backers, convinced that support for Banks had peaked, or even eroded, knew if they could hold their votes and persuade enough House members to be conveniently absent when the roll was taken, they might prevail.

On November 2, 1856, Clerk Forney began to call the roll for the 133rd and, as it turned out, last ballot of the long standoff: 214 of the possible 234 votes were cast (some members having absented themselves) and 11 votes were scattered among candidates who could not win. Mr. Aiken had 100; Mr. Banks, 103. The sergeant-at-arms raised his mace; the clerk passed the gavel. Old Joshua Giddings, the senior member of the body, administered the oath to Nathaniel P. Banks, who had celebrated his 40th birthday the week before. "A proud, historic moment," Charles Sumner wrote. "For the first time during years there seems to be a North. I fancied I saw the star glittering over his head. His appearance, voice, and manner were at admirable harmony with the occasion."

Congressman Alexander H. Stephens, who would become the vice president of the Confederate States, downplayed the Banks victory as purely sectional. In fact, it was a significant defeat for the legislative leaders of slave power and the first national victory of the Republican Party. If Robert Winthrop's defeat in the 31st Congress had advanced the cause of slave power one step, the election of Banks in the 34th took it a step backward. While dispensing fairness to both sides in the slavery issue, Banks did accomplish one goal of the Free-Soilers: He appointed a majority of antislave power congressmen to the Kansas Investigating Committee. His Speakership gave antislavery forces much needed time to better organize.

Banks's single term as Speaker was marked by his consummate skill in presiding with fundamental courtesy and fairness over a dramatically divided House. The man who had defeated Winthrop in 1849, former Speaker Howell Cobb of Georgia, said Nathaniel P. Banks "was in all respects the best presiding officer I have ever seen." "The best," others asserted "since Henry Clay."

After his defeat for reelection to the Speakership in 1849, Robert Charles Winthrop continued in the House until July 1850, when he was elected to the U. S. Senate to complete the unexpired term of Daniel Webster, who had been appointed secretary of state. The time for compromise on the slavery issue having passed, Winthrop lost his bid for reelection to that seat in 1851 to the radical abolitionist, Charles Sumner. With the exception of an occasional word of advice, Robert Charles Winthrop usually stayed away from politics after that defeat and devoted his remaining years to the advancement of education. He wrote incessantly, was a long-serving vestryman of the Trinity Church in Boston and continued his membership of 55 years (30 of them as president) in the Massachusetts Historical Society. He died on November 16, 1894, at the age of 85.

A supporter of Lincoln who in turn admired him, Banks served during the Civil War as one of the president's "political generals." His wartime service was probably not as defensible as his admirers would wish, nor as horrid as summed up by General William T. Sherman: "It seems but little better than murder to give important commands to such men as Banks . . . and yet it seems impossible to prevent it."

In 1879 Banks was appointed by President Hayes as U.S. Marshal for the District of Massachusetts. The veteran political warhorse and retired general served as marshall for ten years, his last reappointment made by Democratic President Grover Cleveland. By that time Banks was either incapable or unwilling to give the proper time and attention to the supervision of a government agency quite susceptible to patronage and corruption. The U.S. Attorney General had reason to believe all was not well in Boston. Upon investigation, he learned that Banks's chief deputy and his cronies were engaging in substantial fraud. Banks, who was beginning to show mental feebleness, ran once again for Congress in 1888 and won. By the time he stood for reelection, his infirmities were so apparent that he was denied renomination. His last political act was to cast a vote as a presidential elector for Benjamin Harrison in 1893. He died shortly thereafter, on September 1, 1894, at age 78.

Mr. Associate Justice Benjamin Curtis

Benjamin Robbins Curtis was born in Watertown, Massachusetts, on November 4, 1809, the son of a ship's captain, Benjamin III and his wife Lois Robbins Curtis. The Curtis family had first arrived in Boston on the *Lyon* in September of 1632, and Benjamin could list among his ancestors the Reverend John Eliot, the 17th century Puritan "apostle of the Indians." The death at sea of Benjamin's father threatened to silence the Curtis clan's boast of having produced a Harvard College graduate in every generation since 1738, but his uncle, George Ticknor, a professor at the college, and author and publisher, came to Benjamin's aid with generous loans. Those funds, supplemented by the income from a student boardinghouse his mother opened in Cambridge, allowed young Benjamin to enter Harvard in 1825. From the class of 1829, where he graduated with second honors, Curtis entered Harvard Law School but left in 1831 before completing the course both to gain practical experience by taking over the law practice of a county attorney in Northfield, Massachusetts, and to secure an income so that he might marry his cousin, Eliza Maria Woodward. Curtis did complete his studies at the law school and moved to Boston in 1834 to become a partner in the law firm of a distant relative, Charles Pelham Curtis. Benjamin's wife died in 1844. Two years later he married his law partner's daughter, Anna Wroe Curtis, also a cousin. In all, Curtis married three times and fathered 12 children.

Early American presidents took regional representation on the U. S. Supreme Court into consideration when appointing justices. When the "New England" seat became vacant on the death of Justice Woodbury of New Hampshire in September 1851, Secretary of State Webster proposed to President Fillmore that he nominate Curtis. Benjamin Curtis was 41 when he took his oath of office on October 10, 1851.

Justice Curtis distinguished himself by writing the Court's majority opinion in the *Colley v. Board of Wardens* case, which held that when the objective of regulating commerce is to establish a uniform national rule, the power to do so is in the hands of Congress, but where such a countrywide rule is not necessary, the power to regulate is in state control. Five years later, in 1857, Justice Curtis was to write a dissenting opinion for which he would be praised, condemned, and driven from the Court. Dred Scott, a Negro slave, had brought suit against his owner to gain his freedom. Scott contended that since his former owner had taken him to Illinois, a free state, where he had resided for several years, he was a free man. Scott first won, then lost on appeal, and the case eventually was brought to the Supreme Court. Whether the High Court would even hear the case was problematical. The Court had previously ruled that state courts had jurisdiction in determining the status of Negroes living within their borders. The justices had only to refer to that decision in refusing to take on the Dred Scott case. For a combination of reasons—two Northern justices indicated that they would rule in favor of Scott and affirm the constitutionality of the Missouri Compromise; Southern sympathizers were pressing for a pro-slavery verdict, and the Southern justices were anxious to have a go at the Compromise—the Supreme Court decided to rule.

At the conclusion of the arguments in the case (the advocate for Scott being Benjamin's brother, George Ticknor Curtis) but before Chief Justice Taney had released the majority decision, Justice Curtis's dissent appeared in the Boston press. Taney's majority, in a sweeping and devastating opinion, held that Scott was not a citizen, that residence in a free territory did not make him a free man, and that, under the Constitution, Congress had no power to ban slavery from the territories as it had done in the Missouri Compromise. Curtis's long and well-reasoned dissent cited 14 instances where Congress had legislated with respect to slavery in the territories prior to the Missouri Compromise. It stated that because there was no federal citizenship clause in the Constitution, it followed that such was created by the conferring of state citizenship, thus Scott could be a citizen within the meaning of Article III; and that after the Court had ruled that Scott was not a citizen, it could not proceed to decide the case on its merits.

Chief Justice Taney was livid, not only because Curtis's dissent had been released to the press before Taney's ruling, but also because Curtis's argument forced him to re-work some of his. The bitterness between the two carried on through lengthy and acrimonious correspondence. Justice Curtis resigned from the Court in September 1857, six months after the *Dred Scott* decision, giving as the reason his inability to support a large family on the paltry salary of an associate justice of the nation's highest court. As true as that may have been, many believed the enmity engendered between him and the chief justice over the *Dred Scott* case had a substantial bearing on Curtis's leaving the bench.

In 1868, Curtis presented the opening argument in President Johnson's defense against impeachment. Curtis later declined the president's offer of the attorney generalship and died while vacationing at his summer home in Newport, Rhode Island, on September 15, 1874, at age 65.

"A knockdown argument; 'tis but a word and a blow." —John Dryden

Charles Sumner and his sister Matilda were born in Boston on January 6, 1811, the premature twins of Charles Pinckney Sumner and Relief Jacob Sumner. Charles's father was a graduate of Harvard and studied law in the office of Josiah Quincy, the second mayor of the city of Boston. A stern man seemingly incapable of any outward expression of love toward his children, he was nevertheless a progressive thinker. He believed Negro children were entitled to the same education as white children and that laws against intermarriage between the races ought to be repealed.

Through the patronage of Governor Levi Lincoln, Charles Pinckney Sumner was appointed sheriff of Suffolk County, a lucrative office that allowed him to send his son to Harvard. Young Sumner went on to the law school after receiving his undergraduate degree and while there, came under the influence of Justice Story. Despite some early success at lawyering, Charles surprised his friends by borrowing enough money for a two-year sojourn in Europe. Like George Bancroft before him, Sumner managed to meet many of the political and intellectual elite on the continent. In the style of Bancroft, Sumner returned to Boston besotted by European culture and disdainful of American society.

A bachelor until he married at age 55, Sumner thrived in the company of men such as Story, Henry Wadsworth Longfellow, Samuel Gridley Howe and Francis Limber. As the years passed and more of his beloved circle of male friends took wives and moved on, Sumner became isolated and, so it seemed to some of his contemporaries, bitter. More and more attracted to causes such as school and prison reform, he began to assume the role of an uncompromising ideologue. A lonely role when taken to the extreme Sumner took it, he held positions that not only created bitter enemies but antagonized friends.

That was to be his destiny, for, like the biblical prophets of old, Sumner, using his magnificent voice and finely honed intellect, and in singular possession of a writ from almighty God, would call a nation to account for its evil without regard for personal consequence. When Sumner first gave a public oration, at Boston's Fourth of July celebration in 1845, the reaction of the city's former mayor, Samuel A. Eliot, the father of the future president of Harvard, Charles W. Eliot, was that "The young man has cut his throat." Sumner ignored, perhaps in defiance, the many military men and descendants of Revolutionary War soldiers on the platform, to the awe of the thousands gathered on the Boston Common, and proceeded to declaim on his theme that in that age there was no dishonorable peace nor honorable war.

The results of the 1849 Massachusetts elections were clouded by an attempt on the part of a coalition of Free-Soilers, Conscience Whigs and Democrats to wrest control of the state from the regular Whig Party. The result was that no candidate for governor or lieutenant governor had the clear majority required for election. Election to those offices then fell to the legislature, where the coalition had gained control. After proceeding to divide up the contested state offices among themselves, Henry Wilson, the leader of the coalition, turned to the biggest prize of all: a full term in the U. S. Senate beginning on March 4, 1851. The coalition put forth the name of Charles Sumner, setting off a prolonged and bitter contest that was to have historic national significance.

The Honor of the Commonwealth

In July 1850, in the days before popular election of U.S. Senators, Robert Charles Winthrop had been elected to the U.S. Senate by the Massachusetts Senate to fill the unexpired term of Senator Daniel Webster, who had recently resigned to serve once more as U.S. Secretary of State. Winthrop served until February 1, 1851, when the Senate replaced him with Robert Rantoul, Jr. When the election for a full U.S. Senate term came up, Winthrop presented himself as a candidate. Opposition to Charles Sumner, who played the reluctant suitor in the drama, was widespread and vehement. The leader of the opposition, Caleb Cushing, warned of sending "a red-hot Abolitionist . . . like a firebrand, for six years into the senate chamber of the United States . . ." Such would be "a death-stab to the honor and welfare of the Commonwealth." It took several weeks and 21 ballots before the Senate chose Sumner, under pressure from the House of Representatives and influenced by the voters at several town meetings who insisted on his election.

Caleb Cushing was proven correct in his assessment of the consternation the "red-hot Abolitionist" Charles Sumner would raise in the Senate. Sumner took his seat on December 1, 1851. Five days before the end of the session, the junior senator from Massachusetts took the floor. The visitors' gallery was nearly empty when he began his speech; it was filled with nodding heads and shaking fists by the time he finished three hours later.

The object of the awe and anger was Sumner's defense of an amendment he had offered to the appropriations bill forbidding the expenditure of federal funds in enforcement of the Fugitive Slave Law. Using his considerable forensic powers and armed with a plethora of legal and classical references, Sumner attempted to vocally flog that perfidious statute to death.

If it was for the votes of his fellow senators that Sumner made his appeal he failed: only four voted for his amendment. The awakening of America's conscience was another matter. Horace Mann wrote in his diary that "the 26th of August, 1852," the date of Sumner's speech "redeemed the 7th of March, 1850," the date of the passage of the Kansas-Nebraska Act. Senator Salmon P. Chase of Ohio declared that Sumner's speech would mark the day in American history when the advocates of the restriction of slavery "no longer content to stand on the defensive in the contest with slavery, boldly attacked the very citadel of its power in that doctrine of finality."

Sumner was not finished. He would have further words in a later speech in condemnation not only of those who would extend slave power but also of those who, despite professed moral objection, would allow slavery to continue. The subversive writings of Samuel Adams and the call of Thomas Paine to liberty or to death were as soft whispers in inattentive ears in comparison to the tumult Sumner's polemics let loose.

"This session will not pass without the Senate chamber's becoming the scene of some unparalleled outrage." So said Sumner before the gathering of the 34th Congress on December 5, 1855. That outrage would come the following May, and Charles Sumner of Massachusetts would be both perpetrator and victim.

On May 20, 1856, rising to his full six-foot height, Sumner first paused to scan the attentive Senate chamber and expectant gallery and then began a speech he titled "The Crime Against Kansas." He began slowly and softly, but soon, now surely the dooming prophet of old who was righteously armed with the wrath of an angry God, merciless and unmitigated, the powerful voice thundered. Like drops of his Savior's blood from that ancient cross of infamy, the words fell one by one—not in cleansing, redemptive flow, but with vituperation, condemnation and scorn. His enemies, those within and without the chamber, were subjected to terrible vilification. They represented ". . . the mingled meanness and wickedness of the cheat" in their support of ". . . the incredible atrocity of the Assassins and of the Thugs." Quickly, and without care, the senator attacked his absent colleague and defender of slave power, Senator Andrew P. Butler of South Carolina, as one who had ". . . chosen a mistress to whom he had made his vows, and who, though ugly to others, is always lovely to him; . . . the harlot, Slavery."

Abandoning any pretense of civility, Sumner went on to ridicule the elderly Butler's speech impediment and described the senator's comments about the representatives of a free Kansas as those with incoherent phrases, discharged the loose expectoration of his speech . . . he cannot open his mouth, but out there flies a blunder."

Turning to face him directly, Sumner then loosed his fiery tongue on the senator from Illinois and leader of the Democrats, Stephen A. Douglas. "If Butler was the Don Quixote and made his vows to the harlot slavery," then Douglas was "the Squire of Slavery, its very Sancho Panza, ready to do its humiliating offices."

The incendiary words of Sumner's speech crackled like electric thunder over the telegraph wires. The South was in an uproar, its rights condemned, the code of personal honor it so dearly held cast rudely to the floor. The abolitionists and antislavery Free-Soilers in the North were in ecstasy. Now it had been said: there it was. No longer could the "harlot slavery," like the Victorian whore, be allowed in the surreptitious company of the gentleman liberty. No longer, in the cause of the Union, or profit, or peace, or in the hope of its natural demise, could human bondage be tolerated with the wink of compromise or the glance of accommodation. Charles Sumner had blown away the middle ground.

Two days after he had delivered the speech, while at his desk in the Senate, Sumner was viciously attacked with a cane by Senator Butler's cousin, Congressman Preston S. Brooks. It was not until three years later that Sumner was able to return to full duty in the Senate. In October of 1861, he was the first statesman of prominence to advocate emancipation, and he never ceased to urge President Lincoln to take action. When the Republican Party achieved a majority in the 37th Congress (1861-1863), Sumner became chairman of the Foreign Relations Committee. A vehement opponent of President Andrew Johnson's reconstruction policies, Sumner, who rightly considered it a political rather than a judicial proceeding, was a leader in the failed attempt to impeach the president. Charles Sumner died in office on March 11, 1874, at the age of 63.

A Mr. Adams Once Again

When his appointment as U.S. minister to the United Kingdom became public, those in England with any historical memory immediately recognized the family name—Adams. It could be assumed with some degree of certainty that in Charles Francis Adams, grandson of John and son of John Quincy, both of whom served as ministers to the United Kingdom, the same family traits would be found: those of a classically educated, intelligent and literary man. An Adams who would conduct himself with all the expected social graces but would endure neither fool nor sycophant; once he had determined the correctness of it, he would stay his course with a resoluteness and stubbornness that was as certain as it was hereditary.

Charles Francis Adams was born in Boston on August 18, 1807. When he arrived at the Boston Latin School, the scholastic incubator of so many renowned leaders, young Charles already possessed an informal education of some depth. While with his father in St. Petersburg he had mastered French; journeying with his mother by carriage from Russia to Paris, he had witnessed the "Hundred Days" and Napoleon's return and had spent two fruitful years at an English boarding school. After graduating from Harvard, class of 1825, Adams engaged in literary pursuits, oversaw what little estate his father had accumulated, and came rather late and somewhat reluctantly to agree with the old curmudgeon congressman on the slavery question. Displeased with the Massachusetts Whig leaders, Charles Francis

Adams founded the *Boston Whig*, a publication that, in opposition to the opinions of such men as Webster and Winthrop, pointed out that unless some great and unlikely change took place, the country must face up to the alternatives of either disunion or war.

Elected in 1858 to fill the seat formerly held by his father, Adams came to believe that only the Republican Party had the newness and capacity to provide policies that would prevent the breakup of the Union. The situation at the time was fluid. The financial and political clout of slave power was immense. The Southern states had taken their stand, but the border states were hesitating. The possibility that the newly elected president, Abraham Lincoln, could not be peaceably inaugurated was real. As leader of the House Committee on the Union, Adams managed with tact and moderation to limit the epic differences in the House between the North and South to discussion and debate rather than violence.

A supporter of William H. Seward for the Republican nomination for president in 1860, Adams was not particularly pleased with the election of Lincoln but did concede him to be honest and with "fair capacity." It was to Adams, on the recommendation of Secretary of State Seward, to whom Lincoln turned for the most important diplomatic assignment at that moment in American history: the ambassadorship to the Court of St. James. In the equation that existed at the commencement of the Civil War, the highly industrialized North held the advantage over the rural, agricultural South. If the war were to last for any great length of time—and few believed it would—the rebellious Confederate states could not hope to prevail unless they could acquire the hardware of war from Europe.

Here England was to be a key player. Great Britain's clothing mills consumed great quantities of southern cotton. The English, in their usual opportunistic, diplomatic maneuvering, seemed ready to take advantage of the rupture of the American Union. The most important instruction Adams received from Lincoln before his departure for London was to prevent recognition of the Confederacy as a "belligerent." The status of belligerent, one step up from that of pirate, which would make confederate vessels outlaws on the high seas, and one step down from full recognition as a sovereign nation, would allow the Confederacy to legally trade with European States. Adams arrived in

England on the evening of May 13, 1861, and was chagrined to learn from the next morning's newspapers that the status of "belligerent" had already been granted to the Confederacy.

The official policy of the English government of Lord Palmerston, as carried out by the minister of foreign affairs, Lord John Russell, was to appear neutral in the American civil war only so long as circumstances dictated it. The dissolution of the Union or the appearance of an impending Southern victory would quickly change that course. Adams found Russell to his liking and Russell was at ease with Adams. Their manner was quite similar—reserved, intelligent, logical, unimpassioned. Both were reasonable men. Adams also found English society quite supportive of the Southern cause, with many willing to go all the way toward recognition of the Confederate states. Adams was also confronted with the fact that two Confederate agents in London, James Murray Mason and John Slidel, had the attentive ear of the foreign minister. The continuing military frustrations of the North, which led to a belief on the part of some British leaders that it could not win the war, made Adams's task all the more difficult.

Despite its official policy of neutrality, the British government was allowing large quantities of war supplies to be shipped to the Confederacy. The Confederate naval agent in England had been able to have two large men-of-war, the *Alabama* and the *Florida*, built and outfitted in England. The two ships, especially the *Alabama*, wreaked havoc on Union shipping up and down the Atlantic. Emboldened, the agent, James D. Bullish, then contracted with the Lard shipyard in Liverpool for the building of two double-turret ironclads to hurl against the Union blockade of Southern ports. As a result of Adams's persistent protests to Russell on the true purpose of the ships—and not coincidentally on the British government's learning of the Confederate surrender at Vicksburg and Lee's defeat at Gettysburg, July 3-4, 1863—on September 3, Russell ordered the British ships detained.

The United States and Great Britain came dangerously close to hostilities themselves during Adams's ambassadorship when Captain Charles Wilkes, on the U.S.S. *San Jacinto*, boarded the British ship *Trent*, removed the two Confederate agents, and sent the ship on its way. The British public was in an uproar, with the press demanding an apology or war. Adams succeeded in keeping things from getting too far out of hand in London until President Lincoln and his cabinet were persuaded to instruct Secretary Seward to dispatch a letter of apology and assurances of freedom for the Confederate captives.

When news of Lincoln's emancipation of the slaves reached England, Adams expected jubilation in a country that had for so long compared its noble effort to suppress the slave trade with America's continued sufferance of it. But the high Tory and commercial interests in England still believed the North might lose the war, so Lincoln's action was futile, even foolish for the U.S. economy. The reception given to the proclamation convinced Adams of the hollowness of English condemnation of American slavery. It was a disappointment that prompted him to write in his diary, "It is impossible for me to express the contempt I feel for a nation which exhibits itself in this guise. It is a complete forfeiture of the old reputation for manliness and honesty." Yet British public opinion was slowly shifting to the Northern cause, first that of the working class and then that of societies and organizations. Expressions of support for the United States and President Lincoln were sent to Adams at the American embassy from a great public meeting at Exeter Hall in London. An indication of the esteem in which Ambassador Adams was eventually to be held came during parliamentary debate on the *Alabama* in March 1868. When Adams's name was mentioned, the House of Commons broke into spontaneous cheers.

In June 1868, Adams resigned his ambassadorship and returned to the United States. He refused the presidency of Harvard and resumed his life in Quincy. In 1871 President Grant appointed him as one of the two American arbitrators in the attempt to settle disputes between the United States and Great Britain. One dispute concerned what compensation, if any, Great Britain would pay for its culpability in the *Alabama* raids. The calm and reasonable efforts of Adams had much to do with the completion of an agreement that included $15.5 million dollars for the damage caused by the *Alabama*, *Florida* and *Shenandoah*. In his more than seven years as ambassador in England, Charles Francis Adams, like his grandfather and father before him when sent to that most comfortable and challenging of American diplomatic posts, showed himself equal to the British foreign ministry.

In 1874 Adams began the publication of a 12-volume compilation of his father's diaries. He died at Quincy on November 21, 1886.

Big Bad Ben

Some time after the seizure of the British ship *Trent* by an American frigate on high seas, which almost precipitated war with Great Britain, Charles Francis Adams received an extraordinary letter. That its author, Lord Palmerston, in violation of the British religious adherence to protocol, would correspond directly with the American ambassador, bypassing the British foreign office, was itself extraordinary. The letter's contents were even more extraordinary, for the letter contained a denunciation by the prime minister of Great Britain of the actions of an American army general. In undiplomatic language, the incensed lord declared, "If the Federal government chooses to be served by men capable of such revolting outrages, they must submit to abide by the deserved opinion which mankind will form of their conduct." The object of Palmerston's angry reprimand, and similar ones from other equally sensitive European heads of state, was Benjamin Franklin Butler.

Born at Deerfield, New Hampshire, November 5, 1818, and later removed to Lowell, Massachusetts, where his widowed mother ran a factory boardinghouse, Butler was a graduate of Colby College (called the Maine Literary and Theological Institute when it was chartered by the Massachusetts General Court in 1813). He became a successful criminal lawyer, with offices in Lowell and Boston; a shrewd investor, who accumulated a fortune despite his lavish spending; and a yachtsman who once owned the cup-winning *America*. An impolitic politician with an instinct both for creating enemies and great skill in refuting them with undiminished gusto, Butler was elected as a Democrat to the Massachusetts House in 1853 and the state Senate in 1859. An advocate of the ten-hour day and a friend of laboring men and women who had few such in those days, Butler cultivated support from his French-Canadian and Irish-Catholic constituents by favoring such things as compensation for the nuns who had been burned out of their convent in Charlestown in 1834. At the 1860 Democratic National Convention, Butler opposed the nomination of Stephen A. Douglas and voted for the future president of the Confederacy, Jefferson Davis. It was characteristic of the politician Butler that when the convention adjourned in chaos, he joined Caleb Cushing and others in nominating John C. Breckinridge, thus placing two candidates of their party on the ballot, with the unintended result of assuring the election of the Republican candidate, Abraham Lincoln.

Benjamin Butler was a strong defender of the Union and anticipated that its preservation might require war. Much to the consternation of Massachusetts Republicans, he managed to get himself elected brigadier general of the militia and made himself ready with men and money. When news reached Boston of the firing on Fort Sumter, Butler, resplendent in the best and most colorful uniform money could design, marched his troops out of Boston and off to glory. He hoped to receive financial and political rewards, including perhaps the Unionist presidential nomination in 1864. The day of his departure, April 17, 1861, was the first day of a spectacular military career that would bring him both glory and disgrace.

Before Ulysses S. Grant became the darling of the national and international press, it was Benjamin Butler who was the best known of the Northern generals. Brash and bold, Butler performed brilliantly, relieving the blockade of Washington by landing his Massachusetts 8th at Annapolis, and, more vital to the Union cause, repairing the railroad leading to the South. On May, 13, 1861, General Butler peacefully occupied Baltimore and three days later was promoted to the rank of major-general of the Union volunteers. As the Union army moved farther into Confederate territory, it was confronted with growing numbers of fleeing slaves. Neither the Army high command nor Lincoln's government seemed to have a solution to the volatile situation, but Butler did. He declared the former slaves "contraband of war," and organized them into work gangs.

The fortunes of war turned foul for Butler with a disastrous failure at the battle of Big Bethel, and on August 8, 1861, he was replaced. Butler was then given the command of military forces in the attack on the forts at Hatteras Island. Sent back to Massachusetts with the authority to enlist troops, which greatly displeased Governor Andrew, Butler planned, with little or no authority from above it seems, to use his independent command to reduce rebel presence on the eastern Virginia peninsula. Instead he was dispatched to command the land forces against New Orleans. General Butler entered the city on May 1, 1862, and inherited the onerous task of governing a very hostile population.

Ignoring army policy, with little interference from a government that found it difficult to discipline a prominent Democrat fighting for the Union cause, Butler proceeded to rule his domain with characteristic and troublesome elan. He assumed financial control of New Orleans, levying and collecting taxes and expending funds. He seized $800,000 in bullion and turned it over for safekeeping not to the United States but to the French consul. When a citizen of New Orleans, William Mumford, had the temerity to haul down the U.S. flag, Butler had the man hanged. Fed up with the verbal abuse and disrespect some of the female population of the conquered city were showing his troops, General Butler decreed that henceforth "When any female shall, by word or gesture, or movement, insult or show contempt for any soldier of the United States, she shall be regarded and held liable to be treated as a woman of the town plying her avocation." Others may have hesitated to consign patriotic ladies of the South to whoredom, but not Ben Butler. It was that order, Number 28, that caused so much discomfort to the more genteel Europeans. Despite his successes, Butler had caused enough trouble for the higher-ups. On December 16, 1862, he was ordered to relinquish his New Orleans command.

After the war, Butler joined Charles Sumner and other radical Republicans of Massachusetts in their attempt to seize control of the reconstruction of the defeated South from President Johnson and place it in the hands of Congress, which the Republicans controlled. Elected to the House of Representatives in 1866, Butler and Thaddeus Stevens of Pennsylvania were the House managers of the impeachment process against Johnson. Stevens was in ill health and weak at the time and Butler, bombastic and belligerent as ever, became the dominant prosecutor of the president. On questions of the reconstruction of the post-war South, Butler without fail took the most drastic position. The contempt the residents of New Orleans had for their former master was matched in Massachusetts by the conservative elements of both the Democrat and Republican parties. Butler was not one of them: he was too radical, too unconventional and, many were convinced, dishonest to boot. He was even accused of stealing the silverware from the New Orleans mansion where he had been headquartered.

In 1866 Butler was elected to Congress. In 1871 he ran for the Republican nomination for governor of Massachusetts and lost. He lost again in 1872 and lost his congressional seat in 1875. Three years later he went back to Congress as an independent member of the Greenback Party. That same year he again ran for the governorship, this time as a Greenback, and lost again, and again in 1880. Nothing if not persistent, he finally garnered the undivided support of the Democratic Party and was elected governor of Massachusetts in 1882. The fact that all the other constitutional offices, the governor's council and the legislature remained in control of the Republicans doomed his administration to failure. When the Butler-hating Harvard Corporation decided to break with their long tradition and not award an honorary degree to the sitting governor, Butler nevertheless showed up at commencement in full military regalia with a mounted escort.

In 1884 Butler received the presidential nomination of both the Anti-Monopoly Party (which advocated an income tax and elimination of tariffs) and the Greenback-Labor Party and he received a mere 175,370 votes. Even that small number may be counted a celebration of the different drummer to whom Butler had marched his whole life. General Benjamin Franklin Butler gained 1.8 percent of the vote; Grover Cleveland's margin of victory was 0.3 percent. Butler died in Washington on January 11, 1893, at age 84.

Politics in Peace and War

At the commencement of the Civil War the Republican Party was, practically speaking, the political arm of the North's attempt to preserve the Union, and the Democratic Party was the political arm of the secessionists. The fortunes of both parties would rise or fall on the military outcome of the struggle. Prior to the 1864 presidential election, with the military fortunes of the Union at low ebb and the reelection of Abraham Lincoln in doubt, the leaders of the national Republican Party took two measures to broaden the party's base. The first was to change its name to the National Union Party and the second was to choose as its vice presidential candidate the "War Democrat," Andrew Johnson of Tennessee. The reelection of Lincoln and the eventual victory of the Union left the Republican Party triumphant and the Democratic Party in shambles. In the 68 years between Lincoln's reelection in 1864 and Franklin Roosevelt's election in 1932, the Republican Party would control one or both Houses in 29 of the 34 Congresses and elect 13 of the 18 presidents. The post-Civil War dominance of "The Grand Old Party" began in grand style in the elections of 1868, when Ulysses S. Grant garnered 52.7 percent of the popular vote and 214 of the 294 electoral votes. Grant's party dominated the Senate 56 to 11 and the House 149 to 63.

The office the hero general entered into on March 4, 1869, was one under siege. The Senate, having flexed its legislative muscle against the executive during the Johnson administration had little inclination to retreat. In the North the electorate had grown weary of the ongoing roil of Reconstruction. In the South, the freed slaves had their liberty but not their rights and were being legislated into legal nonentities and subjected to unprosecuted violence, even death. What the nation needed was a strong, politically acute chief executive: a president who would effectively use the power of his office to bring the nation to the approaching centennial of its birth in as much harmony and prosperity as was possible. It was a capability found wanting in President Grant. The post-war situation the new president found himself in provided compost for the flowering of as grand a garden of thieves as the nation had ever seen. In order for power to corrupt, the corrupt must have power, and the Republicans had it. In the words of Senator James W. Grimes of Iowa, the Republican Party in 1870 was "the most corrupt and debauched political party that has ever existed"; thorns and thickets of evil the range and depth of which caused Henry Adams to lament, "The worst scandals of the 18th century were relatively harmless by the side of this which smirched executive, judiciary, banks, corporate systems, professions, and people, all the great active forces of society."

In Massachusetts, the Republican Party assumed a vise-like grip on all levels of government: local, legislative and executive. In the years of its ascendancy that party would send to Washington an extraordinary number of influential federal officeholders. There were eight during

Grant's two administrations: two cabinet secretaries, an attorney general, four ministers to foreign countries, and a vice president.

The Tax Collector

Not all the buds in the flowering of Massachusetts Republicanism opened in the conservatory of inherited wealth and privilege. As part of the distribution of Massachusetts constitutional offices after Henry Wilson's coalition of Free-Soilers, Democrats, and Know-Nothings took control of the legislature in 1851, George Sewall Boutwell was elected governor. Born in Brookline of old Massachusetts stock on January 28, 1818, Boutwell had little formal education beyond the few weeks each winter he could steal from his job clerking in a store to attend school. Like Nathaniel Banks before him, much of any other spare time the young man had he devoted to vociferous reading. General suffrage is a leveler, and the low as well as the high can aspire to the votes of their fellows. At age 24, Boutwell, already the author of several articles and speeches on the political situation in Massachusetts, was elected as a Democrat from the town of Groton to the state House of Representatives. He became a leader of the young anti-slavery element of his party and was thus positioned to throw support to Henry Wilson's coalition. Charles Sumner's reward for his participation in that political upheaval was a seat in the U. S. Senate; the 33-year-old Boutwell's was the governorship of Massachusetts. Governor Boutwell served two terms as the state's chief executive, was a key figure in the organization of the Massachusetts Republican Party and a member of its radical wing. The self-educated Boutwell was appointed secretary of the state's board of education following his terms as governor, and was admitted, at age 44, to the Suffolk County Bar in 1862.

Boutwell began his national political career as a member of the failed peace convention held prior to the outbreak of the Civil War and as a military commissioner in the War Department during the war. Wars are costly undertakings. As a measure to finance the Civil War, Congress enacted a tax on income "derived from any source whatever" in August of 1861. Lincoln appointed Boutwell as the country's first Commissioner of Internal Revenue. Elected as a Republican to the 38th and the three succeeding Congresses (March 4, 1863, to March 12, 1869), it was in the 40th Congress that he made his mark.

By that time the battle between the executive and legislative branches, between the "War Democrat" Johnson and the overwhelmingly Republican Congress had come to a head. In defiance of the Tenure of Office Act, which in effect forbade the president from removing from office an official whose appointment had been subject to Senate confirmation, President Johnson attempted to remove Secretary of War Edwin Stanton. Although such an action was established as presidential prerogative by President John Adams's firing of Secretary of State Pickering, some Republican radicals, Charles Sumner in the Senate and Benjamin Butler and George Boutwell in the House among them, saw the president's attempt to rid himself of holdover Stanton as an opportunity to remove the detested Johnson from office. With Sumner leading the proceedings in the Senate, and Boutwell and Butler agitating in the House, Articles of Impeachment were brought against the president. Boutwell was chosen as one of the seven House managers of the proceedings. In contrast to his reputation as being one of the few radicals open to political compromise, George Boutwell abandoned any pretense of statesmanship in his attack on the president. Andrew Johnson was, Boutwell declared, "an enemy of two races of men" whose appropriate punishment would be his projection into "a hole in the sky" near the Southern Cross. In the end, Johnson retained his presidency by one vote, but Boutwell's leadership among the radicals brought him the post of secretary of the treasury in President Grant's new administration.

Boutwell was no friend of civil service reform at a time when many thought it was sorely needed, and despite the fact that he had served as State Banking Commissioner, his appointment to the treasury was more because of his political skills than for any financial expertise. Nevertheless, his tenure at the treasury department was marked by four years of diligent effort to improve the efficiency of the department. Among his more successful efforts was the redemption of $200 million of 6 percent bonds and their replacement with an equal number of 5 percent bonds. Millions of dollars in "greenback" currency, a species used in the financing of the war, were still in the hands of the public. The question arose as to whether the government would redeem them in gold or allow their continued circulation. Speculators preferred the former; farmers and debtors the latter. If the choice were to be redemption, money was to be made by those who held the gold the government would need for repurchase. Two New Yorkers, Jay Gould and Jim Fisk, more gamblers than investors, with the connivance of persons in Grant's confidence, set out to corner the market in gold. By Friday, September 24, 1869, the premium on gold reached $163.50 an ounce, and Grant, following Boutwell's advice, ordered that $4 million of government gold be sold. That action thwarted Gould and Fisk's effort to corner the market but also had the adverse effect of triggering the infamous "Black Friday," with its ensuing financial panic and damage to the Grant administration.

When his old political comrade, Henry Wilson, resigned from the Senate in 1873, Boutwell left the Treasury to serve out what remained of Wilson's term. He served in the U. S. Senate from 1873 to 1877, and later was appointed by President Hayes as commissioner to codify and edit the existing federal statutes. Boutwell also served as U. S. counsel before the French and American Claims Commission in 1880 but declined the appointment as secretary of the treasury in 1884. At various times, he was involved with questions of international law in cases involving Haiti, Hawaii and Chile. Boutwell's concern over the Republican stand on the question of the Philippines, which he considered imperialistic, caused him to break with the party. From the time of its founding in 1898 until his death at age 87 in 1905, George Sewall Boutwell was president of the Anti-Imperialist League.

Mr. Richardson's Reputation

When George Boutwell first arrived at the Treasury, he brought with him as assistant secretary William Adams Richardson, a friend of many years. When Boutwell resigned, Grant elevated Richardson to secretary of the treasury. The date on which one came to or left the Grant administration was proof of the adage that in politics, timing is all-important: Boutwell left in time to have his reputation generally unsullied; Richardson came in time to have his besmirched.

Born in Tyngsborough, Massachusetts, in 1821 and raised by his stepmother, the sister of his departed mother, William Richardson prepared at the Pinkerton Academy in Derry, New Hampshire, and what is now the Lawrence Academy in Groton, Massachusetts, and at Harvard, class of 1843. His nature as a painstaking and methodical man helped him to excel at such tasks as consolidating the statutary laws of Massachusetts and the preparation of Supplements to congressional legislation that bear his name. As assistant secretary, Richardson was sent to London to oversee the treasury's funding operation with bankers there, and as secretary he managed to preserve the gold reserves of the United States by retiring government bonds simultaneous with the receipt of 15 million from the Geneva Award settlement having to do with Civil War claims. By 1873, however, both the nation and its secretary of the treasury had fallen on hard times.

One of capitalistic America's periodic financial panics had struck. Banks were failing, businesses were contracting, and three million men were out of work. As it ever was (and is) at such times, farmers and laborers wanted the government to pump more money into the economy to get it going. This time, to the classic fear of industrialists and businessmen that such action would trigger inflation, strikes and industrial violence added to the panic. After first resisting, Secretary Richardson finally succumbed to the turmoil and reissued $26 million of the $44 million in uncanceled greenbacks still held in government coffers. It was a stopgap measure many considered of dubious legality.

Meanwhile, in an action that seemed on its surface good policy but in the hands of its sponsor, Benjamin Butler, had a nefarious outcome, Congress passed a law authorizing the secretary of the treasury to employ three persons to assist in collecting unpaid taxes. It was a grand contract because each of the three holders of the monopoly were to be awarded with a "moiety"—one-half of what they could recover. Ben Butler, by whatever means, persuaded Richardson to grant one of the contracts to Butler's friend, John D. Sanborn. It is far easier to collect money from those who have it than from those who do not. The value of Sanborn's contract was further enhanced by the inclusion on his list of deadbeats almost all the country's railroads.

An energetic district attorney in New York did not like the smell of the matter and sought to bring an indictment against Sanborn. When the district attorney attempted to get pertinent papers from Secretary Richardson, Richardson shrugged him off with the claim that supplying documents might "affect the interests of private parties," which was just what the district attorney had in mind. The Ways and Means Committee of the House of Representatives was convened to investigate the matter with the possibility of recommending Secretary Richardson's impeachment. In a public report issued on May 4, 1874, the committee found Richardson's handling of the affair worthy of "severe condemnation" but found no evidence substantial enough for impeachment. In private they advised President Grant to get rid of Richardson, which the president did by means of a rather unsavory nomination of Richardson to be a judge on the U.S. Court of Claims. It was an appointment the magazine the *Nation* derided as "one other illustration of what General Grant means by the purification of the civil service."

In 1885, the courteous, unassuming, learned and terse Richardson became the chief justice of the Court of Claims. He also served as a Harvard overseer and taught law at Georgetown University. An active Mason and a member of the Unitarian Church, Richardson, whose wife had died 20 years earlier in Paris while returning from a trip the couple had made to China, died on October 19, 1896, at age 75.

Too Soon Gone

Ebenezer Rockwood Hoar took the oath of office as attorney general of the United States on March 5, 1869, one day after Ulysses S. Grant took his oath as president. A year and three months later, June 23, 1870, Hoar would be gone—an ill-timed departure of an honest man from an administration that would be increasingly in need of honest men.

E. Rockwood Hoar was born in Concord, Massachusetts, on February 21, 1816, the son of Samuel Hoar and Sarah Sherman Hoar. Both his father and his younger brother, George Frisbie Hoar, were U.S. Representatives, with the latter also serving in the U.S. Senate. In those years before the popular elections of U.S. senators, when a candidate had only to please the state legislators and not the wider electorate, many were beholden to the powerful interests of bankers and industrialists. Not so George Hoar or his older brother. Integrity was a family trait that one day would cost Ebenezer Hoar a seat on the Supreme Court of the United States. He graduated from Harvard at age 19, taught for a year and studied law in his father's office. He then entered Harvard Law School, where he received his LL.B. in 1839.

Ebenezer was appointed a judge of the court of common pleas in Boston and was the sitting judge in the trial of the abolitionists who had stormed the federal courthouse in an attempt to free the fugitive slave, Anthony Burns. Judge Hoar's carefully worded charge to the jurors did nothing to help the prosecution's case, and the accused were acquitted. His rise among the eminent members of the Boston Bar was rapid. An opponent of the annexation of Texas with its potential extension of slavery, he was elected to the Massachusetts Senate in 1846 as an antislavery Whig. (It was Hoar who first put words to the distinction by declaring on the floor of the Senate that he was a "Conscience" Whig, not a "Cotton" Whig.) Hoar resigned the judgeship in 1855 to resume the practice of law, but climbed back on the bench as an associate justice of the state Supreme Judicial Court in 1859, where he remained until called to Washington by the president. Grant's appointment of such an accomplished lawyer and jurist from one of the nation's most prestigious courts was among the finest the president would make in his two terms in office. Hoar proved a most effective administrator but a poor politician.

Politics, policy and professionalism, in differing order and to a lesser or greater degree, are the criteria for the appointment of federal judges. During weak presidencies such as Grant's, politics often outweighs the other criteria. The Judiciary Act of 1869, which created a separate circuit court judiciary, called for the appointment of nine new federal judges to that court. To powerful members of the Republican-controlled Senate (56 to 11), which had to confirm the president's nominees to the new circuit courts, that presented the patronage opportunity of a lifetime. Hoar's insistence that the appointments go to men of high character and ability thwarted more than one senator's grab for the judicial gem. Payback time came a few months later, when Grant nominated the highly qualified Hoar for one of the two additional seats on the U.S. Supreme Court created by the Judiciary Act. Hoar's nomination failed, 24 to 33. The Democrats in the Senate were not any more pleased with Hoar than the Republicans were.

It was the duty of the U.S. Attorney General to enforce the Fourteenth and Fifteenth Amendments to the U.S. Constitution, which guaranteed liberated slaves their rights in a free society. The Southern Democrats wanted a man more sympathetic to their cause than Hoar, and when Grant found he needed their support on other matters, Hoar's fate was sealed. As would be expected of a man of his quality—and as he would expect of himself—Ebenezer Hoar resigned his cabinet post. The following year he yielded to the president's request that he serve as a member of the joint high commission that concluded the Treaty of Washington between the United States and Great Britain regarding the *Alabama* claims and Canadian-American fishing rights.

Ebenezer Hoar served one term in Congress (1873-1874) along with his brother George. In 1876, Ebenezer, allowing his abhorrence of the man and his politics to overrule his better judgment, stood for Congress against Benjamin Butler. The dignified former cabinet member proved no match for Bad Ben Butler, who won handily. As a devoted son of Harvard and for nearly 30 years either an overseer or member of the college corporation, Ebenezer Hoar was also a dominant force in the American Unitarian Association. The youngest of the seven children from Ebenezer's marriage to Caroline Dowes Brooks in 1840, Sherman Hoar followed his grandfather Samuel and his father to Congress in 1890. Ebenezer Rockwood Hoar died on January 31, 1895, at the age of 79.

Recalling Mr. Motley

If ever there was a man with the pedigree, education, intelligence and accomplishment to prepare him—mold him really—to represent his country in the capitals of Europe, it was John Lothrop Motley. Despite those attributes, or perhaps because of them, Motley's assignments to Austria and to the Court of St. James would not be remembered for their successes: they were marked by the fact that from each of them he was recalled.

J. Lothrop, as he styled himself, was born on April 15, 1814, in the historic town of Dorchester before it was annexed to Boston in 1869. His father, Thomas, was a wealthy merchant, and his mother, Anna Lothrop Motley was the daughter of the minister of the Old North Church. His early education was at private schools such as Round Hill, where one of his masters was George Bancroft. The bright young Motley entered Harvard at age 13 and graduated at 17. Like many who do well in college, his college years made little impression on John except for the introduction it provided to the great literature of the world, to writing and to the improvement of his social graces. For a youth of scholarly ways and financial means, Europe was the place for further erudition. Off J. Lothrop went, following in the footsteps of other Harvard men to Gottingen, Germany. During that journey and in future trips to Europe, Motley would, like others before him, carry the proper letters of introduction and make the acquaintance of the political and social leaders, of the gentry and nobility of England and the Continent. The Boston to which he would return offered him the company of men such as Holmes, Longfellow, Emerson, Hawthorne, Agassiz, Dana and Amory. Boston was a place where, family fortune having been made and matured, a son could pursue noncommercial interests. Motley chose history, and he would become a historian of international reputation by producing such well-received works as *The Rise of the Dutch Republic* (1856) and the four-volume *History of the Dutch Republic* and *The United Netherlands*. The long gap between publication of the first (1860) and last two volumes (1867) of his Netherlands work is explained by the intervention of the Civil War.

At the urging of Senator Charles Sumner, a titan of patronage in the Lincoln administration, Motley was appointed minister to Austria in August, 1861. The president had once protested to the senator "I suppose you . . . think your State could furnish suitable men for every diplomatic and consulate station the Government has to fill." Although it was not in his brief as America's new representative in Vienna, on his way there Motley spent some time in England conferring with Lord John Russell and visiting the Queen at Balmoral Castle in Scotland.

Motley's position in Vienna, where he stayed from November 1861 to July 1867, was the object of some maneuvering in 1862. Gustavus Korner, recently appointed U.S. minister to Spain and by birth a German, would have preferred to go to Vienna and offered to swap positions with Motley. The enticement Korner used was the availability in Madrid of research material Motley could use to further his studies of the Dutch revolt against Spain. Motley already had all the material he wished for that project and wanted to stay put so he might research his proposed history of the Thirty Years War. Motley also believed that, as a German, Korner might not be welcome in Austria.

One of Minister Motley's main duties was to report on the European reaction to the American Civil War, which he did with thoroughness. He was also to articulate his country's position on the election of Maximilian to the Mexican throne, and the later American efforts to prevent Maximilian's execution. In 1866, Motley reported to Secretary of State Seward about rumors in Vienna that Austria was preparing to send troops to Mexico. Seward sent instructions that Motley was to withdraw from Vienna if the rumors proved true. It was another dispatch from the secretary later that year that proved the minister's undoing. On November 21, 1866, Seward wrote to Motley that an American in Paris had informed President Johnson that during his recent travels in Europe he had observed U.S. ministers and consuls openly expressing their hostility toward the president and his administration. The informant—George W. McCrackin—singled out Motley for expressing his disgust with the president's conduct and categorizing Seward as "hopelessly degraded." McCrackin, alleged Motley, showed general contempt for American democracy. Seward wanted an explanation. On December 11, Motley sent a strong denial of the charges as being a "vile calumny." One did not question the integrity of a man of the upbringing and character of J. Lothrop Motley without consequence—the questioning itself was beyond acceptance—thus in his lengthy reply to Seward the minister included his resignation. On January 5, 1867, Seward wrote to Motley that the president did not find Motley's answers to the charge of disloyalty unsatisfactory and it was up to him, Motley, whether he should consider his resignation absolute. Before Seward's dispatch could reach Motley, however, the president had Secretary Seward recall it. Motley waited for a reply to his defense until April 18, 1867. When it came it was an acceptance of his resignation.

In March of 1869, again at Charles Sumner's urging, President Grant appointed Motley to be the U.S. minister to Great Britain. Motley presented his credentials to the ever-reigning Queen Victoria 11 months after Charles Francis Adams had departed from the ageless sovereign. At the time, relations between the two countries were in one of their periods of strain, the main cause being the dispute over the

Alabama claims. Before his departure to London, Motley reviewed all the pertinent official correspondence on the matter, drew up a memorandum and submitted it to Secretary of State Hamilton Fish. Fish, however, had other ideas. He laid aside Motley's work and handed him specific instructions the minister was to carry out. What happened next, or at least what Motley's motivation for his actions were, is unclear. Either because Fish's instructions were ambiguous or because Motley did not fully understand their intent or because of his own well-settled opinions as to what should be done in the matter, the American minister failed to convey to the British Foreign Secretary the true position of his government. Fish's reaction was to take the matter out of Motley's hands and request of the British government that negotiations be transferred to Washington.

Despite that setback, Motley was convinced he still had the confidence of Fish and Grant. As late as May 17, 1870, he had been congratulated by Fish for his success in negotiating a naturalization treaty. One can imagine the minister's surprise when he picked up the *London Times* in June and read that he was about to be recalled to Washington. On June 30, Motley received a dispatch informing him that the president wanted to make a change in Great Britain and offered Motley the opportunity to resign. This Motley refused to do, explaining in a letter to Fish that to do so would leave the impression that he had failed in his duty to properly represent his country. For four months more he remained in London under the strained conditions created by the attitudes of Fish, Grant and himself. On November 10, 1870, Motley received a copy of a letter from Grant to the queen announcing his recall and additional instructions for him to turn over the property of the embassy to the secretary of the legation. Motley's response was a letter of protest to Fish; Fish's reply was a litany of complaints, many of them frivolous. There was some talk in Washington that Motley's fate had something to do with Grant's anger at his patron, Sumner, over the senator's opposition to the president's Santo Domingo policy. The Senate had the pertinent correspondence published, and the matter was dropped.

John Lothrop Motley died in England at his daughter's home on May 29, 1877, and was buried beside his wife in Kensal Green Cemetery, just outside of London. Witnesses to the internment included English royal and political figures and the ministers of the Netherlands and Belgium. The distinguished gentleman of letters and diplomacy was 63 when he died.

Over the Bounding Main

In 1820 the American Board of Commissioners for Foreign Missions, founded in Boston by New England Congregationalists ten years earlier, sent its first missionaries across the Pacific to bring Christianity and Western education to the native peoples of the islands of Hawaii, a place described by Mark Twain "as the loveliest fleet of Islands that lies anchored in any ocean." Four years later the brig *Griffon* sailed out of Boston and reached Honolulu after a five-month voyage. Among its crew was 16-year-old Henry Augustus Peirce, brother of the captain. Henry was born in Dorchester on December 15, 1808, the eleventh of 13 children of Joseph Hardy Peirce and Frances Temple Peirce. Augustus's delicate health as a child led to his leaving school at age 14 to go to work under the watchful eye of his father, the clerk of the Boston Municipal Court.

The maiden sailing by the young lad, grown strong and motivated by his wide reading, was the beginning of a life of great voyages over vast seas, of fortunes made and lost, and of diplomatic missions for his native land and as foreign minister of the Kingdom of Hawaii.

For the next three years, Henry, promoted to ship's clerk in charge of stores and trade goods, cruised between Alaska and Mexico trading for hides and furs. Returning to Hawaii in 1828, Peirce was hired by the prosperous Boston merchant, James Hunnewell, to be his clerk. Two years later, at age 22, young Peirce became the partner of Hunnewell, who left the young man $20,000 to manage the business of bartering New England goods for sandalwood while Hunnewell returned to Boston. In 1833, Hunnewell withdrew from the firm, and Peirce opened a lucrative triangular trading business among the United States, China and Siberia. In February of 1836, Peirce returned to Boston, leaving the business in the hands of his partner, Charles Brewer. The next year found Peirce in Valparaiso, where he sold an armed brig before crossing the continent on horseback to Buenos Aires. By 1838 he was back in Boston, where he married Susan Thompson. In 1839 he was back in Hawaii and trading along the Mexican and California coast. In Mezatlan, Mexico in 1842, he sold a vessel and cargo before going overland to Vera Cruz, whence he sailed home to Boston and retired from the sea.

During his almost two decades of sailing and trading, Henry Peirce had amassed a considerable fortune—$100,000—enough for him to become one of the leaders in Boston's shipping industry. When the news of newly discovered gold in California reached Peirce's ears, he was too much the adventurer not to heed the call of further riches. Quickly buying, outfitting and manning a suitable ship, he set sail from Boston to San Francisco. His ship's lines were scarcely secured to the dock before the crew to a man ran off to the gold fields.

A year passed before Peirce managed his way back to Boston by way of Hawaii and Canton. Settling down finally to the life of merchant and ship owner, Peirce was for a number of years consul to Hawaii for New England. At the outbreak of the Civil War, Peirce used $50,000 of his fortune to outfit a contingent of Massachusetts volunteers. Many of his large fleet of merchantmen fell prey to the marauding ships of the South, and by war's end, Peirce was relatively poor. With what money he had left, he invested in a Mississippi cotton plantation, which failed, very nearly wiping him out. Forced to sell his Beacon Hill mansion to satisfy his debtors, Peirce lived in retirement until called by President Grant to become U.S. minister to the Kingdom of Hawaii in 1869.

Ever since whalers from Europe and America came upon Twain's "loveliest fleet of Islands" their governments realized the importance of the islands as a resting place and way station on the great trade route to China, and Hawaii's strategic importance in the event of war. The time of Peirce's tenure as American minister to Hawaii (1869 to 1877) were the decisive years in the contest for dominance over the islands. In February of 1874, following the election of King Kalahaua, riots broke out, although perhaps they were not as spontaneous as some American merchants led people to believe. Peirce's response was to call out the U.S. Marines and surround the king's palace. Some months later, the minister accompanied the king on a trip to Washington, the result of which was the signing of a reciprocity treaty between the United States and the Kingdom of Hawaii. The ownership of the coveted islands was finally settled in June of 1898, when Congress passed a joint resolution annexing them.

Henry Peirce resigned his post in October of 1877 and left Hawaii for Boston, only to return in a few months because of illness. On March 1, 1878, the man who had for so many years been caught up with the economic and political life of the Kingdom of Hawaii was appointed its foreign minister, a post he lost the following July as a result of a quarrel between the legislature and the king. Peirce returned to Boston, but it was the Pacific, not the Atlantic, that pulled his heart. Peirce went West once more, settled in California, and died in San Francisco on July 29, 1885, at the age of 77.

CHAPTER V

Barbarians at the Ballot Box:
A Cobbler's Journey

FOR THE BETTER PART OF A CENTURY, WITH SETTLED FORTUNES AND aristocratic families in the halls of the university they so dominated, and in continuation of a long-standing culture of public service, the leaders of the Republican Party of Massachusetts would make a unique contribution to the governance of the United States. As the party matured, it came to symbolize an institutional rectitude that was strikingly absent from the tumult of its creation. The birth of the Republican Party in the Commonwealth was a breach birth; the party was yanked a bawling, cantankerous child, strong enough to survive where its siblings and sires had failed. At its nativity and through its infancy the party was attended by an array of men whose names can be found in any comprehensive American history book: poets and writers such as James Russell Lowell, John Greenleaf Whittier and Richard Henry Dana Jr.; the education reformer Horace Mann; and the industrialists Abbott and Amos Lawrence. For agitation it produced Charles Sumner, for embarrassment Ben Butler, for acerbic comment and intellectual stimulus an Adams—Charles Francis, the nineteenth century Adams. Yet it was not a poet or an aristocrat, or an educated or wealthy man of station or pedigree who set in motion the events that were to lead to the establishment of the Republican Party in the Commonwealth. Rather, it was a humble cobbler, Jeremiah Jones Colbath, born in poverty in Farmington, New Hampshire, on

February 16, 1812. Jeremiah spent 11 of his first 21 years in indentured servitude. He died in Washington, D.C., on November 2, 1875, as vice president of the United States.

Winthrop Colbath, Jeremiah's father, was a day laborer in a saw mill—when he could get the work—and a hard drinker who fathered more children than his constantly impecunious condition could support. There was nothing to do then but to indenture young Jeremiah, a rude and profane boy, to a neighboring farmer. With his indenture completed on February 16, 1833, Jeremiah, hard of body from the years of farm work, sold for $85 the six sheep and yoke of oxen that were his due for that labor. He earned another $65 hiring out on local farms, and, with a fortune in his pockets, left Farmington for the opportunity he believed he could find in Natick, Massachusetts. Jeremiah departed from bad memories as well as from the place of his birth. As if to emphasize its finality, he went to court and had his name changed. The former Jeremiah Jones Colbath arrived in Natick as Henry Wilson, having walked the 100 miles in four days having spent one dollar and five cents.

At the time Natick was in transition from a farming community to a manufacturing town, and the otherwise unskilled farmhand had difficulty finding employment. When he did find work, it was in making "brogans," a rough workman's shoe, for a manufacturer who promised to teach Henry Wilson the trade in return for five months' work. The young man's ambition was to save enough money to study law, and he drove himself unceasingly in the effort. That and his devotion to reading (he claimed to have read 700 volumes during his indenture) and the improvement in speaking and diction he sought in the Natick Debating Society combined to break his health. He went south to Virginia to recuperate, and during a visit to Washington, D.C., witnessed a scene that was to greatly influence his political future. There on a platform in a public market in the capital of the Land of Liberty, Negro families were being sold in part or in whole to the highest bidder. "I left the capital of my country with the unalterable resolution to give all that I had, and all that I hoped to have, of power, to the cause of emancipation." Power was to become Wilson's mistress and politics the aphrodisiac feeding his passion.

Returning to Natick, Wilson eventually opened his own shoe business and in 1840 married Harriet Malvin Howe, in a union which produced one child, Henry Hamilton Wilson. Throughout their lives together, Harriet Howe was never in full possession of the man she married: the public's business was. Henry Wilson was first elected to office in the state House of Representatives in 1840. The man who arrived on Beacon Hill had only the thinnest of formal educations—three brief terms at three New Hampshire academies during his indenture—and he could scarcely write his own speeches. Yet by applying pragmatism and shifting principles when necessary through hard work, with a common touch and an astute political mind, Henry Wilson's star shone as brightly as any other in a galaxy filled with them.

In 1845, Wilson was a delegate to the Concord, Massachusetts, convention called to protest the extension of slavery, and, along with John Greenleaf Whittier, he was chosen to present a petition with 65,000 signatures protesting the annexation of Texas. In 1848, he was elected a delegate to the Whig National Convention in Philadelphia. Wilson and other Massachusetts "Conscience" Whigs were unalterably opposed to the nomination of the Mexican War general Zachary Taylor for president, which seemed inevitable. Wilson, as he always did, had a plan. The antislave power delegates should advocate the nomination of Daniel Webster in the hope that when Webster lost, as he surely would, they would rally behind Wilson and others in the creation of a new party dedicated to "free soil, free speech, free labor, and free men."

When Taylor was nominated, Charles Allen, a Wilson coconspirator, leapt to his feet and shouted over the din that on this day the Whig party was "dissolved." Wilson himself waited until nominations for vice president began. One of the leading candidates was Massachusetts industrialist Abbott Lawrence. Just as the nominating process began, Wilson, amid catcalls and hisses, demanded the floor and hurled the allegation that Lawrence's nomination was meant as a bribe for Massachusetts and the North. Hardly heard over the crescendo of invective shouted at him, Wilson proclaimed that Massachusetts could not be bought and that he personally would work to defeat Taylor. With that, he and Allen marched out. True or not, the accusation had its effect. Nathan Appleton blamed Lawrence's failure to get the nomination for vice president on the furor caused by Wilson's "disgraceful piece of political swindling."

Back in the Commonwealth, the target of bitter comment in the Whig press and thus the spreading of his name that attention assured, Wilson set out to organize a new party. In that movement he was joined by other "Conscience" Whigs and dissident Democrats upset about their party's nomination of Lewis Cass for the presidency. The dissidents called for a convention to meet in Worcester in June and hopefully watched for similar movements in other states. The Worcester convention appointed a committee to coordinate a state campaign and elected delegates to the national convention in Buffalo that was to form the Free-Soil Party. Martin Van Buren was nominated as its candidate for president and Charles Francis Adams for the vice presidency. The party garnered 30 percent of the Massachusetts vote, more than the Democrats but far behind the Whigs. On a national level, the embryonic party carried no states but received enough votes in New York to enable the Whigs to deny that state to Cass.

Henry Wilson had once given a speech, which Charles Francis Adams thought laudatory but fruitless, in which Wilson threatened to join with others, be they "Democrats, Abolitionists, Christian, or Infidel," to overthrow the entrenched Whigs unless that party took a firm stand on emancipation. Henry Wilson now set out to do just that. Unfettered by the social restraints that would have prevented others from doing so, Wilson stumped the state in social clubs, public meetings, factories, restaurants and even taverns, although he himself was a lifelong abstainer from spirits.

Using the friendship of newspaper reporters, who genuinely liked him, and the pages of the *Boston Republican*, which he had made over from the defunct *Boston Whig*, Wilson preached coalition. He ranted against the "selfish, conservative and corrupt money power" of the Boston Whigs when he was in the western part of the state and advocated more public control over Harvard when he was in Boston. By the time of the 1849 Free-Soil Party convention, support for a coalition was growing. The Democrats furthered it along by adopting an antislavery plank in their party platform. The idea of a coalition with Democrats, the party of Southern slave power, did not sit well with some of the more prominent antislavery Whigs and new adherents to the Free-Soil Party. Charles Francis Adams, John G. Palfrey and Richard Henry Dana, Jr., prevented the Free-Soil Party from endorsing Wilson's proposed coalition. While there would be no formal coalition with dissident Democrats, Wilson won tacit approval for informal, local alliances. When the ballots were counted in the 1849 election, the Whigs were astonished to see 13 alliance senators and 130 representatives elected to the Massachusetts legislature.

Henry Wilson was quick to see that with a few more Free-Soilers and Democrats under proper management, the de facto coalition could gain control of the legislature, a power of enormous significance, for if no candidate for state office received the required majority, the choice devolved to legislature. With each of the three parties—Whigs, Democrats and Free-Soilers—fielding candidates, a clear majority would be hard to come by. Wilson, with the aid of Democrats George Boutwell and Nathaniel Banks, kin to Wilson in their lack of formal education and humble birth as well as in guile, philosophical flexibility and burning ambition, pressed for a populist agenda. It called for establishing a mechanic's lien, regulation of corporate stock issues, capitalization of railroads, abolishment of capital punishment except for murder and more popular control of Whiggish Harvard. They lost on most of their agenda but in losing gained what they most wanted— a dynamic platform to run in the 1850 elections. Wilson's scheme had received a significant if unexpected boost in March of 1850 when word reached Boston of U.S. Senator Daniel Webster's soon-to-be-famous speech of March 7th. Webster's endorsement of Henry Clay's compromise proposal on several slavery issues incensed the "Conscience" Whigs, gave fodder to the abolitionists and little comfort to antislavery Democrats.

The writing was on the wall for the outmaneuvered Whigs when the coalition took comfortable control of the House (filling ten no-elections with their own) and dominated the Senate 22 to 8. Henry Wilson sat in the chair as president of the Senate at the convening of the legislature in 1851. As presiding officer, the cobbler from Natick held the position once occupied by such stalwarts as Josiah Quincy, Leverett Saltonstall, great-grandfather of the future U.S. senator, Harrison Gray Otis and Levi Lincoln.

The time had come to fill the offices where no candidate had received the required majority or, as the Whig governor Briggs, who was about to be coalitioned out of office, sneered, the "trading and swapping of oxen."

The Democrats gained the governorship (George Boutwell) and the lieutenant governorship (Henry W. Cushman), the Speaker of the House (Nathaniel Banks), a majority of the governor's council, and the few weeks remaining of Daniel Webster's senate term (Webster had resigned to become secretary of state). The Free-Soilers received the remaining seats on the governor's council and—the plum in the pie—a full term in the U.S. Senate, which eventually went to Charles Sumner. Caleb Cushing lamented that the state had been "shoemakerized." Charles Francis Adams exulted that the "domination of Webster is finished." To the seething Briggs, Wilson replied, "So long as the people were satisfied with the trade, it did not become the oxen to complain."

What the preeminence of the Whigs and the settled opposition of the Democrats had previously brought to the arena of the Commonwealth's politics was stability and predictability. Henry Wilson and his successful coup brought that situation to an end, but its demise was at hand anyway: the times were on the side of turmoil. The capital city of the Commonwealth had begun its turn from Yankee, Protestant and Republican to Irish, Catholic and Democratic. The abolitionists would not let anyone be: make up your mind; be slave or be free.

Unfettered by little restraint of the law, industrial greed corrupted the system. The Free-Soil Party, so full of promise at its conception, sputtered in the 1852 presidential elections by gaining only 5 percent of the popular vote, its dream of national influence forever ended. Henry Wilson, in a practical sense, had used the fortunes of that party to fuel his own political ascendancy. With its fall, he also fell. Wilson longed for the party's nomination for governor in 1852, but his enemies in the party nominated Horace Mann. Wilson then put his hope in succeeding Mann when the latter retired from his seat in Congress, but the refusal of Ben Butler to step aside and clear the way assured Wilson's defeat. The future of his coalition looked bleak. He waited for the call of patronage from Washington from the one to whom he had been patron, Senator Charles Sumner, but he heard none.

A Political Phoenix

"In 1852," reads the entry in the *Manual of the General Court* "on the 7th of May, another act [a similar one having been rejected the previous year] called upon the people to vote upon the question of calling a Constitutional Convention. A majority of the people having voted in favor of the proposed convention, election for delegates thereto took place in March, 1853." The call for election of delegates set the political master's heart aflutter. Henry Wilson, taking advantage of the fact that such delegates did not have to be residents of the town they would represent, placed popular Free-Soilers in the most promising positions. Outmaneuvered once again, the Whigs found themselves with a third of the delegates to Free-Soilers' two-thirds. Wilson and his supporters (Nathaniel Banks was in the chair) managed to get most of their agenda adopted. The Whigs were galvanized into action, their powerful press hammering away at the proposed constitution. Ebenezer Hoar considered it a threat to an independent judiciary and called a meeting to organize opposition. United States Attorney General Caleb Cushing sent instructions from Washington that the Democrats were not to support the agenda. Charles Francis Adams hesitated, large-town representatives, facing the loss of legislative clout, turned out in great numbers to defeat it, and Irish Catholics voted no because they feared a specific prohibition of state funding for parochial schools. The result was close, but the final entry in the *Manual of the General Court* notes that the "committee appointed to receive and count the votes and make thereof to the General Court . . . found that the proposed Constitution had been rejected." Henry Wilson, thrice defeated and without income from public office, returned to Natick to what was left of his once-thriving shoe business, a lone shop on Central Street.

Not too many blows had been struck on the soles of Wilson's customers' shoes before the cobbler was back banging away with his political hammer. United States Senator Steven A. Douglas had proposed legislation that would end the ban on slavery in Kansas and Nebraska, which appalled the Massachusetts antislavery forces and forced the whole question out into the public. Wilson attacked Sumner's colleague in the Senate, Edward Everett, as being "down among the dead men" for his failure to condemn Douglas's proposal. Everett resigned under pressure, and the sitting governor, William C. Plunkett, appointed Julius Rockwell as Everett's temporary replacement until the legislature-to-be elected in the fall could make its own choice. In response to Henry Wilson's call for a fusion meeting with the

"Republican Party," founded the previous February in Ripon, Wisconsin, a meeting was convened in Mechanic's Hall in Worcester on July 20, 1854. Wilson's effort met with little success. Many of the anti-slavery Whigs and Democrats preferred to follow their own paths in opposition to slave power. Many of the old Free-Soilers refused to follow their former leader into the Republican Party, and Adams feared the whole exercise was just a ruse to save old coalitionists. There then entered into what was fast becoming political disintegration in Massachusetts a new element, first noticed when little bits of heart-shaped paper began appearing in the streets of the Commonwealth's towns.

The mysterious bits of paper were a signal to the members of an equally mysterious and clandestine organization to meet at a predesignated time and place. "Know-Nothings" they came to be known as because of their persistent assurance that they knew nothing about anything untoward going on. When they did become strong enough to assume the role of a political party, they hid their anti-Catholic, anti-immigrant purpose behind appealing words of nativism, nationalism, and the protection of the jobs and morals of true Americans. How strong the party would be in the coming elections was beyond the reckoning of most Massachusetts politicians. But not Henry Wilson. His superb network of observers told him that the new party would be formidable. Early in 1854, Wilson secretly joined the group and in the March elections, the Know-Nothings seized political control of several cities and towns in eastern Massachusetts.

At its second convention, the new Massachusetts Republican Party nominated Henry Wilson for governor, which would cause acute embarrassment in its future. For the time being, however, the Republican leaders were pleased that Wilson, while he had attended the Know-Nothing convention in October, had declined to accept that party's gubernatorial nomination. At that point a story appeared in the *Springfield Republican* claiming a deal had been struck between Anson Burlingame, Wilson, and Henry Gardner, a Boston wool merchant. Under the deal the Know-Nothing Party would support Gardner for governor, Burlingame for the U.S. House of Representatives and Wilson for the U.S. Senate. True or not, the allegation of Wilson's continued consorting with the Know-Nothings upset Republican party leaders. Charles

Allen deserted his old friend and attacked Wilson at a Republican meeting. Others urged Charles Sumner to speak out, but that gentleman owed too much to Wilson to do so. A few days before the election, Wilson sent a letter to the party's leaders declining the Republican nomination for governor. In the ensuing elections, the Know-Nothing's Gardner received 80,102 votes compared to a combined total for Republicans, Democrats and Whigs of 35,000.

The criticism, indeed condemnation, heaped upon the head of Henry Wilson for his dance with the Know-Nothings took its toll. It was a dubious alliance the master of the art would later deplore. At a Know-Nothing dinner in late November, Wilson voiced the hope that the party would help to eliminate bloc voting and make the Irish and German immigrants into Americans. He then declared that the party should not use its power "to the prejudice of foreigners, simply because they are foreigners . . . wherever he was born, and whatever might be the complexion the Almighty has impressed upon him."

When the legislature, which was to elect a new U.S. senator, met in January, the Know-Nothings in control of the House put forth the name of Henry Wilson for the office. The House was solid Wilson, the Senate not so: there the opposition was both extensive and varied. Some members feared putting a radical Free-Soiler in the Senate; others wanted a more dedicated nativist. There was speculation—dread on the part of some—that the combination of Charles Sumner and Henry Wilson in the Senate would so radicalize the Massachusetts congressional delegation that it would lose any national influence it then had. The possible election of Wilson took on national importance. New York papers such as the *Evening Post*, the *Tribune*, and the *Times* all supported it. *The Know Nothing* and the *American Crusader* damned Wilson, the "scheming, fraud, humbug and injustice" that he was. To the *Boston Chronicle*, Wilson was "the Talleyrand of Massachusetts politics."

On January 12, 1855 the House nominated Wilson without any trouble. The Senate four days later voted to defer action until January 31—a mistake in that it gave the most astute politician in the state, perhaps the nation, time to advance his cause. Wilson wrote an open letter to the Boston newspapers insisting that the nativist movement did not seek to deny anyone equal rights under the law but only to protect America from the adverse consequence of the arrival of thousands of immigrants reared under different religious, social and political conditions.

On the 23rd of January, the House elected Henry Wilson without a contest. The Senate was to vote on the 31st. The day before the Senate was to vote, Amos Lawrence opined that, humanly speaking, Wilson could not win, but given his own and his manager's political art, he probably would. Complaints were heard outside of the Senate chamber just down the hall from the governor's office that Henry Gardner was holding up patronage until he saw how the vote went. The visitor's gallery was overflowing, with an extraordinary number of the press vying for the few seats available to them on the floor. A man could get a bet on the outcome at any tavern in town, but not with odds—it was even money. "For Mr. E. M. Wright," the Senate clerk intoned to the hushed Senate, "fifteen votes. For the Honorable Henry A. Wilson, twenty-one"—21 of the 40 eligible votes. Cannons boomed on the State House lawn announcing the choice of a new U. S. Senator. The Whig *Boston Atlas* thought it knew how Wilson had won "by intrigue, by duplicity, by bargain and sale of his own party, by denying his own language, ignoring his own language." If that were true it was only true in tactic. For Henry A. Wilson, beyond his masterful use of political expediency, was at heart constantly faithful to his beliefs: no man should be a slave and everyone, no matter his birth or station, was due the dignity bestowed on him by his Creator.

Once in the U.S. Senate, Wilson was a whirlwind of energy, a great help to President Lincoln as chairman of the committee on military affairs. The senator traveled back to Massachusetts to raise soldiers and money and was constantly urging an emancipation proclamation on the president. Wilson shaped legislation to bring freedom to thousands of slaves years before ratification of the Thirteenth Amendment; he was later a bitter and vituperative opponent of President Johnson's Reconstruction polices. Yet Wilson the consensus maker, the coalition man, conferred quite openly with leaders of the vanquished South and urged education and homesteading to solve the problem of the freed slaves in their midst. In 1872, in a move to strengthen a ticket that needed none, Henry Wilson was nominated to be Ulysses S. Grant's vice president. Wilson proved a highly efficient and popular presiding officer of the Senate. On November 10, 1875, while on his way to the Senate he suffered a paralyzing stroke and lay in his office for 12 days until his death on November 22nd.

"No statue will keep my form and face for friends to sometimes recall my name," Henry Wilson once said. Its history's gain that he was right, for statues are immobile. Jeremiah Jones Colbath's true memorial lies not in stillness but in motion: a cobbler's journey.

CHAPTER VI

A Poet in Piccadilly

"FORTUNATELY FOR AMERICA ALSO, IN ALL TURNS OF OUR POLITICS there has been the same sense of the value of literature and of the sphere of men of letters which has given the world about all the good diplomats which the world has ever had. Somewhat as Franklin was sent to France because the French had heard of him before, quite as Motley was sent to Vienna because he knew something about the history and could speak the language of Germany, exactly as Mr. Irving had been sent to Spain as our minister, the new administration made advances to Mr. Lowell to ask him if he would not represent us at one of the European courts."

This passage from Edward Everett Hale's *James Russell Lowell and His Friends* gives hint of the participation in local and national politics by "men of letters" of Massachusetts—that extraordinary group that so lit up the literary sky of Boston, New England and the nation for so many years of the nineteenth century. Of these, the historians George Bancroft, J. Lothrop Motley and Charles Francis Adams held high appointive office. Others, such as Henry Wadsworth Longfellow, Richard Henry Dana, Jr., John Greenleaf Whittier (who served in the state legislature), and Edward Everett Hale (himself the author of *The Man Without a Country*) were enthusiastic participants in the stimulating game of politics as played in the Commonwealth. Their participation in the political culture of Massachusetts afforded many of them national influence as well. Toward the end of the nineteenth century, however, such men were being replaced by a new breed of political leaders: industrialists, manufacturers, men of commerce, men of wealth—inherited or newly acquired. James Russell Lowell, author, teacher, wit, satirist and bardic poet, was one of the last of "them littry fellers" who journeyed forth from Massachusetts in the service of his country.

James Russell Lowell was born on February 22, 1819, in the family home, "Elmwood," in Cambridge. His father was minister at the Old West Church in Boston, and his grandfather was Judge John Lowell. To the blood of that distinguished heritage of lawyers and clergymen, James's mother, Harriet Brackett Spence Lowell, added a sensitive, even mystical strain. Mrs. Lowell was a lover of bardic poetry and old ballads and was thought by some to possess the gift of second sight.

James's early participation in politics took the same shape as that of his fellow literati in Boston and Cambridge: the club meetings, a polemic, an article in the *Atlantic Monthly*. For Lowell, it was the witty rhyme, the sarcastic verse. As the years went by and Lowell gained recognition as one of America's leading poets, the vigor of his writings on public affairs made him a sought-after political ally. In 1876, the Republican leadership of Massachusetts asked him to stand for election in the South Middlesex congressional district, the same seat once held by Edward Everett. Lowell refused, estimating, quite correctly, the limitations of such a personality as his in a legislative body. He did, however, accept the Republican nominating convention's offer to be a presidential elector. Lowell supported the Republican nominee, Rutherford B. Hayes, in the famous (or infamous) election of 1876. Samuel J. Tilden, the Democratic nominee seemed, at first count, to have received the majority of both the popular and electoral vote. Challenges were made in several states and a congressionally appointed commission, voting along party lines, awarded sufficient votes to Hayes to make him president. Lowell had worked hard for Hayes and, after some maneuvering (Hale wrote that Lowell was offered and refused four ministries), he finally, with the laconic observation that "I should like to see a play in Caldron," accepted one he fancied—that to Spain.

Relations between the United States and Spain had been rocky for a number of years. In 1873, the summary execution by Spanish authorities of 53 men of the U.S.-owned vessel *Virginius*, a filibuster ship carrying arms and men to Cuban rebels, almost led to war. Lowell's stay in Madrid (1877-1880) came during a lull before the storm that saw the two countries at war in 1898. Lowell was accepted by the cultured aristocracy of Spain and formed a genuine liking for the Spanish people in general, if not for their philosophy of "manana" and the studied duplicity of Spanish officialdom. In October of 1853, Lowell had lost his first wife, Maria, a gifted poet and an ardent reformer who greatly influenced her husband's outlook on the social and political issues of the day. In 1857, he married his daughter's governess, Frances Dunlop, who during the third year of their stay in Spain fell ill and took to her bed. In January of 1880, Lowell received word that Hayes wanted him as minister to the Court of St. James. The perception that the change in climate would be beneficial for Mrs. Lowell greatly influenced his decision to accept.

The new U.S. minister came to the Court of St. James with considerable baggage when he presented his credentials to Queen Victoria. During the American Civil War, Lowell had been quite outspoken in his criticism of the English flirtation with the South. Lowell was, however, as were many of his circle, the American equivalent of the English aristocrat, so he found ease among his cultural cousins in London. As for his English hosts, the university-educated, erudite, man of letters was their kind of American. The minister's presence was much sought after at both private and public dinner tables. On October 6, 1884, Lowell was given the honor of the presidency of the Midland Institute, where he delivered a brilliant address titled "Democracy." Past differences now put aside, Lowell's ship of diplomacy sailed placidly along tranquil waters until it was hit broadside by a wave from across the Irish Sea.

Taking their name from Fianna, the legendary band of warriors led by the mighty Finn MacCool, Irish rebels had been waging a campaign to rid their land of English rule. In an effort to suppress it, Parliament had passed a "Coercion Act" which permitted the arrest and indefinite confinement of anyone under the merest suspicion of involvement. Into this broad net, thrown about with great enthusiasm and little discretion, fell several naturalized American citizens. When caught, these mythical miscreants invoked their status as citizens of the United

States and forthwith complained to their protector at the embassy in London, Ambassador Lowell. To the liberal-minded Lowell, a law that allowed such arrest and detention was "arbitrary and despotic." Still, Lowell the diplomat thought that the United States was bound to abide by an act of Parliament. "It would be manifestly futile to ask the government here to make an exception on behalf of an American who brought himself within the provisions of any law thus sanctioned," he wrote in a dispatch to Washington.

In Washington, the administration was under pressure from increasingly powerful Irish-American political forces, a pressure that included accusations of an undue anglophilic and anti-Irish Catholic attitude on the part of Lowell and demands for his recall. The minister's answer was a declaration that "all such persons should be made to understand that they cannot be Irishmen and Americans at the same time, as they now seem to suppose. . . ." Which is not to say that Lowell did not attend to Irish-Americans in their time of need. "You are," he wrote to the American consul in Limerick, "to go without delay to the jail to see John McInerny and Patrick Slattery, and if they should be put at liberty, to draw forty pounds on the embassy account and give it to them for their passage to the United States."

On February 19, 1885, Lowell's second wife succumbed to her long illness. James Russell Lowell had served his country in the foreign service with distinction during three presidential administrations. In 1885 he received word that the newly elected president, Grover Cleveland, had replaced him in London with Edward J. Phelps. Lowell lived out the remaining years of his life until his death in 1891 at the beloved sanctuary of Elmwood, where he had been born 72 years earlier.

From Another Part of the Commonwealth

The leaders Massachusetts had provided the federal government in the years leading up to the nation's centennial had for the most part come from within the boundaries of the colony at Massachusetts Bay rather than from Plymouth Colony. In 1841 a young man whose ancestors first settled in the Plymouth Colony in the middle of the eighteenth century traveled up to Cambridge to attend Harvard. Thomas Russell was born in Plymouth in 1825, graduated from

Harvard College in 1845, studied at Harvard Law School and commenced practice in the office of William Whiting in Boston.

Russell's rise in the legal life of the city to both financial success and prominence was rapid. By 1853, he was a judge on the Boston Municipal Court. When the legislature created the modern superior court in 1859, Governor Nathaniel Banks chose Russell as one of the court's first judges. Eight years later, President Andrew Johnson appointed Russell to the lucrative post as Collector of the Port of Boston. Later, President Grant appointed him American ambassador to Venezuela, a position in which he served from April 1874 to January 1877. At the time of his death, on February 9, 1887, Thomas Russell was chairman of the Massachusetts Board of Railroad Commissioners.

The General

Charles Devens was given the title of "General" twice: the first time as an officer in the Union Army and the second as Attorney General of the United States. Charles was born in Charlestown, on April 4, 1820, the son of Charles and Mary Lithgow Devens and the grandson of the patriot Richard Devens. Young Charles graduated from the Boston Latin School and went on to Harvard College and Harvard Law School. Admitted to the bar at age 20, he opened an office in Northfield, was elected to the first of two terms to the state senate at age 28, and was appointed by President Tyler as U.S. Marshal for the District of Massachusetts a year later.

The demon that harassed so many antislavery officials and officeholders of the day—moral imperative versus enforcement of the law—caught up with Marshal Devens in 1851. When the Boston police had collared a runaway slave, Thomas Sims, the U.S. Commissioner, ordered the fugitive returned to his master. It fell upon Devens to escort the miserable fellow to the ship that would transport him back to Georgia and again to bondage. The duty was repugnant to Devens, but duty it was, and Sims was marched to the dock. For several years thereafter, Charles Devens attempted to aid Sims by offering to pay for his freedom. When the Emancipation Proclamation succeeded where Devens had failed, Devens was in a position to obtain a government job for the former slave.

Devens resigned his federal post as marshal and returned to the practice of law at Worcester in 1854 in partnership with George Frisbie Hoar and served as city solicitor for three years. From his youth, however, Devens had been attracted to things military. He joined the state militia and he rose steadily in its ranks, eventually reaching the rank of brigadier general. When the news came of Lincoln's call for 75,000 volunteers at the outset of the Civil War, Devens turned over his practice to another lawyer and offered his services. On April 16, 1861, Devens was commissioned colonel of the Third Battalion of Massachusetts Rifles and departed for the South on April 20th. In Devens, Lincoln found what he lacked in many other politically-connected citizen-soldiers: a man who could, and would, fight. General Devens's military service lasted five years and three months, during which time he fought in the peninsular campaign, at Fredericksburg and at Chancellorsville. Wounded thrice, he was brevetted a major general after leading the Union advance on Richmond.

While Devens was away at war, a loose combination of dissident Democrats and a few Republicans nominated him for governor of Massachusetts but he lost to the incumbent, John Andrew. Devens was appointed to the Massachusetts Superior Court in 1867 and elevated to the Supreme Judicial Court in 1873.

Justice Devens was a strong supporter of Rutherford Hayes in the 1876 presidential election. When Hayes prevailed he offered Devens the position of secretary of war. Devens refused that appointment but was subsequently offered and accepted the office of U.S. Attorney General. As attorney general, he was considered one of the strongest members of a strong cabinet, serving from March of 1877 until the expiration of Hayes's term in 1881 and then reappointed a justice of the Massachusetts Supreme Judicial Court, where he served until his death on January 7, 1891. He was buried with full military honors from the Trinity Church in Boston.

Mr. Justice Gray

Horace Gray's reward for having earned his degree from Harvard College was the same as that of other classmates of his social and economic class: a trip to Europe. The year was 1845, his father was prosperous, and Horace was 17 years old. For two years the young man traveled about Europe furthering his interest in natural history at museums and in the field. In 1847 Gray's idyllic life of wandering and note-taking was abruptly ended with a summons from home. He was to return immediately not to a comfortable home where he might continue to indulge his intellectual curiosity, but to a family that had suffered disastrous financial reverses. Gray would now have to support himself. Of the professions acceptable to someone of his class—medicine, teaching, the clergy or the law—Horace Gray chose the law and entered Harvard Law School in 1848. With his inquisitive and scientific bent of mind, it was not what the young man would have preferred, but his natural ability, enthusiasm and industry combined to make Gray one of the law school's best scholars. At the time of his attendance at the school, the method of learning the law was to study all existing cases pertinent to the one under consideration. It was a discipline apparent in Gray's later judicial decisions—and a very unpopular one with the lawyers who had to wade through the many previous cases the judge thought germane enough to cite.

Soon after Gray's admission to the bar in 1851 at age 23, the Reporter of Decisions of the Massachusetts Supreme Judicial Court, Luther Cushing, became ill. Young Horace Gray was given the task of preparing Cushing's last volume of the *Reports* and permanently succeeded to that important job himself in 1854. Gray's personal conservatism and social circle might have been expected to draw him into the ranks of the Whigs, yet when he did enter the political vortex that was pre-Civil War Massachusetts he did so as an original member of the Free-Soil Party. In 1860 Gray had been the unsuccessful nominee of the Republican Party for state attorney general. The Commonwealth's Civil War governor, John A. Andrew, relied heavily on Gray for legal advice, and when a vacancy occurred on the Supreme Judicial Court in 1864, Horace Gray at age 36, became the youngest man ever to be appointed an associate justice of that distinguished body. In 1869, following a series of deaths and resignations, Gray found himself the senior associate justice, and after the death of Justice Chapman in 1873, chief justice.

The state's high court at the time was a court of original jurisdiction as well as an appellate body. The justices conducted trials individually and also sat together to hear appeals. It was a dual experience that was to serve Justice Gray well in the future. Acute of mind, quick to absorb and retain long briefs, Gray in his 18 years on the court wrote more than his share of its opinions. Thought to be a bit of a martinet, at least by the lawyers appearing before him, and unyielding in his insistence on proper dignity and decorum in his courtroom, Gray often employed recent Harvard Law School graduates recommended by his half brother, Professor John Chapman Gray. Among the temporary law clerks from 1879 to 1881 was a young Louis D. Brandeis.

It was Senator George Frisbie Hoar, a classmate at Harvard in 1881 who advanced the name of Horace Gray to the newly inaugurated President James A. Garfield for nomination as an associate justice of the U.S. Supreme Court. Before he could act on the recommendation, however, Garfield, barely six months into his term of office, was assassinated. His successor, Chester A. Arthur, did not hesitate to effectuate the appointment of such a well-qualified and widely supported candidate. Horace Gray took his oath as an associate justice of the Supreme Court on January 8, 1882.

The Court Justice Gray joined was moving away from its previous conservative interpretation of the federal structure to a court increasingly willing to find new reservoirs of national power in the Constitution. Gray's reputation as a "nationalist" lay in his findings that no constitutional prohibition limited the power of Congress to issue paper money or deal with aliens. Of all the decisions in which Gray played a major role, one of the most notable was *United States v. Wong Kim Ark* (1898). An Act of Congress holding Chinese immigrants ineligible for naturalization while at the same time conferring citizenship on their American-born children was being challenged. Using Anglo-American common law as his guide, Justice Gray wrote that the Fourteenth Amendment to the Constitution commanded that citizenship be made a birthright no matter the claimant's race or national origin.

Gray's long and sometimes ponderous opinions, with their surfeit of citations, often took on the essence of historic scholarship. As the years went by, the effort to produce such tomes exacted its toll on the man who took so many hours to produce them. On February 3, 1902, after sitting in Court, Justice Gray suffered a stroke from which he never recovered. He died the following September. Gray tendered his resignation following his stroke, the time of his departure from the Court contingent on the appointment of his successor. The man who President Theodore Roosevelt chose to succeed Gray was himself from Massachusetts and, like Gray, at the time of his appointment was the chief justice of the Supreme Judicial Court: Oliver Wendell Holmes.

The Multifaceted Mr. Loring

George Bailey Loring is as fine an example as one can find of the self-promoting, opportunistic politician infused into the persona of an intelligent and accomplished man of diverse interests. Physician, agriculturist, and noted orator, George was born on November 8, 1817, into a family that could trace its American roots back to the arrival of Thomas Loring in Hingham in 1634. Educated at the Franklin Academy at North Andover, at Harvard College (1838) and at Harvard Medical School (1842), Doctor Loring began his medical practice in his hometown but soon transferred his surgical skills to the Marine Hospital at Chelsea. When agitation for reform of the marine hospital system arose, it was Doctor Loring who was given the task of seeing to it. The medical life, however, no matter how successful he had been at it, was not for Loring. In 1851 he moved to Salem to begin a new life as an agriculturist and politician. Two years later, having rapidly made himself a factor in the Massachusetts Democratic Party, George Loring was appointed postmaster at Salem by President Franklin Pierce.

A "war" Democrat, Loring used his considerable oratorical skills to promote preservation of the Union at any cost (while making sure his speeches were printed for subsequent distribution). To have been a Union-defending Democrat before the war was one thing, but being a member of the party of rebellion during it, was quite another. With his nose always sniffing the prevailing political winds, Loring went over to the Republican Party in 1864. For others less adroit or accomplished, such a defection might have been politically debilitating, but not for the good doctor. Loring was elected to the Massachusetts House in 1866; made chairman of the Republican state committee in 1869; was a delegate to the national party convention in 1868, 1872 and 1876;

was president of the Massachusetts Senate for three years (1873-1876) and served two terms as a Representative in Congress. When he failed to gain reelection to that office in 1880, President Garfield selected him to be U.S. Commissioner of Agriculture, an appointment that turned out to be one of the doomed president's finest. Loring's interest in things agricultural was sincere and his expertise in the field very real. Under Loring's administration great efforts were made to improve husbandry, efforts Loring made certain were conspicuous enough to keep him in the public eye. Loring's tenure ended with the inauguration of President Cleveland in 1885.

Together with his friends Ralph Waldo Emerson and Louis Agassiz, Loring held an aesthetic love of nature, and much of Loring's life was devoted to the promotion of the rural life. He wrote extensively, and despite much sentimentality, his works are filled with sensible essays on many aspects of husbandry. In his capacity as representative (1860-1877) of the Essex Agricultural Society and on the Massachusetts Board of Agriculture, Loring did much to further the interest of the fledgling Massachusetts Agricultural College (now the University of Massachusetts at Amherst). For a brief period (March 1889 to May 1890), Loring was President Benjamin Harrison's appointee as U.S. minister to Portugal. George Bailey Loring died on September 14, 1891, the year of the publication of his very informative if rambling travelogue, *A Year in Portugal*.

The Typical Mr. Washburn

If there were not so many of them and the choices were fewer, John Davis Washburn would be as good an example as there was of the Yankee-Harvard-Republican-lawyer-politician who so dominated Massachusetts politics from the post-Civil War years until far into the twentieth century. A descendant of one of the early settlers of the Plymouth Colony, Washburn was born in Boston in 1833, received his early education in Lancaster, Massachusetts, where his parents had moved, graduated from Harvard College in 1853 and from the law school in 1856. From 1876 to 1879, Washburn was a state representative, and in 1884 was elected to the state senate from Worcester, serving on the insurance committee. When Alexander H. Bullock was elected governor of the Commonwealth in 1866, he appointed Washburn his chief of staff and adjutant, with the rank of colonel. The governor also, in the way such matters were decided by such men in those days, assigned Washburn the field of his private practice, in which he was the attorney for several large insurance companies.

In 1899, President Harrison appointed the ever loyal party man Washburn as American ambassador to Switzerland, a rank later advanced to that of envoy extraordinary and minister plenipotentiary. In 1892, having carried out his diplomatic duties quite respectably, Washburn returned to private life and to a long list of directorships of banks and insurance companies, trusteeships of charitable and historical institutions and societies, including that of an overseer of Harvard University. John Davis Washburn died at Worcester in April of 1903.

Life and Death at Sea

Augustine Heard, born at Ipswich on December 7, 1827, was the nephew and namesake of Augustine Heard, one of America's most renowned China traders and founder of the trading, banking and shipping firm of Augustine Heard & Company. Graduated from Harvard in 1847, young Augustine spent ten years in Canton and Hong Kong working for his uncle's firm and is said to have been the first Western businessman permitted to trade in Siam.

For several years Heard represented the family firm in Europe, traveling on business to England, France, Belgium and Russia. The years 1870-1872 witnessed the failure of many American firms doing business in Asia, including that of Augustine Heard & Company. The failure of his uncle's firm did not diminish Heard's deep attachment to the Far East, and he continued to spend much of his time there. In 1858, he had married Jane Leep, the daughter of the Belgian consul at Havana, Cuba. In January of 1890, President Harrison appointed Heard as U.S. ambassador to Korea, where he served until June of 1893. One of Augustine's five children, Helen Maxima Heard, married Max von Brandt, German ambassador to Japan and China. As befitted a man so involved with the sea, Augustine Heard died aboard ship off the coast of Gibraltar on December 12, 1905.

The Elite Mr. Coolidge

"I believe myself," Thomas Jefferson Coolidge once wrote, "to belong to a superior class, and that the principle that the ignorant and poor should have the same right to make laws and govern as the educated and refined was an absurdity." Mr. Coolidge's first and middle name came from the fact that he was, on his mother Eleonora Wayles Randolph's side, a great-grandson of Thomas Jefferson. Unlike some of his peers, young Thomas took his grand tour of Europe first and then entered Harvard as a 16-year-old sophomore, graduating in 1850, 17th in a class of some 60 fellows. Coolidge's career decision was quite simple: He would become as wealthy as he could.

In such an endeavor in the Commonwealth of the 1850s a proper marriage did no harm. In 1852, Thomas married Hetty, the daughter of William Appleton of the eminent family of New England industrial pioneers. In 1852, at the suggestion of his father-in-law, Coolidge accepted the position as treasurer of Boott Mills. At different times, Coolidge was treasurer of the Lawrence Manufacturing Company and of the famous Amoskeag Mills. His involvement in the cotton-spinning industry eventually led to his involvement in banking. He was a director of Merchants National Bank of Boston and of the New England Trust Company, and was one of the original incorporators of the Old Colony Trust Company. He was also heavily involved in railroads and served for a short time as president of the Atchison, Topeka & Santa Fe.

As he grew older and richer, Thomas Jefferson Coolidge's belief in his aristocratic superiority mellowed somewhat, and he took on some social obligations, manifested by an increasing dedication to the public welfare. He was a member of the Boston Parks Commission, which, under the guidance of Frederick Law Olmsted, had laid out the systems of parks and parkways that would become known as the Emerald Necklace. Coolidge was a substantial donor to the public library of Manchester-by-the-Sea; and he funded research in physics at Harvard where he served on the board of overseers. Appointed a member of the Pan-American Congress by President Cleveland in 1889, Coolidge was sent to France as United States ambassador in 1892. He stayed in France for the remainder of Cleveland's term. Coolidge's fluency in French, his tact, gentlemanly courtesy and solid judgment pleased both the French government and the U.S. Department of State. Before he died in his 90th year (on November 17, 1920), Thomas Jefferson Coolidge served on the Massachusetts Taxation Committee and the Joint High Commission of the United States, Great Britain and Newfoundland to study the myriad problems of the fisheries, the destruction of seals, Alaskan boundaries, armaments on the Great Lakes, and over-water transportation of goods.

The Unnecessarily Obscure Mr. Olney

In the city of Boston, amid the schools and government buildings, statues and parks dedicated to the likes of John Winthrop, George Bancroft, John Adams and John Kennedy lies a street in the Dorchester section running from 212 Bowdoin to 44 Rosseter named Olney Street. Richard Olney was born in Oxford, Massachusetts, on September 15, 1835, and died on April 8, 1917. His obituary, shortened somewhat by news of the declaration of war with Germany two days previously, told of a man who had accomplished much: he was a successful corporate lawyer, a trusted adviser to railroad barons, and attorney general and secretary of state of the United States. That the obituary lacked any reference to personal loss by Olney's friends was due to the fact that he had so few of them. In his professional life he was cold and standoffish and of stern and uncompromising discipline. Olney neither developed close friendships nor encouraged intimacy. In his home he was an absolute autocrat whose command was not to be disputed. Olney did not serve in the Civil War: he had managed to buy his way out of the draft.

Richard Olney received his early education at Leicester Academy, his undergraduate degree at Brown University, and his LL.B. from Harvard Law School in 1858. Admitted to the bar, Olney entered practice in the Boston firm of Benjamin Thomas, whose daughter Olney eventually married. Neither Olney's party nor pedigree assured him a place in the upper social and political strata of the city. Olney's grandfather, a Democrat, had been a follower of Roger Williams, and his mother was by birth connected with the Huguenot settlers of Oxford. The young lawyer would have to make it on his own way in Boston, and by dint of skill, intelligence and an extraordinary work ethic, Richard Olney did. He became not only one of the city's most successful lawyers, but a trusted adviser to many of Boston's preeminent members of the Brahmin-Republican aristocracy. In those days of railroad expansion, acquisitions, mergers, stock manipulation, fanciful financing and outright thievery, lawyer Olney was the man to keep his influential and affluent clients, to the extent they felt it necessary, inside the law.

Olney served in the Massachusetts legislature in 1873, was twice defeated for reelection and lost a bid for the state attorney general's office. When President Cleveland had an opportunity to fill a vacancy on the U.S. Supreme Court he was lobbied by some Democratic leaders to appoint Olney to restore the "New England" seat previously held by Justice Morrison Waite of Connecticut, who died in March 1888. Cleveland did appoint a New Englander, but it was Mellville Weston Fuller of Maine, who became chief justice. In the 1892 election, Olney was active to the extent of raising campaign funds and persuading John Quincy Adams II (son of Charles Francis and grandson of John Quincy) to campaign for President Cleveland.

In January 1893, Olney wrote to the president-elect's campaign manager (and fellow director of the Boston & Maine Railroad), William C. Whitney, that he hoped the president ". . . in making up the cabinet for his new administration," would not "forget how many people at the east, including numberless widows and orphans, are interested in railroads and require and deserve a reasonable amount of consideration." As sincere as Olney's concern may have been for impecunious widows and ill-fed orphans without number depending on railroad stock dividends for food and lodging, his interest in the make-up of the Cabinet was not entirely altruistic. In 1887, in an attempt to stop abusive practices by the railroads in rate setting and other practices, Congress had created the Interstate Commerce Commission, the first federal regulatory commission in American history. Although at the outset it was generally ineffective and quite susceptible to manipulation by skillful lawyers such as Olney, its very existence was thought by some inimical to railroad interests.

Richard Olney's chances of a cabinet post in President Cleveland's second administration were enhanced by the president's decision to award an office to the New England constituency. The posts that seemed available were those of secretary of the navy and attorney general. At a meeting with Cleveland at his preinaugural headquarters in Lakewood, New Jersey, a friend of Olney's, former Congressman John E. Russell, suggested that the Navy post be offered to John Quincy Adams II and that the attorney generalship go to Olney. The president believed however, that should the Navy post go to Adams, he should give the attorney generalship to a southerner. There followed a bit of political intrigue, with Adams being accused of blocking the appointment of prominent New Englanders by informing the president's men that if asked to serve they should refuse—with Olney fending off feelers with one hand and encouraging them with the other. When finally asked, Adams flatly refused the Navy post. When the attorney general position became a distinct possibility, Olney acted as would have been expected of him: he pointed out that relinquishing his lucrative private practice ($50,000 a year) for a cabinet post that paid $8,000 would be a great financial sacrifice—unless, or course, he could retain the practice while serving in Washington. Benjamin H. Bristow, a former secretary of the treasury and solicitor general, informed Olney that it was customary for a serving attorney general to continue his private practice. That Olney would have less time to serve his private clients was of little concern to them. "It seems to me," John Murray Forbes, chairman of the board of directors of the Burlington Railroad, wrote to the line's president, Charles E. Perkins, "rather for our advantage to have him in Washington." Richard Olney took his oath of office as Attorney General of the United States on March 6, 1893, two days after President Cleveland had been sworn in.

The railroad barons would have a friend as the chief law enforcement officer of the United States in the person of Richard Olney, but not one so subservient to their interests as to abandon the principles of law as he saw them. Olney believed that labor disputes should be settled by arbitration without government intervention, and refused the plea of railroad interests to apply the Sherman Anti-Trust Act to labor unions. Events, however, conspired to persuade the attorney general as to where the danger to civil order and the country's welfare stood, and it was not with the capitalists.

In 1893, one of the financial "panics" that periodically roiled the United States in the nineteenth century broke out. In the spring of

1894, Jacob S. Coxey, an Ohio manufacturer, raised an "army" of workers and began a march on Washington to force the Cleveland administration to do something about wide-spread unemployment. Olney took the ragtag bunch—there were only about 100 of them—more seriously than most authorities, and ordered Secret Service agents to slow them down. Elsewhere, disgruntled railroad workers, engaged in wage disputes with their employers, took to seizing railroad trains and headed to the nation's capital. Most of the stock seized belonged to bankrupt companies that were under the protection of the federal courts. When local authorities and U.S. marshals were unable, or unwilling, to control the mounting violence, railroad officials asked the president to intervene with federal troops. The president's policy was to do that only if a federal court order had been clearly violated. Olney, at least at that point, held to the conservative view that labor disputes should be settled by the parties to them, and doubted the federal government had jurisdiction except when there was interference in the transport of the U.S. mail.

In June 1894, the Pullman Company, in an effort to reduce costs, cut the wages of its workers without a commensurate reduction in rents for company housing. The American Railroad Union, newly formed by a man abhorred by the capitalists, socialist Eugene V. Debs, voted to boycott all trains carrying Pullman cars. Amid charges by the union that its members were being viciously attacked by management goons, and in some states by the militia, and by the railroads that the property was being destroyed, the railroads took to coupling mail cars to all their trains. When the workers attacked them, they sought federal injunctions.

On July 2, the U.S. Marshal in Chicago deputized 400 men, armed them with rifles and attempted to read an injunction. The marshal was hooted down and promptly called for federal troops. Olney's reply was that such a request had to be accompanied by the signatures of the U.S. attorney and a federal judge. The requisite telegram reached Olney on July 3, giving a somewhat distorted picture of the situation. No real violence had occurred, and the governor of Illinois was assuring Washington that he had enough state forces to quell any outbreak. Before the telegram had arrived, however, Olney, who feared a wide-spread breakdown of civil order, was lobbying a reluctant president and his cabinet for military intervention. When it did come, debate ceased and the U.S. Army was ordered in.

The commander of the troops and future general, Massachusetts-born Nelson Appleton Miles, was personally sympathetic to the plight of the impoverished strikers and reluctant to fire on his fellow Americans. Miles organized his corps into squads of 20 to 50 soldiers, each accompanied by a U.S. marshal, with orders not to fire unless fired on first. The sight of the soldiers, bayonets at the ready, served to enrage the strikers even further. By July 6, the rampaging men had destroyed thousands of dollars of railroad equipment and had set fire to the great halls of the World Columbian Exposition at Jackson Park.

The governor of Illinois, devoid of the restraint Miles was exhibiting, ordered in the state militia. In a bloody clash on July 7, four rioters were killed and five militia men seriously injured. Eugene V. Debs and other strike leaders were arrested and jailed, and the federal troops were withdrawn. Criticizing Miles's hesitation to fire on the strikers, Attorney General Olney said, "If Miles would do less talking to the newspapers and more shooting at the strikers, he'd come nearer to fulfilling his mission on earth and earning his pay." As to whom should be paid for carrying out this duty, one newspaper editorialized that the railroad barons "could pension him [Olney] for life for this one service."

When Secretary of State Walter Q. Gresham died in the summer of 1895, President Cleveland gave the post to Olney. To some of the president's advisers, it was an ill-conceived appointment of a man with no experience in diplomacy at a time when the country was faced with several serious foreign relations problems. But Cleveland had great confidence in the man whose advice he had come to rely on so heavily.

Olney's greatest challenge as Secretary lay in the American belief that Great Britain, by withholding from arbitration territory that was in dispute between Venezuela and British Guiana, was constructively extending its colonization in the Americas. With the active and sometimes threatening support of the president, Olney reaffirmed the Monroe Doctrine in the strongest possible terms. Olney told the British, "the United States is practically sovereign on this continent, and its fiat is law upon the subjects to which it confines its interposition."

After the election of Republican William McKinley in 1896, Olney left Washington and resumed his law practice in Boston, devoting considerable time to charitable and philanthropic works. There was a boomlet to secure the Democrat Party's presidential nomination for

Olney in 1900, led for the most part by the Irish-born mayor of Boston, Patrick A. Collins. Olney received 38 votes at the convention, 32 of those from the Massachusetts delegation. His last political battle was to be as leader of Boston's Citizen Municipal League, which sought through changes to the city charter, to rein in the growing political power of the city's Irish ward bosses. Richard Olney died before he could see what a futile effort that would be.

The Introspective Mr. Long

Perhaps it was the circumstances of his birth and childhood in the bucolic village of Buckfield, Maine, that developed in John Davis Long the cheerful and tolerant personality he displayed in later years. If so, the shrewd understanding of human nature and the dreams and poetry of blue skies and green meadows were tempered by the discipline and ambition imposed by his father. From his education at the academy in nearby Hebron, Maine, his four years at Harvard College, and a term at the law school, young Long achieved an excellent academic record but suffered personal dissatisfaction. He considered his days in Cambridge an educational failure and an unhappy experience. He was insatiably eager for self-improvement, a discipline that included enhancing his vocabulary by translating into English blank verse Virgil's Aeneid.

John Long taught for two years at the academy at Westford, Massachusetts, after leaving Harvard before the irresistible pull to "express the consciousness of power" drew him to Boston to answer the question, "Can such a man as I succeed, get rich, and acquire a reputation?" Before he died in 1915 at age 77, he attained all three.

Long arrived in Boston in 1862, and in 1870, by then financially comfortable with a lucrative law practice, he married Mary Woodward Glover of Hingham. The Longs made their home in the pleasant village of Hingham, not so far from Boston as to prevent John from commuting most days. Mary died in 1882, the mother of two daughters. Four years later John married Agnes Peirce, of North Attleboro, with whom he had a son.

In 1871 Long accepted the Democratic Party's nomination for a seat in the state legislature and lost. For the rest of his political career the heart and loyalty of the conservative and cautious John Davis Long would rest with the Republican Party. He was elected as a Republican to the Legislature in 1875, rose to the Speakership of the House a year later and advanced steadily up the traditional political ladder to lieutenant governor in 1879 and then to three terms (1880-1883) as the Commonwealth's chief executive. Long went from the Massachusetts State House to Washington, where he served six years in the House, until he declined to be a candidate for reelection in 1888.

Never politically venturous, Long stuck close to the party line, supporting James G. Blaine in 1884 and opposing Theodore Roosevelt in 1912. In 1897, President William McKinley appointed him secretary of the navy. Adopting the philosophy that a cabinet secretary does not so much represent the department he heads to the people, but rather the people to the department, Long wrote in his diary that his plan was "to leave all such [technical] matters to the bureau chiefs" and limit himself to the general direction of naval affairs, especially personnel matters. Long's patient and tactful administration did much to promote cooperation and diminish friction among competing forces in the naval service. To Secretary Long goes much of the credit for the U.S. Navy's success in the Spanish-American War.

After President McKinley was assassinated, Long stayed on as Secretary of the Navy for the first year of President Theodore Roosevelt's term, and resigned in May of 1902. He devoted much of his later life to writing on naval affairs, and the history of the Republican Party. In 1909, he penned a personal memoir for the *Proceedings of the Massachusetts Historical Society* titled *Reminiscences of My Seventy Years' Education*, which best described who and what he was. The life-long scholar and former politician also found time to advocate for prohibition, woman's suffrage, world peace and the elimination of the death penalty.

CHAPTER VII

The Rise of the Celt

THE MASSIVE WAVE OF IMMIGRANTS WHO FLOODED THE GREAT Eastern and Midwestern cities of America in the last decade of the nineteenth century brought more than cheap labor and high hopes. They brought with them the numbers and energy to raise the minority post-Civil War Democratic Party from its place as the "party of rebellion" to the majority "party of the people." Of all the immigrant groups none was more populous or more instrumental in the revival of the party's fortunes than the English-speaking Irish, and none did so earlier in a significant role than a man born in Ireland, at Ballinafauna, Fermoy, County Cork, on March 12, 1844.

From atop his high mount upon the equestrian statue sculpted by Thomas Ball standing in the Boston Public Garden, George Washington may peer all the way down Commonwealth Avenue to the statue of another heroic figure, Leif Erickson. In between, on the green mall flanked by old brownstones that once gave shelter to the city's aristocracy, there are other statues in honor of men with more intimate connections to the city's history. Among those is a statue commemorating the life of a man who was a congressman before John F. Fitzgerald, a mayor before James Michael Curley and a diplomat to the Court of St. James before Joseph P. Kennedy.

General Collins

'Twas grand altogether on that island in those days to be a lease-holder of two hundred acres, as was Bartholomew (Matt) Collins. Then God sent the hunger to try one's very soul, and old Matt Collins, who had the learning and could read and write, died of the consumption and the widow Collins, Matt's second wife, sold the lease, and left Ballinafauna in 1848 to sail to America with her four-year-old son Patrick. The Boston in which she arrived, and the nearby town of Chelsea, where she settled were not welcoming places for what the natives saw as "thick Micks" and statue-worshiping Papists. Young Pat was the target of ridicule and sometimes worse on his way back and forth to school, and his mother fared little better at the hands of the tormentors' parents. Mrs. Collins moved the family to Ohio in 1857, and when Pat was 13 and able to do so, he went to work in the fields and coal mines of the area. From his mother and other Irish immigrants, Pat heard tales of the oppression of his people by the English occupiers of their land. When he was 20, Collins joined the American branch of the Fenians and became one of its foremost American spokesmen.

The Collinses stayed in Ohio for two years before moving back to Boston, where Patrick was apprenticed to an upholsterer. Quick to learn and hard-working, he became an expert at his trade and was highly compensated. He also became an organizer and charter member of the local upholsterers union. The family at the time lived comfortably in South Boston among their own kind. For whatever reason, Patrick Collins was possessed by that element of discontent present in some exceptional young men of his day that propelled them along the determined road of self-education. On many a night after his supper, Patrick would trek the several miles to the Boston Public Library in Copley Square to expand his knowledge. Somewhere he made the acquaintance of Robert Morris, the first Negro to be admitted to the Boston bar, who suggested that Collins take up the law. As a result of his oratory on behalf of the Fenians, Collins was known in Boston political circles and increasingly sought after by the Democratic party leaders to sway his fellow Irishmen to their cause. A prominent Democrat and lawyer, James A. Keith, invited Collins to study in his office. Following Keith's tutelage, Collins was elected to the legislature in 1867, served in the House in 1868 and 1869 and in the Senate for two terms, 1870 and 1871. With what Collins learned, and after two years of attending Harvard Law School (LL.B. 1871), he was able to open his own office. Lawyer Collins's first client on the first day of opening his practice was a prosperous Boston merchant, Leopold Morse, whose business and political connections (he would later be elected to Congress) would prove of great value in Collins's rise to political leadership.

The anti-Catholic prejudice that prevailed in the Commonwealth at the time was embedded in law. There were no Catholic chaplains appointed to the state's charitable and penal institutions, and permission was often withheld for a Catholic priest to give the last sacraments to a dying prison inmate. Collins worked hard to remove those obstacles and to change the special form of oath Catholics had to take as witnesses in court. As a reward for his services in the election of Governor William Gaston in 1874, Collins was appointed judge advocate general. Such titles continue long after the occupant of the office leaves it, thus Collins was thereafter addressed as "General," despite his oft-expressed disdain for the title. When Charles Francis Adams ran for governor of Massachusetts, Collins defended him against charges of prejudice in the former ambassador's handling of Irish-American prisoners of the British. Abandoning his previous stand, Collins told his fellow Irishmen that their interest now lay in American, not Irish, issues.

Collins's first appearance on the national political scene, where he was destined to become a significant player was as a delegate to the Democratic convention, which nominated Samuel J. Tilden in 1876. By the time of that election thousands from the great wave of Irish immigrants who had fled the famine and come to America were either naturalized citizens or had native-born sons. The Irish, amassed in the large cities, could have a major impact on which presidential candidate would carry several key states. In local contests that most affected their lives, the Irish-Catholics' votes were almost invariably for Democrats.

On a national level, the Democratic Party did not take that vote for granted, and in casting about for a spokesman to exhort his countrymen and their sons to party loyalty, Tilden's handlers chose Patrick Collins. A gifted orator with the Irish touches of wit and self-deprecation, Collins spoke on Tilden's behalf in New York, Ohio, Indiana,

New Jersey and Connecticut. With his enthusiasm, eloquence, honesty of purpose, and great devotion to the principles of Jeffersonian democracy, the Boston Irishman became a darling in the Tilden camp and a participant in the higher councils of the party. To the extent such things are done by the overconfident and less superstitious in a close political campaign, there was talk, should Tilden win, that Patrick Collins would have his choice of a cabinet post, an ambassadorship, or (the one Collins would have wished for) the Collectorship of the Port of Boston. Any chance of Patrick Collins's elevation to high federal office disappeared along with Tilden's apparent victory in that disputed election with Rutherford B. Hayes.

A member of the American Land League in support of Irish farmers against their mostly absentee English landlords, Collins actively supported Charles Stewart Parnell when he came to America in 1880 seeking funds for the Irish Nationalist Party. Elected to the U.S. Congress in 1882, Collins was an unenthusiastic member of the House, where he found the procedures of the body frustrating, the work seemingly fruitless, and Washington rentals very high. In 1884 the congressman was chosen as one of the four Massachusetts delegates to the Democratic Party's national convention in Chicago.

That city's many abattoirs had hardly witnessed anything more bloody. When the awful battle was over, the party had nominated Grover Cleveland. In the coming national election both parties faced the possibility of large defections; the Republicans because many of their adherents questioned the honesty of the party's nominee, James Blaine, and the Democrats because of the belief on the part of their Irish-American supporters that as governor of New York, their nominee had been unduly harsh on the so-called "Irish bosses." Collins himself expressed such enmity when he wrote to a friend in July 1884: "I think I will go out [to the Democratic convention] as a looker-on, perhaps as a slayer in case Cleveland be not quite dead." A summons to Albany and a talking-to by nominee Cleveland persuaded Collins otherwise, and he became the party's most effective worker in its attempt to stem any large defection of Irish-Americans.

The Republican campaign to woo the Irish vote was dishonest and insidious. Cleveland was a bigot, an enemy of the working class, a monopolist and an implacable foe of organized labor. Blaine, on the other hand, was a stalwart enemy of England who would pursue a vigorous foreign policy that was sure to make John Bull quiver. A Blaine administration, they were assured, would result in great moral and material benefits for the Catholic Church in America. The admission by Cleveland that he had fathered a child out of wedlock did nothing to enhance his standing among the sexually puritanical Irish.

The Democratic Party's answer to the Republicans wooing the Catholic vote was Patrick Collins, who exhorted and cajoled, charmed, entertained and persuaded in city and town, meeting hall, and outdoor rally. Cleveland won, if only barely. When the debits and credits were being calculated, everyone from the president-elect down through the campaign hierarchy knew that there was a large chit outstanding in the hands of Patrick Collins.

Cleveland's victory, the first by a Democrat in 24 years, brought in from the political wilderness an extraordinary number of party office seekers. Congressman Collins, who had been elected head of the Massachusetts Democrat Party in July 1883, and who reputedly had the ear of the new president, was deluged with requests. On a higher level it was believed that one cabinet post would be allotted to New England, specifically to Massachusetts. In addition to what regional balance that would bring to the president's cabinet, it would also constitute the Bay State's reward for its contribution to the Democratic victory. Surely Collins, who had so effectively represented a constituency so key to President Cleveland's election and to the party's future was more than worthy of the post.

In February 1885, a delegation of leading Democrats traveled to New York to urge upon the president-elect the selection of Collins for a cabinet post. Initially, Collins opposed the move, citing the financial sacrifice involved and his intention to abandon public life at the end of his present term in Congress. Collins relented, however, and got his Irish up when he learned of opposition to the appointment to such high office of an Irish immigrant over a native-born scion from one of the old "families" of Massachusetts.

The opposition to Collins was formidable, and Cleveland's temporary White House was peppered with protests against his appointment, including blatantly false attacks on Collins's honesty. Even during the worst days of discrimination against the immigrant Irish in

Massachusetts they did not go without their defenders on all levels of society, nor would Collins. Judge Josiah Abbott, James Carleton, Reuben Noble and other Yankee Democrats threw their support to the Congressman. Among the more passionate of Collins's Irish supporters was a fellow Fenian who had escaped British exile in Australia to become one of America's better known journalists and political leaders, John Boyle O'Reilly.

The ultimate selection by the president of Judge William C. Endicott of Salem to the open cabinet post—secretary of war—was more of a disappointment to Collins's supporters than it was to the reluctant candidate himself. There is no question that in the appointment of William Crowninshield Endicott, of the impeccably pedigreed Salem, Massachusetts, Endicotts, over that of Patrick Andrew Collins, of the lease holding farming family of Ballinafauna, Cork, Ireland, the element of ethnic and religious prejudice played its dark part. A good number of the erstwhile Massachusetts Democrats who had opposed Collins were Mugwumps, Republican Yankees whose disdain for Blaine had caused their defection to Cleveland. Patrick Collins was soon to witness another example of the sway the Brahmin political aristocracy, be they Democrat or Republican, held over the political fortunes of Massachusetts.

Collins did not get a cabinet appointment and the post of Collector of the Port of Boston went to Leverett Saltonstall of Newton. Despite this, Collins and the president remained close friends, and Collins was often invited to the president's summer home at Buzzards Bay. Collins presided as permanent chairman of the 1888 Democratic National Convention, which renominated Cleveland, who lost to Benjamin Harrison in that year's election. Cleveland, however, was nominated and elected again four years later. In that process no one was a more enthusiastic and effective advocate for Cleveland than Collins. Cleveland was returned to the White House in 1892, and Collins was rewarded for his hard work and loyalty by a most unexpected and somewhat daring appointment. If the government of Her Majesty Queen Victoria did not consider an avowed Fenian and opponent of her rule in the land of his birth persona non grata, Patrick A. Collins would go to London as American Consul-General to the Court of St. James. The British government did not, and he went—the climax of an extraordinary journey.

Collins's stay in London kept him out of the rancorous 1896 election, which pitted the free-silver-advocating Bryan, with whom Collins had little sympathy, against the Republican McKinley. Later, in 1901, Collins was elected mayor of Boston and reelected in 1903. Both Collins and his Irish-born Democrat successor in that office, Hugh O'Brien, were aligned with the reform movement in the city personified by the Yankee mayors Josiah Quincy and Nathan Matthews.

Collins died suddenly while vacationing at Hot Springs, Virginia, on September 14, 1905. He was an honest man untouched by the improprieties of which some of his succeeding mayors of Boston with a Celtic background would be accused. Loyal to his family, to his church, to the country of his birth and to the country of his manhood, Patrick Andrew Collins was, as much as any other Irish-American, the progenitor of the Rise of the Celt in American politics.

PART II

The American Century

MAN REACHED TO THE MOON AND TOUCHED IT, SOUGHT OUT HELL
and dwelled there. In its conflicted history, the twentieth century witnessed scientific and technical advances that made the most creative
futurist seem cautious. It revealed the ease with which man could
embrace the harlot of death and fall into the arms of the purveyors of
deliberate genocide and merciless war. In the great contradiction that
of all nature's species only humankind could survive, empires were
toppled, freedom was generally extended and the welfare of man,
although not universally, at least significantly, improved.

The United States of America entered the twentieth century hardly
out of its adolescence and just beginning to exercise the developing
muscle of what was to become an extraordinary capacity to produce.
A young nation of the new world ensconced in the pleasant cocoon of
its isolation as yet unaware that it would soon enough be called upon
for the salvation of the old, and from that stampede emerge triumphant and preeminent.

On January 1, 1900, the United States of America was a union of 45
states, several territories, and the overseas possessions of Hawaii, the
Phillipines, Puerto Rico and Guam. Its domestic population had grown
to 76 million, with 3.6 million having immigrated to America over the
previous decade. The country's work force was split almost evenly
between farm and industrial workers: its median age was 22.9 years; its

gross national product $18.7 billion. There were 8,000 automobiles registered, and the country would face myriad domestic problems.

To the traumatic consequence of recessions and the Great Depression, presidential assassinations and a resignation, racial upheaval and civic unrest were added: the question of the fair distribution of the nation's growing wealth; the power of monopoly; the consequence of immigration; the extent to which the government could suppress dissent it regarded detrimental to the general welfare; the demands of women for the vote, and of reformers for the prohibition of alcohol; the hope of African Americans to be liberated from their status of slave but not to gain full citizenship. In much of the role the federal government would play in both the domestic and international upheavals of the twentieth century, Massachusetts men and women would play a significant and often vital role.

CHAPTER I

The Commonwealth's Century:
A Question of Continuity

"If you do not rise to the head not only in your own profession but of your country, it will be owing to your own laziness, slovenliness, and obstinacy."

— John Adams of Massachusetts
to his son, John Quincy Adams

"I bequeath a father's experience, and I entreat them to take no public or active part in the disputes of their country beyond a vote at an election."

— Benjamin Rush of Pennsylvania to his sons

IN HIS *PURITAN BOSTON AND QUAKER PHILADELPHIA*, E. DIGBY BALTZELL, professor emeritus of sociology at the University of Pennsylvania, contrasts the intellectual, educational, and political leadership emanating from Massachusetts and Pennsylvania in the eighteenth and nineteenth centuries and concludes that the greater contribution came from the smaller of the two commonwealths. This gap is particularly wide in the political field, an effect, the professor postulates, of the cultural difference between the Puritans' emphasis on a hierarchical participation in structured government, and the Quakers' more democratic and egalitarian philosophy that the individual better serves the community by being a good person than a good judge or statesman.

The structure and persona of the political leadership of Massachusetts and of those it sent to the nation's capital in the eighteenth and nineteenth centuries was familial and aristocratic. The ever astute John Adams wrote in his *Defense of the Constitution*, "Go into every village . . . . And you will find that the office of justice of the peace, and even of representative, which has ever depended from generation to generation, in three or four families at the most." As the years went on, Mr. Adams's "three or four families at the most" grew into an identifiable political aristocracy—a hierarchy of leaders made up, with but few exceptions, of men of English ancestry, Puritan ties and Brahmin standing, initially educated at private or classical public schools and graduates of Harvard College.

The leadership of the Commonwealth and of its capital city, Boston, the hub and foment of its social, political and cultural existence, was in the declining decades of the the nineteenth century contentedly homogeneous: Yankee, Protestant and Republican. The city and state in which they prospered, and, the prosperity that provided the means and time for public life, were centers of commerce, finance and manufacturing. Soon enough, much of the source of that prosperity would be lost, exported to more convenient ports or given over to cheaper labor. At the same time a more dramatic, monumental demographic change was taking place: from Canada for opportunity, from the poverty of Italy, to escaping the pogroms of Poland and Russia, fleeing starvation in Ireland. They came, these foreigners, not in streams but in torrents. The French and the Poles, the Italians and the east European Jews were at the borders of the changing landscape of Boston and the Commonwealth: at its heart were the Irish. In the decade from 1846 to 1856 the Celts disembarked at the Port of Boston, the second busiest point of entry for immigrants after New York, at the rate of a thousand a month, and succeeded in changing the relatively small, insular and self-assured city of Boston in hardly the wink of history's eye, from Yankee, Protestant and Republican to Irish, Catholic and Democrat.

What then was to happen to the culture of participation in public life born of the Bay Colony's Royal Charter, seeded in its town meetings and nurtured by its legislature and Constitution if the progeny of its continuity went into decline? Would the political culture of Massachusetts that demonstrated itself so well in the widespread participation of the governed in their governing and produced national leaders far out of proportion to the size and national importance of the

Commonwealth decline as its traditional participants declined in presence and power? Or would the heritage of that ethic be assumed in the way their own heritage would dictate by the emerging political leadership? The domination of the focused and disciplined Yankee Massachusetts Republican Party would last far into the nineteenth century, its demise at least slowed by the incestuous feuding of the Irish-Democrats. Yet neither the decline of the one nor the ascendancy of the other degraded the Commonwealth's extraordinary national political presence.

From the day in 1902 when Oliver Wendell Holmes was sworn as an associate justice of the Supreme Court of the United States, until the retirement of Thomas P. O'Neill Jr. as the Speaker of the national House of Representatives, in 1987, Massachusetts enjoyed a triumph of national leadership that set in gold the continuum of such leadership begun at the birth of the nation. Indeed, in comparative numbers and extent of influence, the Commonwealth's contribution to the governance of the nation exceeded in those nine decades of the twentieth century that of all the eighteenth and nineteenth.

For a remarkable 15 Congresses (29 years in all) four Massachusetts men, Frederick H. Gillett, Joseph Martin, John W. McCormack and Thomas P. O'Neill Jr. presided over the U.S House of Representatives, twice when the occupants of the White House, Calvin Coolidge and John Kennedy, were fellow Bay-Staters. For 60 continuous years, sometimes alone and sometimes with another, four Massachusetts lawyers: Oliver Wendell Holmes, William Henry Moody, Louis Dembitz Brandeis and Felix Frankfurter sat on the Supreme Court of the United States concurring or dissenting in over 1,500 decisions, and writing more opinions than any other of that number in the history of the Court. In 20 presidential administrations, 13 Massachusetts men and 2 women served 29 times as cabinet secretaries, including one, Elliot Richardson, who presided over three. Over 50 men and women from the Commonwealth held high office in the U.S. State Department or represented their country as the chief diplomat in 47 countries.

It was not from the great immigrant populations of New York or Philadelphia or Chicago that the first Catholic Irish-American president of the United States or Speaker of the U.S. House of

Representatives came, nor the first African American ever popularly elected to the U.S. Senate; they came from Boston, Massachusetts.

CHAPTER II

Striking a Balance

FROM ITS INCEPTION, IN ITS CONSTITUTION, LAWS AND ADMINISTRATION, the government of the United States of America had been devoted to the promotion of commerce. To that end, Congress subsidized railroads, built canals, passed protective tariffs, constructed roads and dredged harbors. Beyond the physical contribution to the growth of business and industry, the legislatures, both federal and state, either by benign neglect or specific legislation, allowed the growth of increasingly powerful trusts, monopolies and financial combines. By the waning years of the nineteenth century the power, political and financial, of American capitalism had created an enormous imbalance between its interests and the legitimate aspirations and basic needs of working men and women. The rise of the Progressive movement in its various manifestations was an attempt to redress that imbalance within the constitutional structure of the American democracy. Others—communists, socialists, radical labor leaders and anarchists—had neither the patience for nor the need for methodical restructuring. Tear down and build anew, that was their way. The social upheaval that tore the nation—from the second presidency of Grover Cleveland to the start of the Great Depression—was a civil war, less bloody (but not bloodless) than the War between the States; mortal combat nevertheless.

The Supreme Court of the United States, an institution that by its very nature can scarcely render an insignificant decision, would, in those years, be repeatedly called upon as the final arbiter of what was, and what was not, constitutionally permissible among the conflicting claims of opposing segments of American society. From Theodore Roosevelt in 1902 to Franklin Roosevelt in 1939, seven presidents would appoint 20 justices to the Court. No list of the more outstanding and influential of those justices could be compiled without the inclusion of three from Massachusetts: Justices Holmes, Brandeis and Frankfurter. There was a fourth justice from Massachusetts during that period, William H. Moody, whose significant contributions on the Court were cut short by illness. Taken as a whole, the work of Holmes, Moody, Brandeis, and Frankfurter constitutes an unequaled contribution to American jurisprudence—a contribution perhaps best realized if the story of their incumbency is related in its sequential whole, uninterrupted by chronological considerations.

The journey to the Supreme Court would take each of the four through Harvard Law School, their way of arrival at that institution dictated by who and what they were. Oliver Wendell Holmes and William Henry Moody's path was that of the Brahmin: talented sons of long established and financially secure New England families, educated at the best of grammar schools, at Harvard College and the law school. Louis Dembitz Brandeis, son of a Jewish family aristocratic in its own culture, and Felix Frankfurter, a poor Jewish immigrant, would find their ways to the law school in a less structured fashion. They were critically helped along by what Holmes had in abundance, Moody possessed in good measure and the two Jews exhibited to an extraordinary degree: intelligence and ability.

Please Rise: Brahmins and Jews—A Pair of Each

Oliver Wendell Holmes Jr. was born in Boston on March 8, 1841; William Henry Moody on December 23, 1853 at Newbury, Massachusetts; Louis Dembitz Brandeis, in Louisville, Kentucky, on November 13, 1856; and Felix Frankfurter on November 15, 1882, in Vienna, Austria.

Holmes was the namesake son of Dr. Oliver Wendell Holmes, whose fame as an essayist (Autocrat of the Breakfast Table) far exceeded that of his profession as a physician, and of Amelia Lee Jackson Holmes, the daughter of Judge Charles Jackson. Holmes was born at home, No. 8 Montgomery now (Bosworth) Place, Boston. The street is short and narrow, and in other cities it might be designated an alley. As a youth, Holmes, on his way to becoming tall and thin unlike his short, stout father, walked to school. First to a dame school and then to Reverend T.R. Sullivan's little classroom around the corner on Beacon Street, then to Mr. Dixwell's private latin school. If one wished to research Wendie (as he was addressed by his peers) Holmes's ancestry, the records of the King's Chapel Burial Ground just down Tremont Street would show descendence from families such as Quincy and Bradstreet. In the privileged and aristocratic society of Holmes's childhood, his education was exquisitely enriched by the conversation of learned men of the caliber of Ralph Waldo Emerson, who came to dine with his father. Sunday in a home that still observed the strict Puritan Sabbath was given over to quiet diversion. He would read, Holmes would say in later life, the works of writers John Ruskin and Thomas Carlyle and Emerson, the sort of men Holmes most admired. The writings of Charles Darwin must have also impressed the young Holmes: he early on became a devotee of the principles of evolution and survival of the fittest.

Holmes entered Harvard in 1857, at age 16, six feet tall and 130 pounds, a self-styled "seeker of the truth" full of high jinks and pranks. He graduated as the class poet in 1861, not to indulge in a European tour or to pursue further studies, or even to engage in a gentleman's employment, as might be expected of his social class, but to fight in the fields of war. Holmes, like so many of his classmates, heeded President Lincoln's call to arms and enlisted in the Union Army, an action that made him, in the words of his father, one of the ". . . poor Brahmins . . . pallid, undervitalized, shy, sensitive creatures, whose only birthright is an aptitude for learning . . . even these poor New England Brahmins of ours . . . count as full men, if their courage is big enough for the uniform which hangs so loosely about their slender figures." It was as a "full man of courage," not a Harvard gentleman, that Holmes returned from war; a thrice-wounded veteran of the awful carnage, once and forever changed. Holmes began his study of the law and graduated from Harvard Law School in 1866.

William Henry Moody's forebears first landed in America at Ipswich, in 1634, moved to Newbury in 1635, where, in the very same homestead over two centuries later, William Henry Moody was born on December 23, 1853. William Moody received his early education at Danvers, graduated from Phillips Academy at Andover in 1872, earned a degree in history cum laude from Harvard College in 1876, and matriculated to the law school. The young man's stay there was of short duration, just four months before he continued his study of the law in the office of Richard Henry Dana Jr., lawyer and author of *Two Years Before the Mast.*

In Europe, when the abortive 1848 democratic revolution against the Austro-Hungarian Empire collapsed, Louis Dembitz Brandeis's father and two related families thought it politic to leave their cultured and sophisticated life in Prague and journey to America. Arriving in Kentucky with plans to engage in farming (inappropriately accompanied by two pianos and numerous boxes of books), the families moved to Madison, Wisconsin, where Adolph Brandeis and Frederika Dembitz were married. Farming was not in the nature of the Brandeises so they returned to Kentucky, to Louisville, where Adolph built up a very successful wholesale grain and produce business and where Louis was born on November 13, 1856.

Anticipating the coming financial difficulties in America, Adolph Brandeis sold his business in 1872 and took his family on a three-year tour of Europe. While in Italy, young Louis traveled alone to Dresden, Germany, and presented himself to the headmaster at the Annen-Realschule. With neither birth certificate nor proof of vaccination, and lacking an entrance exam but exuding the intelligence and persuasiveness that were to become his hallmarks, Brandeis talked himself into admittance, and graduated as the most outstanding student in all subjects. On his return to America in 1875, Brandeis, without a college diploma, entered Harvard Law School, where he duplicated his academic success in Germany by earning grades never before seen at the school. Brandeis received his law degree in 1877 and stayed at the school the next year, tutoring and proctoring exams.

Holmes, Moody and Brandeis, aristocrats of their particular cultures, were never in material want or lacking in intellectual stimuli. Felix Frankfurter's background was, at least in a material sense (his uncle was chief librarian of the University of Vienna), more common. Felix's father, Leopold, was a rabbinical student turned businessman. The change did not bring the financial success that Leopold, somewhat an impractical dreamer, had anticipated, so he brought his family to New York City in 1894 and became a linen merchant. His father's naturalization four years later conferred American citizenship on 16-year-old Felix as well. For Felix that status marked the birth of an extraordinary love affair with the adopted land of his youth.

Frankfurter began his American education in P.S. 25 in New York City. Because of his short stature (he was less than five feet five inches) he was immune to the periodic beatings administered by the Irish kids on the "kikes" on their way to and from classes. Young Felix had the good fortune to have as his teacher an indomitable woman by the name of Miss Hogan, who threatened dire consequences to any student who would address Felix in any language other than English.

Felix augmented his formal education with frequent trips to the reading rooms of the Cooper Union and neighboring libraries, and attended lectures and debates and listened to the incessant arguments by self-styled socialists, communists, and assorted revolutionaries in the coffee houses frequented by the Jews. In 1902, the year his future friend and confidant, Oliver Holmes, first took his seat on the U.S. Supreme Court, Felix Frankfurter received a B.A. from City College, New York, having completed a combination high school/college course.

Frankfurter worked as a clerk in the tenement housing department of the city of New York for a year after his graduation and somehow managed to raise the necessary funds to attend Harvard Law School. The new student was initially ill at ease, as if his short height and small weight were a metaphor for his inferior social standing among young men of much more impressive backgrounds. He regained his self-esteem the old fashioned way: through hard work and application of his considerable intellect. At the end of his first term, Felix Frankfurter led his class.

The Legal Litterateur

Oliver Wendell Holmes made a rather unenthusiastic entrance into the legal profession after graduating from Harvard Law School. The lofty freedom of the philosopher rather than the settled drudgery of the lawyer was the life he truly wanted. It was a conflict that was not resolved until he was older and could write that he "no longer had any doubt—that a man may live greatly in the law as elsewhere; that there as well as elsewhere his thought may find its unity with infinite perspective." The young lawyer believed in the Malthusian theory that on its present course, the world's spawning population would outgrow resources, and he considered for a brief time the benefits of euthanasia.

Holmes was convinced that in the inevitable struggle between master and man, race and race, class and class, the fittest would survive. He was opposed to both labor unions and socialism on the grounds that the former would destroy his class, or that the latter would claim so much of its wealth that the leisure class so necessary for the development of music, art and literature would cease to exist. Yet he believed in mankind's slow and sometimes imperceptible movement to law and legislation to settle its disputes; and that even labor unions and socialists had the right to have their claims respectfully heard and adjudicated. To the extent that the work of the Anglophile Holmes, on or off the bench, had any effect on social progress in America, it was comparable to the measured advance in Britain of Disraeli's Conservatives rather than of Gladstone's Liberals.

A worker of almost feverish intensity (but one who believed that truly creative labor could be pursued no more than four hours a day) Holmes was for three years (1870-1873) editor of the *American Law Review*. In that capacity he displayed a talent given to few legal luminaries of his day (or of this): a compelling literary style. Holmes's early writings addressed issues vital to any society claiming devotion to justice according to law. What are the sources of law and its sanctions? How much lawmaking is appropriate to the courts and how much is the exclusive province of legislatures? What are the ingredients, conscious and unconscious, of adjudication? When should precedent rule and when, in the circumstances of the time, should it be abandoned? Initially a rather disorganized writer, Holmes used an invitation to give a series of lectures at the Lowell Institute in Boston to systematize his ideas into a "connected treatise." In 1881, just before he reached his fortieth birthday, Holmes was able to reach one of the goals he had set for himself: He published *The Common Law*, a seminal work that gave powerful direction to legal science, marked an epoch in law and learning and reoriented legal inquiry. The validity of its fame as a classic is confirmed by the fact that following generations of legal scholars saluted Holmes's perspicacity when he wrote, ". . . the life of the law has not been logic: it has been experience" influenced by the necessity of the time, the existing moral and political theories, public policy and "even the prejudices that judges share with their fellow men." "The law embodies the story of a nation's development through many centuries. In order to know what it is, we must know what it has been, and what it tends to become." Many of his contemporaries believed such a mind as dwelled in the person of Oliver Wendell Holmes belonged in academia, and much through the efforts of Brandeis, secretary of the newly formed Harvard Law School Alumni Association, a chair was endowed for Holmes at the law school.

As attractive as the law school was in affording Holmes the opportunity to influence young law students, teaching lacked the immediacy of writing judicial decisions. Holmes's influential friends, aware of his preference for the bench over the lectern, waited for the opportunity to secure a judgeship for Holmes. In July 1878, the death of Federal Judge George Shepley created a vacancy in Massachusetts, and the choice as to who would fill it was political and intense. John Gray organized a campaign on Holmes's behalf and enlisted the support of his half brother, Horace Gray, at the time chief justice of the Supreme Judicial Court. The two key figures whose support Holmes needed were his fellow war veteran, U.S. Attorney General Charles Devens, and Massachusetts U.S. Senator George Frisbie Hoar. Hoar had his own candidate in mind, and when he and Devens met with President Hayes, it was the senator who prevailed. A vacancy again appeared on the Supreme Judicial Court subsequent to the publication of *The Common Law* and Holmes's name was again proposed and passed over. Time for a judgeship, at least as it was calculated by Holmes in his list of "by when I should have accomplished what" was running out.

Yet hope existed that if a vacancy on the state bench occurred during the incumbency of Republican Governor John D. Long, he would fill it with the loyal and dutiful Republican Holmes. No such opportunity presented itself during Long's three one year terms (1880-1883), and when Long did not stand for reelection, the Democratic candidate, the ever busy Benjamin Butler, was elected governor. On

Friday, December 8, 1882, Holmes was interrupted while having dinner in Cambridge with his fellow Harvard professor, James Barr Ames, by the arrival of George Shattuck. Hurrying the surprised Holmes into his carriage, Shattuck set out for the State House in Boston. Justice Otis Phillips Lord of the Supreme Judicial Court was retiring. If the lame-duck Long could be dissuaded from appointing a Democrat out of deference to his successor, and if it could be done that day so that the governor's council could act before it adjourned for the year, Oliver Wendell Holmes might finally sit on a court.

Within an hour of their hurried leave from Cambridge, Holmes and Shattuck were in Long's office, the appointment papers signed, and the nomination forwarded to the council. No objection arose in that body, and one week later the appointment became effective. On the same day that Judge Holmes took his oath of office, his letter of resignation from the law school was accepted, but not graciously. He had taught there for only three months and was leaving in the middle of the term. It was a long time before Harvard President Charles W. Elliot forgave Holmes for such bad behavior.

When Holmes took his seat on the highest court of the Commonwealth on January 3, 1883, the Supreme Judicial Court was 108 years old, having been established in 1775 to succeed the Superior Court of Judicature of the Province of Massachusetts Bay which had first sat in 1692. Chief Justice Horace Gray, having been appointed to the Supreme Court of the United States, resigned his seat on the Supreme Judicial Court. The court's seven justices began each yearly session sitting in Boston as a court of appeals. That done, two justices would be dispatched to sit individually as trial judges in the Western Massachusetts counties. In the spring, all of the justices would go on "circuit" to preside over trials, divorce cases and criminal cases, where the sentence could be execution. Despite the exhausting schedule, Holmes so loved the work that he volunteered to take other justices' assignments and welcomed even the most dreary and technical disputes. The speed with which he wrote his opinions astounded his fellow judges, and lawyers marveled at his quick and penetrating intellect. One lawyer remarked that he could not get halfway through even the most complicated of arguments before he became convinced that Judge Holmes had already mentally reached its conclusion.

Justice Holmes fashioned himself less a "scientist" of the law than a "farmer" of it. In his 20 years on the bench of a court whose influence went beyond the Commonwealth, Holmes's ideas and precedents, his clarity of thought and extraordinary presentation, fertilized the whole vast field of law. Holmes's Massachusetts decisions, some 1,300 in number, when considered as a whole, constitute the most comprehensive and philosophic body of American law written by any judge not only during the time they were rendered, but also, arguably, during any period of American history. In July 1899, Chief Justice Walbridge Field died, and the governor, Roger Wolcott, submitted Holmes's name as Field's successor to the governor's council, which, without objection, promptly approved it.

Among the chief justices of the Massachusetts Supreme Judicial Court two—William Cushing and Horace Gray—had been elevated to the Supreme Court of the United States. That was where Holmes wanted to be: sitting on the highest court of the land had been his lifelong ambition. An opportunity seemed to present itself in February 1902, when Justice Gray, elevated from the state bench to the Supreme Court in 1882, suffered a stroke. The ailing jurist submitted a letter of resignation in July subject to the appointment and confirmation of a successor. Overtures on behalf of several candidates, Holmes presumably among them, were made to President Theodore Roosevelt. The president, while amenable to keeping tradition and naming a New Englander to the post, seemed to have been leaning toward a Boston lawyer, Alfred Hemenway. Of all the factors that go into securing an appointment as a justice of the Supreme Court—politics, party, personality and standing in the profession—the controlling factor is opportunity. If the president used the opportunity of Justice Gray's retirement to appoint someone other than Holmes, even if another vacancy occurred in the near future the chances of the sixty-year-old Bostonian being appointed were probably nonexistent.

Henry Cabot Lodge, already a power in the U.S. Senate, took up his friend Holmes's cause by warning off all other potential supplicants from New England and formally proposing Holmes to the president. Lodge's senior Massachusetts colleague in the Senate, George Frisbie Hoar, had a candidate of his own, his nephew Ebenezer, son of a man whom President Grant had unsuccessfully proposed for the Supreme

Court many years before. In his process of selection, President Roosevelt consulted neither Senator Hoar nor his attorney general, Philander Knox. Roosevelt had been much impressed by Holmes's speech, "The Soldier's Faith," which the president felt proved Holmes to be with him on the questions of the glories of war and patriotism; President Roosevelt wanted assurances that the candidate was of sound Republican principles and called on Lodge to endorse a man of honor. Lodge insisted that Holmes had always been a stalwart party man: he had never been rebellious and was solid on American expansion. "I would not appoint my best beloved—unless he held the position you describe," Lodge assured the president. Justice Holmes was invited to meet Roosevelt at Oyster Bay, Long Island, on July 25, and the president proffered the appointment.

On August 11, the president announced that Holmes's name would be submitted to the Senate after its summer recess. The Democratic newspapers, noting Holmes's dissents in the Massachusetts court that favored labor, did not oppose the nomination. The Nation and one New York newspaper questioned whether Holmes was too literary, or even too brilliant for the practical duties of the Supreme Court. The *Boston Evening Transcript*, the bible of Brahmin Boston's births, deaths, suitable marriages and proper conduct, opined that while Holmes could not be expected to be as fine a justice as Horace Gray was, it was content to see him succeed to the Justice Gray court. That comment was painful to Holmes, as was the speculation (which he himself harbored) that he would not live long enough to influence American jurisprudence in any meaningful way. Horace Gray died on September 15, 1902, and Holmes was sworn as an associate justice of the Supreme Court on December 8. "Wendie" Holmes had reached his Olympus, and he would soon be master there.

The Special Prosecutor

Oliver Wendell Holmes first came to prominence in his profession via the pen; William Henry Moody by the bloody end of an axe. Lizzie Borden, a 32-year-old unmarried woman in Fall River, was accused of taking an axe to her mother and father on August 4, 1892. She was accused of administering a fatal 40 whacks to the former, the same number and a redundant 41st to the latter. The now orphaned Lizzie, who had lived alone with her parents, was indicted for the double murders; there was no other suspect. Law enforcement authorities believed the evidence to be compelling but feared a jury of locals might be obdurate. The prosecution acquired the services of the U.S. Attorney for the Eastern District of Massachusetts, William Henry Moody, to assist them in convicting Lizzie Borden. They failed to do so, but Moody's handling of his part in the matter brought him wide public recognition. Three years later, in a special election to fill a vacancy caused by the death of William Cogswell, Moody was elected as a Republican to the 54th Congress (1895-1897).

Moody's personal credo during his years of practice of the law was that "the power of a clear statement is the greatest power at the bar." The implementation of that belief and an extraordinary grasp of the subject matter of legislation gained for Moody a seat on the important House Appropriations Committee in his second term. His work in Congress so impressed President Theodore Roosevelt that he appointed Moody secretary of the navy in May 1902. Like the president, William Moody was pugnacious and virile, traits that brought the men together in a close friendship. When the Attorney General of the United States, Philander Knox, resigned in 1904, Roosevelt chose Moody for the post. Moody's closeness to the president and his vigorous pursuit of Roosevelt's antitrust agenda soon led to the praise (and condemnation) of Moody as truly being "the president's lawyer."

Roosevelt's antitrust crusade was at its peak while William Moody served as the nation's chief law enforcement officer. In 1905 the attorney general personally argued the case, *Swift and Company v. United States*, the so-called Beef Trust Case, before the Supreme Court. The government contended that a combination of corporations and individuals, after purchasing livestock and converting it into fresh meat, sold the product interstate in such a manner as to preclude competition both in the purchase and conversion of the cattle. The company countered with the argument that the statute under which the charges had been brought, the Sherman Anti-Trust Act, was vague. Further, since the company's activities (buying the cattle and converting it into meat) were entirely intrastate, they were outside the reach of federal power to regulate commerce as that power had been previously adjudicated. The Supreme Court found otherwise, and in a unanimous decision authored by Justice Holmes held that a combination that excluded competitors with intent to monopolize interstate commerce was in violation of the Sherman Anti-Trust Act. In his official role, Attorney General Moody also instituted restraint of trade charges against the paper, fertilizer, tobacco, oil, lumber and other businesses.

When Associate Justice Henry Billings Brown announced his decision to retire from the high court in 1906, few doubted that William Moody would be at the top of the president's list to succeed him. Moody's nomination came soon enough, to the great displeasure of those commercial interests that feared his attitude toward "big business" during his tenure as attorney general. The business segments were afraid that Moody's personal prejudices would be carried over into the Court and the new justice's decision would reflect Roosevelt's radical ideas. The president prevailed, however, and William Henry Moody's appointment to the Supreme Court was confirmed by the Senate on December 12, 1906.

A Reforming Jew

Louis D. Brandeis departed Harvard Law School and Cambridge in 1878 to practice law in St. Louis, where his sister Fannie and her husband Charles Nagel (later Secretary of Labor and Commerce under Presidents Theodore Roosevelt and Taft) lived, and found it deadly dull. Within the year Brandeis returned to his stimulating friends in Boston and Cambridge and to a partnership in the law firm of Warren and Brandeis. Samuel Warren Jr., a classmate of Brandeis at Harvard, was a proper and affluent Bostonian. The young Jewish lawyer's association with Warren attracted friends and acquaintances that Brandeis would have had difficulty acquiring on his own. Among those with whom Brandeis was to become close were two future associate justices of the U.S. Supreme Court—Horace Gray and Oliver Wendell Holmes. During his first two years practicing law, Brandeis had served as a part-time clerk to Horace Gray, then chief justice of the Supreme Judicial Court of Massachusetts. "He was," Justice Gray was later to say about his clerk, "the most ingenious and most original lawyer I have ever met."

By the time he was 34, the "original and ingenious" lawyer was earning more than $50,000 a year, a princely sum that would give him the financial independence to indulge in other interests. Brandeis joined the Union Boat Club and sailed on the Charles River; he was an organizer of the Dedham Polo Club, and he rode often. Very much the Puritan in his moral values and work ethic, Brandeis was one of those energetic men, the boon and bane of society—a social reformer. Other men might have found satisfaction in collecting art or in sports; Louis Brandeis found his in trying to right social and political wrongs.

Brandeis used his skills in the cause of labor—often working pro bono, a tradition of the American bar he helped pioneer, against the abuses of the life insurance companies; and he concerned himself with the problems of rates and services of the company supplying gas to Boston. Perhaps his greatest efforts on behalf of good as opposed to evil was his opposition to long-term monopolies for the Boston Elevated Railway Company and his attempt to reform what he saw as corrupt political practices in the city. In the latter pursuit, Brandeis was a moving force behind the Good Government Association (whose members their archenemy, James Michael Curley, in dulcet and dripping tones, derided as the "goo-goos"). In the eyes of sincere reformers such as Brandeis and the merchant A. Lincoln Filene, the GGA was a mechanism to sponsor and elect good and honest public servants. In the eyes of the ascending Boston Irish, it was a means for the Yankee Republican political structure to hold on to their waning power. Much to Brandeis's chagrin, in his efforts at reform, he could not count on his fellow Jews. In the 1905 mayoral election, the goo-goos put up Louis A. Frothingham, Republican, against John F. Fitzgerald, Democrat. Not only did the grandfather of President Kennedy soundly beat the Yankee, but did it with the strong support of the Jewish precincts in the West End and Roxbury.

In 1891, Brandeis married his cousin, Alice Goldmark. A nonreligious Jew who was as totally assimilated into the Protestant community as a non-Christian could be, Brandeis nevertheless accepted the leadership of the American Zionist movement. In his vision of a future Jewish state in Palestine, Brandeis, who remained an active Zionist throughout his life, saw a small-scale egalitarian society, protective of the rights of both Jews and non-Jews, highly educated and agrarian, with common ownership of land. In many ways they were the embodiment of the democratic values Brandeis considered vital to the well-being of his own country.

Brandeis had a prodigious memory, nurtured as a matter of necessity when his eyes began to weaken during his days at Harvard Law School, and he turned to fellow students to read text to him. "A lawyer is far more likely to impress clients by knowledge of the facts than by knowledge of the law," he once wrote in a memorandum.

Lawyer Brandeis first came to national attention in 1910, when a young government employee, Louis R. Glavis, went to Richard A. Ballinger, the secretary of the interior, to report what he considered a sweetheart deal between some department officials and mining interests seeking land in Alaska. The secretary rebuffed Glavis, but the whistle-blower, emboldened by ardent conservationists, then took his case to President William Howard Taft. After consulting his attorney general, George Wichersham, the president not only supported Ballinger but ordered Glavis fired. There the matter might have ended had not the editor of *Collier's Weekly* published Glavis's charges. In the ensuing uproar, a joint committee of Congress was created to investigate. Editor Norman Hapgood retained his friend, Louis Brandeis, to represent Glavis. The extensive hearings proved highly embarrassing to the Republican members of the committee and the president. The rationale for exonerating any misdeeds on the part of Secretary Ballinger and for the discharge of Glavis was contained in an elaborate opinion given the president by the attorney general, and it was on that the president had based his actions. The president's men had not counted on the tenacity of a fact-finder as dedicated as Brandeis. The attorney general's opinion, Brandeis was able to show, was drafted after the president's rebuff and firing of Glavis.

In a case before the Supreme Court where he defended the state of Oregon's right to set a maximum of ten hours of labor a day for women, Brandeis was to present an argument that thereafter would be known as the "Brandeis Brief," for which a rare compliment came from the justices of the Court. After spending three pages on the applicable principles of the law, Brandeis proceeded to write over 100 more pages exposing the facts concerning the effects of excessive hours of labor on the women's health, comparable experiences of other countries, and the opinions of various experts. It was a form of augmentation the Court rarely heard. Brandeis was successful in having the Oregon law upheld. (*Muller v. Oregon*, 208 U.S. 412 (1908).

When the Progressive Party (Bull Moose) nominated Theodore Roosevelt in 1912 and the Democrats countered with Woodrow Wilson, Brandeis found himself more attracted to Wilson's unambiguous stand against monopolies as opposed to Roosevelt's distinction between good trusts and bad trusts. A notable meeting took place between candidate Wilson and Brandeis at Sea Girt, New Jersey, on August 28, 1912. During the discussion Brandeis was able to expand Wilson's philosophical position on the regulation of competition with the specifics of his personal experiences. Brandeis campaigned for the Democratic nominee throughout the Eastern states. When Wilson prevailed expectation was high that Louis Brandeis would be the next attorney general of the United States. Wilson made detailed inquiries to that end, but in too many influential quarters, even in Democratic circles, the Boston Jew was thought to be a dangerous radical.

In 1913 and 1914, Brandeis and a friend, George Rublee drafted a bill which, if it were to become law, would greatly strengthen the government's power to enforce antitrust laws and enjoin unfair and destructive trade practices. With President Wilson's strong backing, legislation was passed creating the Federal Trade Commission. When Supreme Court Associate Justice Joseph Lamar died on January 2, 1916, many names—including that of former President William Taft, who was known to covet the appointment—were put forward. Brandeis's name was among those proposed. If there was to be an appointee from New England, President Wilson wanted Brandeis, radical or not.

When the president announced his intention on January 28, 1916, to appoint Brandeis to the Court, consternation ensued among the business and conservative communities: Brandeis was certainly a radical, and probably a socialist. The best representation of the business interests' reaction was a cartoon by Rollin Kerby appearing in the *New York World*. Pictured was a large-stomached, side-burned man, dressed in frock coat and bow tie, lying in a state of swoon in a chair labeled "Wall Street" with a ticker tape machine fallen across his desk, under a picture, frame askew, of the New York Stock Exchange. In his limpid hand the man holds a newspaper with the bold headline: Brandeis for the Supreme Court. The cartoon bears the inscription: "The Blow That Almost Killed Father."

Much of the vehement opposition to Brandeis's appointment from the banking, railroad, insurance and other corporate interests was a rehashing of the grievances against him printed by *Barron's* magazine in its years-long effort to tarnish Brandeis's reputation. The New York press reflected the near apoplexy of their owners. Brandeis was "a man of furious partisanship, of violent antagonisms, and of irresponsible prejudice," screamed one. "If Wilson," huffed the *New York Tribune*, "does not withdraw his nomination, the Senate should throw it out." From on high, the *Boston Transcript* pontificated that it was indeed unfortunate that the exigencies of a forthcoming presidential campaign should force the Senate to put on the Supreme Court of the United States a man who was reported to have refused to consider a position on the cabinet.

In Boston there was not a word written nor publicly spoken, nary a wink or a nod, that any of the opposition to Brandeis's appointment had anything to do with the fact that he was Jewish. Yet in an era when even Justice Holmes, in a letter denying that Brandeis had undue influence on him, could refer to his friend as the "Hebe" one cannot doubt its existence. A respected segment of the city's aristocracy—A. Lawrence Lowell, Francis Peabody and Charles Francis Adams— signed a remonstrance against the appointment. In the manner in which gentlemen did such things, they graciously admitted that Louis Brandeis was an able and energetic lawyer but "ruthless in the attainment of his objectives [and] not scrupulous in the methods he adopts and not to be trusted." It took a former district attorney in Boston, Arthur D. Hill, to label that lofty rhetoric for what it really was.

To Hill, the real reason for such opposition was that Brandeis was a reformer and a Jew. The fact that he had spent a large part of his career attacking established institutions of the Commonwealth helped account for such antagonism. Brandeis was not "one of them," not a member of the legal or social aristocracy of Boston or New England. Such a man who so readily attacks his enemies, also gathers about him good friends of similar thinking. Frances Perkins, a social reformer and future secretary of labor in Franklin Roosevelt's administrations, gathered the supporting signatures of dignitaries such as Walter Lippman, the Reverend Percy Stickney, Rabbi Stephen S. Wise and Belle Moskowitz. On the last day of the Senate hearings on the Brandeis nomination, the Senate committee chairman read a very weighty communication in which the signatories "painfully" opposed Brandeis "as not being fit to be a member of the Supreme Court" because "of his reputation, character, and professional career." Every one of the seven people named on the document had served as a president of the American Bar Association, including such distinguished Americans as Joseph H. Choate, Elihu Root, and former president William Howard Taft. All of which amounted to naught. The full Senate met to consider the nomination on June 1, 1916. In 15 minutes and without debate, Louis Dembitz Brandeis, age 59, by 47 yeas to 22 nays, became the first of his race to be elevated to the Supreme Court of the United States.

The Little Judge

Small in stature, but large in presence, Felix Frankfurter left Cambridge after his graduation from Harvard Law School in 1906, and worked for a brief time in a New York law firm before leaving to work at the office of the U.S. Attorney for the southern district of New York, Henry L. Stimson. Frankfurter's association with Stimson, who would serve as secretary of war under Present Taft, of State under President Hoover, and of War again under Franklin Roosevelt, was a defining one and the beginning of a lifelong immersion in federal law and public affairs. Stimson put his assistant to work on antitrust and criminal work, and of the legal problems of immigrants. Felix accompanied Stimson on the campaign trail during his unsuccessful run for governor of New York in 1910. When Taft appointed Stimson secretary of war, Stimson hired Frankfurter as legal officer of the Bureau of Insular Affairs. Over time, Frankfurter's role was expanded to include that of the secretary's personal confidant in affairs of the War Department.

Frankfurter was retained at the war department by the incoming Wilson administration, albeit with diminished responsibilities that hardly satisfied his interests or consumed his energy. It was at that time that he became involved in the intellectual foment that accompanied the early days of Woodrow Wilson's "New Freedom." He was one of the first contributors to the new *New Republic*, and he began a lifelong and pro-foundly influencing friendship with Justices Holmes and Brandeis. In 1914, Frankfurter was offered, and accepted, the appointment as the first Byrne Professor of Administrative Law at Harvard Law School. With the exception of three years of government service (1917-1920), Frankfurter taught at the school for 25 years with characteristic zest and love of dialectic. The professor brought a holistic approach to case study by expanding the then existing method of logically critiquing appellate opinions to include the full records of the cases, including briefs of coun-sel, interplay of legislative, administrative, and judicial interventions and even biographies of judges. One of the tasks in which Frankfurter took much delight was the selection each year of a law clerk for Justice Holmes and following his appointment to the Supreme Court, for Justice Brandeis. During his years at Harvard Law, Frankfurter and Louis Brandeis became increasingly close. Brandeis continued his interest in Zionist affairs after his elevation to the High Court, and Frankfurter often served as his spokesman. As the five published volumes of their cor-respondence attests, their relationship was by no means limited to a mutual interest in Jewish affairs.

The great wave of patriotism, even jingoism, that swept America during the first World War fueled an hysteria against anyone or any-thing perceived by the public to be a hindrance to the country's noble war effort. German-Americans, socialists, conscientious objectors and labor unions with enmity against the latter encouraged by business interests, were the targets of public wrath. In San Francisco, on "Preparedness Day," July 22, 1916, a powerful bomb exploded, killing ten and wounding forty. Thomas J. Mooney, a labor organizer with an affiliation to the Industrial Workers of the World (the "Wobblies"), and Warren Billings, a shoe worker and migrant radical, were arrested, tried and convicted for the heinous crime. Even if the prosecution team, headed by the city's district attorney, Charles Marron Fickert, a former Stanford football hero, had wished it, they could not have found two men so ripe for conviction as were the defendants. The two had participated in strikes, consorted with known anarchists, opposed the war and had only recently been acquitted of the charge of bomb-ing a power line. Fickert presented his case as the final confrontation between middle-class law and order and the revolutionary proletariat of San Francisco. The trial was quick, the verdict certain, and the punishment expected: Mooney was sentenced to hang.

After much agitation and some evidence of an unfair trial, President Wilson instructed Frankfurter in his capacity as head of the government's war time mediation committee to look into the matter. Frankfurter's report was the work of a legal scholar who wished neither to inflame nor excuse but to seek the truth. It was the injustice of the trial and conviction of the two, not the question of their guilt or innocence, Frankfurter wrote, that required Mooney be pardoned and retried on one of the remaining open indictments. "War is fought," Frankfurter wrote, "with moral as well as material resources. We are in this war to vindicate the moral claims of unstained process of law, however slow, at times, such process may be. These claims must be tempered by the fire of our own devotion to them at home."

The reaction to Frankfurter's recommendations from leading conservatives was to label the comments treasonous, with the most damning of words coming from former president Theodore Roosevelt, who had lost a son in combat. Frankfurter was, the former president charged, engaged in excusing men precisely like the Bolsheviks in Russia who are "murderers, encouragers of murder, traitors to their allies, to democracy and civilization." Frankfurter stood his ground, and reminded Roosevelt that American workers demanded a larger voice in industrial America and unless the nation saw to the correction of "grave and accumulating" injustice in the workplace, the disintegrating forces in the country—that is, anarchists and communists, would gain ground.

The denunciation of Felix Frankfurter's writings in the Mooney (who was never hanged but stayed in prison until 1939) case was to be repeated with equal venom some years later by another former president and the sitting chief justice of the Supreme Court of the United States. On May 12, 1927, William Howard Taft wrote to Elihu Root that Frankfurter was "an expert in attempting to save murderous anarchists from the gallows or electric chair." The chief justice's ire was raised by an essay Frankfurter had written for the *Atlantic Monthly* criticizing the trial, conviction and sentencing to death of two Italian immigrants who had allegedly committed murder during a payroll robbery in Braintree, Massachusetts on April 15, 1920. On August 23,

1927, despite widespread protests in major cities of both Europe and America, Nicola Sacco and Bartholomeo Vanzetti were taken from their cells in the state prison at Charlestown, and put to death.

Five years later the Democratic governor of Massachusetts, Joseph B. Ely, reopened the wounds of the controversy when he unexpectedly nominated Frankfurter to the Supreme Judicial Court. The reaction was swift and bitter. Alvan T. Fuller, who, as governor of the Commonwealth, had appointed a commission that had upheld the convictions of the two anarchists, went so far as to say that he would rather cut off his hand then see "an open sympathizer with murderers on the supreme bench." Frankfurter turned down the nomination on the grounds of his higher obligation to the education of more enlightened future lawyers and judges as a professor at the law school. There may have been other reasons, including the avoidance of what would have been a very nasty confirmation proceeding. By the summer of 1932, Frankfurter was deeply involved with the campaign to elect Franklin Roosevelt president, despite the fact that Governor Ely was a supporter of Roosevelt's rival, Al Smith.

Frankfurter was, as much as anything else, a cultivator of friendships—some with the mighty, a few with the common people. In 1906, while Franklin Roosevelt was a student at Columbia Law School, he and Frankfurter had lunch at the Harvard Club in Boston. From that initial meeting, through Roosevelt's service as Assistant Secretary of the Navy in Wilson's administrations, while he was governor of New York and during his presidencies, Frankfurter was a confidant and adviser to F.D.R. The importance of their relationship led General Hugh Johnson, Roosevelt's appointee to head up the National Recovery Administration, to remark that Frankfurter was the "single most influential [man] in the United States." Journalist John Franklin Carter wrote that "Felix is the legal master-mind of the New Deal." Frankfurter claimed that, despite his relationship "of the utmost intimacy" with Roosevelt, he never made a suggestion or advocated an appointment without the president's asking. The one exception was to urge on the president the hiring of Frankfurter's "favorite student," Tommy "The Cork" Corcoran.

The sweeping victory of Franklin Roosevelt in 1932, with its accompanying election of an overwhelming Democratic majority in

Congress, was in many ways the most significant of all American national elections. For Bostonians Frankfurter and Brandeis, who also had the new president's ear, it offered an extraordinary opportunity to reform the federal government. Reform, not replacement, was the operative word in the economic and social thinking of the two. What their enemies condemned as "radical," other members of Roosevelt's circle of advisers, some of whom supported the nationalization of industry, belittled as too moderate.

Franklin Roosevelt offered Frankfurter the office of solicitor general, accompanied by a hint from that master of the hint, nod and wink, that he would find it easier to elevate a solicitor general to the Supreme Court than a Harvard professor. Frankfurter turned the offer down, balking at the idea of endless hours managing litigation that would prevent him from attending to the more important matters the president might want him to address. Besides, Frankfurter's anglophilia was about to be satisfied by his appointment as Eastman Visiting Professor at Balliol College, Oxford, for the academic year 1933-1934.

For several weeks in the summer of 1935, Felix Frankfurter was in residence at the White House, helping to draft New Deal legislation in such a way that it might pass muster before an increasingly hostile Supreme Court. Frankfurter's temporizing approach did not always prevail: the Court proceeded to strike down as unconstitutional some of the more ambitious New Deal programs. A frustrated Roosevelt attempted to get around the conservative court by allowing the president to appoint one new judge for each sitting justice who did not retire at age 75 up to a maximum of 6. Frankfurter was personally opposed to the "court packing," fearing destruction of the Court's independence from the executive. During the fury that Roosevelt's plan ignited throughout the country, Frankfurter kept his silence, while supplying the president with material sharply critical of the Court's frustrating of social reform. Much has been written about Frankfurter's failure to speak out publicly against Roosevelt's plan. Some attributed it to cowardice; others to blind loyalty to his chief; still others to a practical application of Frankfurter's considerable political acumen, knowing, as he did that any support from a man with his reputation would just supply more ammunition to Roosevelt's enemies.

The heart of Frankfurter's feeling on court packing was that, although he believed that the tendency of the sitting Court in ruling against New Deal proposals was as much a statement of the political philosophy of the justices as it was good law, weakening the independence of the Court was not the solution. Education of the people, the bar and judges as to the necessity of groundbreaking social legislation was the way to reform. As it was, Frankfurter's action in helping Roosevelt make his case for the Court's expansion strained the relationship between Frankfurter and the man whom he had considered a father figure and mentor, Louis Brandeis.

When Justice Benjamin Cardozo died suddenly in January of 1938, the "Holmes" seat on the Supreme Court became vacant. Soon after, at a lunch at Roosevelt's residence in Hyde Park, the president informed Frankfurter that he would have to fulfill a promise he had made to Western senators and appoint a man from that region. Like a good soldier, Frankfurter, who by that time in his life really wanted the appointment, went to work writing reports for the president on the legal opinions of prospective appointees. In the meantime, some of his very powerful and influential friends began a campaign to get the president to choose Frankfurter. That he was able, had great legal intellect and would, if he sat on the Court, probably dominate it for years to come, had to be considered against the controversy his appointment would engender. The fact that he was a "Boston Jew," and that there was already a "Boston Jew" sitting on the Court in the person of Louis Brandeis, weighed against the appointment. That problem might solve itself in a short time, however, as Justice Brandeis was known to be ailing and probably would soon retire.

President Roosevelt announced Felix Frankfurter's nomination as an associate justice of the Supreme Court on January 5, 1939. In a departure from past practice and the setting of a precedent, the nominee was invited to appear before the Senate Judiciary Committee to supplement his past record with a declaration of his present views, a procedure Frankfurter regretted but complied with. On January 30, 1939, having been approved by a unanimous vote of the Senate on the 17th, Frankfurter swore his oath. Louis Brandeis retired on account of ill health two weeks later. Before Frankfurter took his seat, Germany marched into the city of his birth, Vienna. For a brief time the masters of the new *Anschluss* imprisoned his uncle, the distinguished Jewish scholar, Solomon Frankfurter.

Death, resignation, or a tortured, and never used, process of impeachment: these are the only ways of terminating the tenure of a justice of the U.S. Supreme Court. An amendment to the Constitution or an adjustment in legislation to meet its objections: these are the only ways to reverse a ruling of the Court. To the Court of such awesome power, each new justice brings with him the cumulative influence of political leanings, of social philosophy, of learning, of practical experience, and of a concept of jurisprudence. Those influences are not shed with the donning of the robe, yet the knee no longer needs to bend at the altar of their constancy. On occasion, Justices Holmes, Brandeis and Frankfurter disappointed their friends and confounded their enemies by concurring or dissenting from a position expected of them. In that, though, they paid to themselves and to the Court the ultimate compliment of being true to the Constitution as they saw that truth to be, and in doing so they were true to themselves.

Justice Holmes died on March 6, 1932, "And so the great man is gone," was Brandeis's tribute. William Moody spent the last seven years of his life at his home in Haverhill, Massachusetts, where he died on July 2, 1917. Louis Brandeis died on October 5, 1941, in Washington, D.C., and his ashes were interred beneath the law school at the University of Louisville. Felix Frankfurter, when he died in Washington on February 21, 1965, had, for years, been like Brandeis, fully assimilated into the nonsectarian culture of the America he so passionately loved. That son of a rabbinical student nevertheless asked that a Hebrew prayer be said at his funeral. "I came into the world a Jew and . . . I want to leave it as a Jew." The Kaddish would be fine, the teacher instructed, but because some of the mourners might not understand the prayer, it could be explained in terms of the Catholic Magnificat.

CHAPTER III

The Honorable and Formidable Mr. Lodge

HENRY CABOT LODGE, GREAT-GRANDSON OF THE FEDERALIST SAGE George Cabot and grandfather of Henry Cabot Lodge, was born in Boston on May 12, 1850, in the family's residence at the juncture of Winthrop Square and Otis Street at a time when that now-commercial district housed such luminaries as George Bancroft and Rufus Choate.

After graduating from E.S. Dixwell's Latin School, young Lodge accompanied his parents on a tour of Europe with a tutor in tow to prepare Cabot, as he was called, for the examination for admittance to Harvard College. Lodge received his degree in 1871 and almost immediately after took as his bride his cousin, Anna Cabot Davis, the daughter of Rear Admiral Charles H. Davis. Uncertain as to what endeavor to pursue, Lodge sought the advice of Henry Adams, who suggested that he take up the pen. Lodge published articles and reviews in the *North American Review* and the *Atlantic Monthly* and went on to author more substantive historical biographies and books. In 1874, Lodge took his degree at Harvard Law School.

Cabot Lodge's first entry into politics was his election in 1880 to the state House of Representatives from Nahant, where his family maintained a summer home. Lodge was elected a delegate and later secretary of the Massachusetts delegation to the 1880 Republican National Convention. At that meeting he worked hard against the nomination of Senator James G. Blaine of Maine, whom Lodge held in contempt because of Blaine's alleged improprieties while he was serving as Speaker of the House. The convention nominated James A. Garfield, a congressman from Ohio, on the 36th ballot. Flushed with victory, Lodge returned to the Commonwealth and set his eyes on a new congressional district that had been created by the 1880 federal census, thus there would be no incumbent to challenge. Running out of Nahant, Lodge led on the first ballot, taken at Monument Hall in Charlestown. He believed he would win when he obtained a commitment from one of the fading other candidates, giving him what he thought were enough votes on the 130th. Not only did those votes not materialize; they went to his nearest rival, who was the winner. Lodge absorbed that painful lesson in practical politics with the remark that his loss was due to "that dastardly crowd of lying villains from Chelsea," which was also part of the district.

The impetus for Lodge's political comeback was his management of an intensive campaign to defeat Governor Benjamin Butler's attempt at reelection in 1883. Mostly through Lodge's efforts and his heeding of Senator George Frisbie Hoar's previously unacceptable advice that Lodge go after "the foreign vote"—that is, those of the recently naturalized Irish and French Canadians, Lodge's candidate, George B. Robinson, beat Butler.

On his return from the 1884 Republican National Convention, which this time nominated Blaine, Lodge faced a dilemma. The great men of the Commonwealth in almost all fields—Charles Elliot, Moorfield Storey, William Everett, Thomas Higginson and Gamaliel Bradford—all vigorously opposed Blaine. There was even open talk of defecting to the Democratic Party. If Lodge, who was at the time chairman of the Republican State Committee, listened to his peers and deserted his party to join the dissident Republicans—"mugwumps," as they were called—he probably would forfeit any chance he had of obtaining what he so ardently wanted: nomination for a seat in Congress. In the ". . . bitterest thing I ever had to do in my life," Lodge opted to support the party's nominee.

Lodge was nominated for Congress by acclamation at the party's convention in September 1884. Blaine carried the state, but barely, and Lodge lost by a margin of less than 1 percent.

Two years after he lost his bid for a seat in Congress, Lodge defeated the man, Henry J. Lovering, who had previously defeated him by a few hundred votes. He arrived in Washington as a freshman in the 50th Congress (1899-1901). The 36-year-old Lodge quite impressed his peers with his frequent and effective appearances in floor debate. In 1887, Lodge was the leader of an attempt to depose the sitting Republican senator, the 71-year-old Henry Lovering. The "young" Republicans, of whom Lodge was the leader, put up former governor John D. Long. To muddy things up, the opposition proposed outgoing governor George Robinson, while Democrats put forth the name of Patrick Collins.

On the first ballot, Collins led with 89 votes; Dawes and Long tied with 53 each. On the second ballot the Democratic senator from Cambridge, Alpheus Alger, switched from Collins to Dawes. It was a signal that the other Democrats followed, giving Dawes the necessary votes to win. Once again Lodge felt betrayed by the obvious deal Dawes had made with Collins. "If the Republicans will sell or buy a senatorship in this way," he protested, "what can be said?" What can be said is that Lodge was the ultimate winner. If Long had been elected, he and the incumbent senator, George Frisbie Hoar, who died in office in 1904, would shut out any rivals for years to come. Dawes, however, then 77, decided to retire in 1893.

Lodge mounted a massive and successful campaign and went off to Washington to the office he so coveted—the office that had also been held by his great-grandfather, George Cabot, and that would eventually be filled by his own grandson and namesake, Henry Cabot Lodge— United States senator of the Commonwealth of Massachusetts.

Until Death Do Us Part

Some United States senators are participants; others are leaders and a few a true force. Henry Cabot Lodge was the last. From the beginning of his 31-year tenure, at first tentatively and then with increasing effectiveness as he gained seniority, Lodge directed his attention to the day's "great questions" and became a player, sometimes the key player, in their resolution. He was an influential supporter of the Sherman Anti-Trust Act and the Pure Food and Drug laws. He was also an advocate of tariff measures and an uncompromising protectionist. Usually partisan, often unyielding, and, when the occasion called for it, completely independent, Senator Lodge voted against popular election of U.S. senators, opposed women's suffrage and voted against the 18th Amendment (Prohibition). He deserted his fellow Bay Stater, President Coolidge, by helping to override the president's veto of the World War I Soldier's Bonus legislation.

Senator Lodge's particular interest was in international affairs, a field for which his knowledge and competency won him a seat on the Foreign Relations Committee. When his seniority lifted him to the chairmanship of the committee, Lodge became a central figure in one of the nation's historic controversies—the question of America's joining the League of Nations.

Lodge initially supported the harsh terms the Allies had imposed on the Central Powers but opposed its coupling with the covenant creating the League. Lodge went public with his objections, and because of his standing in European capitals, his reservations received widespread attention. In March of 1919, Lodge outlined his reasons for his objections in a proposed Senate resolution co-signed by one-third of his fellow senators. In the face of such strong opposition, President Wilson reacted by sending a modified version of the covenant to the Senate. Lodge's committee adopted it, but still with reservations. Wilson found the counterproposals unacceptable and urged Senate Democrats to defeat the modified covenant, which they did. The result of those moves was to effectively end any possibility of the United States entering the League of Nations. What effect the spirit of compromise each side had initially shown if it had resulted in the United States' entry into the League would have had on the world carnage to come cannot be known. Lodge believed in his position as passionately as Wilson did his. When Warren G. Harding was elected president in 1921 with over 60 percent of the vote and the Republican Party took control of Congress, Lodge took those victories as vindication of his position.

In 1913 the U.S. Constitution was amended to end the practice of election of U.S. senators by state legislatures and to give that choice to the voters directly. For the first time in his 20-year senatorial career, Lodge would have to face a popular election. The patrician Lodge was not a good "pol" in the sense of closeness and warmth to his constituents. He had neither the patience nor personality for working the crowd or going to public meetings when asked, or avoiding the small slights that people took personally. He was fortunate to have as his mentor in such matters Elihu B. Hayes, mayor of Lynn and practical politician. "I have never," Hayes once wrote to Lodge, "had a fear that you would deal with the great questions that you may meet. It is in the little matters that small men thrive on that is a danger to you."

That year the Democrats nominated John F. "Honey Fitz" Fitzgerald over the loud protests of James Michael Curley, who also wanted the job. Fitzgerald had no illusions about his chances to unseat the venerable Senator Lodge, especially because of Lodge's attention to the needs of his large Irish-Catholic constituency. "He's more Irish than O'Connell," one wag declared, a reference to the Irish statesman, Daniel O'Connell. Lodge won, defeating Fitzgerald by thirty thousand votes out of the half-million cast.

Henry Cabot Lodge died at age 74 with the status he would have wished, United States senator from Massachusetts, at the Charlesgate Hospital in Cambridge on November 9, 1924.

CHAPTER IV

In the Diplomatic Service:
Political Appointees and Careerists

AFTER JAMES G. BLAINE ASSUMED THE OFFICE OF SECRETARY OF STATE in the administration of James A. Garfield, he wrote to the mother of Henry Cabot Lodge, his political enemy, with a request. Could the gracious lady recommend to him a gentleman of good breeding and manners who spoke French, and preferably German as well, who could spend perhaps $2,500 or a little more of his own money annually? If so, the man might become assistant secretary of state, a delightful sinecure of some prestige and high social standing. That social standing and wealth were two of the qualifications Secretary Blaine listed for a government post that was, at least on the face of it, of some importance was symptomatic of the condition of the U.S. Department of State at that time.

A "Department of Foreign Affairs" was established by the Constitutional Convention in 1787, its purpose and structure were defined further and its name changed to the Department of State under legislation introduced by Congressman James Madison of Virginia and enacted in 1789. When the first man to hold the position of secretary of state, Thomas Jefferson, took office he did so with a chief clerk, three assistant clerks, a translator, a messenger and a domestic yearly budget of less than $8,000. By 1791, the United States of America had established diplomatic missions in five countries—England, Spain, France, Holland and Portugal—and consulates in 16. A new structure for the consular service, which Mr. Jefferson had found wanting, was established by leg-

215

islation in April 1792. Consuls, in addition to providing commercial reports, were charged with meeting the needs of American citizens within their jurisdictions. Consuls in foreign cities were not paid nor given any allowance for room and board or expenses, but they were expected to support themselves from the fees they charged. In 1856 Congress enacted a reform of the diplomatic and consular services, prescribing regular if highly inadequate salaries for consuls as well as for ministers—$17,500 per annum in London and Paris, and $10,000 elsewhere. The amounts defied increase until 1946.

The historic neglect, often far from benign, of the U.S. Department of State was in good measure a reflection of American citizens' isolationistic disdain for foreign, especially European, affairs. Except when a U.S. interest, real or perceived, was involved, they were there and we were here, with a full ocean in between. In 1895 President Cleveland attempted to put the consular service on a more professional basis by requiring candidates for employment to have had previous Department of State service, or to pass a qualifying examination. Cleveland's limited merit system, which included changes in tenure and promotion policies, was enhanced by congressional action and executive orders in the administration of Theodore Roosevelt in 1906. President Taft subsequently extended the requirements for employment in the consular service to foreign service officers below the rank of minister, and initiated a rating system for promotions.

It was in that slowly changing climate of the American foreign service that 11 Massachusetts men were appointed to serve as heads of 18 foreign missions in the two decades between 1900 and 1920. Some were politicians out of office or contributors of money or influence to successful candidates for president, a few of whom spoke French or German and may have had the extra wherewithal to live in the style expected of those representing an increasingly important nation. There were also several to whom the diplomatic service was neither a political reward nor a prestigious sinecure, but life and livelihood. A good number of the latter were sons of Massachusetts merchants or industrialists for whom the family business had no attraction and elective office was too common a pursuit. Graduates of Harvard mostly, and if not, of Yale or Princeton, many of them joined the diplomatic service to broaden their experience, to travel, or to become proficient in a foreign language. Those who stayed on were the beneficiaries of the increasing professionalization of the service, and made steady, sometimes painful, progress to high posts. One of them, Joseph Grew, had the unenviable dual distinction of having to shepherd the American diplomatic corps out of Berlin upon his country's declaration of war against Germany in 1917, and being marched off to internment in Tokyo after the Japanese bombed Pearl Harbor in late 1941.

Meyer to Italy

George Von Lengerke Meyer was one of the Boston aristocrats of the nineteenth century whose paternal lineage was not English but German. George's grandfather had left Germany for New York. His father, George Augustus Meyer, moved from there to Boston, where he wed Grace Helen Parker. Young George was born on Beacon Hill in Boston on June 24, 1858, "prepared privately" for Harvard College, graduated in the class of 1879, and six years later married Marian Alice Appleton. Meyer's business success, the locus of his education, his most acceptable marriage, and his conservative Republican politics brought him acceptance in the centers of influence in both Boston and Essex County, where he maintained "Rock Maple Farm" in Hamilton as a showplace of good taste and affluence.

The life of a city swell and country squire did not entirely satisfy young George Von L. Meyer's idea of "making something of himself," so he turned to elective office. He served as a member of the Boston Common Council, as an alderman and Speaker of the Massachusetts House of Representatives (1894-1896). In 1899 he was chosen as National Republican Committeeman from Massachusetts and proved a valuable liaison between the party and the business community. Meyer's position in the party, both local and national, was considerably enhanced by his steady and generous personal contributions to its coffers.

In December 1900, at the urging of the state's then junior U.S. senator, Henry Cabot Lodge, President McKinley appointed Meyer American ambassador to Italy. During his almost five-year stay in Rome, Meyer managed not only to raise the influence and popularity of the embassy there, but also to become a warm friend of the king. He made several valuable contacts in important circles in Europe and another royal friend in the person of Emperor William II of Germany. When McKinley's successor, Theodore Roosevelt, was contemplating the role of peacemaker in the Russo-Japanese War and wanted someone at St. Petersburg "who, while able to do all the social work . . . can do, in addition, the real vital and important things," he chose George Meyer. The president's man, whose diplomatic success, or so it was said, was enhanced by his skill at bridge, managed, without causing offense, to cut through the nearly impenetrable bureaucracy surrounding the Russian court and to present the U.S. president's proposals to the czar personally.

Back home, Senator Lodge, always a player in such matters, was urging an appointment to a cabinet post for George Meyer from President Roosevelt. While in Europe, Meyer had provided a valuable listening post for the foreign policy-minded Lodge through extensive correspondence, more so than with the president. On March 5, 1907, Meyer was sworn in as postmaster general of the United States. In that position he applied the efficiencies of a paying business: he initiated parcel post, special delivery, and the postal savings system. Appointed by Taft as Secretary of the Navy, Meyer held that post until the end of Taft's term. Meyer was far more attracted to the physical and flamboyant Roosevelt than he was to the corpulent Taft, but he stayed loyal to his chief during the political upheaval in the Republican Party in the election of 1912. In 1916 Meyer supported Roosevelt in his unsuccessful attempt to secure the Republican nomination for president. He died on March 9, 1918, at age 60.

Peirce to St. Petersburg

In his ultimately successful and Nobel Peace Prize-winning effort to see a negotiated end to the Russo-Japanese War of 1904, President Theodore Roosevelt had the invaluable services of another Massachusetts man. Roosevelt, without the knowledge of Congress, had been working through friends and acquaintances in various European diplomatic services to bring the disputing parties to the table. By the summer of 1905, with Russia's distress at home and impending financial crisis in Japan, the time seemed ripe for a peace conference. George Meyer as American ambassador extraordinary and plenipotentiary to Russia may have been able to bring the president's proposals directly to the czar, but the ever-difficult and delicate arrangements for such a peace conference would be in the hands of a professional diplomat. For that mission the president was fortunate to have in St. Petersburg at the time one Herbert Henry Davis Peirce.

Herbert Peirce was born in Cambridge in 1849, the son of Professor Benjamin Peirce, reputedly the leading mathematician of his day. His mother was the daughter of Elijah Hunt Mills, who had represented Massachusetts in the U.S. Senate from 1820 to 1827. Young Peirce was educated at Exeter, New Hampshire, in the Harvard class of 1871, and at the Royal School of Mines in London, where he studied geology. Peirce's long association with Russia began with his appointment in 1894 as secretary to the U.S. Legation at St. Petersburg during the second Cleveland administration. In 1896, he attended the coronation of Czar Nicholas II, and two years later he was made First Secretary of the Embassy, subsequently serving as charge d'affaires. In 1901 Peirce was elevated to the post of third assistant secretary of state.

It was in that capacity that Peirce was chosen by the president to take charge of the plenipotentiaries of Russia and Japan and of the arrangements for their deliberations at the peace conference to be held in Portsmouth, New Hampshire, in November of 1905. It was Secretary Peirce to whom the parties first reported their successful negotiations and he, in turn, had the honor to communicate the news to a highly pleased president. After serving as special counsel for the claimants and counsel for the United States in arbitration cases between the United States and Russia, Peirce was American ambassador to Norway from June of 1906 to May of 1911. At the time of his death on December 5, 1916, Herbert Henry Davis Peirce was making his home in Petrograd, Russia.

Climates Warm and Frozen:
Mr. Dodge and Mr. Brown to Honduras

The first of the Massachusetts career diplomats, H. Percival Dodge, was born in Boston on January 18, 1870, into a family descended from English immigrants, who came to Salem in 1636. Educated partly in the public schools of New York and Boston, as well as schools in France and Germany, Henry Dodge received his A.B. magna cum laude from Harvard in 1892, and an LL.B. from Harvard Law School in 1895. He was admitted to the Massachusetts bar the same year and began to practice law in the offices of Hutchins and Wheeler. In 1897, Dodge went to Europe to further his studies. While there he was chosen by President McKinley as third secretary of the American Embassy in Berlin, advancing by 1900 to the post as the embassy's first secretary. From Berlin Mr. Dodge was assigned to Tokyo, as first secretary.

In 1907, President Roosevelt sent the by-now-seasoned diplomat to Honduras and El Salvador as envoy extraordinary and minister plenipotentiary headquartered in El Salvador. In 1909 Dodge was transferred by President Taft to see to American interests at Morocco, with his residence at Tangier. In his long and distinguished diplomatic career, Henry Percival Dodge also represented his country as minister in Panama from 1911 to 1913, and minister to Yugoslavia from 1919 to 1926.

In 1908, while Henry Dodge was representing the United States in both El Salvador and Honduras, legislation was passed creating a separate legation in Honduras. The first secretary at the new post was another diplomat from Massachusetts, Philip Marshall Brown. Brown had distinguished careers in both diplomatic and academic fields. Born in Hampton, Maine, in 1875, Brown took degrees from both Williams College (B.A. 1898, LL.D. 1918) and Harvard (M.A. 1912). He entered the diplomatic service in 1900 as private secretary to the second secretary of the American Legation at Constantinople. Thereafter followed assignments as secretary of the legation at Guatemala and Honduras, back to Constantinople as secretary and sometime charge d'affaires there and eventually minister to Honduras, from 1908 to 1910.

In 1912, Brown returned to Harvard as first an instructor in international law, then as an assistant professor in law and diplomacy in 1913, before taking up the position as professor of international law at Princeton, where he taught for 14 years. An associate editor of *The American Journal of International Law*, he authored *Foreigners in Turkey*, *International Realities*, *International Society*, *La Conciliation Internationale* and other works. He died on May 10, 1966, at age 91.

The Wandering Coolidge

John Gardner Coolidge was born in Boston in 1863 into the same family as Thomas Jefferson Coolidge and was thus the great-great-grandson of Thomas Jefferson. At a time when such was often neither convenient nor comfortable, young John (A.B. Harvard, 1884) gave new meaning to nineteenth century world travel. Starting from Boston in 1887, he spent three years traveling in the Far East, four years in South America, and an additional four mainly in Europe. July of 1898 found Coolidge in Cuba, and in 1899 visiting Samoa, the South Sea Islands and Australia. In 1900 the administration of William McKinley thought to put such familiarity with the world to some good and appointed Coolidge as vice-consul at Pretoria, South Africa, an assignment that coincided with the start of the Boer War. For the next decade the ever-moving Coolidge was charge d'affaires in Peking, secretary of the embassy and charge d'affaires Mexico City and, from July to November 1908, envoy extraordinary and minister plenipotentiary to Nicaragua. But he resigned the same year because of a disagreement with the policy of the U.S. Government. In 1909, Coolidge married Helen Granger Stevens and was back in the diplomat service by 1914 as special assistant to the American ambassador in Paris, where he stayed during most of World War I. Coolidge's diplomatic career ended as special assistant to the secretary of state (July 1918 to August 1919). The inveterate traveler wrote of his many journeys in *Random Letters from Many Countries* (1924), and of his experience in wartime France in *A War Diary in Paris*, 1914-1917 (1931). He died at home in Boston on February 28, 1936.

A Digression for the Postmaster General

When President Taft moved George von L. Meyer from postmaster general in the Roosevelt administration to Secretary of the Navy in his own, the president assigned the vacant post to Frank Harris Hitchcock. Frank Hitchcock was born on October 5, 1867, in Amherst, Ohio, in Lorain County, where his father was pastor of the Congregational Church. Despite his midwestern birth, Frank Hitchcock was of old New England stock in a line from Matthew Hitchcock, who had emigrated to Boston from London in 1635.

Young Frank's family returned to Massachusetts and he graduated from Somerville Latin School, and Harvard in 1891, the A.B. degree he received was hardly indicative of his preferred activities at college, which were boxing and precinct organization for the Republican Party. The 24-

year-old Hitchcock launched his public career almost immediately after graduation, landing a minor position in the treasury department in Washington and after qualified for an appointment as a biologist in the Department of Agriculture. While at the Department of Agriculture, Hitchcock, who was tall, broad-shouldered, red-headed, rather aloof, and given to foppishness in dress, studied law and received both an LL.B. and LL.M. from what is now Columbia (George Washington) University. His new degrees helped Frank in his bureaucratic advancement. By 1897 he was chief of foreign markets in the Department of Agriculture. When the Congress established the Department of Commerce and Labor in 1903, Frank Hitchcock was made its chief clerk.

In 1904, Hitchcock was tapped to be assistant secretary of the Republican National Committee in charge of the party's Eastern head-quarters in New York City. Appointed first assistant postmaster general in 1905, he was a member of the Keep Commission, established by President Theodore Roosevelt to investigate the efficiency of government departments with an eye to improvement. Hitchcock rose to national prominence in 1908 when he was chosen to manage the successful presidential election campaign of William Howard Taft, and subsequently was elected chairman of the party's national committee. Managers of successful presidential campaigns merit substantial rewards: Hitchcock's was an appointment as postmaster general in Taft's cabinet. Consummate politician he may have been, but Frank Hitchcock was far from a political hack. His administration of the government agency that has the most frequent contact with the public was business-like and innovative.

Postmaster General Hitchcock reorganized the department's accounting procedures, consolidated star routes with rural free delivery, began the transportation of magazines by freight, and put the new postal savings system, previously created by George Meyer, into gradual and efficient operation. It was Hitchcock who inaugurated the first airmail route in 1911 from Garden City to Mineola, New York, and put into operation the parcel-post system. It must not be assumed, however, that Frank Harris Hitchcock, the efficient public administrator, had subsumed Frank Hitchcock, the adept political operator.

As forward-looking in his political machinations as in his official position, the postmaster general set out to gain control of Southern delegates to the next Republican National Convention through the time-honored method of political appointments to government jobs. President Taft refused to approve many of them on the grounds that to do so would violate his policy of choosing the most decent and qualified men. The postal service was well served by Taft's reluctance to approve Hitchcock's recommendations. If the rumors that began to circulate around Washington were true, it was Teddy Roosevelt, not William Howard Taft whom Hitchcock wanted as the party's nominee in 1912. A brooding and private person who kept his own counsel, Hitchcock as postmaster general was forced to choose sides at the end of a cabinet meeting when the president looked directly at him and demanded, "Frank, are you for me or against me?" Sincere or not, the job-saving answer was "yes." Hitchcock practiced law in New York City after Taft's defeat in 1912, and managed the pre-convention campaigns of both Charles E. Hughes in 1916 and General Leonard Wood in 1920. He moved to Arizona in 1928 to pursue his long-held interest in mining and served as Republican National Committeeman from there in 1932 and 1933. Frank Harris Hitchcock, who never married, died of pneumonia in the Desert Sanatorium in Tucson on August 5, 1935.

Guild to Russia

In the last half of the nineteenth century, when every American city of moderate size had more than one newspaper, Boston had several—in daily, direct and sometimes fatal competition. In 1857, Curtis Guild, an example of the proper Bostonian, properly educated, of a literary bent, urbane, upholder of the city's traditions, and raconteur of its anecdotal history, set about to consolidate some of them. Although he did manage to merge the *Boston Evening Traveller*, the *Boston Daily Atlas*, the *Daily Evening Telegraph*, the *Evening Traveller*, into the *Boston Morning Traveller*, it took only a few months for the enterprise to fail. But by January 1859, Guild was back in the newspaper business with a new concept: his *Commercial Bulletin* would publish tabulated stock market quotations, market reports and general banking news. After his death, and that of his brother, the management of the by-then influential paper, passed into the hands of Guild's son, Curtis Guild Jr.

Young Guild was educated at a Dame school, Miss Lewis's in Roxbury, the Chauncy Hall School, and Harvard, where he was the class orator and editor of both the *Crimson* and the *Lampoon*. He graduated with highest honors in 1881. A tour of Europe, of course, was the young man's next venture and on his return he became an apprentice in every department of the family newspaper.

Curtis's membership in the Harvard Rifle Club led to his enlistment in 1891 in Troop A of the Massachusetts Militia, and an eventual appointment to the staff of Governor Roger Wolcott with the rank of brigadier general. After the explosion of the Maine in Havana Harbor, Wolcott sent Guild to Washington to ascertain what would be required of Massachusetts in the anticipated war with Spain. Guild's service in the war was as an administrator, not a combatant. He served mostly as inspector general of VII Army Corps with the rank of lieutenant colonel, and later was inspector general of the Department of Havana.

In 1895, the 35-year-old Guild began what was to be a distinguished public life as president of the Republican State Convention. At the Republican National Convention of 1896, delegate-at-large Guild was elected a vice president of the conclave, and was instrumental in securing a gold plank in the platform. Elected lieutenant governor of the Commonwealth in 1902, Guild later went on to serve three terms as the state's chief executive.

From the second term of Abraham Lincoln far into the twentieth century, with only an occasional lapse, the reigns of the government of Massachusetts were firmly in the hands of the Republican Party. As could the progressive governments of Wisconsin and New York, the Commonwealth's Republicans could boast of forward-looking social legislation. Between 1886 and 1888, the General Court enacted 36 laws relating to labor interests, including the establishment of the State Board of Arbitration and Conciliation, provision for wages to be paid on a weekly basis, the establishment of Labor Day as a legal holiday; imposition of factory safeguards, and authorization for the incorporation of labor organizations. An activist governor, Curtis Guild Jr. may have initiated more legislation than any of his predecessors during his terms as chief executive as he concerned himself with improving the plight of laboring women and children, the infirm and the insane.

In 1910, President Taft sent Guild to represent the United States at the Mexican Centennial, and on July 21, 1911, appointed him ambassador to the Imperial Court of Russia. Curtis arrived at a time when Czar Nicholas II was attempting to reverse the new freedoms exacted from him a few years before, after his government had experienced a series of decisive defeats by Japan. Guild left Russia in April 1913, before the events of World War I and its subsequent upheaval gave birth to the Russian Revolution. He died on April 6, 1915, at age 55, having received the designation of Grand Officer of the Crown of Italy for his efforts in enacting legislation for the protection of immigrants from fraudulent banking practices; the Grand Cordon of the Order of St. Alexander Nevski from Czar Nicholas for his service as American ambassador, and the plaudits of his fellow citizens of Massachusetts for being one of the most efficient and forward-looking governors in the Commonwealth's history.

The Wealthy and Worthy Andersons

For years Harvard students have crossed the Nicholas Longworth Anderson bridge, which was constructed to allow access from the Cambridge campus to the playing fields across the Charles River, and people still skate in winter and play ball on the 60.2 acres of what once was the estate of Larz Anderson in Brookline. Born in Paris on the 15th of August, 1866 to Civil War hero Nicholas Longworth Anderson and Elizabeth Coles Kilgour Anderson, Larz was part of a family that included William Clark of Lewis and Clark fame, Robert Anderson, who had the onerous duty of surrendering Fort Sumter, and the first millionaire in the Northwest Territory, Nicholas Longworth. Young Larz prepared at Phillips Exeter Academy and received his A.B. from Harvard in 1888.

With a friend in tow, Anderson expanded the near requisite post-graduate excursion to Europe enjoyed by those of his family's means into a world tour. He was a first-year student at Harvard Law School when he was summoned by one of his father's friends, Robert Todd Lincoln, son of the martyred president, to become Ambassador Lincoln's second secretary at the U.S. legation to the Court of St. James in London. In addition to his formal secretarial duties, the handsome and exquisitely-mannered Anderson was called on to represent the ambassador and America in the never-ending swirl of social events and to mingle with England's governing and literary elite. When Democrat Grover Cleveland replaced Ambassador Lincoln in London in 1893, the new ambassador, Thomas Baynard, recognized Anderson's valuable role in the public presentation of diplomacy so valued in Europe, and kept him on.

In 1894, Cleveland promoted Anderson to the post of first secretary of the American embassy at Rome. Several times the charge d'affaires in the absence of Ambassador Wayne MacVeagh, Anderson's urbane and steady hand had much to do with the settlement of the explosive issues between the United States and Italy raised by the mob lynching of three Italians awaiting trial for murder in Holmesville, Louisiana. When a new ambassador arrived in Rome in 1897, Larz Anderson resigned his post and returned to America to marry Isabel Weld Perkins, who was wealthy in her own right, having inherited $17 million from her shipping-magnate grandfather.

At the outbreak of the Spanish-American War in 1898, Anderson volunteered his service. He turned down a commission as major because he deemed it inappropriate for one with no military experience. He did, however, accept a commission as captain and was engaged during that brief conflict as assistant adjutant and acting adjutant general on the staff of the commander of the Second Army Division.

Larz Anderson and his wife were substantial contributors to the 1908 presidential campaign of William Howard Taft and in 1910 the couple accompanied Secretary of War Dickinson and General Clarence Edwards on their official visits to China and Japan. In 1911 Taft offered Anderson the opportunity to return to the diplomatic service as ambassador to Germany, but he turned down the appointment in the belief that his personal disdain for German militarism and authoritarianism would limit his effectiveness in Berlin. Anderson did, however, accept the ministership to Belgium, where his greatest accomplishment was to persuade the Belgian State Railway to end its discrimination against American crude oil, which was a violation of the Belgian-American tariff agreement.

Taft sent Anderson as American ambassador to Japan in the fall of 1912, an assignment for which Anderson, who had traveled extensively in Asia, was well qualified. Politics ruled, however, and when Woodrow Wilson was elected president later that year, Anderson resigned from what was to be his last venture in the diplomatic world after only four months in Tokyo.

Between his diplomatic assignments and after their termination, Larz and Isabel Anderson, who had no children, spent their time traveling, attending charity balls and hosting formal dinners at their Florentine-style villa on Massachusetts Avenue in Washington and at "Weld," their estate in Brookline. If one were looking for an example of wealth wisely used to great benefit, the Andersons' use of theirs would more than suffice. The Andersons donated their estate, which became the 60.2 acre Larz Anderson Park, to the people of the town of Brookline.

Larz Anderson, a talented writer who kept extensive journals, many accompanied with sketches and cartoons, was the recipient of many honors, including the highest awards from Italy, Belgium and Japan. He died at White Sulphur Springs, Virginia, on April 13, 1937, at age 71.

The Man Who Might Have Been King

The road that led George F. Williams to diplomatic service of his country was filled with far more ruts and turns than the smooth straight path of Larz Anderson, and all the more colorful for it. George's father, William Wenigmann, ran away as a boy from his home in Prussia and stowed away on a ship bound for America. Fortunately for him, the ship's captain took a liking to the young lad and brought him up as a member of his family, the Williamses, who eventually adopted William Wenigmann. George Williams, as he was known after his adoption, married Henrietta Whitney (a niece) and their son, George Fred, was born at Dedham, Massachusetts on July 10, 1852.

George entered Dartmouth College in 1868, matriculated to the universities of Heidelberg and Berlin after his freshman year, then rejoined his Dartmouth class and graduated with an A.B. in 1872. After teaching for a year on Cape Cod, Williams became a reporter for the *Boston Globe* while studying the law in a private office and at Boston University. Practicing in partnership or alone, Williams's legal career reached its peak when he successfully argued before the

Supreme Court of the United States on behalf of Oregon and several other states the question of the legality of the initiative petition and popular referendum provisos of the Oregon constitution.

George Williams was among those Massachusetts Republicans who could not abide the thought of the nefarious James G. Blaine becoming president of the United States, so he left the party to support the Democratic nominee, Grover Cleveland, in the election of 1884. Unlike some of the others who went back to where they belonged, Williams's defection proved permanent. For many years he was one of the Commonwealth's most prominent Democrats. Williams served in the Massachusetts House in 1889 and in the 52nd U.S. Congress (1891-1893). Three times the unsuccessful nominee of the Democratic Party for governor of Massachusetts, Williams was a national committeeman from Massachusetts, a convert to and ardent supporter of William Jennings Bryan's bimetallism, spoke for U.S. House Speaker Champ Clark in the preconvention campaign of 1912, and most vigorously supported Woodrow Wilson after he obtained the party's nomination for president.

In December 1913, Wilson rewarded Williams's loyalty with the American ministership to Greece and Montenegro. Williams abruptly resigned that post less than a year later, occasioned not by any trouble in Greece or Montenegro, but by a massacre of Albanians carried out by Greek soldiers. In most public, undiplomatic and embarrassing (to the Wilson administration) terms, Minister Williams condemned the killings and denounced the six leading European Powers who had placed Prince William of Wied in power, accusing him of stirring up religious warfare, and establishing a government by force rather than by popular support. The beleaguered Albanians hailed the Boston lawyer as their savior and wished to crown him king. The offer of royalty was refused, but Williams took up the Albanian cause, acted as their counsel in America and in 1919 made a most stirring appeal at the Paris Peace Conference on their behalf.

A handsome man possessed of a tenor voice of beautiful tone and power, George Williams excelled in his renderings of the German Lieder. In expressing himself he was always frank and vigorous, and both in party and personality a friend of the poor and oppressed. He died on July 10, 1932.

Another in the Line

We are certain that George Fred Williams was born in Dedham, but of Frederic Jesup Stimson, there is some doubt. Although it is usually written that Stimson was born there in July of 1855, records of the town do not bear that out. Whether the two had a common place of birth, other similarities mark their lives. Both were lawyers; both studied in Europe; both left the Republican Party at the time of the Cleveland-Blaine election and became Democrats. Stimson's loyalty to the party of his conviction rather than to that of his birth, however, was not lifelong, as was Williams's. He lasted only until the arrival of Franklin Roosevelt's New Deal.

The only child of Dr. Edward Stimson, a graduate of both Harvard College and the Medical School, and Sarah Tufts Stimson, young Fred led a privileged life of travel. For a while the elder Stimson practiced in New York but eventually, because of the weak health of his wife, the family moved west to Dubuque, Iowa, where he entered the banking business and became president of the Dubuque & Pacific Railroad, which he sold in the mid-1860s and then retired to Dedham. Young Frederic studied at the Dedham public schools, and a boarding school in Lausanne, Switzerland, before entering Harvard. He was awarded his A.B. from Harvard in 1876, and his LL.B. from the law school two years later.

An incorporator and general counsel of the State Street Trust Company, on many corporate boards, a sometime partner of Francis Cabot Lowell and A. Lawrence Lowell, Frederic Stimson fought for full legal rights for the American Indian and protested the growing American imperialism. His dilemma lay in his sincere desire to see justice done for the laboring man without the government interference he feared would subvert individual liberty and property rights. In his *The Modern Use of Injunctions* (*Political Science Quarterly*, June 1895) Stimson argued against the use of the Sherman Anti-Trust Act against labor organizations, and in *Labor in Its Relation to Law*, written the same year, while supporting labor's aspirations, he strongly suggested labor do so through non coercive collective bargaining rather then through the non competitive closed shop. In 1897, Stimson was appointed to the U.S. Industrial Commission and during his two year tenure there, compiled two volumes on American and European labor legislation.

The Republican phase of Frederic Stimson's political life began soon after his graduation from Harvard with his election as one of Dedham's delegates to the party's state convention, and progressed to his becoming financial manager for Congressman Theodore Lyman. In 1884, Governor Robinson appointed Stimson assistant attorney general of the Commonwealth. When James Blaine was nominated for president by the Republican Party, Stimson resigned from both his state office and the party. The fiscally conservative Stimson supported the "Gold Democrats" rather than William Jennings Bryan, and in 1896 and 1900 was instrumental in reuniting the badly divided State Democratic Party. In 1914, President Wilson appointed Stimson ambassador to Argentina. He resided in Argentina almost seven years in that office. His most important accomplishment came when he was able to persuade the officially neutral Argentinians to sell large quantities of wheat to the allies during World War I.

Frederic Stimson had a second career as a contemporarily popular but historically forgotten author of several short stories, novellas, and novels. Perhaps the best of these was *King Noanett* written in 1896. A historical romance, the book was praised by Carl Van Doren in the *Cambridge History of American Literature*. Frederic Jesup Stimson died at age 88 on November 19, 1943, and is buried in Dedham at the Old Village Cemetery there.

CHAPTER V

The Speaker, the President, and It All Came Tumbling Down

Frederick Huntington Gillett

ON MAY 19, 1699, THE TOWN OF WESTFIELD, MASSACHUSETTS, WAS carved out of a section of Springfield called Woronoake. It was there that Frederick Huntington Gillett was born in October 1851. The Gillett family had first settled in Dorchester in 1635 and by the time of Frederick's birth boasted a line of successful lawyers. Frederick graduated from Westfield Academy, spent a year of study and travel in Europe, and received an A.B. from Amherst in 1874. He then completed three years of study at Harvard Law School and was admitted to the bar. An assistant attorney general of the Commonwealth from 1879 to 1882, a member of the Springfield common council in 1890 and of the state House of Representatives 1890 and 1891. After he won against a strong Democratic opponent a seat in the U.S. Congress in 1892, Frederick Gillett was to serve in that body for 16 congresses—a total of 32 years. It might be said that he was wed to the U.S. House of Representatives until, much to the surprise of his friends, he married the widow of Congressman Rockwood Hoar in 1915 at age 64. While residing in Washington before he married, Gillett lived in a bachelor's house with the other two of the "Three Musketeers," as Teddy Roosevelt dubbed them: future associate justice of the Supreme Court William Moody and future army general William Crozier.

Congressman Gillett came to the attention of the House in the waning days of his freshman term, when he rose to speak against a Southern member's attempt to repeal all laws relating to federal supervision of elections by federal marshals. The measure was obviously meant to remove laws that, at least theoretically, protected the voting rights of Negroes. In the evenhanded way that was a hallmark of Gillett's tenure in the House, the congressman added a scathing denunciation of the voting fraud perpetrated by Tammany Hall and the big-city bosses. Candid and constructive, hard-working and knowledgeable, Gillett opposed partisanship in foreign policy. He teamed up as chairman of the House committee on civil service with the chairman of the Civil Service Commission, Theodore Roosevelt, to defeat old guard Republicans' efforts to thwart reform. In perhaps the most significant contribution in his long years of service in the House, he was instrumental in the establishment of a bureau of the budget. As his years as a congressman grew longer, Frederick Gillett, as a reasonable and pragmatic nonpartisan, rose in both responsibility and influence to assignments on key committees, such as the judiciary, appropriations and civil service reform committees.

The Democrats won a majority in the House in 1911 and continued to control it during all but the last two years of President Woodrow Wilson's two terms. In 1919, in the 66th Congress, the Republicans held a comfortable majority of 50 votes, more than enough to elect the Speaker. They would have done so in the unified manner they wished if it had not been for a looming specter—the ghost of Old Joe Cannon.

Joseph G. Cannon, Republican of Illinois, had served as Speaker of the U.S. House from 1903 to 1911. An affable man well liked by his peers, "Uncle" Joe Cannon was unyielding in his conservatism in the face of the rise of progressivism. He held autocratic control of the House through his power to appoint committee chairmen, who in turn controlled the introduction, procedure and ultimate fate of all legislation. Cannon had barely survived a revolt in the ranks of Republican members in 1910, and he and his partisans were determined to return a "Cannonite" to the Speaker's chair in the person of the minority leader in the previous Congress, James R. Mann, also of Illinois. They could not have chosen more wisely. A formidable legislator of whom a future Democratic Speaker and Vice President, John Nance Garner, had said, "The most useful legislator I ever knew . . . the hardest worker and the most adroit parliamentarian." Yet Jim Mann had been Speaker Cannon's right-hand man, and many Republicans feared the legacy of old Joe Cannon and what he stood for would be raised in the presidential election of 1920.

Looking for a compromise and an electable alternative, Congressman Nicholas Longsworth of Ohio led a group of distrustful regulars into a coalition of insurgents and farm state Republicans and, assisted by the chairman of the Republican National Committee, Will C. Hays, and Senator Boise Penrose of Pennsylvania, engineered the election of the second ranking Republican (after Cannon in seniority), Frederick Gillett, as Speaker of the U.S. House of Representatives.

When he first took up the gavel of presiding officer, Gillett said, "I would rather be Speaker of the House than hold any other position in the world." There is no doubt that he would have remained in the office he so loved as long as his party retained control of the House. Yet his tenure, three congresses and six years, succumbed to the call of party loyalty issued by the Republican presidential candidate in 1924, fellow Bay Stater Calvin Coolidge. Coolidge believed that because he, as a former governor of Massachusetts was heading the national Republican ticket, the incumbent first-term Democratic senator, David Ignatius Walsh, was vulnerable. In an extraordinary sacrifice, Gillett agreed to leave his beloved House and its Speakership to oppose Walsh. Gillett, 73 at the time, beat Walsh. Coolidge's attempt to at least slow down the progress of the Massachusetts Democratic Party, with its hordes of Irish-American adherents, ended in a bit of irony.

Senator Henry Cabot Lodge died on November 9, 1924, and Governor Channing Cox appointed William Morgan Butler to fill his unexpired term. In 1925 David I. Walsh was elected to a full term in the seat once held by Lodge, the symbol of Massachusetts Republicanism.

Gillett was not happy in the Senate. He missed the House, a place of comradeship and controversy, kindness and rivalry, where he had spent a good portion of his adult life. He did not seek reelection to the Senate, and died in Springfield on July 31, 1935 at age 84.

Diplomatic History

If one wished to recreate the history of twentieth century American diplomacy he or she could do no better than to recount the diplomatic careers of William Phillips and Joseph Grew. From the administration of Warren Harding to that of Harry Truman, in ministries and ambassadorships, in the executive of the State Department, as presidential envoys and on special assignments, from the prelude to World War I to the planting of the seeds of the Vietnam conflict, those two Massachusetts men of aristocratic background played key roles.

Mr. Phillips

It was written of William Phillips in the gentle way that such things once were written, that he "had the means and the connections to forge a distinguished public career without undue concern for compensation." Born in Beverly, Massachusetts in May of 1878 to a family of both wealth and accomplishment, William was educated at private schools: Milton Academy and Noble and Greenough School, in Boston. He earned his B.A. from Harvard in 1900 and attended Harvard Law School for two and one-half years. In 1903 Phillips joined Joseph Choate, at that time the ambassador to the Court of St. James, as an unpaid private secretary. In 1910 he married Caroline Astor Drayton, the granddaughter of William Astor and, a second cousin to Franklin D. Roosevelt.

Alternating assignments between Washington and the field, Phillips rose to assistant secretary of state in 1914; was envoy extraordinary and minister plenipotentiary to the Lowlands from 1920 to 1922; Under Secretary of State from 1922 to 1924; ambassador to Belgium and minister to Luxembourg from 1924 to 1927; the first-ever minister to Canada from 1927 to 1929; Under Secretary of State again in 1933 and ambassador to Italy from 1936 to 1940. In Italy he unsuccessfully labored to dissuade Europe's first 20th century Fascist dictator, Benito Mussolini, from entering World War II against the Allies. During the war Phillips was his friend President Franklin Roosevelt's personal representative and then ambassador to India (1942 to 1944), resident director of the Office of Strategic Services in London, and ambassador to Supreme

Headquarters, Allied Expeditionary Force, where he assisted the Supreme Commander, General Dwight D. Eisenhower, in diplomatic dealings with allied governments. At one point during the absence of Cordell Hull, Phillips was acting U.S. secretary of state.

During his stay in India, out of deference to Prime Minister Winston Churchill's attempt to suppress that country's movement for independence from Great Britain, Ambassador Phillips was forbidden to meet with its leader, Mahatma Gandhi. The ambassador became so frustrated with the condescending and obdurate attitude of the British toward the aspirations of so vast a number of people to govern themselves that his life long Anglophilia soon turned to Anglophobia. Such a man as William Phillips had not advanced in a diplomatic career by rocking the boat, at least not in public. Yet, on July 25, 1944, his personal report to the president, one that contained explicit criticisms of Winston Churchill not only for his stand on India but also for the prime minister's disregard for the Atlantic Charter, was leaked to the *Washington Post* and appeared in the widely syndicated column of Drew Pearson. The dissemination of the letter made Phillips, who, at the time was serving at Supreme Headquarters of the Allies in London, highly unpopular with the British.

In 1944, the 66-year-old Phillips retired from the diplomatic service. He might have spent his remaining years in genteel retirement in bucolic Beverly had he not received a summons from President Truman in 1946. The problem the president wished Phillips to address seemed quite insolvable then and has continued to prove so many years and many deaths since. A number of Jews who had escaped Hitler's genocide remained homeless and displaced in Europe and wished to immigrate to Palestine. The Jewish organization, the Yishuv, was determined to remove the then-existing restrictions against unlimited Jewish immigration and to establish a Jewish State. The Arabs were adamant that no further Jewish immigration would occur and that an independent Arab state be created. The British, under whose mandate such matters came, were primarily concerned with their country's strategic interest in the Middle East and Asia. The British secretary of state for Foreign Affairs, Ernest Bevin, who opposed Jewish immigration and the establishment of an independent Jewish state—partly to establish American co-responsibility in the region and partly to pull British chestnuts out of the fire—called for an Anglo-American Committee of Inquiry. The State Department supported the British position, but the president wanted to ensure that Jews displaced by the war were permitted to enter Palestine. He nominated Phillips to the Committee of Inquiry.

During extensive hearings in Europe and the Middle East, it was often Phillips's tact and diplomacy that kept the committee together. Its final ten-point report, unanimously adopted, recommended the admission of 100,000 Jewish refugees, both the division of Palestine and the establishment of either a Jewish or Arab state, and that controlled immigration should be accompanied by aid to the Palestine economy so that the Arabs might close the economic gap between themselves and the Jews. Only the first recommendation was adopted, resulting, as Phillips feared it would, in seemingly perpetual violence and death.

Phillips's diplomatic skills would be summoned once again to a part of the world that would not see peace for many years and would eventually directly involve his own country. In 1947, he headed a commission to help a boundary dispute between Siam and French Indochina (Vietnam). The French were unable, like Churchill, to recognize the end of empire, and they proved intransigent and the mission failed. William Phillips lived to be 90. During his long retirement he busied himself writing his memoirs, *Ventures in Diplomacy* (1952). He participated in various international conferences and published occasional pieces about his career for the Massachusetts Historical Society, of which he was a long and valued member. He died while on vacation in Sarasota, Florida on February 23, 1968.

Mr. Dresel

Like John Adams and John Quincy Adams, who had been sent to represent their government at the conclusion of its wars with Great Britain, a pair of Massachusetts men, Ellis Loring Dresel and James Bryant Conant, would be chosen U.S. High Commissioners to a defeated Germany after World War I and World War II, respectively.

Ellis Loring Dresel was born in Boston on November 28, 1865, graduated from Harvard in 1887 and the law school five years later. In 1915, he was sent by the U.S. Department of State to Berlin as an attache in the American embassy to represent the interests of British prisoners of war held by the Germans. In the spring of 1917, with America's entry into the war growing more likely, Dresel was dispatched to Vienna. President Wilson had signed a declaration of war on April 6, and Dresel settled what embassy affairs he could, closed the legation, and had left for Switzerland. He had worked with the Red Cross during the war in caring for American prisoners. At the Paris Peace Conference in 1919, Dresel was in charge of the political information section and made two inspection tours of the defeated country. In 1921 he was appointed U.S. Commissioner for Germany, and as relations between the United States and Germany normalized, Dresel's title was changed to charge d' affaires, and in that capacity, signed the Treaty of Berlin ending World War I. Dresel left Germany and the diplomatic service in 1922, and died at Pride's Crossing, Massachusetts on September 19, 1925. He was 59 years old.

Mr. Grew

On February 10, 1917, precisely at 8:10 P.M., a train pulled out of Berlin, and headed south toward the Swiss border. At 1:00 o'clock in the morning of June 25, 1942, a Japanese ship, the *Asama Maru*, slipped its moorings in Yokohama Harbor and sailed to Hong Kong, Saigon, and, eventually, to a rendezvous with the Swedish vessel *Gripsholm* off the southeast coast of Africa at Mozambique. As had the train from Germany so many years before, the ship leaving Japan was carrying American diplomats ordered out of a country with which their own was then at war. In an irony of history, the first secretary of the embassy who led the evacuation from Berlin and the ambassador who was expelled from Tokyo a quarter of a century later was the same man, Joseph Grew, the definition of an extraordinary diplomatic career, and a chronicle of the formation of a professional and effective American foreign service.

In the dawning years of the century, the term "foreign service" could hardly be applied to that aspect of the U.S. State Department. With no entrance examination, no tenure and no system of promotion, the ambassadors and ministers representing the nation abroad were a collection of friends of the president, financial contributors to the party, and out-of-office politicians. In 1899, of the 17 men at the State Department in Washington and the 149 chiefs of mission around the world, there was not one careerist. American businessmen and travelers were constantly complaining that their needs were unmet by a consular corps that consisted of minor officials who were forced to live on meager salaries augmented as best they could by fees and private business ventures. In 1906, an investigation of consulates in Asia revealed widespread incompetence, dishonesty and drunkenness.

In 1906, President Theodore Roosevelt, by executive order, instituted rules that opened the way for a professional consular service, an order kept in place by his successor, President Taft. In 1924, Congress passed legislation, the Foreign Service Act, that was designed to establish one completely professional organization encompassing the diplomatic and consular corps with their separate and different functions, characteristics and perspectives. It was in that ever-more professional and organized state department where Joseph Grew would spend his adult life.

Joseph Clark Grew was born in his family home on Marlborough Street between Dartmouth and Exeter Streets in Boston's Back Bay on May 27, 1880, to Edward Sturgis Grew, a wealthy banker and wool merchant in the city, and Annie Crawford Clark Grew. The Grews had an estate in the adjacent and then still somewhat rural town of Hyde Park (annexed to Boston in 1911) surrounded by a large wooded area where, long after the family had moved on, this author used to pick wild blueberries. When the city's heat rose, the Grews fled to their summer home, "All Oaks" at Manchester-by-the-Sea.

It was on to the familiar and expected path for the son of a banker such as Edward Grew: Groton, where the purpose of education was as much to inculcate social responsibility as it was to arouse intellectual curiosity, and Harvard where along with his fellow Groton graduate, Franklin Delano Roosevelt, Grew served on the staff of the Harvard *Crimson*. The tall, thin, mustached, pipe-smoking and handsome Joseph Grew took a world tour following his graduation in 1902. While in Amoy, China, Grew shot a tiger, which, as it turned out, would be of future significance.

Joseph Grew was of the time and the temperament of many of his social class, sons of the well-to-do graduates of Harvard, Yale, Princeton, or a foreign university, to whom the commercial life was unattractive, the pursuit of political office demeaning, and the successful literary life attainable only by the gifted. A good number of these young men were to conclude that the obligation for public service they felt their position and prosperity placed upon them might be honorably discharged in the foreign service. That was Grew's preference, a choice in which he was handicapped by a serious loss of hearing. When Edwin V. Morgan, consul general in Korea, let it be known through the clubby world of Harvard faculty and alumni that he needed a private secretary, he was advised by a Professor Coolidge that Grew would be a good man for the job if he were not deaf. After Professor Coolidge's misunderstanding of the extent of Grew's disability was corrected, and when Edwin Morgan's brother, Fred, serving in Cairo, needed a clerk, Grew was offered the position. The temperature at Cairo when Joseph Grew arrived at his first diplomatic post on July 10, 1904, was 118 degrees—out of the sun.

In the fall of 1907, Grew returned to Boston to accomplish a deed that was to immeasurably enhance his effectiveness as a diplomat in every post to which he would subsequently be assigned—he married Alice deVermandois Perry. Alice Perry was articulate, beautiful, charming, and well bred: her mother was a Cabot, her father a scholar, critic and eminent Brahmin; and she could trace her ancestry back directly to Benjamin Franklin. The fact that she had lived in Japan and spoke Japanese and was the great-grand niece of Admiral Matthew Perry, who had opened Japan to Western trade and influence, was to prove of great value to her husband in his most fateful assignment: that as ambassador extraordinary and plenipotentiary to the Imperial Court of Japan in 1932.

While in Cairo, Grew had attended to his consular clerkship in orderly and disciplined fashion, organizing records, categorizing correspondence and keeping meticulous files. His work was the nitty-gritty and unthanked daily task of a minor functionary. What he wanted was a career in a structured foreign service; he longed to be a diplomat.

Grew's opportunity to start on that path came when the wife of a friend of his, Bellamy Storer, whose husband was at the time ambassador (a title first adopted by the United States in 1893) to Austria-Hungary, wrote to her friend, Alice Roosevelt, the president's wife. Mr. Storer, she wrote the first lady, was in need of a third secretary and felt that young Joseph Grew would be ideal for the position. The president, in his blunt fashion, replied to Mrs. Storer that he had made his own opportunities in life, had never heard of Grew, and he had other worthy young men in mind for the post. Once again, and not for the last time, Grew's Harvard connections came to his aid. The president's assistant attorney general, Alford Cooley, a companion on his vigorous bike rides, and a classmate of Grew's brother Randolph at Harvard, managed to shout into the president's ear a recounting of Grew's hunting adventures in China. The result was Grew's appointment not to Austria-Hungary, but as Third Secretary of the Embassy in Mexico City in March of 1906.

In 1907 Grew was Third Secretary in Moscow; Second Secretary in Berlin a year later; in that same capacity at Vienna in 1911 and 1912, and back to Berlin that year. In Germany the cultured and urbane Grews were welcomed into the closed society of European diplomacy. Members of the diplomatic corps dined with each other, socialized with each other, communicated in the native tongue or in French, and believed their basic mission was to keep their country from the ultimate failure of diplomacy: war. The Grews, however, in the near obligatory fashion felt by representatives of a democracy, expanded their circle of friends beyond the aristocratic and powerful. Which is not to say that those so admitted went beyond the educated and accomplished to the charwoman, chauffeur, gardener or common citizen; they did not.

By August of 1914, with the gunshots of the assassination of the Austrian Archduke Ferdinand and his wife echoing down the corridors of Europe, Berlin was taking on the excited expectations of impending war. Troop trains came and went, soldiers marched, and long lines of Americans anxious to flee the country formed around the embassy. Grew at the time had a pro-German bias. "My sympathies," he wrote his mother, "are mostly [in] all of this [on the German] side, though they are perhaps founded more on admiration of their marvelous organization and the fact that they are fighting against enormous odds than anything else." Those words were not what his mother or his anglophile friends in Boston wanted to hear from one of their own, and the return mail brought censure and criticism of his gullibility. Grew's response was to claim that his position as a neutral diplomat required him to avoid all moral, ethical, or political judgments. By the spring of 1915, the growing evidence of German brutality, a sense of the country's animosity toward America, and the sinking of the

Lusitania, had brought his attitude full circle. With the probability of war between the United States and Germany growing ever stronger, the task of removing the American diplomatic presence in Berlin fell to Joseph Grew, charge d'affaires in the absence of the ambassador, who had been called home for consultation.

During the war, Grew was chief of the State Department's Division of Western Europe Affairs, and, at its conclusion Secretary of the United States Commission to the Peace Conference at Versailles. It was a thankless task of enormous tension considering the insistent and often conflicting demands of an American delegation consisting of the president's men, academics, and the Army all vying for the superior position; but it was one that Grew handled with consummate tact and finesse. In 1920 Grew received the promotion he had so long desired, which insured his career, when he was appointed minister to Denmark, the first careerist in the State Department's history to be so elevated. In 1921 he became minister to Switzerland and as the principal American diplomat at the Lausanne Conference on Near Eastern Affairs (1922-23), distinguished himself as a skillful and accomplished negotiator, notably in his efforts to thwart British attempts to dominate the conference in the matter of oil concessions from Turkey.

In 1924, Grew returned to the United States as Under Secretary to Secretary of State Frank B. Kellogg, with whom he did not get along. Nevertheless, he creditably carried out his duties, which were to see to a restructuring of the department. Named ambassador to Turkey in 1927, Grew was sent to Japan five years later, the first career ambassador to what was considered a major power. He sailed for Tokyo on March 13, 1932 and would remain as American ambassador to the Imperial Court of Japan for a decade until his repatriation in June 1942.

Grew arrived in the land of the Rising Sun as the old world order was sinking into the abysmal darkness of destruction and death. Years of tact, decades of protocol, forever conscious of the etiquette of international society, seemed to make Joseph Clark Grew an ideal choice for the posting. But Tokyo was not Berlin, not Vienna, not Copenhagen, not Bern, not even Istanbul; the Japanese thought process was not that of the Westerner. Conclusions and consensus were arrived at in a different way and the pervasive deference of decision-makers to their inferiors in the bureaucracy was, even to a perceptive diplomat like Grew, baffling. The new ambassador arrived at a time of crises. The military seemed to control the government, China had been forced into unfavorable trade and political treaties, the Kwantung Army, Japan's surrogate military force, had occupied Manchuria and declared an independent state ruled by a puppet government for Japan. Despite some periods of calm, Grew was to face numerous problems: the failure of a Western-style economy in the wake of the Great Depression; the resentment against American laws restricting Japanese immigration; the limit on Japanese naval power in the treaties following World War I; Japan's desire to be recognized as the leading Far Eastern power with legitimate spheres of influence; its militarism, its expansionism, and also the matter of trade policy.

By 1937, Japanese-American relations were on a downhill spiral. The second Sino-Japanese war had broken out. In December, Japanese naval aviators sank the U.S.S. *Panay* in the Yangtze River above Nanking. The Japanese government blamed renegade pilots (the question of the civilian government's control of the military was an ongoing one), and the crisis passed. The Japanese credited Grew for helping restrain American reaction to the incident, and Grew, in turn, in no uncertain terms, warned the Japanese of the growing revulsion of the American people to the actions of the Japanese military. Despite the tension, the two countries maintained profitable commercial ties. Yet, within and without the State Department, and in the Roosevelt administration, the sentiment was growing that appeals to law, treaty or principle were no longer adequate to the increasing aggression. The situation grew more ominous when the Japanese government joined Nazi Germany and Fascist Italy in the Tripartite Pact in September of 1940.

The Japanese military was on the move, determined to conquer China. Grew believed that they would not stop there but would move south to Indo-China. He opposed military or economic sanctions against Japan, arguing that they would be subject to misinterpretation and that they would raise the possibility of a war the American people opposed except in defense of American territory. In short, he believed that America's Far East interests did not justify war with Japan.

In a speech given at a dinner in his honor by the American-Japanese Society in Tokyo on October 19, 1939, Grew was at his diplomatic best. With true conviction, he assured his audience he felt that by . . .

"the very deep affection for Japan and [his belief] that the real, the fundamental and abiding interests of both countries called for harmony of thought and action in their relationships. Those who know my sentiments for Japan, developed in happy contacts here during the seven years in which I have lived among you, will realize, I am sure, that my words and actions are those of a true friend."

In December 1939, Japan made overtures to begin talks on a settlement of the differences with the United States, but nothing came of it. Early in April 1941, a series of private and semi-official efforts toward the same end were initiated. The two countries engaged in official talks at the highest level through the fall and early winter even as the American embassy in Tokyo was noting straws in the wind pointing to a military move southward. The German embassy had predicted a Japanese attack to knock out the British Empire's interests in the Far East in conjunction with its own country's invasion of England. Grew was holding to the conservative theory that Japan would wait until Germany had defeated England before taking any massive military action. In that spirit he passed on to Washington the "rumor" picked up by a Peruvian colleague who considered it "fantastic" that the Japanese were planning an all-out surprise attack on the American military installations at Pearl Harbor, Hawaii. Grew remained in the dark about the ongoing negotiations taking place in Washington because of the belief by the State Department that the Japanese had broken the American Diplomatic Code.

On Sunday morning, December 7, 1941, the American secretary of state, Cordell Hull, went to his office, as was his custom almost every Sunday since he had entered the State Department as Secretary in 1933. The Americans also had broken the Japanese diplomatic code and Hull was able to read a series of decoded intercepts that indicated the answer the Japanese government would make to the latest American peace proposals. The heart of the answer was in the concluding paragraph, which stated that in view of the attitude of the American government, the Japanese government found it impossible to reach an agreement through further negotiations. There was a further message instructing the Japanese ambassadors to present the note of rejection at one o'clock in the afternoon, but not after. Ambassador Nomura telephoned to request a meeting at that time, which was granted. A few minutes after 1:00 P.M., he telephoned again asking the meeting be postponed until 1:45, but he did not arrive until 2:05 and was ushered along with a colleague into the diplomatic waiting room. They had hardly settled in their seats when Hull's phone rang again. This time it was the president. "There is a report that the Japanese have attacked Pearl Harbor," FDR said.

During the ensuing war, Grew served as special assistant to Hull, and after 1944 as head of the Far Eastern Division of the State Department. In that capacity he argued strenuously with President Truman not to continue to demand unconditional surrender from the Japanese because that would enable the fanatics to claim the emperor would be disposed of and thus there was a need to continue the war. In his memoirs, Grew claimed that had he been listened to, the United States would not have felt compelled to use the atomic bomb.

After the war, he became a hard-liner against the Soviet Union. Believing a war between the United States and Russia a distinct probability, "The most fateful thing we can do," he was quoted as saying, "is to place any confidence whatsoever in Russia's sincerity, knowing without question that she will take every opportunity to profit by our clinging to our ethical standards."

Joseph W. Grew had spent 41 years in the diplomatic service of his country when he retired in 1945, then wrote his memoirs and served for a while as chairman of the board of Radio Free Europe. He died at his family home at Manchester-by-the-Sea on May 25, 1965. He was age 85.

The Versatile Child

Educated at Milton Academy, Harvard University, and Harvard Law School; lawyer, writer of magazine articles, short stories and novels; an organizer of the Massachusetts Progressive Party; speechwriter for Warren Harding; employee of the British government; admirer of Mussolini and contributor to the dictator's autobiography; isolationist; president of the American Arbitration Society; organizer of the "Republicans for Roosevelt" in 1932; special adviser to the secretary of state; chairman of the U.S. delegation to the London Economic Conference; four times married, and a convert to Roman Catholicism as the Angel of Death turned the handle on his sickroom door—Richard Washburn Child's life was peripatetic and productive.

He was born on August 5, 1881, in Worcester, to the shoe manufacturer Horace Walker Child, and Susan Sawyer Messinger Child. His father's family had settled in 1630 in "the Town upon the river," which the Puritans decreed should be called Watertown. Richard's first employment after graduating from Harvard was as the Washington correspondent for *Ridgeway's Weekly* and similar publications. Although he practiced law intermittently, and eventually founded a law firm in New York in 1933, Child's reputation was made in the literary field. A prolific writer in various forms—he published articles in *Collier's* and the *Saturday Evening Post* and wrote short stories and books—Child soon became one of the most popular writers of his day. The subjects he chose to write about—crime prevention for example—also revealed an active social conscience.

In 1911, as associate state chairman of the effort to organize the Progressive Party in Massachusetts, Child became acquainted with Frank A. Vanderlip, who drafted him to aid in the U.S. Treasury Department's financing of World War I. Child also traveled to Europe as a war correspondent. A supporter of General Leonard Wood at the 1920 Republican National Convention, Child became a confidential adviser and speechwriter for the eventual nominee, Warren Harding, and organized a committee of writers and journalists to support him. In 1919, Child was employed by the British government to study the problems of post-war reconstruction. In that year he became editor of *Collier's*, in which capacity he served until 1921. On May 26, 1921, President Harding appointed him as American ambassador extraordinary and plenipotentiary to Italy. It was to be a rich and rewarding experience for the writer, a phase in which he was to become a great admirer and advocate of the Fascist dictator, Benito Mussolini.

Ambassador Child almost immediately gained a sincere and deep affection for the Italian people. To them and to their government he was a "persona gratissima." With a blind eye to the dark and evil side of the Black Shirt dictatorship of Mussolini, Child extolled the energy, efficiency and discipline of the movement: its breadth of youth, its national spirit, and its joy and service. The Italian government conferred on Child both its Order of St. Maurice and St. Lazarus and the Order of the

Crown of Italy. While serving in Rome, Child represented the United States as an observer at the Geneva and Lausanne conferences.

Child continued his active literary and diplomatic life after he returned from Italy. He wrote extensively for the Hearst newspapers, helped organize the National Crime Commission, promoted industrial arbitration and became president of the Arbitration Society of America. In the 1932 election, Child organized the Republicans-for-Roosevelt League and campaigned vigorously for the Democrat. In 1934, Roosevelt appointed him a special adviser with the rank of ambassador to Secretary of State Cordell Hull in Hull's capacity as chairman of the U.S. delegation to the London Economic Conference. Child's first three marriages ended in divorce. On September 28, 1931, at age 50, he married Dorothy (Gallagher) Everson, with whom he had a daughter. He died of pneumonia in New York City on Janaury 31, 1935, at age 53.

John Wingate Weeks

In February of 1925, John Wingate Weeks, in his capacity as Calvin Coolidge's secretary of war, was called before an investigating committee of the U.S. House of Representatives to answer criticisms of his office and of the military hierarchy from the Army's assistant chief of staff for air service, Brigadier General William Mitchell. "Billy" Mitchell, America's most outstanding combat air commander in World War I, advocated an independent air force under a united control, a system opposed by the military chiefs and Secretary Weeks. Mitchell would lose his battle and go on to be court-martialed and convicted of insubordination; Weeks would continue to oversee American's War Department through the years of Coolidge's presidency.

John Wingate Weeks came from a family with a history of public service, his great uncle and namesake having served New Hampshire in the U.S. Congress from 1829 to 1833, his cousin, Edgar Weeks, was a Representative from Michigan in the 56th and 57th Congresses (1899-1903). The younger John Wingate Weeks was born on April 11, 1860, on a farm near Lancaster, New Hampshire, and educated at the local schools. In 1877 he entered the U.S. Naval Academy and graduated in 1881. Any hope Weeks had of a naval career came to an end when cutbacks in personnel precipitated his resignation in 1883. In 1885, while working as a surveyor in Florida, he married Martha Sinclair, with whom he had two children. Martha found the Florida climate not to her liking, so when an opportunity presented itself for her husband to enter the banking and brokerage business in Boston, the couple moved north. Weeks eventually became a partner in the very successful and prestigious banking-brokerage firm of Hornblower and Weeks.

In Boston, Weeks joined the Massachusetts Naval Brigade and was active in the protection of the state's shoreline during the Spanish-American War. Before that, in 1896, Weeks was named to the Board of Visitors of the U.S. Naval Academy. The Weeks family had moved to the Boston suburb of Newton in 1893, and in 1899 Weeks was elected to the city's Board of Aldermen and served as mayor of Newton in 1902-1903. Weeks then was elected as a Republican to the 59th Congress (March 4, 1905) and served in four succeeding Congresses until his resignation on March 4, 1913, when the Massachusetts Legislature elected him to succeed the retiring U.S. Senator, Winthrop Murray Crane. Weeks became the first senatorial victim of the rise of the Irish Democrats when he was defeated by former Governor David I. Walsh in 1918. While in the House and Senate, the tall, powerfully built and ever cordial Weeks—"the smiling statesman" he was some-times called—generally followed the orthodox faith of the Republican Party: for high tariffs, against independence for the Philippines, a pro-ponent of the Aldrich Plan for banking and currency, and a reluctant supporter of President Wilson's Federal Reserve Act.

Weeks's yeoman work for Harding in the 1920 presidential cam-paign and his association with the Navy gained him sufficient notice from the president-elect to appoint him secretary of war, an office he also held under President Coolidge until ill health forced his departure in October of 1925. He died where he was born, in Lancaster, New Hampshire, on July 12, 1926.

The Other Mr. Washburn

Albert Henry Washburn was born in 1866 in the town of Middleborough, Massachusetts, to Edward and Ann Elizabeth White Washburn. Albert's father operated a small manufacturing business in the town, and for the most part young Albert received his early education there. The quality of his scholarship—and of his intellect—was evidenced by an academic career that extended beyond his undergraduate degree, a PhD. degree from Cornell in 1899, an LL.D. from Dartmouth in 1924, further studies at Georgetown University, and an LL.B. from the University of Virginia.

Washburn entered the diplomatic service as U.S. Consul at Magdeburg, Germany, in 1890. Three years later he received an invitation from Henry Cabot Lodge to return home to become the senator's private secretary. In 1901, he left that position to serve as the U.S. Attorney for the District of Massachusetts. From 1901 to 1904 Washburn was counsel for the U.S. Treasury in matters of tariff legislation and imports. He resigned his federal post in 1904 and, in 1906, he married Florence B. Lincoln. The couple had one daughter.

Washburn took up the practice of law, wrote scholarly pieces on a field of law in which he had expertise: that of customs law. For three years—1919 through 1921—he was a professor of international law and political science at Dartmouth College.

In 1922, at the end of World War I, the time had come to reestablish diplomatic relations with former enemies. President Harding sent Albert Washburn to Austria as American minister, where Washburn spent eight years in Vienna. They were productive years, with the signing of treaties of friendship, commerce and consular service. When a commission of jurists met at The Hague from 1922 to 1923 to consider amendments to the laws of war, Washburn was the U.S. representative. The minister's reports to Washington were literate, incisive and objective. The Austrian authorities consulted him often on the difficulties of a new republic in its formative years. In January of 1930, Washburn resigned his position in Austria not to leave the diplomatic service but to await submission of his nomination as ambassador to Japan. Washburn died in Vienna on April 2, 1930, before the nomination was made, and the Japanese assignment went to another Massachusetts man, William Cameron Forbes.

Expectations

Even from the least of "the poor New England Brahmins of ours" the senior Oliver Wendell Holmes's paean to the Yankee youths who were off to save the Union from destruction, much was expected and much was delivered. How much should be expected from a youth whose ancestors excelled in public service and business? Whose father was president of the Bell Telephone Company and whose mother a daughter of Ralph Waldo Emerson?

William Cameron Forbes was born in the well-to-do Boston suburb of Milton on the 21st of May, 1870, and received his early education at Milton Academy and at the Hopkinson School in Boston, before going on to Harvard. He received his degree in 1892. In his youth, sports, not business or public service, was the object of Forbes's passion. He coached Harvard's freshman football team for two years before taking over the varsity eleven in 1897. For a young man to whom horses were readily available, polo was the sport of choice, and Forbes was to become a player of international caliber. The Boston brokerage firm of Jackson and Curtis took him on as an unpaid clerk in 1894. Three years later, at 27, he proved that there was more to him than a saddle, wooden ball or mallet by becoming the chief of the financial department of the utilities and electrical engineering company, Stone and Webster, and, in 1899, he became a life partner in the family investment house of J. M. Forbes Company.

The pace of activity in an investment house was not exciting enough for young Forbes, so he sought more excitement by applying for an appointment to the Panama Canal Commission. The appointment was not forthcoming but did result in President Theodore Roosevelt's sending Forbes to the Philippines as Secretary of Commerce and Police with a seat on the governing Philippine Commission. By 1908, Forbes was vice governor-general of the islands and a year later, by appointment of President Taft, governor-general. Governor Forbes approached his stewardship—"the big central thing in my life"—as would be expected from one of his economic background and point of view. If progress, efficiency and modernity were introduced, if the economy could be made to prosper, he reasoned, then not only would the plight of the inhabitants improve, but it would also neutralize the growing Filipino agitation for independence. The governor set out on a vigorous program of road and rail building and water transportation. He also tried to establish an effective system of land registration and irrigation to deal with animal disease and encourage foreign investment.

In a political adjunct to his economic program for the Philippines, Forbes befriended Sergio Osmena and Manuel L. Quezon, leaders of the rising Nacionalista Party, Forbes going so far as to counsel the two on government appointments.

For all its effort and enthusiasm, Forbes's plan did not work. He was vilified not only for his obstinate and public opposition to Philippine independence, but his unwillingness to encourage and fund universal education lessened his influence. Tension, much of it racial, deepened between the Americans and the Filipinos. In 1911, Forbes became ill, exhausted from his work and unable to maintain the administrative efficiency he had initiated. When Woodrow Wilson was inaugurated in 1913, American anti-imperialists joined with Filipino independence leaders, and even some of Forbes's former supporters, in demanding a governor-general more supportive of independence for the islands. Wilson first announced Forbes's successor, Francis Burton Harrison, to the press, and then requested that Forbes promptly resign.

William Cameron Forbes became a bitter man, unable despite his position as a sometime-consultant to Stone and Webster, as a receiver of the Brazil Railway and as director of several corporations, to retrieve his heart from the Philippines. A backstage mover of the Republican Party, Forbes was chosen by President Harding to join General Leonard Wood in a mission to report on the American administration of the Philippines under Wilson's appointee and, in an indication of its underlying bias, the performance of Filipinos in a wide range of posts they had filled under Governor-General Harrison. The report recommended the retention of the colonial status of the Philippines, giving as the rationale, consolidation of past reforms. The report became the basis for the Philippine policy of both the Harding and Coolidge administrations.

In 1930, Forbes was appointed by President Hoover to head a commission for the study of conditions in Haiti. At the completion of his work in Haiti, Forbes was asked by Hoover to take an appointment as ambassador to Japan. Only a few Americans knew much about the Chrysanthemum Empire at the time and by no means was William Cameron Forbes among those who did. Despite being warned that hostilities between China and Japan over Manchuria might be soon breaking out, Forbes left Tokyo for home on a planned leave on

September 14, 1931, the day after the fighting actually began. In his analysis of what was needed in America's diplomatic relations with Japan, Forbes agreed with the position of the majority of the Tokyo staff that foreign pressure would only result in uniting the Japanese behind the military and compromise the liberal foreign policy of the government. In that stand he differed from Secretary of State Henry L. Stimson and so was reluctant to deliver the secretary's harsh protest over Japan's actions in Manchuria to the Japanese government. Forbes became openly critical of Stimson, and Stimson, for his part, dismissed the ambassador's reports, which he considered obscure and filled with alien sympathies. Forbes had tendered a standing offer to resign to Stimson, and in early 1932, it was accepted. Forbes's ambassadorship to Japan ended in March of 1932, after Joseph Grew had been appointed to the position the month before.

Forbes lived to see the fall of the Japanese empire in 1945 and the proclamation of Philippine independence on July 4, 1946. Wealthy, intelligent, energetic, and accomplished in his own right, he did not disappoint those who expected much from him. A polo player well into his 80's, he died on the day before Christmas, 1959, at age 89.

The Consummate Pol

The man was a professional politician who spent the greater part of his adult life seeking and holding appointed and elected public office: 11 of them in a quarter of a century. A believer, long before the maxim was articulated by Tip O'Neill, that "all politics is local," he was an inveterate doorbell ringer, a street campaigner to whom everybody's vote was important and never to be taken for granted. Had he lived in a different era, Calvin Coolidge would be the scorn of those who look with self-righteous disdain on the "professional pol."

In 1898, the voters of Northampton, Massachusetts, elected a 26-year-old transplanted Vermonter to the board of aldermen. For the next 30 years until the term of his last office expired, that consummate officeholder would be, in turn, mayor, state senator, president of the Massachusetts Senate, lieutenant governor, governor, and vice president and president of the United States. During those 30 years he was never out of office.

Fittingly for someone whose career trajectory resembled that of a rocket, John Calvin Coolidge was born on the Fourth of July, 1872, in Plymouth Notch, Vermont, in the back room of a cottage attached to his father's general store and post office. The young man, who later dropped his first name in his preference for Calvin, was educated at the Plymouth district school and at the Baptist-supported Black River Academy. While illness prevented him from entering college immediately following secondary school, he arrived on campus at Amherst College to join the class of 1895. An excellent student, Calvin had developed an interest in politics by the time he graduated. He was inspired somewhat by the galaxy of Republican leaders who attended the 1891 dedication of the Bennington, Vermont, battleground memorial commemorating the Vermont Green Mountain Boys' defeat of the British in 1772.

Coolidge studied the law, then moved to Northampton, where he enjoyed success as a lawyer. It was there that he began his political journey that was to end at the White House in Washington, D.C. As a progressive, at least during his years in the Massachusetts legislature and as lieutenant governor and governor, he was a supporter of women's suffrage, the popular election of U.S. senators, and the expansion of workers' compensation. In defending his support of legislation to curb the power of Standard Oil Company, he said: "You forbid a union to injure a man's business, but a giant corporation can do the same thing."

The year 1919 was one of labor strife all over the country. The most troubling dispute came in Boston when 80 percent of the city's police force walked out over poor wages. Legislation enacted earlier by the Republican-controlled legislature to curb the growing power of the "Irish bosses" was still in effect, so the police commissioner, Edwin U. Curtis, was answerable to Governor Coolidge. Curtis, a stiff, rather pompous man, was a former mayor, but the situation soon got beyond him with growing reports of violence and open crime. When the governor signaled that he did not wish to interfere, the sitting mayor, Andrew J. Peters, as was his right, called out the city militia and seized control of the police, at the same time publicly criticizing Coolidge for his lack of action.

Coolidge had always gotten along with the Irish politicians, who respected the governor's integrity, the value of his word and his progressive position on the issues that were dear to the Irish. When he got word from Jim Timilty the boss of the Roxbury district of Boston, that Timilty would support any action Coolidge took, the governor sent in the state militia to restore the peace. It was in an exchange with labor leader Samuel Gompers that Coolidge issued his famous statement: "There is no right to strike against the public safety by anybody, anywhere, any time."

At the 1920 Republican presidential nominating convention, neither of the two leading contenders could muster the necessary votes needed for nomination, and the party bosses, meeting in what was literally a smoke-filled room, engineered the nomination of Warren G. Harding. The vice presidential nomination was offered to Senator Hiram Johnson of California, who refused it. The bosses' next choice was Senator Irvine L. Lenroot of Wisconsin, who, in an example of bad timing, removed himself from contention before he knew he would have the backing of Harding. Enter Henry Cabot Lodge, ever alert to unexpected opportunity. Lodge rushed over to the Oregon delegation, which had been pledged to Hiram Johnson for president and Lodge for vice president.

By this time, many of the delegates were on their way to the exits. The chairman of the delegation having gained the recognition of the chair told the delegates that although they had come to Chicago to nominate Lodge, that estimable gentleman had requested that his name not be mentioned. Instead, he proposed another distinguished son of Massachusetts who stood for all that the Republican Party held near and dear, Governor Calvin Coolidge, who won 674.5 votes to Senator Lenroot's 146.5 and went on to become vice president under President Warren G. Harding.

Mr. President

"On the night of August 2, 1923," Calvin Coolidge was later to write in his autobiography, "I was awakened by my father coming up the stairs, calling my name. I noticed that his voice trembled. As the only times I have ever observed that before were when death visited our family, I knew something of the gravest nature had occurred." It was not about a family member, but the president of the United States.

President Harding, sick at heart at the growing realization that the very men who had put him in the White House were engaged in large-scale corruption, had died in San Francisco.

In serving out the remaining two years of Harding's term, Coolidge worked at carrying out the dead president's program, but without much success. The cloud of scandal that had hovered over the nation's capitol finally lifted with the resignation of two cabinet members the new president had inherited from Harding. In 1924, Coolidge became president in his own right, receiving 54 percent of the popular vote, defeating Democrat John W. Davis and the Progressive Party's Robert M. La Follette.

It was President Coolidge's Republican philosophy that business was the nation's business and government its protector and promoter. High tariffs were maintained and Secretary of the Treasury Andrew Mellon saw to the reduction of taxes and made an effort to reduce the national debt. Abstinence was the creed in matters of regulation of business in the restrained hands of Secretary of Commerce Herbert Hoover.

On August 2, 1927, over a year before his term was to expire, President Coolidge's secretary passed on to the reporters covering the White House a short document she had transcribed from a note he had scribbled: "I do not choose to run for president in nineteen twenty-eight." He had told no one about his decision, not even Mrs. Coolidge.

After attending the inauguration of his successor, Herbert Hoover, Calvin Coolidge left immediately for the town that had elected him to public office three decades before. John Calvin Coolidge, 30th President of the United States, died on January 5, 1933, in Northampton and was buried in the family plot in Plymouth Notch, Vermont.

In Massachusetts politics there had been a contemporary of Coolidge, a so-called ward boss in Boston's West End, named Martin "the Mahatma" Lomasney, who had a rule to keep the practitioners of the dangerous business of holding public office out of trouble: "Never write when you can speak; never speak when you can wink; never wink when you can nod." It was good advice diligently followed in the long public career of the man who became known as "Silent Cal."

The Caretaker

When Coolidge's Secretary of Commerce, Herbert Hoover, resigned in August of 1928 to begin his campaign for the Republican Party's presidential nomination, he was replaced as secretary by William Whiting. Whiting, like the president a graduate of Amherst College, was born at Holyoke, on July 20, 1864, the son of Congressman (1881-1889) William Whiting and Anne Marie Fairfield Whiting. Educated in the local schools, at Williston Academy in Easthampton, and Amherst, William went to work at his father's paper mill and eventually became president of the Whiting Paper Company. Whiting was a delegate to four successive Republican National Conventions, from 1920 to 1932. In his capacity as Commerce Secretary, he served as chairman of several commissions, including the Federal Oil Conservation Board, the Federal Narcotics Control Board and the U.S. Council of National Defense. Whiting was replaced at Commerce in the Hoover administration by Robert P. Lamont on March 5, 1929. In retrospect, one might say just in time.

Not in Time

Charles Francis Adams, financier, yachtsman and statesman, was the great-great-grandson and great-grandson of Presidents John Adams and John Quincy Adams. His grandfather was the diplomat, Charles Francis Adams. Like his illustrious ancestors, he was born in Quincy (Braintree) Massachusetts, on August 2, 1866. The younger Adams graduated with an A.B. cum laude from Harvard in 1888 and from Harvard Law School in 1892. "Charlie" was captain of his class crew, president of his class for all four years, and had the honor of being class marshall until he died in 1954. Both Charles and his father were Democrats. Charles the son, as the *New York Times*, long convinced that the family never had one, commented on February 22, 1929, had "a heavenly sense of humor . . . [a] rather unusual variation on the Adams theme."

It goes without saying the one thing "Charlie" Adams would do after college was to take a tour of Europe. After a year of meandering he returned to Boston, was admitted to the Suffolk Country bar and took up the practice of law in the office of Judge Everett C. Bumpus.

In 1893, Charles F. Adams the yachtsman skippered *The Pilgrim* in an unsuccessful attempt to become the America's Cup defender. When Charles's father died in 1894, he assumed, like many another sons of a wealthy Brahmin, the family trusteeships. He also served two terms as a member of the Quincy City Council (1893-1895) and two terms as mayor (1896-1897).

Eventually Adams became the treasurer of the Corporation of Harvard College, where his financial acumen raised the school's endowment from $15 million to $120 million. In 1899, Adams married Frances Lovering, daughter of Congressman William C. Lovering, with whom he fathered two children: Charles Francis Adams, Jr., a prominent industrialist, and Catherine, who married Henry S. Morgan, son and partner of J. P. Morgan the younger.

Popular among the voters—when a state constitutional convention was called for in 1917, he received more votes than any other candidate at large—Adams was nevertheless a political anomaly: a national leader of American banks and corporations while at the same time an avowed Democrat. In 1920, when the leadership of the state Democratic Party put forward his name as a presidential elector—supposedly without his knowledge or consent—Adams switched to the Republican Party.

When Herbert Hoover was elected president in 1928, there were few men in America with a greater reputation for rectitude than Charles Francis Adams. In appointing Adams his Secretary of the Navy, the president gained the additional advantage of having a man thoroughly devoted to things of the sea and who had made an extensive study of naval warfare. Adams came to the Navy at a time when, on the one hand, Japan's increasing militancy seemed to require that the Navy's strength be maintained at the level allowed by the post-World War I treaties, and a time when the service was increasingly restrained by the deepening Depression. Adams did manage, however, to oversee the modernization of several battleships, the construction of eight cruisers, the keels laid for seven more, and the close-to-completion of the aircraft carrier *Ranger*.

In 1931, Secretary Adams announced an ambitious building program that, if implemented, would lead to American parity with the British fleet within five years, only to see it drastically cut by the president. Early the next year, in an appearance before Congress, Adams argued strongly for more naval appropriations, so strongly, in fact, that his advocacy barely avoided an open break with Hoover.

Charles Francis Adams served for the entire Hoover presidency before returning to Boston for a life devoted to trusteeships in numerous major corporations, member and chairman of several philanthropic and charitable organizations, president of the Harvard Alumni Association and of the university's Board of Overseers. He died on June 11, 1954, at age 88, having given, according to his son Charles Francis Adams Jr., only one piece of professional advice: "Charlie, you've inherited a reputation for honesty. God help you if you ever lose it."

A Boston Banker

Abraham Captain Ratshesky was neither prep school nor Brahmin, neither Harvard nor Yankee, but the son of a Russian Jewish immigrant and a graduate of the Boston public schools. Born in the city on November 6, 1864, Abe, or "Cap," as he was known because of his middle name, went to work in his father's clothing manufacturing company as an office boy and eventually rose to a full partnership. In 1895, with capital of $255,000 and deposits of $55,000, the 32-year-old Ratshesky founded the United States Trust Company in Boston, which by 1942, under his careful and conservative management, grew to $2,250 billion in capitalization and deposits of almost $20 million. A Republican at a time when such were still electable in the city, Ratshesky was a successful candidate for the Boston Common Council in 1889, 1890 and 1891, served in the state Senate from 1892 to 1894, and was chosen a delegate to six Republican National Conventions.

In January 1930, President Hoover appointed Ratshesky as American minister to Czechoslovakia, where he served until May 1932. He was awarded the Order of the White Lion, first class. It was not as a successful banker or an effective diplomat that Abe Ratshesky made his greatest contribution, however, but as a humanitarian.

When word reached Boston in December 1917 that a ship loaded with munitions had blown up in the harbor at Halifax, Nova Scotia, causing great damage and loss of life (the toll would eventually mount to 1,800 dead and property loss of $30 million) Governor Samuel W. McCall set up a relief commission to aid the province, which had long had many historical and cultural ties to Massachusetts. The governor asked Ratshesky, who had served on the national relief commission at the time of the San Francisco earthquake and fire, to head up the relief effort. Within a few hours of his appointment, the efficient Ratshesky had gathered a corps of physicians and nurses, assembled a special train, and was on his way to Halifax. There he set up an emergency hospital and stayed on, administering both Massachusetts's and other relief efforts.

In 1894, Ratshesky married Edith Shuman, the daughter of a clothing merchant. The couple was childless. In 1916, Ratshesky established a philanthropic foundation that bears his name founded "to promote the well-being, to assist in the education, to give aid and comfort, and to relieve the suffering of the needy and deserving poor." An active member of many organizations, Ratshesky was the first president of the Federated Jewish Charities of Boston, vice president of the Associated Charities of Massachusetts, a member of the executive committee of the American Jewish Committee, director of Beth Israel Hospital, and a trustee of Boston University, among others. An avid reader of history, philosophy and biography, he contributed articles on business topics for several magazines. He died in Boston on March 15, 1943.

PART III

The American Revolution—
Continued

STUPENDOUS STORMS, THOSE THAT METEOROLOGICAL HISTORIANS with confidence designate the "storm of the century," require for their viciousness a confluence of elements: a full moon, a rising tide, moisture-saturated clouds, specific wind direction, and force. In the fury of their power, secondary phenomena are created: here a tornado, there a whirlwind, here a place of calm. Beginning with the deepening of the Great Depression in 1931 and for a half century thereafter, an awesome fury of economic despair, nascent insurrection, war, racial hatred, accusations of disloyalty, of presidential assassinations and a resignation would crash against the very foundations of the American democracy, bringing forth demagogues to the right and demagogues to the left with their strident advocacy of this or that "ism."

The beginning of those turbulent years found the Commonwealth of Massachusetts in great decline—its once flourishing port a maritime backwater, its capital city unmodernized and drab, its industries departed to more profitable venues. Changing demographics made it a voting midget among the more populous states of the Union, and any national influence it might have exerted, doomed to pass from moment to memory. Massachusetts's past, in the stirring tribute of Daniel Webster, was indeed secure, there to behold. But what of its future? Despite, or in defiance of, all that beset the now-ancient Commonwealth, the next half-century would be among the most glorious years of its national political influence.

From 1932 when Franklin Delano Roosevelt took the oath of office for his first term as president of the United States until Thomas P. O'Neill relinquished the gavel of the Speaker of the U.S. House of Representatives in 1987, Massachusetts would send to the federal government an array of men and women who, in number and consequence, constitute a contribution to the political history of this nation unequaled by any other state in the union.

A president, nine cabinet members, two attorneys general, two solicitors general, one special prosecutor, thirty-eight ambassadors and foreign ministers, charge' de affaires and other high-ranking members of the diplomatic corps, one justice of the Supreme Court, and, for twelve congresses and twenty-three years, three Speakers of the House of Representatives.

CHAPTER I

Bad Times—Worse Times

I am prepared under my constitutional duty to recommend the measures a stricken Nation in the midst of a stricken world may require . . . but in the event that the Congress shall fail to take one of these two courses, and in the event that the national emergency is still critical, I shall not evade the clear course of duty that will confront me. I shall ask the Congress for the one main instrument to meet the emergency-broad Executive power to wage war against the emergency . . . .

— *Franklin D. Roosevelt, First Inaugural Address, March 4, 1933*

To my mind this is all wrong. We live in a representative Democracy and all are laborers. The employer of today is the laborer of yesterday . . . The experience of the past proves conclusively that the best government is the least possible government, that the unfettered initiative of the individual is the force that makes a country great and that initiative should never be bound except where it becomes a menace to the liberty and initiative of others.

— *M. D. McGuire, President of the Real Estate Board of the City of New York, in a dissent from the report of the State Commission investigating safety conditions, wages and hours of factory workers, 1914*

BY 1921, THE ECONOMIC BOOM THAT HAD FOLLOWED THE END OF World War I was coming to an end. Inventories were high, demand in decline, commodity prices down. American loans to war-ravaged Europe to encourage purchase of American goods were being used to buy American gold. European finances were in chaos, its currencies in disorder, devaluation widespread. In the United States, money in circulation and bank credit had expanded exponentially, resulting in inflation. When, to protect its own interests, America cut back on its loans to Europe, the countries there could no longer buy American goods, so manufacturers cut back production, workers were laid off, and farmers were left in a disastrous state. Yet, as things turned out, the "panic" of 1921 entered the history books as just another in a series: 1837, 1857, 1861, 1873, 1884, 1893, 1901, 1907, 1913. All were years of severe economic downturns that caused the engine of American free market capitalism to huff and puff until it could pull itself up from the valley of decline to a new and higher peak.

In the exuberant last years of the roaring 20s, few could see, and fewer yet cared to see, the forming of the nucleus of an economic storm. A financial and social disaster of epic proportions, so deep that the reality of its destruction would go beyond stock markets and wealth, unemployment and hunger, to the serious questioning by serious men of the very viability of the democratic form of government. Capitalism in its American manifestation had failed. By 1933 it was quite apparent: the stock market had lost 83 percent of its valuation; and the average wage of the American worker had been cut in half. Fortunate indeed were those among the growing army of the idle who could find work. The unemployment rate reached 25 percent.

The solution, some cried, was in government control of all industry, in socialism, in fascism, in communism, and many listened, for the hungry man has a fine-tuned ear and a fine tempered belly. Among the reformers there were the gradualists and the burn-down-and-rebuild-from-the-ashes radicals. Labor leaders marched on the factories; others would try to negotiate. Serious liberals took seriously the opportunity to restructure the role of government, and saddened conservatives bemoaned the end of what America was meant to be. Tumultuous times bring forth great leaders, but in the American democracy of the 1930s and 1940s they also brought forth all manner of both demagogues to the right and radicals to the left. Most of them amounted, in the long run, to naught, since what was to be done was in the hands of the president, the Congress, the nine black-robed justices of the Supreme Court, and, ultimately, in the hands of the American people.

Goodbye, Grand Old Party

When order was called for at the organizing session of the 72nd Congress in 1931, the clerks could count 220 Democrats and 214 Republicans in the House; 48 Republicans and 47 Democrats in the Senate. It was a net loss for the GOP from the previous Congress of 53 congressmen and 9 senators. The disappointment in the ranks of the political party that had controlled both houses of the national legislature in 11 of the previous 15 sessions turned to despair two years later, when the Grand Old Party was reduced to legislative insignificance with only 117 of 427 members in the House and 35 of 96 in the Senate. The center of American public policy, with its conservative bent, its mantra of the individual's innate ability to withstand society's social ills, and its bias to corporate America, had been jolted abruptly toward the left, replaced by conviction of the government's duty to enact laws for the general welfare of the people and to rein in the excesses of corporate America.

Happy Days Are Here Again—Somewhere

The day Franklin Delano Roosevelt was sworn in for the first of his four terms, in March 4, 1933 (an amendment to the Constitution would subsequently change the inauguration date to January 20), the Senate met and quickly confirmed the new president's cabinet appointees. The unprecedented haste of that usually deliberative procedure emphasized both the economic situation: the banking system had collapsed and an ever-increasing number of farms were in foreclosure. The growing number of unemployed was fast becoming an army of desperate men. The new administration addressed the situation with lightening speed. In just 100 days, the president proposed, and the Congress enacted, 13 laws that created emergency economic aid, abandoned the gold standard, addressed the problem of the farmers, and created an authority to bring electrification to the Tennessee Valley, compelled truth in the securities market, and provided credit for home and farm loans. One of the members of the hastily sworn cabinet who was to play a significant role in the creation and implementation of much of that legislative blitzkrieg was a woman born in Boston, Frances Perkins.

The Permanent Miss Perkins

Fannie (or Frances as she later chose to be known) Coralie Perkins was born on April 10, 1880, the daughter of Fred W. Perkins, a merchant, and Susan Bean Perkins. Both Frances's mother and father were natives of Maine, where they retained property to which they often returned. When Frances was two years old the family moved to Worcester, where Fred Perkins established a successful stationery business. Frances was educated at Worcester Classical High School from which she matriculated to Mount Holyoke College where she received a B.A. in 1902. In her senior year, Frances had become active in the National Consumer's League, which sought to abolish the then-prevalent use of child labor, and to eliminate sweatshops. A speech by the general secretary of the League, the social reformer, Florence Molthrop Kelley, first planted in young Frances the seed that was to flower into a lifetime devoted to social justice. Frances addressed particularly the elimination of the exploitation of women and immigrants, that at the time contributed so much to the profits of capitalist America.

Frances Perkins was rejected for a position as a family visitor with the Charity Organization of New York City due to lack of experience. She spent the next few years teaching at girls' schools in New England and Illinois. On weekends and vacations, she devoted her time to volunteer work at Hull House, a settlement house in Chicago. In 1907 she became executive secretary of the Philadelphia Research and Protective Association formed to protect young girls arriving in the city. She also took courses with economist Simon N. Pattern at the University of Pennsylvania, won a fellowship to the New York School of Philanthropy, and in 1910 used her study of malnutrition among the children of Hell's Kitchen for her master's thesis at Columbia University.

On a Saturday afternoon, March 25, 1911, Miss Perkins, who then lived on Waverley Street near Washington Square in New York City, heard the loud wail of fire engines demanding passage through the congested streets of the city. Running across a small park Frances and her neighbor beheld 50 yards away a scene of enduring horror. The 8th, 9th and 10th floors of the building that housed the Triangle Shirtwaist Company were engulfed in flames. Perhaps a cigarette carelessly thrown into a pile of remnants discarded by the woman shirt-cutters caught fire. The company had never before seen the need for conducting fire drills; consequently the confused and panicked employees found the fire escapes either locked or jammed. Two freight elevators were shut down, and there were only two passenger elevators for 430 workers. Ironically, several of the stairway exits were usually kept locked as a precaution against the girls leaving their machines for a quick smoke. Before the firemen could reach them, 47 women had jumped to their deaths, many of them landing with such force that their bodies splattered, drenching the firemen with blood. In all, 146 workers, most of them young immigrant girls and women, died.

A Committee of Safety of the City of New York was created, and Miss Perkins was appointed its executive secretary. In that capacity she was the committee's representative to the state's Factory Investigation Commission, which had among its members assemblyman Alfred E. Smith. For the previous two years, Miss Perkins, as secretary of the New York City Consumer's League, had been that organization's legislative liaison—lobbyist—at the capital in Albany.

Al Smith was derided by some as just another Irish pol—a product of the corrupt Tammany Hall but was admired by those who knew him, enemy and friend alike, as a shrewd, intelligent, well-informed and honest public servant. Smith coached Frances Perkins on the ways, means, pitfalls, and procedures of lobbying legislation. (And, good pol that he was, he checked to see if she were a registered Democrat and upbraided her when he found she was not.) The product of the Factory Investigation Commission was a model for modern state regulation of industrial working conditions.

In 1913, Perkins married Paul Caldwell Wilson, an expert on municipal administration. The marriage produced a daughter and another child who died in infancy. In 1918, Paul Wilson suffered a mental breakdown and was to spend the rest of his life in and out of mental institutions. Frances' life as a homemaker ended for all practical purposes, and she was forced to support herself and her surviving child. When offered by then-Governor Al Smith, she was delighted to accept the position as an industrial commissioner and a governing member of the state Labor Department. When Franklin Roosevelt succeeded Smith as governor of New York in 1928, he appointed Perkins

Industrial Commissioner of the state, with the responsibility of administering its labor department.

Miss? Mrs? Secretary? Madame? Madame Secretary? Ah!

If the first months of the Roosevelt administration were to become known for their inventive derring-do, the tip-off came the day the appointment of Frances Perkins as Secretary of Labor was announced. A woman in a presidential cabinet was spectacular enough—but in the Labor Department? The Department had been carved out of the old Department of Commerce and Labor of a few years before and was the bailiwick of the labor bosses—the cigar-smoking, tobacco-chewing, spittoon-filling macho-men, the representatives of construction workers and dock-wallopers. The labor unions were aghast and angry at her appointment. They had not been consulted, and those who knew her to be an advocate of a minimum wage opposed her on the grounds that the minimum to a social worker such as she was maximum to the corporate bosses.

Yet Frances Perkins came not without credentials in labor-management matters. One example was her great skill in settling a strike of copper workers in Rome, New York, which had not only shut down the city, but also threatened serious violence. She was also a seasoned political operator and a fixture at Democratic conventions. She had many friends and supporters nationwide from her work with the great women social reformers of her day, and she had been an enthusiastic campaigner for Al Smith in his 1928 presidential bid. Despite her work for the elevation of working women and her considerable contribution to the effort to gain women the right to vote, one significant sign of her independence was her insistence on retaining her maiden name after her marriage. Yet she was not a radical, but rather a progenitor of the coming political and social emancipation of American women. Demurely attired in her trademark simple black dress, white bow, and small tricon hat, she proceeded cautiously in the man's world of Washington power, determined to be taken seriously. To the not infrequent slights she had to endure in the social world of the capital, Frances Perkins invariably reacted with equanimity. When reporters asked how the new secretary should be addressed (surely not as "Mr. Secretary") the Speaker-elect of the House,

Henry T. Rainey, after a long-winded explanation of the origins and definitions of such public address, decreed she should be "Madame Secretary." In later years, opposition newspapers would on occasion drop the "Secretary." As time went on and labor leaders and business executives became accustomed to the idea of having a woman in charge of the government department so intimately interested in their affairs, Secretary Perkins would be judged on her performance and not her gender. But not always, and not by everyone.

In her relations with her several constituencies—organized labor, Congress, the press and the president, Secretary Perkins's record was ambiguous. Although they reached a level of cooperation and civility, labor leaders continued to believe that advancement in wages and working conditions could best be obtained through unions. Government programs to achieve those ends, as advocated by Perkins, weakened their organizations. The attitude of Congress toward Madame Secretary very much reflected the attitudes of individual congressmen and senators toward a woman in a man's job. The criticism ranged from syrupy patronizing to outright hostility. As time went on, however, she gained from many respect and admiration. But what counted, however, was a constituency of one—the president of the United States, whose approval was more important then all others combined. With Roosevelt, Frances Perkins had a standing of singular note.

The relationship of Frances Coralie Perkins and Franklin Delano Roosevelt, between the elected official and the appointed bureaucrat, began when Roosevelt was elected governor of New York in 1928 and endured until his death in 1945. The very nature of Perkins's appointment as the highest ranking woman in his administration, as the first female secretary of a department in a presidential cabinet, made that relationship unique. But it went far beyond its uniqueness to a genuine friendship and confidence on Roosevelt's part. Roosevelt brought Frances Perkins with him from Albany; he knew her, trusted her, and listened to her, and allowed her unfettered access. To the extent that complex man confided with any degree of sincerity in anyone, he did so to Frances Perkins. Her relationship with Eleanor Roosevelt was less than ideal, however. Frances always felt that Eleanor resented the opportunities Frances had had as a young woman to obtain a college degree and work on her own at what she wanted to do. That Perkins had more direct influence on the policies and accomplishments of the Roosevelt administrations than did the president's wife was apparent to both of them.

There is no doubt that Secretary Perkins's role in several of the Roosevelt era's social legislation, particularly the Social Security Act of 1935, and the Fair Labor Standards Act of 1935 and the Fair Labor Standards Act of 1938, was critical. Even-handed and a stickler for fairness, she opposed, without success, the National Labor Relations Act (1935), sponsored by her old friend from New York, Senator Robert F. Wagner, on the grounds that it too heavily favored the interests of labor against employers.

Personally devout, Frances Perkins became, after a brief flirtation with Catholicism, a convert to the Episcopal Church, the lesser of two evils in the eyes of her Protestant parents. On occasion Frances would retire to a convent for prayer and reflection. She believed that people with a religious motivation were better at dispensing charity to the needy than government officials: the former were more accepting of the admixture of both good and bad in all people. She resigned as Secretary of Labor on July 1, 1945, less than two months after her friend Franklin had died, to make way for President Truman's choice of her successor. Frances Perkins served as Secretary of Labor for 12 years, longer than any other cabinet appointee in the nation's history except Harold L. Ickes, Secretary of the Interior, who had been appointed at the same time as she had been and who stayed on until 1946. Madame Secretary passed her years of retirement from public life in writing a well-received book about her former boss, *The Roosevelt I Knew*, serving on the Civil Service Commission, and teaching at Cornell's School of Industrial and Labor Relations. She died in New York City on May 14, 1965, at age 85.

Certainly Not One of Us

It was a path taken so often by other Massachusetts men that its journey was, by the time he took it, routine, even mundane: preliminary education in a good grammar school, in this case the Boston Latin School; Harvard; his father's banking business; party politics; a government job or two—all climaxed by a prestigious diplomatic appointment. This case, however, was different, for the traveler was not the son of an eminent Brahmin family, he could trace his American ancestry back only two generations. He was not a Congregationalist or a Unitarian, or a Republican or even a Yankee Democrat, but an Irish-Catholic son of a ward boss, and tavern keeper from East Boston.

Joseph Patrick Kennedy was born in Boston on September 6, 1888, and died at Hyannis on Cape Cod on November 18, 1969, having been a witness to and often a participant in many of the most tumultuous events of the twentieth century. His father, Patrick Joseph Kennedy, who served in the Massachusetts House and Senate, was one of the fractured, feuding, clannish Irish political sachems of Boston who dominated and roiled the city's politics in the early years of the century. Upon his graduation from Harvard in 1912, young Joe, who was athletic, energetic and ambitious, got a job as a state bank examiner, with the help, one can safely assume, of his father's political connections. Two years later Joe assumed the presidency of the Columbia Trust Company, a bank founded by his father and others as a depository for, and lender to, the immigrant population of the city. In the same year that Kennedy started his career in finance and business, which would bring him wealth and display both his great energy and acumen, he married Rose Fitzgerald, who was the daughter of another of Boston's Irish-American politicians, the sometime mayor and congressman, John F. ("Honey Fitz") Fitzgerald. It was a union that was to produce nine children.

Joe Kennedy cultivated and was accepted by many of Boston's Brahmin business community but not by its social elite. It was easier for them, it seemed, to deal with the likes of a James Michael Curley. The Brahmins could deride Curley as a demagogue who found attacking their bastions of social elitism more politically profitable than joining them. Joe Kennedy, on the other hand, was a Celtic graduate of their college, with a newly acquired fortune unpurified by the passage of time. He wished to sit among them, saloon keeper's son that he was. In 1924, Joseph Kennedy moved his wife and to-then-seven children from Brahmin Boston to New York. And just to show them, he did it with a stylish finger up, in a private railway car brought to a siding near his Brookline home.

During World War I, the hard-working (the maritime unions said "ruthless") Joe Kennedy was called on to help manage Bethlehem Steel's huge shipyard at Quincy, a job in which he excelled and during which he made his first contact with the then-Assistant Secretary of the Navy, Franklin Delano Roosevelt. By the early 1930s Kennedy was many times a millionaire. His fortune enabled him both to provide for the financial security of his large family and to free him to do what he always had a passion to do—be a mover in the political world.

London Bridges Falling Down, Falling Down, Falling Down

It was often difficult to discern the reasoning behind Franklin Roosevelt's actions, and some who had wondered about his appointment of Joe Kennedy to oversee the reform of a stock market in which he had thrived as the first chairman of the Securities and Exchange Commission, shook their heads again when he appointed the brash, outspoken, personally ambitious Boston Irish-American to represent the United States as Ambassador to the Court of Saint James in London. There had been some dissatisfaction with the Anglophobia of the former ambassador, something Kennedy could not be accused of. He was, when he wanted to be, a most charming man with a large and lively family, and he had the financial wherewithal to cover the substantial expenses of conducting the office in the style both he and the English would wish. Also, there was the theory that Roosevelt, forever looking over his political shoulder, thought Joe had presidential ambitions of his own and was best out of the country.

The new American ambassador arrived in an England still suffering from the loss of a generation of its sons in a war that had ended just two decades before. He arrived in Europe as the dark clouds of the German Chancellor, Adolph Hitler's Third Reich were thickening. There were those in high places in England who saw a growing cancer that must be exorcised even if it meant war. Others wished to address the growing German military might and territorial aggrandizement by accommodation. Joseph Kennedy chose to join the latter.

Kennedy, the conservative American businessman, was much attracted to Neville Chamberlain, the leader of the British Conservative Party, who himself had come from a successful business background. After the fall of France, with Germany having already conquered much of Western Europe, Kennedy convinced himself that England was doomed should Germany attack it. It was an opinion held by many others. Kennedy was concerned about the real possibility that the British fleet might fall into German hands. Kennedy's increasingly pessimistic, if mostly accurate, reports on the situation were a growing annoyance to those in the Roosevelt administration who were of a mind that the United States could not allow England to fall. More and more, the president and his State Department bypassed their ambassador in England and conducted relations with Great Britain through other avenues. For a man like Joseph P. Kennedy to be ignored by the president who had chosen him to serve was intolerable. Several times he signaled the president of his desire to resign and return to the United States. Diplomatically, the president demurred. The resignation of the ambassador at the time of England's deepest danger would seem an abandonment. Politically, the possibility of Kennedy's contesting Roosevelt's unprecedented try for a third term was real in the minds of the president and his advisers.

In the compilation and editing of her grandfather's papers, (*Hostage to Fortune*, published in 2001) Amanda Kennedy Smith lays out the process of Joseph P. Kennedy's resignation. On October 17, 1940, the president wrote the ambassador to tell him that he thought that he was aware of the ". . . increasingly severe strain you have been under during the past weeks and I think it altogether owing to you that you get a chance to get away and get some relief ." In his roundabout way of doing such things, FDR in the same letter told Kennedy that "no matter how proper and appropriate your statements might be, every effort will be made to misinterpret and distort what you say . . . and I am . . . asking you specifically not to make any statement to the press."

On November 6, Kennedy tendered his resignation, which was accepted by the president as of December 1. On December 1, Kennedy met with Roosevelt, and in a good summation of how he felt about the situation, Kennedy told the president that he believed that the prime minister who had followed the discredited Chamberlain, Winston Churchill, was "keeping the fight going only because he had no alternative as Churchill the fighter, whether there is hope in the future or not, but his real idea is that he'll get the U.S. in and then the U.S. will share the problem."

Joseph P. Kennedy's only other ventures directly into public service were his senatorial appointments as a member of the Hoover

Commission in 1953 and 1957. On December 19, 1961, he suffered a coronary thrombosis that left him an invalid. He died at Hyannis on November 18, 1969 at age 81. Few families in American history, the Adamses being the prime example, have given so many of their progeny to high public office; or in the case of Joseph Patrick Kennedy and his two sons, John and Robert, so tragically.

CHAPTER II

In and Out with Speaker Martin

ON SUNDAY, JUNE 25, 1950, SEOUL TIME, THE COMMUNIST-RULED North Korean Army moved south across the thirty-eighth parallel and invaded the territory of the Republic of South Korea. On the 27th, President Harry S. Truman, without consulting Congress, ordered U.S. forces to go the assistance of South Korea, calling the move a "police action." Truman recalled 70-year-old General Douglas MacArthur to active military service, and the conqueror and post-war ruler of Imperial Japan managed to run the North Koreans back to the 38th parallel. Truman allowed the general to continue pursuit of the Communist forces north to the Chinese border but, fearing that an escalation of the conflict could lead to World War III, forbade him to go further. The army of communist China, under no such restraint, crossed the border into North Korea and drove the United Nations' forces back toward the 38th. MacArthur became increasingly strident in his criticism of the president's decision not to allow the blockading of China's coastline and the bombing of its Manchurian bases. The general addressed a letter to that effect to the then-Republican minority leader in the House of Representatives, Joseph W. Martin of Massachusetts, who promptly made the letter public. In writing the letter to Martin, MacArthur had crossed the line, thereby poisoning the relationship between him, the acclaimed military hero, and his commander-in-chief, President Truman. Even so, when Harry Truman relieved MacArthur, Congressman Martin was appalled.

A leader in his party's isolationist wing prior to the United States' entry into World War II, Joseph Martin opposed Roosevelt's efforts to arm American merchant ships and his Lend-Lease program; and further urged the 1940 Republican candidate for president, Wendell L. Wilkie, whose campaign Martin was managing, to oppose a peacetime draft. After the war, Martin became a staunch opponent of Communist expansion. The true measure of Martin's contribution to American political history is found in his role as a leader in the great legislative battles waged in the middle years of the twentieth century. It was Martin, elected in 1947 as the first Republican Speaker of the House since 1931, to whom the task fell to try to legislatively reverse, or at least contain, the perceived excesses of the New Deal.

Joseph William Martin Jr. was born in North Attleboro, Massachusetts, on November 3, 1884, to Joseph Martin, a blacksmith, and his wife, Catherine Katon Martin. Young Joe worked at various jobs during his high school years; as a newsboy, and in one of the local jewelry factories as a night telephone operator. As captain of his high school baseball team, Martin showed enough talent to be offered an athletic scholarship to Dartmouth College. He turned it down in favor of the newspaper business as a printer's apprentice, copyboy and reporter at the *North Attleboro Evening Leader*. When the *Leader* failed, Martin found work as a reporter for the rival Sun and as a correspondent for both the *Boston Globe* and the *Providence Journal*. In 1908, he and a group of local investors purchased the North Attleboro *Evening Chronicle*, and Joe was installed as editor and publisher. By 1914, Martin was the sole owner of the *Chronicle*, and he continued on as its publisher until his death.

Martin's *Chronicle* and his later acquisition, the *Franklin Sentinel*, were but two of the large number of daily and weekly newspapers of the commonwealth that were at the time religiously dedicated to the promotion of the Republican Party. Martin went beyond politics in print and to politics in person. He was elected to the state House of Representatives (1911-1914), and the state Senate (1914-1916). While in the Senate he was secretary of the Joint Rules Committee under the chairmanship of Calvin Coolidge. Coolidge, who was older by 16 years, and Martin formed a life-long association both as friends and political allies. While Cal may have been a political loner, Joe was a joiner, a doer, a mover. He supported the regular Republican Taft over the Progressive Theodore Roosevelt in 1913. Martin managed the election in the state Legislature of John Weeks to the U.S. Senate in 1912, the last such campaign before a constitutional amendment mandated popular election of U.S. senators. Martin was a delegate to the Republican National Convention in 1916 and 1917 and a presidential elector in 1920. He also ran the Massachusetts legislative committee to elect Republicans and was executive secretary of the Massachusetts Republican Party in 1924. That year Martin was elected to Congress to fill the unexpired term of Congressman William Greene, a Democrat, who had died while in office. Congressman Martin was to serve in the House for 21 successive congressional terms over 42 years.

From 1931, when the Democrats wrested control of the House from the Republicans, until Martin's retirement in 1967, there would be only two times that a Republican was Speaker of the House: both times it was Joe Martin. Martin's rise to become one of the most influential legislators of his generation, both in the minority and majority, was rapid. In addition to his friendship with Coolidge, Martin also became a protégé of House Speaker Nicholas Longworth. In his first three terms in Congress, Martin served on two of the most prestigious House committees, Rules and Foreign Affairs. A protectionist in the New England tradition, he voted for the Smoot-Hawley tariff bill and opposed reciprocal trade agreements. During the 1932 presidential campaign, when it was an important issue to many voters, the teetotaler Martin urged Hoover to support repeal of Prohibition. While others attributed Hoover's defeat to the worsening economic conditions, Martin felt that "More than anything else, it was the wet issue that crushed the Republican Party."

Martin honed his legislative leadership skills in the bleak days of Republican banishment from power, during the seemingly endless Roosevelt years. As assistant leader of the Republican minority in the House and then as minority leader, Martin shrewdly maneuvered the battered regiment of his remaining troops away from the abyss of insignificance. Opposing many of the New Deal proposals he and his party thought anathema to the great principle of American individualism, he nevertheless supported the National Recovery Act, Social Security, and the federal guarantee of bank deposits. He helped write the Hatch Act, which prohibited federal employees from participating in political campaigns. Later explaining his opposition to proposals such as the Tennessee Valley Authority (TVA) and the Agricultural Adjustment Act, Martin said, "Many of the experiments of the New Deal seemed to us to undermine and destroy this society."

Like all the Speakers who had been trained in the way things were done in the Massachusetts General Court, Martin also had a trader's instinct. When the Democrat Speaker, Sam Rayburn, had difficulty bridging the gap between the liberal Northern congressmen and the conservative Southerners of his party on a piece of New Deal legislation, he could count on minority leader Martin to deliver the necessary number of progressive Republican votes to carry the day. A quid for which the quo would come was when Martin was nursing a Republican majority in the House which was split between those who would reverse as much of the New Deal as they could get away with and those who would accept what had been done and go from there.

In 1938, "working the streets" on a national basis, Martin, as head of the Republican congressional campaign committee, identified those national districts he thought were winnable, recruited attractive candidates, raised money, and saw the Republicans gain 75 seats in the House. In the congressional elections of 1946, with the war ended, Roosevelt dead, and a relatively unknown former senator from Missouri having succeeded him as president, the American electorate decided that almost two decades of Democratic Party dominance in Congress was enough. The Republicans were called in from the cold. After successful Republican candidates, the Grand Old Party controlled both branches, and Joe Martin was elected Speaker of the House.

Speaker Martin lost little time in rectifying what he considered Franklin Roosevelt and the Democrats' self-serving defiance of a sacred American tradition—that a president should serve only two terms. Under his tutelage, a bill was introduced and passed in the House legislation proposing the term-limiting 22nd Amendment to the Constitution, which was ultimately adopted in 1951. In the Republican tradition of tenacious attack on income tax rates, Martin produced (as HR 1) a cut of 30 percent in the bottom tax rates and 10 percent in the top. Truman, holding to progressive taxation, denounced the legislation as a boondoggle for the wealthy, and vetoed it. Martin managed to override the veto in the House. He was also able to override Truman's veto of the Taft-Hartley Act of 1947. Both were also overridden in the Senate.

In foreign affairs, Martin supported the Marshall Plan (although he backed his Appropriations Committee's reduction of funds by $1.5 billion) and the president's Greek-Turkish aid program. When the Rules Committee blocked consideration of legislation to allow the United States to participate in the World Health Organization, the Speaker forced it to the floor and saw that it passed. Martin was pleased with the performance of the Republican Congress and, as the 1948 national elections approached, was confident, like almost all Republicans, that after the votes were counted he would continue as Speaker. The country anticipated its first Republican president in 16 long years, Thomas E. Dewey. The pollsters, pundits and almost everyone else agreed that 1948 would be a Republican year of triumph. The party would be fully restored to congressional control and its candidate would be elected president. Everyone, it seemed, thought so except that accidental occupant of the White House, Harry Truman.

Truman had taken his plain-spoken, twangy midwestern act on the road, crisscrossing the country by rail, pouring contempt on the 80th ("Do-Nothing") Republican Congress. Martin was personally and politically offended by the attacks, but Dewey, the racket-busting state's attorney and sitting governor of New York, stayed above the nasty fray as a king waiting to be properly crowned. Much to the dismay of newspapers put to bed with headlines announcing his victory and the nationally respected radio commentators who steadfastly refused to believe the election returns, Dewey lost. Truman pulled a Democrat majority into Congress with him. Joe Martin was no longer Speaker, and he blamed the demure Dewey for his party and his Speakership's derailment.

Joe Martin with his unruly shock of black hair and an oversized gavel became a familiar figure to those Americans watching the televising of the Republican National Convention in the late 1940s and early 1950s. He supported Ohio Senator Robert Taft, son of William Howard Taft, against General Dwight Eisenhower at the 1953 convention, but Eisenhower prevailed and his margin of victory over the Democratic nominee, Governor Adlai E. Stevenson of Illinois, helped return the Republicans to control of the House and Martin to the Speakership. Not for long, though. In the 1954 "off year" congressional elections the Democrats prevailed and Joe Martin became the last Republican Speaker of the House until the election of Newt Gingrich 40 years later.

After the Democratic sweep in the 1958 congressional elections, Martin was ousted from his position as minority leader by his long-time assistant, Charles Halleck of Indiana, who in turn was defeated for the post six years later by Martin, and replaced by a congressman from Michigan and future president, Gerald R. Ford. In 1966, the 82-year-old veteran of the House lost his bid for reelection to a 35-year-old, New York-born, member of the Massachusetts Governor's Council, Margaret Mary O'Shaughnessy Heckler. Joseph Martin died in Hollywood, Florida, on March 7, 1968 and is buried at Mount Hope Cemetery, North Attleboro, Massachusetts.

"Mossie"

In the rationale of the gambler, it follows that the higher the risk, the greater the payoff. In the presidential campaign of 1948, the long-odds bet would have the Democratic Party's ever-so-common Harry S. Truman, defeating the Republican Party's urbane Thomas E. Dewey. One Massachusetts politician who took the long odds and bet his political future (and a good sum of his own money, the rumor went) on Harry Truman was Maurice J. Tobin.

"Mossie" Tobin was born on May 22, 1901, in the Mission Hill section of the Roxbury neighborhood of Boston, as Irish-Catholic and hardscrabble a place as could be found outside of Dublin, Ireland. Both Maurice's parents were born in the "old country," and his father worked as a carpenter. In that family in those days a penny was more than a penny, so Maurice and his brother got up long before the sun rose to hop on the trolley into town to old "Newspaper Row" on Washington Street, where they picked up bundles of daily newspapers to hawk back at Roxbury Crossing. On a good day, counting morning and evening editions, the boys would sell up to 500 copies.

Tall, strikingly handsome and ambitious, young Tobin took the route ever more available to Irish-American boys of Boston in the early years of the 20th century: in 1926 he ran successfully for the Massachusetts Legislature. He was 27 in 1928, when Tobin gave up what was a sure seat in the House, to run for Congress against the Republican incumbent, George Holden Tinkham. Tinkham, one of the notable Yankee "characters" of his day, was a red-bearded lion hunter who often went on safari, even during election time. Tinkham's congressional district had been gerrymandered by the Republican-controlled Legislature in such a way as to preclude a Democratic victory no matter how heavy that party's vote. The Democratic candidate was further handicapped by the fact that Tinkham's secretary assiduously saw to the needs of Tinkham's Irish constituents. The congressman was known for his generosity, having on occasion paid the outstanding campaign debts of the latest Irish-American he had defeated. Tobin lost his bid for Congress, but he carried the Democratic wards handily enough to widen his political base beyond Mission Hill.

In office or out, or for that matter, in jail or out, candidate or commentator, James Michael Curley was always a player in the combat that bloodied the political field of the Boston of that era. Both Tobin and Curley had been Al Smith delegates to the national Democratic convention in 1928, and both worked in that same capacity for Franklin Roosevelt's nomination four years later. Curley and Tobin were close enough for Curley to lend his aid in the 1931 Boston school committee race, contributing to Tobin's topping the field of 12 candidates. Tobin worked hard in 1934 to help Curley accomplish a historically infrequent feat: a mayor of Boston being elected governor of Massachusetts.

No matter how long-standing or hide-bound political loyalty to others may be, it is to one's own ambition all others must give way. Curley, who once had introduced Tobin as "perhaps the next mayor of Boston," now perceived the young up-and-comer as a threat and attempted to buy him off with a gubernatorial appointment and hints that Curley could secure a federal sinecure for him. When neither worked, Curley denied Maurice's brother, James, the appointment as clerk of the Roxbury court, a slot the Tobins thought they had earned.

Governor Curley, while still in office, announced he would once again be a candidate for mayor in the 1937 election. Tobin announced his own candidacy shortly thereafter—on St. Patrick's Day. It was a vicious battle, with tactics of dubious propriety on both sides. When the ballots were counted, Tobin, backed by a coalition of supporters of "Honey" Fitz, New Deal Democrats, and eminent Yankees of the caliber of Henry L. Shattuck and Henry Parkman Jr., had prevailed.

Before his second term as mayor ran out in 1945, Tobin was elected governor. As mayor and governor, Tobin was an eloquent advocate of his party's liberal social doctrine. He was fiscally conservative. During his terms as mayor, Tobin reduced the city's debt by $5 million, and while governor he proposed legislation to make discrimination in hiring illegal, to impose rent control, and to increase unemployment benefits.

Much to the surprise of almost everyone except Truman and his ardent supporters such as Tobin, it was Harry and not Thomas who took the oath of office as president of the United States in January 1949. When Lewis B. Schwellenback, the successor to Frances Perkins as Secretary of Labor, resigned prior to the 1948 election, President Truman appointed Tobin as interim secretary. Tobin had lost his bid for reelection as governor to his Republican lieutenant governor, Robert Bradford.

Tobin's impact on the Labor Department did not begin to be felt until he was appointed to a full term in January 1949. After the departure of Frances Perkins and due to the exigencies of conducting a war, the Department had lost much of its power and influence, and Tobin set about to gain it back. The National Labor Relations Board and the Mediation Service, for example, were not then under the secretary's jurisdiction.

In 1949, the new secretary persuaded the president to transfer the U.S. Employment Service and the Unemployment Insurance Service to his department. A year later, both the Bureau of Employees' Compensation and the Compensation Appeals Board were added. In 1950, the secretary saw to the establishment of a Federal Safety Council in the Bureau of Labor Standards.

A staunch friend of the working man, Tobin, both in his campaigning for Truman and as Secretary of Labor, ardently espoused the cause of labor. While secretary he was active in the unsuccessful attempt to repeal the Taft-Hartley Act. The Act had been passed over Truman's veto, and had changed many of the provisions of the Wagner Act, which the Republican Congress considered blatantly pro-labor.

Tobin was more successful in backing amendments to the Fair Labor Standards Act, which raised the minimum wage to 75 cents an hour. During the Korean conflict, Tobin who had been responsible for federal civilian manpower, created a labor-management committee and instituted the Defense Manpower administration.

Maurice J. Tobin died at his home in Scituate, Massachusetts, on July 19, 1953, at the age of 52, after returning from playing a round of golf. One of the few public officials to have served in high city, state and federal office, he was, like Patrick A. Collins before him, a harbinger of the future influence of Massachusetts Irish-American politicians in the federal government.

The Commonwealth's Presence

When the United States evacuation ship arrived in the United States from Japan on August 25, 1942, returning Ambassador Joseph Grew was not the only Massachusetts diplomat aboard. There were two others: a career diplomat, Charles Eustis Bohlen, and the first secretary of the American embassy in Tokyo, Edward Savage Crocker.

Edward Crocker was born in Fitchburg, Massachusetts on December 20, 1895, served in the U.S. Navy in World War I, received his A.B. from Princeton University in 1918 and studied law at Columbia University in 1921 and 1922. His diplomatic career began with his appointment as assistant secretary of the American delegation to the Conference of Central American Affairs in Washington (1922-1923). Crocker served in various positions of diplomatic importance in San Salvador, Warsaw, Rome, Budapest and Stockholm, and was first secretary in the American embassy in Tokyo at the outbreak of the war. After his release from a Japanese prison and return to the United States, Crocker was appointed first secretary at the embassy in Lisbon, then counselor at Warsaw, Poland, where he became the ad interim charge d'affaires. The climax of Edward Crocker's long career in the foreign service came with his appointment by President Truman as the ambassador to Iraq in 1948, a post he served in until 1952. Crocker later was a consultant to the faculties of both the Air War College (1952-1953) and the Naval War College (1953-1955). He died in Kittery, Maine, where he made his home, on April 7, 1968, at the age of 73.

CHAPTER III

Always Certain, Never Sure:
Massachusetts Men in Berlin

IT WAS NOT PEACE, AT LEAST NOT IN THE SENSE OF INTERNATIONAL tranquility, that followed the Allied victory over the Axis in World War II. For decades to come, the nations espousing democracy and capitalism would stand in opposition to those who believed the world's future lay in the collectivism of communist dictatorship. The struggle would be waged by principal and surrogate, in words and in wars, in many parts of the world. If one were to choose the place that was both the symbol and substance of what was to be known, not always accurately, as the "Cold War" it would be post-war Berlin. There it was that the former allies in the West—the United States, Great Britain and France—and in the East—the Soviet Union—faced each other in physical proximity, on territory that each had occupied by the most ancient and enforceable of rights—that of conquest.

The Ideal Diplomat: Charles E. Bohlen

Charles Bohlen, nicknamed "Chip," which was shortened from "Chipper" to denote his bubbling personality, was born in Clayton, New York, on August 30, 1904, while his family was vacationing. Charles's father was by profession a banker, by avocation a sportsman. His mother, Celestine Eustis Bohlen, had been her widowed father James Eustis's hostess in Paris while he served as Grover Cleveland's ambassador to France. When Charles was eight, his mother took him on the first of several trips to Europe. By the time he reached maturity, Charles had visited almost every country on the Continent, developing a great admiration for European culture, particularly that of France. A family with such a sophisticated son was an easy fit into Massachusetts society when the Bohlens moved to Ipswich, in 1916.

St. Paul's School prepared Bohlen to follow his father's academic footsteps to Harvard. At St. Paul's it was the athletic field and at Harvard the athletic field and the clubs (Hasty Pudding, Porcellian), not academics, that attracted the energies of the young Bohlen. Graduating in the class of 1927 with a degree in European history, he was an undistinguished scholar and was undecided as to what to do next. Bohlen concluded that the best way to find out what he really wanted out of life was to sign on a tramp steamer as an apprentice seaman, and sail around the world. He landed back in Boston after several months, ashore but still adrift as to his future.

One of his cousins introduced Bohlen to William R. Castle, at the time assistant secretary of state for European affairs. From that acquaintanceship began a distinguished 40-year diplomatic career. In 1960, as that career was coming to an end, a poll was taken among senior American diplomats to name the person who came closest to their conception of the "ideal diplomat." The accolade went to Charles Bohlen.

The leaders of the executive branch, elected for a limited term certain and faced with the immediacy of domestic problems, must nevertheless recognize the necessity of stability and continuity in its relations with foreign nations. Administrations change and with the changes come different nuances, or even direction, as to what the nation's foreign policy should be. In the formulation of policy, the professional career diplomat has the responsibility of advice and consent—to make available to the policymaker the facts of the situation, to learn from his expertise, to advise as to the hypothetical results of any given action, and, once policy is made, to carry it out. A lovely canon, subject as all such are, to the vagaries of individual prejudice and pride. Valuable indeed then is the man who understands that dichotomy.

Charles E. Bohlen was a generalist in the area of Russian affairs and spoke the language fluently. From the time he was introduced into the inner circles of the White House by President Roosevelt's intimate adviser, Harry Hopkins, Bohlen sat at the elbow of succeeding administrations while they formed their half of United States-Soviet relations. A "company man," Bohlen was cautious perhaps to the extent of forgoing opportunities to fashion policy more directly. He believed that the interests of the ruling Soviet Communist Party and that of Mother Russia, no matter how much they appeared to be one entity, were not always so, and that ultimately the safety of the state would prevail over the advancement of party ideology. Though pessimistic about its certainty, Bohlen believed that accommodation between the East and West was in many cases possible as long as one remained realistic to the ultimate objective of the Soviet Union—the destruction of democratic capitalism and its replacement with dictatorial communism. It was a diplomatic nuance rendered as "appeasement" by many Americans in the heyday of Senator Joseph McCarthy's hunt to rid the country of all who were advocates, real or imagined, of such a measured and ultimately successful policy, of which its first concrete test would come in Berlin, Germany.

The Involved Chemist: James Bryant Conant

James Bryant Conant was born on March 26, 1893, in the town of Dorchester (annexed to Boston in 1869) to James and Jennet Orr Bryant Conant. While his father could trace his family back to the arrival of Roger Conant at Salem from Devonshire, England, in 1623, he had neither the wealth nor social standing of other Puritan descendants. Rather, Conant made an honorable living as a photoengraver. Young James was sent for his college preparation to the private Roxbury Latin School (founded in 1645), where he came under the tutelage of Newton Henry Black, his chemistry instructor. Black's efforts and Conant's dedication resulted in Conant being accepted, with permission to forgo first-year chemistry, to Harvard College, where he graduated with high honors in 1913. Conant received his Ph.D. at Harvard three years later, and would go on to receive more than 30 honorary degrees from universities around the world. In 1933, by then the recipient of numerous prestigious awards for research in his field, Dr. Conant was elected, at age 40, as one of the youngest presidents of Harvard University.

When World War II broke out in Europe, Conant, who had held the rank of major in the Chemical Warfare Service in World War I, was, to the chagrin of some of his Harvard contemporaries, an outspoken interventionist. He advocated all-out aid to England and military conscription in America. Before America entered the war, Conant, as chairman of the office of the Scientific Research and Development Agency, was charged with organizing chemists into research groups to help the Army and Navy. In that capacity he established a previously unknown relationship between universities and private laboratories and the federal government. It was on Conant's recommendation that President Roosevelt made his decision to proceed with the secret construction of a uranium pile, which would eventually lead to the creation of the atomic bomb. In 1953, President Eisenhower appointed Conant American High Commissioner to post-war Germany.

A Natural Born American: Christian Archibald Herter

Christian Archibald Herter was born in Paris, on March 28, 1895, the son of expatriate American artists, Albert and Adele Herter. Herter's father earned considerable renown as a painter of murals in public buildings in both Europe and America, and his mother was an accomplished portrait painter. Initially educated at the Alsacienne in Paris, "Chris" Herter's American education began at the Browning School in New York City, from which he graduated at such a young age—15— that his entrance into Harvard was delayed a year. Herter majored in fine arts at Harvard, and graduated cum laude in 1915. The 20-year-old Herter matriculated to the School of Fine and Applied Arts in New York with the intention of studying architecture and interior decorating, intentions perhaps having more to do with family loyalty than with personal preference, as evidenced by abandonment a year later. At a Harvard class reunion, Herter met Lithgow Osborne, who proceeded to enthrall Herter with exciting accounts of Osborne's work as a diplomatic attaché in the American embassy in Berlin. When Herter expressed the wish that he could have such an opportunity, in an exchange of cables (a tribute to the efficacy of Harvard graduates' network) and in two weeks' time found Christian Herter with a diplomatic appointment to the United States embassy in Berlin.

Whatever adventures Osborne related to Herter to induce him to make such an abrupt and dramatic change in his career choice paled against the reality of foreign service at that place at that time. Still a fresh young face in Berlin, Herter was sent in December to Brussels to join the Spanish and Dutch members of the Commission for Belgian Relief. For six week during the absence of the U.S. minister there, the inexperienced 22-year-old Herter acted in his place. When the United States broke off diplomatic relations with Germany the following February, Herter tried to catch a train from Mainz to neutral Switzerland, was arrested as a spy and held overnight. His return to America was a time of great joy for him—he married Mary Caroline Pratt, whose grandfather had founded the Pratt Institute. Substantially underweight, and plagued by hip trouble, which was attributed to too-rapid growth, Herter tried to join the Army, but was unsuccessful. In the fall of 1918, he accepted an invitation from Secretary of State Robert Lansing to join Joseph Grew as assistant commissioner and secretary of the American-German Prisoner-of-War Conference. Herter's service with Herbert Hoover while the latter supervised the American Relief Association led to Herter's appointment as Assistant Secretary of Commerce when Hoover became Secretary during the Coolidge administration.

Herter left public service in 1924, having been advised by Hoover that his future would best be served in private enterprise. But his foray into the world of private enterprise was short, however; he became co-editor of the *Independent*, a magazine that devoted itself to "politics, economics, history, literature and the arts," until it was sold in 1929. After lecturing on international relations at his alma mater for a year, Herter commenced what was to become a most rewarding public career, launched from the never-permanently-anchored pad of Massachusetts politics.

Governor Herter

Chris Herter was elected to the state House of Representatives in 1930 and served there until 1942, the last four years as Speaker. In 1952 he was elected governor of the Commonwealth. Herter had been an early supporter of General Eisenhower for the Republican party's presidential nomination in 1952. When some Republicans, upset by reports that the vice presidential nominee, Richard Nixon, had improperly accumulated a political "slush fund," they sought to replace him on the ticket with Herter. But Herter refused and reiterated his support for the ticket as it stood. After his election as governor and Eisenhower's as president, John Foster Dulles, the president-elect's secretary of state, sent a note congratulating Herter and at the same time informing him that he, Dulles, was aware of Herter's interest in the position of Under Secretary of State but that appointment was not available at the time. In 1956, however, after the governor had declined to run for a third term, the-then-under secretary, Herbert Hoover Jr. resigned. With the help of an old friend of Herter's, Sherman Adams, the president's chief of staff, and with the endorsement of Vice President Nixon, who owed him a favor, Herter was appointed Under Secretary of State.

In 1959, Secretary of State Dulles, with whom Herter was never able to forge a close relationship, fell ill with cancer and was forced to retire. Herter had been acting secretary for over two months and it seemed a certainty that he would be elevated to succeed Dulles. When asked, President Eisenhower hesitated, with the observation that others besides Herter were being considered for the position. Herter got angry when Eisenhower asked him to undergo a physical examination, evidently to ascertain the severity of the osteoarthritis that on occasion forced Herter to walk with two canes. Despite all, that on April 22, 1959, Christian Archibald Herter replaced John Foster Dulles as secretary of state.

The City on the Spree: Counselor Bohlen

Although the parts they played—Mr. Bohlen as the diplomat, Professor Conant as the High Commissioner and Governor Herter as the secretary of state—were different, the goal they sought was the same: to keep banking the embers of Berlin lest they burst into a conflagration of catastrophic proportions.

In December of 1947, a meeting of the Council of the World War II Allies—the United States, Great Britain, France and the Soviet Union, broke up in disagreement over the future of a divided Germany. In February, despairing of agreement, the Western powers instituted plans for a West German state, and currency reforms in their respective zones. The Soviet's response was to throw up a blockade of all traffic in the occupied zones of Berlin, which were 110 miles inside the Russian zone. General Lucius D.Clay, the American military commander in Germany, proposed an airlift to supply the now isolated city, and the marshaling of an armed convoy to break the blockade. Bohlen, who at the time held the rank of counselor in the State Department, urged that America stand firm, but he opposed military action. Adding to the dilemma was the question of whether the Western allies would present a united front should the United States opt for a military response that might lead to war.

Bohlen left for London to confer with allied leaders to coordinate a response. Convinced that any surrender to Soviet pressure would be tantamount to admitting that the Western powers occupied Berlin only by Russian sufferance, he nevertheless kept his acutely tuned ear to the possibility of a diplomatic solution. By the fall of 1948, with Berlin sustained by massive airlifts, he believed he might have detected a shift in Soviet policy. Stalin, the Russian Premier, had failed in a recent speech to refer to the currency issue, which he had previously used as a rationale for the blockade. Bohlen brought this to the attention of Secretary of State Dean Acheson, who then instructed the American ambassador to the Soviet Union, Philip Jessup, to approach the Russian ambassador to the United States, Yakov Malik on an informal basis. Malik's response was that he had nothing to report on the matter, but a month later told Jessup that his information on Stalin's remark was not in error. Bohlen had learned over the years that when the Russians were serious about defusing a situation such as that consuming Berlin, they preferred quiet diplomacy. He followed up the apparent opening by instigating intensive secret discussions. The lifting of the blockade depended on the answer the Western allies could give to the Russians' request that the establishment of a West German government be delayed. Bohlen responded that while the West could not halt its plans for such a government, they might be delayed until a meeting of the Council of Foreign Ministers could be convened. The blockade was lifted on May 12, 1949.

Commissioner Conant

The newly appointed American High Commissioner, James Bryant Conant, arrived in Bonn, Germany, on February 11, 1953. The political atmosphere he was to encounter seemed as barren as the naked trees he passed on his way from the railroad station to the West. The signing the previous May of preliminary treaties between the Western Powers and the by-then-established Federal Republic of Germany, which allowed for the rearming of a sovereign Germany, had infuriated the Russians. To make matters even more dangerous, hundreds—and on some days more than a thousand asylum seekers—were daily fleeing East Germany for the American sector. The Russian response was to cut off trolley lines and reduce the number of access points on the autobahn. Eventually, they erected the infamous Berlin Wall.

Dr. Conant's responsibilities as High Commissioner, and later as ambassador to Germany, were both diplomatic and political. He had to deal with the French opposition to German rearmament, and with the always perplexing and rarely consistent Soviets, while staying in the good graces of Konrad Adenauer, the new German state's strong-willed first chancellor. And also, as it turned out, in the good graces of his equally strong—willed boss, secretary of state, John Foster Dulles. No one could have been more enthusiastic about a presidential appointment than Conant was about his new assignment, a job he might have had much earlier had he wanted it. Conant recorded in his diary his reaction when he was informed that President Eisenhower wished to send him to Berlin: "The Day! Oh, Boy!" If he had known then what he would be facing, the more appropriate reaction might have been "Oh, my God!"

Adenauer, Dulles and Conant

On June 17, 1953, a series of uprisings by workers broke out in East Germany. The Russian Army eventually responded to the sticks and stones with guns and tanks, killing many rioters. At the time it was the official policy of Washington to encourage such attempts by the workers to throw off the yoke of Communist rule. It was a policy more in theory than in reality, for neither the president, nor his secretary of state, nor his high commissioner seemed to have any concrete plan to back up the insurrection they were encouraging. Conant, who was in Washington at the time of the troubles, did the best he could to respond to heavy criticism over the failure of America to come to the aid of the beleaguered workers. He went to Europe and drove to the Eastern sector of Berlin in his official limousine with the American flags flapping. In reaction to the resulting criticism in the American press, Conant stated that he could do nothing in view of the division among the Western allies over the matter.

The fact was that there existed in the highest American political and diplomatic circles a division between those who wished to keep things on the boil in Europe—those who were holding out hope that such continued pressure would cause a Soviet withdrawal—and those, including the British and French, to whom such a policy was not only proof of the United States' implacable enmity toward the Soviet Union, but a blueprint for war. The clash of two powerful egos, of Dulles and Adenauer, would put Conant in a difficult position and lead to his leaving his post before he had intended.

In September, in reaction to a proposal to begin a campaign of strident psychological warfare against the East put forth by those advocating continued agitation, a group of senior American diplomats stationed in Europe issued a top-secret memo denouncing the plan. Among the signatories was James Conant. The following January, a conference of the four foreign ministers of the wartime alliance was held in Berlin. Commissioner Conant, as his position required, was much involved in the protocols and arrangements. He also realized that when it came to discussions between Secretary Dulles and his Russian counterpart, that he, Conant, was being left out, indicating Secretary Dulles's lack of confidence in him.

In July 1956, using the rationale that Adenauer had lost confidence in Conant (what Adenauer wanted was someone with Dulles's ear, which Conant did not have), Dulles suggested to Eisenhower that Conant be reassigned as ambassador to Rome. Abandoning that plan a week later, Dulles persuaded the president to offer Conant the same assignment in India. When informed of his new assignment, Conant asked time to think it over, then declined, and was instructed to consider it further. After much thought, Conant refused to go to India.

When the customary leak of the Dulles-Conant discussions reached the press and Conant was asked about them, his reply was that he intended to remain in his post through the remainder of Eisenhower's term and then submit his resignation. For whatever reason, the State

Department considered the statement a de facto resignation. On January 10, 1957, Conant received a dispatch accepting it.

Mr. Herter

On the 10th of November, 1958, Russian Premier Nikita Khrushchev announced that the time had come for the Western Allies to leave Berlin. He gave them six months to do so, after which time he would turn over control of the city to the German Democratic Republic (GDR), the Communist government of East Germany. Later elaborating, the premier said that the Western Allies had violated the Potsdam agreements, rendering their rights as occupying powers in Berlin null and void, that Berlin would become a free city to choose its own way of life. Berlin's location ensured that the city would become part of the GDR and the reunification of Germany would come about by the federalization of the two existing Germanys as represented by the Federal Republic of Germany (FRG) and the GDR. If Khruschev's plan transpired, the expanded influence of the Soviet Union would put into danger the West's positions in all of Europe. The Western powers refused the bait, insisting on both their historical and legal right to be in Berlin, but took note of Khrushchev's offer to negotiate on the status of a demilitarized Berlin. The West might be amenable as long as the talks included all aspects of the German question and the Western powers were not under the threat of an ultimatum. The Russians responded by insisting they had issued no ultimatum, but restated that if the Allies did not remove their occupying forces from Berlin by May 27 but persisted in keeping them there "by force if necessary," the Allies would be threatening a "big war." Once again, as it had been during the blockade a decade earlier, Berlin was the tinderbox where a conflagration of another potentially more horrific world war might ignite. The Russians proposed a meeting of the 22 countries that constituted the allied powers in WW II. The Western Allies countered with the proposal for a meeting of the foreign ministers of the United States, Great Britain, France and Russia, with representatives of both Germanys in attendance as "advisers."

The meeting of the foreign ministers began in Geneva on May 11, and it took two weeks to agree to just who would sit where at what shaped table. What the Russians really wanted, as did Great Britain, was a summit meeting of the four heads of government. President Eisenhower would only consider one if the ministers meeting failed. Word then leaked out of a planned visit by Khrushchev to the United States, followed by one to Russia by President Eisenhower. That news took the steam, if indeed there was any, out of the meeting which broke up on August 1st.

Nikita Khrushchev enjoyed a flamboyant tour of the United States, and furthered his cause for a summit meeting by letting the president know that agreement to such a conference would be justification for his removing the time limit on the Berlin ultimatum. The Western powers agreed to hold such a meeting on May 5, 1960. On May 2nd, while attending a NATO ministerial meeting in Istanbul, the secretary of state was handed a note saying that the CIA was reporting a United States U-2 reconnaissance plane down in Russian territory. There followed a series of missteps by the American government, seemingly incapable of coming up with a unified and plausible story.

On May 3, the U.S. Air Force issued a statement saying that a NASA U-2 weather research plane had apparently gone down in the Lake Van area of Turkey. On May 5, the U.S. ambassador to Russia, Llewellyn Thompson, who was in the dark about what was going on, was a guest at the convocation of the Supreme Soviet when he was startled to hear Khrushchev announce the shooting down of the plane and speculate as to whether it had been sent by the president or by the militarists in the Pentagon.

On the 6th, Herter arrived back in Washington, still not fully informed as to the circumstances of the now torrid international incident, but convinced that Khrushchev's accusations of the previous day required a structured American response. He convinced all parties that any further statements should emanate from the State Department, and that the president must not be involved. That day a statement prepared by the State Department and approved by the CIA, followed that of the Air Force: the pilot of an unarmed weather research plane had trouble with his oxygen supply causing unconsciousness and the plane had gone on automatic pilot, accidentally entering Soviet air space. Forty-five minutes later, NASA, as yet uninformed of the decision that only the State Department was to issue statements, issued one of its own; followed later in the day by one from the Department of Defense echoing the Air Force's statement of the 3rd.

Khrushchev continued to heap ridicule on the obviously confused Americans and threatened "serious consequences to those countries who make their territory available for the takeoffs" of such planes—an obvious reference to Turkey. Herter saw significance in the fact that the premier laid blame on the American military and left out the president in his condemnation. Eisenhower, supported by his press secretary James Hagerty, was inclined to take responsibility for the fiasco. Herter objected and things went back and forth. Khrushchev continued to taunt, and the downed pilot, Gary Powers, admitted that his mission was to spy. Eisenhower faced the unwelcome choice of either admitting the facts, or to the charge, of which he was very sensitive, that it was the CIA and the Pentagon and not the president who were in charge in Washington.

The incident came to a conclusion, quite unsatisfactorily at the previously scheduled summit meeting in Paris. Khrushchev set three conditions: condemnation of the flights, an end to them, and punishment for those involved. He followed that with a loud tirade against the American president. Eisenhower's response was to admit the flights were neither legal nor proper, and added that he was not going to be the one to raise his hand to a promise not to do what everyone else was doing. Khrushchev canceled Eisenhower's scheduled June visit to Russia and postponed participation of the Soviet Union in any summit for six to eight months. How Eisenhower, the great man and general who had led the allied forces to victory in World War II might have affected the Russian people if they had the opportunity to meet him, will never be known.

Christian Herter had conducted himself exceptionally well under the trying circumstances that were not of his own or his department's making. His defense of "coming clean" about the spy plane that otherwise "we would have dug ourselves in deeper and deeper in denial of something that was perfectly self-evident" was one of the few pieces of good advice given by anyone in the whole sorry affair.

Herter left the State Department at the end of Eisenhower's term, but was called back to public service by President Kennedy in December 1962 to be the president's Special Representative for Trade

Negotiations. He continued in that capacity under President Johnson until his death on December 30, 1966. Of all the tributes paid to him, perhaps the one Chris Herter would have appreciated the most was that of President Eisenhower: "When you look at him, you know you are looking at an honest man."

CHAPTER IV

The General's Men

IN ADDITION TO CONANT AND HERTER, PRESIDENT EISENHOWER appointed another Massachusetts man to his cabinet and seven others to diplomatic posts during his two administrations. The appointment of Sinclair Weeks to be Secretary of Commerce continued a family tradition of public service in high office.

Born in West Newton, on June 15, 1893, the only son of John W. Weeks, founder of Hornblower and Weeks and secretary of war in the cabinets of both Presidents Harding and Coolidge, Sinclair was a product of the Newton public schools and Harvard College, class of 1914. After graduation the young man went to work at the First National Bank of Boston, where he rose over the years from messenger to assistant cashier to a seat on the board of directors. Weeks served with the Massachusetts National Guard on the Mexican border in 1916 and in France during World War I as an artillery officer in the 26th Yankee Division. In 1923, at the time he was in charge of the First National Bank's foreign banking business, Weeks instead went to work in the family concern—not his father's but his father-in-law William Dowse's metal manufacturing business. The firm included the silversmith company, Reed and Barton, and the United Fastener Corporation. Weeks helped arrange a merger between United and its chief rival and was made a director of the new firm. In 1945, Weeks was made chairman of the board of Reed and Barton.

Although their routes to business success were different, the paths of the Weekses, father and son, in the political area were strikingly similar. Both served on the Newton board of aldermen and as that city's mayor. John was elected by the legislature to the U.S. Senate to succeed the retiring Winthrop Murray Crane in 1913. Sinclair was appointed to that body by Governor Leverett Saltonstall in 1944 to finish the term of Henry Cabot Lodge Jr., who had resigned to serve in the military. (Weeks did not run for a regular term; he left that to Governor Saltonstall, who did run and won.) The younger Weeks was both chairman of the state Republican Committee and chairman of the executive committee of the Republican National Committee. Active in the unsuccessful presidential campaigns of both Wendell Wilkie and Thomas Dewey, Weeks was one of the party establishment who sought to persuade the early frontrunner for the party's presidential nomination in 1952, Senator Robert Taft of Ohio, to step aside in favor of General Eisenhower. Weeks's extraordinary ability to raise large sums of money played a large role in the general's subsequent election to the presidency.

The president-elect who considered Weeks far more politically conservative than himself, wanted him to take over the chairmanship of the Republican National Committee, but Sinclair held out for the job he wanted, and for which he felt himself eminently qualified, that of Secretary of Commerce. The new secretary set about reducing the departmental budget proposed by his predecessor by more than 16 percent and the department's work force by 24. If businessmen in post-Roosevelt, post-Truman, post-war America were longing for an effective advocate of their interests in high office, they found it in Secretary Weeks. Not only was he the champion of their cause, opposing price controls, for instance, but he also brought them to the seat of power through the creation of the 100-man business advisory council made up of "the blue bloods of industry." Weeks was instrumental in the passage of the president's reciprocal trade program and established a bureau of foreign commerce in his department. His greatest accomplishment in the eyes of the president and others, though, was his overseeing from conception through Congress and on to construction the biggest project ever undertaken by any government up to that time, the building of a 41,000-mile national highway system.

Weeks resigned as Secretary of Commerce in 1958, resumed his seat on the board of directors of the First National Bank of Boston, and became a limited partner in his father's old firm, now Hornblower and Weeks, Hemphill Noyes. During his career, Weeks was an overseer of Harvard and director, corporator or overseer of no less than 17 academic, business, and charitable institutions. Married twice after the death of his first wife in 1945, he retired to his family's beef and dairy farm in Lancaster, New Hampshire, in 1970, and died at Concord, Massachusetts on February 7, 1972.

CHAPTER V

The Party of Inclusion

THE CONTRIBUTION OF MASSACHUSETTS MEN AND WOMEN TO THE government of the United States in the years following the Korean conflict are obvious in the president and three Speakers of the House the Commonwealth sent to Washington. Less well known in number and repute are the 26 men and women who represented the United States in other countries, and more than a dozen who held administrative offices in the Department of State.

John Moors Cabot

John Moors Cabot was of the family sired by John Cabot, who arrived in 1700 at Salem. The Cabot family has produced over the years in various fields of endeavor progeny of excellence: George Cabot, Francis Cabot Lowell, Arthur Tracy Cabot, Richard Clarke and Edward Clarke Cabot, Godfrey Lowell Cabot and the Henry Cabot Lodges.

John Moors Cabot was born in Cambridge on December 11, 1901, and graduated from Harvard, Class of 1923, before going on for further studies at Oxford. Like other Brahmin sons born around the turn of the century, Cabot was to find his satisfaction not in commerce or elected office, but in the diplomatic service. Entering the State Department in 1927, he began his career as vice-consul in Callao, Peru

THE PARTY OF INCLUSION • 301

and went on to fill various posts and ambassadorships until his appointment by President Eisenhower to the important post as Assistant Secretary of State for Inter-American Affairs in February 1953.

Less than a month later, Cabot led the U.S. delegation to the Inter-American Economic and Social Conference in Caracas. At the time, the United States government was conscience-stricken because of its neglect regarding inter-American affairs. Cabot started out at the conference by stating what he thought, wrongly, as it turned out, was the policy of the United States. The Assistant Secretary recommended continued U.S. technical assistance, the movement of public funds and private investments into the area, and equitable trade policies. Later expanding on that as a theme in the United States, Cabot warned that import curbs on Latin American products would only damage the ideals of Pan Americanism and give comfort to Communist subversion in the area. To deal effectively with the Communist threat, he added, the United States had to sever its connection with reactionary and oppressive regimes and seize the high road of social reforms in the Americas.

There were those in President Eisenhower's cabinet who saw things differently. Secretary of the Treasury George Humphrey vetoed the use of the Export-Import Bank for long-term development loans, and the administration imposed import restrictions on Latin American products. Subsequent administrations also failed to heed John Cabot's warning concerning the adverse effect of United States support of repressive governments in the area.

Cabot's conflicts with Secretary Humphrey and others in the administration led to his resignation as assistant secretary in February 1954. Sent to Sweden as ambassador, Cabot set about hosting meetings with Swedish citizens to explain American policy. In April 1957, he was posted as ambassador to Colombia, and in May 1959, in the same capacity to Brazil. Based on his past thinking as to how his country should handle its relations with its southern neighbors, Cabot was the right man to send to Brazil. That nation, however, was undergoing a great surge of nationalism and hostility to the United States. Cabot's efforts—he spoke frequently to groups of hostile students—did nothing to restrain the Brazilian government's adoption of an independent foreign policy. Although President Kennedy asked Cabot to remain in

Brazil, his difficulties with the new Brazil president, Janio Quadros, forced him to leave Brazil.

John Moors Cabot finished his diplomatic career as American ambassador to Poland, having served there from 1961 to August 1965. He died in 1981.

Margaret Mary O'Shaughnessy Heckler

It was a lovely political slogan: "Massachusetts needs a Heckler in the House," especially appealing to those Republicans and Independents who thought the first duty of their congressman was to monitor the excesses of Congress, especially a Democratic Congress.

Born in Flushing, Queens County, New York, on June 21, 1931, the daughter of John and Bridget O'Shaughnessy, Margaret received her B.A. from Albertus Magnus College in 1953; married a stockbroker, John M. Heckler in 1954; earned her LL.B. at Boston College in 1956; and was admitted to the Massachusetts bar the same year.

A female graduate of Boston College Law School in the year 1956 could not reasonably expect to be hired by any of the prestigious old law firms in the city or, for that matter by any of the new and growing number of successful, but chauvinistic, Irish firms. So "Peggy" Heckler, undeterred by such rejection, gathered some of her law school classmates and founded her own firm. In college, she had made practical use of her major in political science by running for Speaker of the Student House, with her future husband as her campaign manager and being elected speaker of the student house. Active in state Republican politics, and early on an advocate of the rights of women: "the one minority group it is still considered fashionable to discriminate against," Margaret was elected a member of the Governor's Council in 1962, and a delegate to the Republican National Convention in 1964 and 1968.

In 1966, Joseph Martin was 82 years old and had been a member of Congress for 42 years. He had been speaker and a revered leader of his party—the only man, in fact, ever to be honored while still living with a bust in the rotunda of the House Office Building. Such a man was due, in the opinion of his peers in the leadership of the Republican Party in Massachusetts, the honor of dying in office or of at least gracefully retiring from public life. Despite warnings from the leadership and a plea from the Republican governor, John Volpe, not to do so, Margaret Heckler challenged and defeated Martin in that year's Republican primary. Heckler was careful not to make an issue of Martin's age, and ran as an outsider with a wide appeal to women voters. Her opponent in the final election was Democratic candidate Patrick J. Harrington, against whom Heckler ran with the toughness and lack of timidity so characteristic of her public career, and she won.

It is expected of freshmen congressmen, properly awed and self-effacing in the presence of the seniority and power of those who got there before them, to accept assignments to minor committees whose work is done with humility and in obscurity. Freshman Heckler was taught that lesson when her bold request for a seat on the Judiciary Committee was met with assignments to the committees on Government Operations and Veterans Affairs. Heckler's opposition to President Nixon's escalation of the Vietnam War and calls for U.S. withdrawal as early as 1972, did not have the effect that subsequent opposition by other congressmen was to have: her protests were dismissed as "a woman's thing."

There was hardly an issue of interest to women that did not find a champion in Margaret Heckler—and it mattered not whether her stand was in conformity with her party or her president. During the 1968 Republican National Convention, she criticized the presidential nominee, Richard Nixon, for his stand on limiting child-care funds for working women, knowing firsthand of the need for such help among the working women of the industrial towns she represented.

With the fiery Congresswoman from New York, Elizabeth Holzman, Heckler founded the Congresswomen's Caucus, a bipartisan group of women representatives devoted "to improving the rights, representation, and status of women in America." The list of those issues and the success of the Caucus in furthering them is long and impressive: legislation to facilitate women's entry into the labor force; revisions in the Social Security system as regards women; violence against women; sexism in public education; betterment in the procedures for monitoring women's health and many others. As hard as they tried, however, the Women's Caucus was unable to accomplish its goal of an equal rights for women amendment to the U.S. Constitution.

In the 1982 election, Heckler lost her seat to a young and articulate Democrat, Barney Frank. In March 1983, President Reagan appointed Heckler as Secretary of Health and Human Services, and two years later as ambassador to the Republic of Ireland.

CHAPTER VI

Neither One nor the Other

THE RISE OF IRISH-AMERICANS TO POSITIONS OF POLITICAL POWER in the Commonwealth, and from that base to national power, far from being any indicator of growing political diversity, was more a substitution of oligarchies. In 1900 the names of the governor, lieutenant governor, secretary, treasurer, auditor, and attorney general of Massachusetts were, respectively: W. Murray Crane, John L. Bates, Henry P. Peirce, Edward S. Bradford, John W. Kimball, and Hosea M. Knowlton. Fifty years later, the same offices were held by men with names such as Paul A. Dever, Charles F. "Jeff" Sullivan, Edward J. Cronin, John E. Hurley, Thomas J. Buckley, and Francis E. Kelly. On occasion, the voters forced the admittance into that exclusive club a man who was neither one nor the other, Yankee or Irish. Of those, two who went on to service in Washington were an Italian hod-carrier and an African-American lawyer.

John Volpe

John Anthony Volpe was born in Wakefield, Massachusetts on December 8, 1908, the son of Italian immigrants Vito and Filomena Volpe. He was married on June 18, 1934 to Jennie Benedetto. John graduated from Malden High School and in the generally ethnic-structured occupations of those days in Massachusetts—Yankee bankers, Irish cops and politicians, Jewish storekeepers, German delicatessen owners, Italian building contractors—Volpe went to work as a hod carrier and apprentice plasterer. Possessed of ambition to better himself, like so many sons and daughters of foreign-born parents, John enrolled at the Wentworth Institute in Boston in 1928 to study engineering and construction. He graduated from Wentworth in 1930. After working for a while for a residential construction company, where he rose to assistant superintendent, Volpe founded his own business in 1933: the John A. Volpe Construction Company, an enterprise that in a relatively short time made him a millionaire.

After World War II, during which he served in the Civil Engineering Corps of the U.S. Navy, Volpe became active in Republican politics, serving as deputy chairman of the party's state committee. Because of the exigencies of the war effort, upkeep and repair of the Massachusetts highway system had been put on hold. In 1953, Governor Herter appointed Volpe as Commissioner of Public Works to oversee one of the largest highway construction programs in the state's history. In the beginning stages of what was to become the creation of a massive federal highway system, President Dwight Eisenhower, in 1956, appointed Volpe as the first federal highway administrator.

In 1960, the incumbent governor of Massachusetts, a Democrat and himself an Italian-American, Foster Furcolo, announced he would be a candidate for the U.S. Senate. Volpe ran for governor to succeed him, defeating his Democratic opponent, Joseph D. Ward by 140,000 votes out of 2,500,000 cast. During his term as governor, Volpe, a deeply religious man who could be seen attending daily Mass at the Paulist Center on Park Street, just down from the State House, increased the supply of low-income housing for the elderly and workers compensation payments, initiated campaign reform by requiring the publication of political contributions and expenditures, and granted financial autonomy to the University of Massachusetts. In one of those soap operas that so enrich the political culture of the Bay State, the Italian-Republican Volpe was defeated for reelection by a Democrat with not one but two distinguished Yankee names, Endicott Peabody, who had defeated the Irish Edward McCormack, nephew of Congressman John W. McCormack, in the Democratic primary. Edward McCormack was himself defeated in the Democratic party primary two years later by Francis X. Bellotti, who lost the final election to his fellow Italian-American and former governor, John A. Volpe.

In his second term, 1965-1969, the first four-year term under an amendment to the state constitution, Volpe reorganized the department of education, established a higher standard for public schools, and secured the passage of a pioneering racial imbalance law, the implementation of which years later would become the flashpoint of bitter division in the state's capital city. The most significant accomplishments of Volpe's second gubernatorial administration, however, were the passage of a sales tax and the shifting of the burden of the cost of welfare from the cities and towns, where it had been since colonial days, to the state.

It has been written that there was talk in the inner circle of advisers to newly nominated Richard Nixon of choosing John A. Volpe to be his running mate in the 1968 presidential campaign. If so, it came to naught. Nixon chose the governor of Maryland, Spiro T. Agnew, who eventually was forced to resign as vice president because of dishonesty. Meanwhile, Volpe the governor had established a state crime commission to rout out what the commission described as "Corruption [that] permeates the state from town governments to the State House and involves politicians, lawyers, and ordinary citizens."

In 1969, Volpe resigned the governorship to become the nation's second Secretary of Transportation. Under appointment by President Nixon Volpe proposed an innovative federal mass transportation program to be funded in five-year periods, and fought for the U.S. development and deployment of a commercial supersonic transport plane. In February 1973, already the recipient of the Vatican's Knight of Malta honor and the Italian government's Knight of the Grand Cross Order of Merit, Volpe journeyed to the home of his ancestors as ambassador to the country that so many had left to find freedom and opportunity—the Republic of Italy.

Climbing the Mighty Mountain

The two men were of similar backgrounds: middle class, possessing undergraduate and graduate degrees, personable, popular, and black. While one, the Democratic Congressman from Harlem, Adam Clayton Powell, was passing through a large and raucous crowd of his supporters who were demonstrating against his expulsion from his seat in the House, the newly elected U.S. senator from Massachusetts, Edward Brooke, was bathing in the warmth of a standing ovation from his welcoming colleagues. Powell's contribution to the cause of African-Americans was as the outspoken pastor of the Abyssinian Baptist Church in Harlem and the effective chairman of the House Education and Labor Committee. Brooke, on the other hand, the first African-American popularly elected to the U.S. Senate and the first to hold office there since Reconstruction, did not, in his own opinion, qualify as a "black leader," at least not in the style of Powell. Adam Powell, with his militant insistence on the rights and acceptance due his people, was a man of his time; Ed Brooke, with his insistence that the voters use only the criterion of who was the best choice in casting their votes, was a man of a future time.

Edward William Brooke was born in Washington, D.C. on October 26, 1919, the son of a lawyer in the Veterans Administration. He was educated in the public schools of the District and at Howard University, where he received his bachelor of science degree in 1941. A member of the Reserve Officers Training Corps (ROTC) at Howard, Brooke was called up to the all-black 366th Combat Infantry Regiment shortly after the Japanese attack on Pearl Harbor with the rank of second lieutenant. He was serving in Italy when hostilities ended. While awaiting his return to the states, he married Remigia Ferrari-Scacco, one of three daughters of a cultured and prosperous Genoa family. Brooke enrolled in Boston University Law School in 1946, and received both his LL.B. (1948) and LL.M. (1949) degrees.

The lawyer Brooke struggled in the first years of his practice. His clients were mostly residents of the black section of the city's Roxbury district and were often unable to pay a fee commensurate with the work required. The ward in which Brooke's law office was located—Ward 12—had a white majority, mostly Jewish, with a smattering of Irish, and a growing black population that had reached perhaps 35 percent. Some of the younger black leaders, veterans of the war like Brooke and concerned with the lack of their community's political clout, persuaded him to run for state representative in 1950.

The district was heavily Democratic and winning that party's nomination was tantamount to election. Brooke, who had never shown much interest in politics, and whose father prior to the New Deal had been a Republican, filed, as was allowed by law, for both the Democratic and Republican nominations and won the latter. In the final election, the Republican Brooke came in third behind two Jewish Democrats, George Greene and Louie Nathanson. Two years later, Brooke came in second to Greene, polling almost 7,000 votes and losing by less than 1,000. For much of the rest of his political life, Brooke would be dogged with the charge that his choice to run as a Republican in Democratic Boston was more practical then philosophical. If he could not win in a contested Democratic primary, which he could not, the nomination of the Republican Party, politically speaking an irrelevancy in that place at that time, was his for the asking.

By 1960, Brooke had a very successful law practice in Pemberton Square, the "lawyer's row" in downtown Boston, and was on the board of directors of several corporations and charitable institutions. That year he chose to re-enter politics as the Republican candidate for Massachusetts State Secretary against a Democrat and future mayor of Boston, Kevin White. Brooke lost again, for the third time, and in so doing proved once again the axiom known to all professional politicians: a loss is not necessarily a defeat. In that year, when the heavily Democratic state's most favorite son, John F. Kennedy, was running for president of the United States, in a state 98 percent white, the African-American Republican Edward W. Brooke garnered over a million votes, losing by a margin of only 112,000.

There was no doubt in the minds of the leaders of the Massachusetts Republican Party that in the handsome, dapper, charming, intelligent Edward Brooke they had a major asset. The fact that the state's most prominent African-American politician was a member of the party that had suffered much from the opposition's playing the ethnic card, and his obvious appeal across racial lines, were duly noted.

Republican governor, John Volpe, appointed Brooke a member of the Boston Finance Commission. The "FinCom" was created by the Republican Legislature in 1909, ostensibly to provide oversight of the city's finances, but in reality to try to get the indictable goods on the likes of John F. "Honey Fitz" Fitzgerald and James Michael Curley. The commission had become more or less moribund over the years, paid its members little more than expenses and for a busy lawyer like

Ed Brooke, was time consuming, but it had, as the ambitious Brooke well knew, the power of subpoena. Commissioner Brooke's diligent pursuit of corruption in the administration of Boston, not difficult to find, soon made his name well known beyond the city, so much so that at the 1962 Republican state convention and in the ensuing primary, Brooke, running for attorney general against the advice and wishes of much of the party hierarchy, defeated Elliot Lee Richardson, a Boston Brahmin of impeccable credentials and the incumbent U.S. Attorney for the District of Massachusetts. In the November election, while the rest of the Republican ticket, including incumbent governor John Volpe, went down to defeat, Brooke beat former attorney general Francis "Sweepstakes" Kelly by over a quarter of a million votes. Well over a million Massachusetts voters, covering a widespread spectrum of race and ethnicity, cast their ballots for Brooke.

The new attorney general found no less corruption to rout out as the chief law enforcement officer of the commonwealth than he had found as the watchdog of the city. By the time he left office, Brooke had indicted more politicians, mostly Democrats, including a former governor and speaker of the House, than any other attorney general in the state's history. Although many of those accused were ultimately found not guilty, with other indictments dropped or thrown out of court, the voters evidently approved of his anticorruption efforts. In his 1964 reelection campaign, Brooke garnered one and one half million votes and beat his adversary, state Senator James Hennigan Jr., by a plurality of 800,000, one of the largest margins of any Republican nationwide.

In late December of 1966, Leverett Saltonstall, a member of the U.S. Senate for 22 years, announced that he would not be a candidate for reelection. The obvious man to succeed him and to retain the seat for the Republican Party was incumbent governor John A. Volpe. If Volpe ran for the Senate, the equally obvious candidate to succeed him as governor was the attorney general, Ed Brooke. Brooke had already decided, however, that if Volpe was not a candidate for the U.S. Senate, Brooke would be.

Brooke asked Volpe about his plans. Volpe wanted time. Brooke did not give it to him. Instead, he announced his intention to stand for U.S. Senate. Brooke's candidacy did not sit well with some of the traditional leaders of the state Republican Party and even less with the conservative element when Brooke, in a nationally televised interview, advocated such heresy as an increase in the minimum wage and funding for the war on poverty, and expressed opposition to the Vietnam War. In the ensuing state convention, Brooke handily beat J. Alan MacKay, a lawyer and national vice president of the conservative Young Americans for Freedom, for the nomination, 1,485 to 215. In the party primary election, all four of the candidates for the four top state offices were unopposed, but the displeasure of the conservatives with Brooke was made evident by the fact that he received fewer votes than the others. The nominee's Democratic opponent in November was former governor Endicott Peabody, who had defeated the mayor of Boston, John Collins, in the primary. In the final election, Brooke, for the fourth time, received over a million votes, defeating Peabody by more than 400,000.

The question naturally arose in the national press whether the voters of Massachusetts had sent back to the city of his birth as their U.S. senator Edward Brooke, an African-American political leader, or Edward Brooke, an African-American in politics. The resolutely middle-class and middle-of-the-road Brooke proved to be more the latter than the former. He supported civil rights legislation but failed to align himself with the more militant black leadership. He denounced both Stokely Carmichael of the Student Nonviolent Coordinating Committee (SNCC) and the Black Panthers, while at the same time deploring the belligerent segregationist leader, Lester Maddox.

As a former state attorney general, Senator Brooke took a heightened interest in the federal justice system. He introduced several bills, including bills to expedite trials, and to establish training centers for prison officials and community programs for the rehabilitation of juvenile offenders. In foreign policy, the senator supported moderate-liberal policies, voted for several anti-Vietnam amendments beginning in 1970, and, in 1972, personally introduced an amendment calling for recall of U.S. troops from Indochina within four months of its adoption.

On April 22, 1973, Brooke entered the tumult of the Watergate scandal in a speech in which he declared that President Nixon could not escape responsibility in the affair. The following November Brooke became the first Republican senator to call for the president's resignation. Senator Brooke's relations with Nixon's successor, Gerald Ford, were more cordial, and for a time until he took himself out of consideration, there was talk of Brooke as Ford's running mate in 1976. Senator Brooke's historic and in some measure, path-making political career came to an end in 1978 with a heavily publicized divorce and reports of possible irregularities in statements he had made regarding disposition of loans, when he was defeated for reelection by the Democrat, Paul E. Tsongas, the son of Greek immigrants.

PART IV

"They Came to the Delectable Mountain"

—John Bunyan, *The Pilgrim's Progress*

The Old Man on the Mountain

FROM HIS SEAT ON THE RAISED PLATFORM, THE OLDER MAN, BORN IN the nineteenth century, his sharp-featured face as solemn as the occasion, looked down on the dais below, where the younger man, born in the twentieth century, stood. Before them were assembled the leaders of the government of the United States of America in its entirety: executive, legislative and judicial. Ambassadors and ministers from every nation of the world with which their own had relations were present; men of importance, women of distinction, and friends of both men. John William McCormack, 45th speaker of the U.S. House of Representatives, born poor and with little prospect in South Boston, Massachusetts on December 21, 1891, was presiding over the 1962 State of the Union message of John Fitzgerald Kennedy, 35th president of the United States, born into wealth and promise in Brookline, Massachusetts on May 29, 1917. Born mere miles and great distance apart, each now atop his own Delectable Mountain.

There were others present in the chamber that day who were to join the speaker and the president in what were destined to be extraordinary contributions to the governance of the United States. Archibald Cox, Solicitor General, was there, along with Attorney General Robert F. Kennedy and Congressman Thomas P. O'Neill, beginning his fifth term in the House seat once held by the president.

CHAPTER I

The Cardinal Rabbi

ON APRIL 3, 1928, THE INCUMBENT CONGRESSMAN FROM THE Massachusetts district that included South Boston, James A. Gallivan, died. Gallivan, who had served continuously since the 63rd Congress in 1914, would certainly, had he lived and chosen to run, been elected to the 71st. It was decided that rather than hold a special election to fill Gallivan's unexpired term to wait until the regularly scheduled November election and to fill that term and elect a congressman for a full term in the 71st Congress. The winner of both of those contests was a 28-year-old lawyer, John William McCormack, who had lost a challenge to Gallivan in the previous election. There was some small irony in McCormack's election to fill Gallivan's unexpired term, since Gallivan himself had first been elected to fill the unexpired term of James Michael Curley, who had left Congress to once again seek election as mayor of Boston. A larger irony of McCormack's election lay in the fact that he could trace his political heritage to, and was a product of, the turbulent days of Boston Irish immigrant politics and the machinations of its self-made ward bosses. Gallivan, on the other hand, was a graduate of Boston Latin School and Harvard College, and was a successful businessman.

It was not uncommon among the Irish immigrant families of the 19th century for a great brood of children to be raised by their widowed, or in some instances, abandoned mother. Many a successful businessman, priest, or politician could point out—indeed, take pride—in the fact that it was the sacrifice and strength of their mother, absent the presence of their father, to which they owed their success. John McCormack's mother, Ellen O'Brien McCormack, was left alone with her brood in 1905, when John was 13. Research by Professor Garrison Nelson of the University of Vermont conclusively shows that she was not widowed but deserted by her husband, Joseph McCormack, a Nova-Scotian-born stonemason much given to the drink. Before he left her, Joe McCormack had fathered eight children, two of whom died in infancy. His son John, out of hurt or pride or anger, would maintain throughout his life that his father had died the year he left. Death or desertion: it made little difference to the young boy; he would have to leave John Andrew Grammar School and get a job.

Young John hawked newspapers at first, found employment as an errand boy in a Boston brokerage house at $3.50 a week, and finally, in a move of great portent, obtained a position as an office boy in the law firm of William T. Way at $4.50 a week. It soon came to the notice of lawyer Way, that his young clerk was spending his spare time between assignments pouring over books in the firm's library. Way encouraged the young man in his law studies, and in 1913, just a few weeks after his mother died, 22-year-old John McCormack was admitted to practice before the Massachusetts bar.

When McCormack, with sophomore standing, took the oath for a full term in the 71st Congress, he brought with him the political experience of a delegate to the Massachusetts Constitutional Convention of 1917-1918, election to the Massachusetts House and Senate, and stateside service as an Army sergeant major in World War I. He also brought with him the commanding presence and eloquence that had enabled him to build up a lucrative practice as a trial lawyer, and was to make him one of the most formidable debaters on the floor of the U.S. House.

The Austin-Boston Axis

The Speaker of the House of Representatives in 1928 was the personable, fine-living, well-bred, talented and highly visible Nicholas Longworth of Ohio, the husband of Alice, the acerbic, witty daughter of President Theodore Roosevelt. Longworth, was a Republican, like the

318 • EXTRAORDINARY TENURE

Speaker before him, Frederick Gillett of Massachusetts, and like none would be after him, with the exception of Joe Martin of Massachusetts, until the election of Newton L. Gingrich in 1995. Longworth's successor as Speaker, Texan John Nance Garner, served until his swearing in as Franklin Roosevelt's vice president in 1933. His fellow Texan and protégé, Sam Rayburn, took a liking to McCormack, the tall Bostonian who so easily met people, made friends, told stories, played a nice hand of poker, and could best most other members in floor debate. Rayburn advanced in the House leadership, and eventually, beginning in 1940, his unprecedented, nearly 17 years in the Speaker's chair John McCormack followed apace.

In only his second full term in the House, and with the blessing and encouragement of Speaker Garner, McCormack in 1931 was elected a member of the powerful Ways and Means Committee, a rare prize for one with so little seniority. McCormack's influence with the urban, largely Catholic northern Democratic congressmen helped Rayburn's elevation to majority leader, and when Rayburn was elected to the Speakership in 1940, McCormack succeeded him as Majority Leader. McCormack became acting Speaker when illness forced Rayburn to return to Texas. "Mr. Sam" died in December 1961, and at the convening of the next Congress, on January 10, 1962, John W. McCormack, Democrat of Boston, became the first adherent of the Roman Catholic faith to become Speaker of the U.S. House of Representatives.

Putting aside which of the two political parties at any given session had majority control of the House, the exercise of power within the body was, for many years of the 20th century, in flux. Strong dictatorial speakers gave way to party caucuses, chairmen of important committees held sway, seniority eschewed democracy. When McCormack became speaker, the movement for reform of the then-existing system, which Ronald Peters Jr. in his *The American Speakership* dubbed "feudal," was growing, a disenchantment fueled by the arrival of an increasing number of younger, more liberal members, many of them veterans of World War II and the Korean conflict. Seasoned observers of the workings of the Congress felt that the new speaker, product that he was of the old school of leadership, would be ill-equipped to deal with that which was emerging. What they failed to take into account was that McCormack was also a product of the "old school" of Boston Irish survival politics and had prospered, long after its demise. To the politically pure, to "go along to get along" is a euphemism for sub-rosa wheeling and dealing, unholy alliances and abandonment of principle. To the ultimate legislative leader such as John McCormack, it was the way to get things done. In a body where every shade of legitimate—and sometimes not so legitimate—opinion dwelt, all had a vote and each was answerable to his or her own constituency. If the ultimate judgment of how effective John W. McCormack was as a leader in the House lies in what was accomplished during his extraordinary stretch of leadership, it might be found in the fact that in all his years as majority leader and speaker, he never once lost a vote on the House floor.

McCormack came to the House in 1928, when Calvin Coolidge was president, and left in 1971, when Richard Nixon was. In those 43 years he served in positions of leadership in the U.S. Congress longer than any other man in its history. From the Depression, through World War II and the civil rights movement, during the presidencies of Franklin Roosevelt with his New Deal, John Kennedy with his New Frontier and Lyndon Johnson with his Great Society, John McCormack participated in the enactment of legislation, which, taken in its aggregate, revolutionized American society. No other man in American public life had the continuity of power, and few the skills, to leave such an imprint, as did the tall, gaunt man from South Boston.

McCormack was married to Harriet Joyce in 1920, and the two of them lived in the same modest house at 726 Columbia Road in Dorchester for 51 years, until her death in 1971. The couple had no children, and when John was in Washington, Harriet lived with him in a residential hotel. It is said that the two never failed to have dinner together. McCormack was an ardent anti-Communist and a defender of the Vietnam war. It was a tribute to the high regard in which McCormack was held by members of the House of both parties, that they appropriated millions of dollars on a project, the construction of the atomic bomb, without knowing what the money was for, based only on his word.

John W. McCormack, sometimes called "The Cardinal" for his loyalty to his church and "Rabbi" by his Jewish constituency for his unfailing support of their community, died in his sleep on November 22, 1980, at age 89.

CHAPTER II

Little Boy Blue

JAMES MICHAEL CURLEY HAD THE GIFT OF SILVER-TONGUED ORATORY with which he could confound his enemies, and a fresh mouth of derision with which to delight his friends, a winning combination, but not always. In 1936, the U.S. Senate seat held by the Democrat with the Republican name, Marcus A. Coolidge, became available, and Henry Cabot Lodge Jr., the 34-year-old grandson of Henry Cabot Lodge, decided to run for it, not it seemed a judicious decision. President Franklin Roosevelt and his New Deal were at the height of popularity, and political pundits were nearly unanimous in their predictions of a Democratic sweep. As things turned out, the Democrats elected more of their party to seats in the House, 331, and the Senate, 76, than at anytime before or since, and Roosevelt would be crowned president with 523 electoral votes with a mere 8 for Alfred Landon, his Republican opponent.

Lodge's rival in his attempt to overcome the Democratic tide in an increasingly Democratic state was governor James Michael Curley, who ran his campaign not on issues but by reverting to, for him at least, the tried and true formula of Yankee baiting. In the process he got off some great one-liners. Lodge was, according to James Michael, "a young man who parts both his name and his hair in the middle," "a very handsome child," "Puny Henry," and the one that hurt, not Lodge but Curley, the most: "Little Boy Blue." The final outcome was that Lodge received 870,000 votes to Curley's 732,000. Jim Curley's personal attacks on the grandson of Senator Lodge who had courted and been supported by Irish Democrats during his long political career was a large factor in Curley's defeat. Until the process in which they were then engaged, the creation of a generational pattern of producing outstanding leaders, in this case political, many Irish-Americans in voting for Henry Cabot Lodge over James Michael Curley, felt that "their man" was better than "our man."

The arrival of Henry Cabot Lodge in the U.S. Senate might be considered as much a right of hereditary passage as a function of a democratic election. No less than five of his ancestors had served in the Senate: George Cabot, John Davis of Massachusetts, Theodore Frelinghuysen and his son Theodore, both senators from New Jersey, and his namesake grandfather.

The younger Lodge, Cabot, as he was called, was born on July 5, 1902, in Nahant, Massachusetts. His father, George, who acted as his own father's secretary, died young, at 35, and Cabot was raised by his grandfather and his mother to be what his deceased father had been—a gentleman and scholar. After graduating from the Middlesex School in 1920, he went on to Harvard and received his degree in 1924.

Cabot's first employment was as a reporter, and later an editorial writer, for the *New York Herald Tribune*. When he initially stood for public office in 1932 for state Representative, Lodge ran a "retail" campaign, complete with voters' names on index cards, street layouts for door-to-door campaigning and the like. As a legislator, he was a reformer, particularly in the workman's compensation law, and was successful in his attempt to extend lifetime benefits to the totally disabled.

An avid horseman who often rode with his neighbor and future general George S. Patton at his country home, Lodge joined the Army Reserve in 1931 with a commission in the Cavalry. He was a pre-World War II isolationist with a rather Irish view of the British, but he was nevertheless a constant campaigner for military preparedness. His status as a U.S. senator had exempted Lodge from active service when the war did come, but on February 1, 1944, he informed President Roosevelt that he was resigning his senate seat to seek active military duty. He also sought assurance from the president that he would be assigned to combat duty. Lodge's departure from the Senate marked the first time since the Civil War that a sitting senator had resigned to fight in a war.

In 1918, David Ignatius Walsh defeated the incumbent Republican and President Harding's future secretary of state, John Wingate Weeks, to become the first Irish Catholic Democrat to represent Massachusetts in the U.S. Senate. Six years later, in 1924, Frederick Huntington Gillett, who had resigned the Speakership of the U.S. House at the behest of President Calvin Coolidge to run, defeated Walsh by 19,000 votes. In the meantime, on November 9, 1924, old Senator Lodge died, and William Morgan Butler was chosen to fill his unexpired term. Two years later Walsh got his revenge on Coolidge by defeating Butler, one of the president's closest advisers, by 55,000 votes. When young Henry Cabot Lodge left for the service his vacant seat was filled by Sinclair Weeks until the next regular election. Former Governor Leverett Saltonstall won the seat that year (he was to serve in it for 22 years) so it was unavailable to Lodge thereafter. If, however, Cabot Lodge could defeat David I. Walsh, who was up for reelection in 1946, he would regain the seat held not only by his grandfather for 31 years, but by his kinsman, George Cabot, in 1791. Weakened by the memory of his opposition to Roosevelt's pre-war preparedness measures, abandoned by many New Deal zealots, and with whispers of a sexual scandal, Walsh was soundly defeated for reelection by Lodge by more than 300,000 votes.

CHAPTER III

Family Feuds

WHEN THE VOTES ALL WERE TOTALED, THE SCORE WAS THE KENNEDYS two million, six hundred and three thousand, nine hundred and fifty-four (2,603,954); the Lodges two million, two hundred and eighty-three thousand, one hundred and ninety-seven (2,283,197). Three times over 50 years the family Cabot-Lodge and the clan Fitzgerald-Kennedy waged the battle of the ballot box as to which of their sons would claim one of the ancient Commonwealth's two seats in the U.S. Senate. Of the three—the senior Lodge's defeat of John "Honey Fitz" Fitgerald in 1916, Edward M. Kennedy's defeat of the younger Lodge's son in 1962—the middle contest, John Kennedy's narrow victory over Henry Cabot Lodge in 1952, was the most significant. Significant nationally because it was from there that Jack Kennedy was to begin his final journey to the presidency, and significant locally, for it forged as good a mark as any of the demise of the Massachusetts Republican Party. Three years previously in 1949, control of the Massachusetts House had passed to the Democratic Party and in 1959, the same would transpire in the state senate. With the exception of Ed Brooke's two terms in the U.S. Senate from 1967 to 1979, no Republican would be sent to that body from a state that had sent to Washington so many distinguished adherents of that party for so many years.

A Contest of Some Consequence

If there was a downside for one's party having a tall, handsome, prestigious prep-school and Harvard graduate, distinguished war veteran, and scion of a famous family as its candidate for the U.S. Senate, it only could be that the other party had one also. If either candidate had an advantage at the beginning of the 1952 campaign for the Senate, timing would seem to better serve Lodge. The time had arrived, every neutral observer agreed, when the Republican Party would emerge from its two decades of insignificance to lead the nation through its post-war trials. At the head of the ticket would be General Dwight Eisenhower, the wildly popular commander of the victorious allied forces. Lodge also had the advantage of incumbency. He was, after all, the sitting U.S. senator, and what had he done or not done to deserve to be unseated?

What Kennedy had going for him were the demographics that had changed the political composition of the state and what he and his managers would create—the best-organized and most effective political campaign in the long history of such contests in Massachusetts. It had begun four years previously, when the word went out to veterans' groups, Knights of Columbus councils, the Rotary Club, the Moose, Odd Fellows and Lions clubs, Holy Name societies, Jewish temples, and Protestant men's organizations: if they needed a speaker, the 31-year-old congressman from Boston would be honored to be asked. When the time came to begin the 1952 campaign, the Kennedy organization had in place hundreds of local organizations all over the Commonwealth that were able to produce, quite literally, hordes of foot soldiers. They were an army of envelope stuffers, addressers and stampers, leaflet droppers, people to stand early mornings at subway stations and bus stops passing out literature, dogged pursuers of the unregistered voter. And of course, the Kennedy women, mother Rose and her daughters, who invited the ladies of the community to come by for coffee so they might meet her son and their brother, Jack. Although the candidate needed only 2,500 certified signatures to get on the ballot, his organization filed 262,324.

Lodge was helped by his identification as one of the men who had persuaded Eisenhower to stand for election, but he was handicapped by the time that the general's nomination took away from Lodge's own business at home. To some extent it was by the animosity from conservatives, who felt that their candidate, Robert A. Taft, had been badly treated at the convention. The differences between the two men, Lodge and Kennedy, on the issues was hardly enough to start a decent fight. Eisenhower swept the state, carrying with him the state's top constitutional offices (including the first Jew elected to state office, Attorney General George Fingold). At 7:30 in the morning after election day, someone in the Kennedy headquarters on Kilby Street in Boston, directly across from Lodge's headquarters, saw the senator leaving. A few minutes later, Bobby Kennedy, the campaign manager who along with so many others had sweated out the long night, received a gracious telegram of concession from Cabot Lodge. In the end, over 95 percent of all eligible voters cast their ballots in the contest, and John Kennedy prevailed by 68,754 out of the 2,345,456 votes cast.

Henry Cabot Lodge, carrying on his family legacy, continued to serve his country: as U.S. representative to the United Nations, ambassador to the Republic of Vietnam (1963), both under President Kennedy; at that post again (1965) under President Nixon; ambassador at large (1967-1968) and head of the U.S. delegation to the Vietnam peace negotiations held in Paris in 1969. Cabot Lodge died in Beverly in February 1985, his last government service, of which his grandfather would certainly have approved, was that of President Nixon's personal representative to the Vatican.

Al Smith to Hubert Humphrey:
Larry O'Brien

Bobby Kennedy, in his capacity as his brother's campaign manager, was able to supply the authority and toughness necessary to bring order and discipline, but he had neither the political knowledge nor the experience to organize it. The Kennedy campaigns, for both senator in 1952 and for president in 1960, were fortunate to have a man with superb skill in the concept, organization and execution of a successful political campaign.

Lawrence Francis O'Brien was born the same year as John Kennedy, 1917, to Lawrence F. O'Brien Sr., a hotel operator and real estate dealer in Springfield, and his wife Myra Sweeney O'Brien. Larry certainly would not have had any idea what 11-year-old prep school students like Jack Kennedy did with their spare time in 1928. As for Larry, his father, a mover in local Democratic politics, had his son on the hustings for Al Smith's presidential bid. After graduation from Cathedral High School, O'Brien earned a Bachelor of Law Degree from Northeastern University, Boston, in 1942. He served in the U.S. Army in World War II, and in 1946 and 1948 ran successful congressional campaigns for his boyhood friend and future governor of Massachusetts, Foster Furcolo. He also served as Congressman Furcolo's Washington administrative assistant from 1948 to 1950.

As related by Kenny O'Donnell, later President Kennedy's appointments secretary and political troubleshooter, O'Brien and Furcolo had a falling out, about what, O'Brien would never say, but the upshot of it was that he arrived at the Kennedy for Senator campaign when O'Brien's political type and campaign expertise were most needed. O'Brien later applied his political instincts and sure hand as director of the planning for the 1960 campaign, and after Kennedy's nomination, he became director of organization for the Democratic National Committee. Unlike some of President Kennedy's other intimates who were quickly shown the door when Lyndon Johnson succeeded him in 1963, O'Brien retained his position as White House assistant for congressional relations. He helped run President Johnson's successful presidential campaign in 1964 and was appointed postmaster general in 1965.

After leaving Johnson's Cabinet, O'Brien managed Hubert Humphrey's unsuccessful bid for the presidency. From 1968 to1969, O'Brien was Chairman of the Democratic National Committee. In 1969, O'Brien joined a citizens group lobbying for reform of the postal service, and was again named chairman of the Democratic National Committee from 1970 to 1972.

CHAPTER IV

A Question of Attitude

No SUBSTANTIAL CHANGE IN THE SOCIAL FABRIC OF A NATION IS EVER made without a change in the attitude of the government, be that government democratic or totalitarian, and the change voluntary or forced. For many generations the attitude of the government of the United States, a reflection of a substantial number of its citizens, the makeup of its Congress and the political practicalities facing its presidents, was to give tacit approval and, sometimes to actively promote discrimination against its Negro citizens. One of the early signs that that attitude might be changing in post-World War II America was the executive order issued by President Truman in 1948 that desegregated the armed forces. While Negro-Americans in the South still could not go to school, or vote with their white American counterparts, they could now at least die in equality.

In 1957, during the presidency of Dwight Eisenhower, Congress established a Civil Rights Commission, an independent bipartisan body. The mandate of the commission was to investigate and report instances of the denial of rights and equal protection of the law, or in the administration of justice because of a person's race, color, religion, sex, age, disability, or national origin. The commission could find fact and issue recommendations, but it had no power of redress. That power lay in the government, specifically in the hands of the government's chief law enforcement officer—the attorney general of the United States. When the problem of the two existing American cultures, black and white, which had been on simmer for a century and a half, came to a scalding boil, it was Robert Francis Kennedy who held that office.

Robert Francis Kennedy

Robert Francis (Bobby) Kennedy was born in Brookline on November 20, 1925, the third boy and seventh child of Joseph P. and Rose Fitzgerald Kennedy. Smaller than his brothers Joe Jr. and Jack, and less athletic, Bobby attended public school in Riverdale, New York, where his family had moved, and then Gibbs School in London, while his father was ambassador to the Court of St. James. He attended Milton Academy, just outside of Boston, and Harvard, before enlisting in the U.S. Navy Reserve in October 1943, just prior to his 18th birthday. After his discharge from the Navy, he returned to Harvard, where he received a B.A. degree in 1948. In 1951, Kennedy graduated from the law school at the University of Virginia. While in his senior year there, he married Ethel Skakel, a young woman with humor and enthusiasm who provided him the security of a safe harbor and 11 children.

In 1960, his work on his brother's successful campaign for the presidency accomplished, Bobby, who had served as assistant counsel to Senator Joseph McCarthy's Permanent Investigations Subcommittee, and chief counsel to the Senate Rackets Committee, found himself without employment, a situation that was remedied when the president-elect appointed his 34-year-old brother as the country's youngest attorney general since President Madison appointed Richard Rush, also 34, in 1814.

Robert Kennedy's 40 months or so as attorney general will be remembered by some for its pursuit of a previously non-existent crusade to rid the country of organized crime. Yet the difficulty in rooting out the entrenched organized crime of the mob bosses and their vicious organizations was nothing in comparison to the problems and players the young attorney general would face in his department's involvement in the explosive struggle to enforce the rights of African-Americans.

What to Do

Robert Kennedy in his thinking on civil rights at that time and in essence was an inheritor of the thinking of those good New England men of another time who tempered their abhorrence of the institution of slavery with the belief that such an evil could not forever endure and that in time and with goodwill it would pass. Surely the growing number of court decisions upholding civil rights gave proper gait and movement to their eventual universal application. But there were those among the increasing number of militants in the civil rights movement in 1960 who believed the man whose duty it was to enforce those rights, the attorney general of the United States, had neither the understanding nor the will to do so. Robert Kennedy, after all, had lived the privileged, educated life of the Northern elite, which was as far from the poor, uneducated, segregated Southern black as Cape Cod was from Cape Hatteras. Nor could these militants, when they looked, find in the political record of the attorney general, or for that matter in the record of his brother, the president, any substantial commitment to end the culture of discrimination against African-Americans in the North, let alone their degradation in the South.

Nor would the attorney general, they believed, even if he did commit the power of his office to the furtherance of the rights of African-American citizens, have the fortitude to require from the FBI's J. Edgar Hoover, his vital cooperation. By 1960, when Robert Kennedy was sworn in, Hoover had been director of the FBI for 36 years. Playing the anti-Communist card like a deck of aces, and accumulating personally embarrassing dossiers on prominent officeholders, Hoover had managed not only to perpetuate himself in office but also to create himself as an American icon. Hoover's attitude toward black citizens was one of disdain. When the new attorney general personally visited each division of the Justice Department and noticed the paucity of black faces, he requested a report on the number of black American employees in each division. After resisting the order, J. Edgar Hoover sent the names of two—both, it turned out, were Hoover's chauffeurs.

The political reality was plainer still: Bobby Kennedy's loyalty to his brother. Jack Kennedy had come to the presidency with the narrowest of margins. If he had any chance of getting a substantial agenda approved by Congress, he would have to avoid offending the entrenched and powerful Southern members to whom segregation was a political mantra. As the drama played out, all those considerations came to naught. For once again, as had happened before in the turbulent pages of American history, the shaping of government policy was overwhelmed by men willing to die and by others willing to kill. Once again the hand holding the power of the law was forced by that holding the trigger of the gun.

> *But Times Do Change and Move Continually*
> —Edmund Spencer, The Faierie Queene (1590)

> *The Negro was willing to face martyrdom . . . . He would force his oppressor to commit his brutality openly, with the rest of the world looking on. . . .*
> —Martin Luther King, Jr., Why We Can't Wait (1964)

Of all the states of the United States carried by John Kennedy in the 1960 election, the one that awarded him the largest percentage of its votes was a state of the Old Confederacy, Georgia. On May 6, 1961, in one of his first major speeches as attorney general, Robert Kennedy, before an audience at the University of Georgia, lamented that the racial incidents accompanying the attempt to integrate public schools in Little Rock, Arkansas, was hurting America's image in the world. Like almost every public happening of that era, he put his words in the context of the nation's fight against the threat of international Bolshevism. He assured his Georgia listeners that the admission of two black students aided the fight against Communist political infiltration. Ending with a promise that his office would not stand aloof; that it would enforce civil rights statutes and Supreme Court decisions, Kennedy sat down to a standing ovation. If Robert Kennedy had any illusions as to the cost to him and the country that the implementation of that promise would have, they were already in the process of destruction.

America, the Ugly

Early in the same month, dozens of black and white men and women, under the leadership of James Farmer, director of the Congress of Racial

Equality (CORE), in a test of compliance with a recent Supreme Court decision outlawing segregation on interstate buses and at terminals began a journey by bus through several Southern states. Not much happened until the "Freedom Riders," as they came to be called, reached Alabama. One of the buses was attacked by an enraged white mob armed with clubs, metal pipes, bricks and chains; a bus was stormed and several of the passengers were badly beaten.

Robert Kennedy's reaction to the outrage, pictures of which were spread on the front pages of every daily newspaper in the country, was to dispatch his administrative assistant and trusted adviser, John Seigenthaler, to the scene. Seigenthaler could not, as the attorney general would have preferred, dissuade the riders from pressing on, even though they had been effectively stopped by the refusal of any driver to take them farther. Kennedy demanded that a driver be found. The ostensibly private conversation appeared in newspapers the next day, convincing many in the South that the Kennedy brothers were the moving force behind the activities in the civil rights movement. When the riders reached Montgomery, the state capital, unprotected by either local or state authorities, they were again met by a mob, dragged from the buses and severely beaten.

The attorney general now began a series of negotiations with the governor of Alabama, John Patterson, the first of many with Southern governors, to at least provide protection for the riders. Patterson was an avowed segregationist who had been quoted as saying that there was ". . . nobody in the whole country that's got the spine to stand up to the god-damned niggers except me," but he promised Bobby Kennedy to see to the safety of the riders. Kennedy did not believe him. Much to the chagrin of some black leaders, the attorney general thought that the dispatching of federal troops or the nationalizing of state militia, either of which would require authorization by the president, was only permissible in the enforcement of an order of a federal court. Until that happened, and if the situation called for it, federal marshals could be used. On May 21, 500 U.S. marshals, many of them hastily deputized federal prison guards were placed under the command of the No. 2 man in the Justice Department and future associate justice of the Supreme Court, Assistant Attorney General Byron White. When the marshals arrived in Montgomery, they found that the Reverend

Martin Luther King was also there. King was to address the support-ers of the riders, who had assembled in the Dexter Avenue Baptist Church.

The marshals were lined up around the perimeter of the church between the 1,500 men and women inside and an estimated 3,000 angry men and women outside. Someone set fire to a car, and the mob rushed the marshals, who forced them back with clubs and tear gas. Kennedy, on a phone to the scene, ordered units of the U.S. Army at Fort Benning, placed on alert. Governor Patterson declared martial law. When the state militia arrived, White put the marshals under its orders, whereupon the commander of the guard dismissed the mar-shals and dispersed the crowd outside the church. That left the belea-guered congregation still inside the church, prevented from leaving by the raised bayonets of the guards.

Attorney general Kennedy requested of Martin Luther King that he try to persuade James Farmer to initiate a cooling-off period, the CORE freedom riders having made their point. Farmer's response, which angered the attorney general, was that the effort was not to make a point but to end segregation in interstate travel. Farmer asserted that the Negroes had been "cooling off" for 150 years and if they cooled off any-more, they would be in a deep freeze. After some negotiation, an assistant to White was finally able to get an agreement from the Dixie Division of the National Guard to escort the detained blacks to their buses or homes. A few weeks later, Kennedy asked the Interstate Commerce Commission to issue regulations banning segregation at interstate bus terminals, which the commission did in September, effective November 1, 1961, but only after intensive lobbying by the Justice Department.

Live in Black and White

Reading at leisure in their daily newspapers about the escalating vio-lence in the South allowed the American people, black and white, to maintain the detached judgment of the personally uninvolved. But not for long. In the privacy of their living rooms, the American public wit-nessed the awful image of bloodied blacks, beaten and bitten by snarling dogs, of women trampled, of children terrorized. In Nazi Germany the police had done that. In Communist Russia the authorities condoned it. But not here, not in America. White America was appalled; black America was outraged. The one weapon beyond the law and above the courts that had been previously denied both militant and peaceful crusaders for justice for the American Negro—the support of the majority of American people—was now theirs.

In late September 1962, at the cost of 35 U.S. marshals shot, 150 injured, and the deployment of 20,000 soldiers of the U.S. Army, James Merideth, an African-American, in forced compliance with a direct order from the Supreme Court of the United States, was admitted as a freshman at the University of Mississippi.

On the night of June 11, 1963, President Kennedy awaited a report from his brother as to whether the University of Alabama had been successfully integrated. Aware of the fact that Governor George Wallace was bodily resisting, the president, overruling the objections of some of his staff, who had argued that his anticipated speech required more preparation, requested television and radio time to address the nation. In a speech that Martin Luther King was to laud as "one of the most eloquent, profound and unequivocal pleas for justice and freedom of all men ever made by any president," the chief executive officer of the government of the United States articulated in words that left no doubt that the attitude of his and future governments toward the implementation of the rights so long promised and so long denied black Americans had changed. Recognizing that new laws were needed, he nevertheless put the thrust of his statement in moral terms: "We are confronted primarily with a moral issue. It is as old as the Scriptures and is as clear as the American Constitution. . . . We face a moral crisis as a country and as a people. It cannot be met by repressive police action. It cannot be left to increased demonstrations in the streets. It cannot be quieted by token moves or talk. It is time to act. . . . Those who do nothing are inviting shame as well as violence. Those who act boldly are recognizing right as well as reality."

A few hours later, the Mississippi field secretary of the National Association for the Advancement of Colored People (NAACP) was ambushed and killed in front of his home. On the same day, June 12, 1963, a caucus of Southern legislators met and voted to oppose any civil rights legislation. On June 19th, the president introduced the most extensive civil rights legislation since the days of Reconstruction.

In 1968, there were, among the large and silent banks of people watching the mourning train take the body of the slain Bobby Kennedy from New York to Washington to rest with the brother he loved and served so well, an extraordinary number of sad faces of color. They did not mourn the Harvard man, the rich man's son, the elite Brahmin Irishman. The man for whom they came to say goodbye had become in the last years of his life an apostle for their cause and for all those in poverty and need, neglect and despair. In gentle and sometimes soaring words he had called America to its promise. "Why?" some Americans asked when the black brethren marched into the violent storm of resistance to their cause. "Why not?" would have been the answer of the man whose body was interred on that June day in 1968.

Oh, Canada

John Kenneth Galbraith had the distinction, among others, of being one of the very few men who were ever fired—or asked to leave as those things were put—by Franklin D. Roosevelt. It seems the young professor of economics from Princeton, at the time deputy administrator at the war-time Office of Price Administration, was advocating, with his usual disdain for "conventional wisdom," a comprehensive program of price controls, of which the Roosevelt administration was very wary.

Galbraith was born on October 15, 1908, at Iona Station, Ontario, Canada. His father was a leader of the other Scots farmers in that isolated Canadian town. Having received his B.S. in agricultural economics in 1931, Galbraith earned a Ph.D. from the University of California at Berkeley and went to work as an instructor at Harvard. While there he took American citizenship, and was greatly influenced by his reading of the works of Keynes, Veblen and Marx. During World War II, Galbraith, rejected for military service because of his height (6'8") served, with George Ball, as a director of the U.S. Strategic Bombing Survey. The survey's conclusion that the extensive bombing of German industrial targets was relatively ineffectual, did not sit well with the advocates of war-time air power.

Prior to the U.S. involvement in the war, Galbraith had sat on the board of editors of *Fortune* magazine, and returned there at war's end. In 1949 he became professor of economics at Harvard, a position he held until his retirement in 1976. A much published, and often controversial author on economic subjects, Galbraith is more popularly known for his political activity. An avowed liberal, the professor was a speech writer for the Democratic candidate, Adlai Stevenson, in his losing campaign against Dwight Eisenhower in 1952. During Eisenhower's administrations, Galbraith was a vocal critic of the president's economic policy.

Long before others, especially his fellow academics at Harvard, took it seriously, Galbraith took interest in the possibility of the election of John F. Kennedy as president. During the campaign, he served as the candidate's agricultural advisor, and in March of 1961, went to India as the United States ambassador; a post he filled until July of 1963. Galbraith returned to Harvard, published several books, produced a television series on economics, and returned to the political area as president of Americans for Democratic Action. He was a vocal opponent of the Vietnam war, and an early supporter of Senator George McGovern's ill fated attempt to unseat President Nixon in 1972.

The Honorable Secretary of Everything:
Elliot Lee Richardson

Elliot Lee Richardson was born on July 20, 1920, into a family that, during its more than two centuries of existence in New England, produced a number of leaders, particularly so in the medical field. Elliot was the son of Dr. Edward P. Richardson and Clara Shattuck Richardson. His mother's family also produced physicians and devoted Republicans. Henry Lee Shattuck, while not one of the former, was a distinguished example of the latter, having had the unusual experience of being at once both treasurer of Harvard and a member of the by-then-Irish-Democrat dominated Boston City Council, one of its last Republican members.

In the eventful years from age 22 to age 32, Elliot Richardson graduated from Harvard with a B.A. magna cum laude, spent three years in the U.S. Army during World War II, with the rank of first lieutenant in the 4th Infantry Division and received both the Bronze Star and Purple Heart. He graduated from Harvard Law School, and then clerked for both Judge Learned Hand in the federal Appeals Court and Justice Frankfurter at the U.S. Supreme Court. In 1949, he joined the

Boston law firm of Gray, Best, Coolidge and Rugg, and was admitted to the bar in 1950. Two years later, he was appointed a lecturer of law at Harvard. On August 2, 1952, he married Anne Frances Hazard.

Richardson had a brief stint in public life as assistant to Senator Leverett Saltonstall in 1953 and 1954, before his appointment by President Eisenhower in 1957 as assistant secretary for legislation at the Department of Health, Education, and Welfare. In his job at HEW, Richardson played a major role in developing legislation in the area of Social Security, public health and juvenile delinquency. After two years (1959-1961) as U.S. attorney for Massachusetts, he entered elective politics as a candidate for Massachusetts attorney general in 1962. He lost the Republican nomination to Edward Brooke. In 1964, with John A. Volpe the gubernatorial nominee, Richardson was elected lieutenant governor. Although that election marked the first time in the history of the Commonwealth that constitutional offices were elected to four-year terms, Richardson left the lieutenant governorship in 1967, having been elected attorney general. He departed that job in 1969 when, on the recommendation of Secretary of State William Rogers, President Nixon appointed him Under Secretary of State.

Although Richardson had no creditable experience in foreign affairs, Secretary Rogers was confident in his administrative ability and organizational skills. In the 17 months Richardson was at State, he immersed himself in the details and nuances of the country's foreign policy and became, before his departure, both Secretary Rogers's most trusted adviser and alter-ego. The Under Secretary represented the United States at the Paris meeting of the Organization for Economic Development, and advanced the administration's policy on free trade. He was also involved in the preparation of the Strategic Arms Limitation Treaty. Richardson personally opposed Nixon's decision to invade Cambodia during the Vietnam War, but vigorously supported it in public. This display of loyalty to his chief was noted by Nixon who highly valued personal and unquestioning loyalty in his appointees, a bit of a miscalculation on the part of the president as future events would prove.

By 1970, the well-intentioned HEW, created in 1953, had grown into an unwieldy bureaucracy overseeing too many agencies overseeing too many programs in too many different areas of the country's social programs. That inefficiency, and the desire of the Nixon administration to rein in some of President Johnson's Great Society programs, resulted in Richardson's appointment as Secretary of HEW. The conservative wing of the Republican Party was pleased with Secretary Richardson's determined effort to bring efficiency to the sprawling department, but not so happy with his support of the Model Cities program, his opposition to welfare test legislation, and his development of a Northern school integration drive. (He personally favored limited busing.)

When Richardson returned to HEW, where he had begun his career in the federal government, he told friends that he was returning "to my old love." It was, after all, the department where the federal government could, as nearly directly as the federal government ever could, affect the lives of its citizens, the poor, the badly educated, the homeless, the old and the infirm. For a man such as Elliot Richardson, with his strong strain of the Puritan creed of man's obligation to man, it was an ideal position.

But efficiency has its punishments, and in January 1973, Nixon moved him over to the Department of Defense as its secretary with the same mandate he was given at HEW: Straighten it out. Another reason for the move may well have been that Republican conservatives were convinced no meaningful moderation of social programs would ever come about under Richardson. Whatever his reason, if there had been one, President Nixon could do whatever he wanted to; in the election of 1972 he had amassed 520 electoral votes to his hapless Democrat opponent George S. McGovern's 17. The one state he did not carry was Massachusetts, the home of Elliot Richardson and Archibald Cox.

Professor Cox

Archibald Cox Jr. was born in Plainfield, New Jersey, on May 17, 1912, the first of seven children of Archibald and Frances Perkins Cox. The senior Cox was a successful New York City lawyer who, during the summer, when the Cox family was in residence at Runnemeade Lodge at Windsor in the mountains of Vermont, took the train up from Manhattan every weekend to be with his family. Archie Cox was introduced to the New England rectitude of which he was to become such a symbol when, at age 14, he entered St. Paul's, an all-boys Episcopal preparatory school near Concord, New Hampshire. St.

Paul's was run on the model of the English "public school": early to rise, cold showers, spartan rooms, compulsory athletics, days in classroom and chapel, early to bed. Archie Cox left St. Paul's with many things, not the least of which was a demanding work ethic.

Cox went to Harvard from St. Paul's, and received his undergraduate degree in 1934. He went on to the law school and graduated magna cum laude in 1937. While at the law school, Cox had the good fortune to have as a professor Felix Frankfurter, the future associate justice of the U.S. Supreme Court, and classmate James Barr Ames, who introduced his sister, Phyllis, who became Archie's future wife. Before his graduation from the law school, Cox took a job in the law firm of Palmer and Dodge in Boston. It was a good, solid firm, where a hard-working and talented young lawyer could gain the financial security to marry and buy a nice home for his bride. Those plans, however, were dramatically changed by a phone call from Professor Frankfurter in December of 1936. "Would he," Frankfurter asked the excited young man, "like to clerk for Justice Learned Hand of the U.S. Court of Appeals in New York?"

Cox finished school, married Phyllis and set off to New York. It was the beginning of a journey that was to take him to Washington in various capacities, including appointment by President Kennedy as solicitor general of the United States, the government's chief advocate before the Supreme Court. In June 1965, Solicitor General Cox, whose existence had hardly been acknowledged by the new Johnson administration, submitted his resignation to the president. Many in high positions in Washington believed that had John Kennedy lived, Archibald Cox would have had a seat on the Supreme Court. The next best thing, of course, would be to teach at Harvard Law School, and Cox was pleased to accept an appointment as the first Samuel Williston Professor of Law at his alma mater. Cox left the political turmoil of the nation's capital not to return to quiet classrooms full of attentive students on the peaceful Cambridge campus, as one might have expected, but to the howling protests of rebellious students.

CHAPTER V

Men of Principle

Oh, what a tangled web we weave,
When first we practice to deceive!
— Sir Walter Scott, 1805

IN 1970, T.C. HOUSTON, A YOUNG WHITE HOUSE AIDE, APPROACHED the president with a plan of covert operations to deal with the president's enemies. In Richard Nixon, Houston had an attentive listener. All successful politicians have their share of enemies, Nixon perhaps more than most. Beyond the identifiable and legitimate foes, Nixon saw many more, real or imagined, who were plotting his undoing. Houston's plan envisioned an array of patently illegal activities: burglaries, electronic surveillance, and mail interception. The president approved the plan.

On Monday, June 17, 1972, at 2:10 in the morning, a security guard making his rounds inside a complex consisting of a hotel, offices and apartments known in Washington as the Watergate, came across five men where they should not have been: in the headquarters of the Democratic National Committee. Four of the men, wearing surgical gloves and ladened with sophisticated electronic bugging and spying devices, were Cuban Americans. The fifth, after his alias was discredited, turned out to be James McCord, a former operative with the CIA and, more recently and interestingly, the chief of security for the Committee to Reelect the President—a name that lent itself to, as things were to unravel, the supremely apt acronym, CREEP.

Before the fallout from that burglary and related crimes had settled, dozens of officials in high federal office, prominent businessmen, and the most intimate confidants of the president would stand convicted of a variety of felonies. There is no hope of cleansing waters in a polluted stream if it flows back to the source of its corruption. As grand juries hauled more and more rotten fish out of the most corrosive river of government corruption since the Teapot Dome Scandal of 50 years past, the putrid stream reached ever more closely to the office of the president. Until forced to face the awful inevitability that truth compelled, that was a place no one, save Richard Milhous Nixon's bitterest of enemies, wished to go.

In January 1973, E. Howard Hunt, a senior White House aide, and the four Cuban Americans, pleaded guilty to complicity in the Watergate burglary. Codefendants G. Gordon Liddy, a White House campaign aide, and James McCord, did not plead. Their trial went on before John J. Sirica, chief judge of the U.S. District Court, in Washington. Liddy and McCord were found guilty of wiretapping, planting eavesdropping devices and theft of documents. Although the trial brought convictions, Judge Sirica did not feel it revealed the whole truth.

On April 30, Nixon announced that he had accepted the resignations of Robert Haldeman, White House chief of staff; John Ehrlichman, White House special assistant on domestic affairs; and John Dean, White House counsel. Haldeman and Ehrlichman were subsequently convicted and Dean pleaded guilty to a variety of charges, including lying to a grand jury and conspiracy to obstruct justice. To the president, the resignations of three of his top aides were proof that he had taken definitive and painful action to put to rest any further speculation as to how far up the scandal went. To others, however, the forced departure of the president's men was scapegoating.

By May, the Washington press corp was reporting increasing anxiety in the White House about the consequence to the president of the rapidly unfolding revelations of his prior knowledge, acquiescence—or worse— in what some had previously derided as a "third-rate burglary."

That month, the Senate Select Committee on Presidential Activities, popularly know as the Ervin Committee after its chairman, Senator Sam Ervin of North Carolina, listened in disbelief as John Dean testified that the then-attorney general, John Mitchell, who had resigned to head up the president's reelection campaign, had ordered the break-in at Watergate, and that a major effort was under way to cover up the White House's involvement. The coverup that included the payment of money to keep the burglars quiet, hush money authorized by no less a personage then the president of the United States.

The departures of Haldeman and Ehrlichman were followed by the resignation of Attorney General Richard Kleindienst, who gave as his reason his friendship with the two men, an intimacy that might hamper him in any future Department of Justice prosecution of the two. The president, faced with the necessity of appointing a new attorney general, looked for a man who would be both acceptable to the Democratic-controlled Senate, which had to confirm the appointment, and at the same time someone who would be loyal to Nixon himself. He found such a man in his cabinet, Elliot L. Richardson, his secretary of defense.

In discussing the appointment with Richardson, who would have much preferred to stay at Defense, the president talked of the possibility of appointing a special counsel to oversee the Watergate burglary and other alleged criminal activity. Nixon's purpose was to have one man, answerable to the attorney general, and thus to the president, who would wrap up the whole affair in one neat package and be done with it. The attorney general agreed in principle: they needed a special prosecutor who would be given great independence to pursue the matter, but ultimately would be subject to the statutory authority of the office of the attorney general. Neither view was acceptable to Senate leaders, who were considering the appointment of a special prosecutor entirely independent of the executive, as Congress had done in the Teapot Dome Scandal. It was not until the nominee assured the Senate Judiciary Committee that he would appoint a Watergate special counsel with the independence they sought that Richardson's appointment went forward.

Richardson's initial search was not fruitful. He received and evaluated hundreds of recommendations, gave considerable thought to the most likely, and reduced his list to a preferred eight. For whatever reasons—most, it is thought, refused because they considered the assignment permeated with lots of trouble and little gain—and all eight turned the attorney general down. One of the names not on Richardson's A list but one more and more often recommended from a variety of parties, was that of Archibald Cox. There were negatives to asking Cox to take the job. It was noted that he had no experience as a prosecutor, was solicitor general under President Kennedy, was not considered very perceptive in his dealings with people, and was infused with "New England self-righteousness." Yet he was known to have good instincts, and was highly respected in all parts of the legal world, was intelligent and as good an example as one might find of the needed measures of rectitude and integrity.

Cox accepted the position and left Harvard Law School to meet with Richardson to discuss the purpose and powers of the independent special counsel. In the months to come, the White House and its defenders would point the finger of bias at both Richardson and Cox. The search for the truth of the matter was in the hands of two gentlemen from Massachusetts, both of whom were products of the suspect "Eastern Establishment," private schools, Harvard and Harvard Law.

Richardson came to the task with the background of having, when U.S. attorney for Massachusetts, successfully prosecuted Boston businessman Bernard Goldfine for tax evasion after Goldfine's gifts to President Eisenhower's chief of staff, Sherman Adams, forced Adams's resignation. Cox's historical relevancy lay in the fact that his great-grandfather, William M. Evarts, had been lead counsel for the defense in the impeachment trial of President Andrew Johnson.

In its essence, the agreement reached between Cox and Richardson, his nominal superior, was to give the special prosecutor an independence that allowed him to go where he wished to pursue what he wanted in search for the truth. On May, 23, 1973, Nixon swore in Elliot Lee Richardson as attorney general, his third cabinet secretariat. Later that day, Richardson administered the oath of office to Cox.

What was to come would be the product of the agreement the two gentlemen had reached, and in the honor with which they, particularly Richardson, under the most excruciating pressure, held to it. Cox and his prosecutorial team were beholden to nothing save the truth and their own consciences, and they were responsible to no other but the people.

> *One Tape, Two Tapes, Three Tapes More; Four Tapes,*
> *Five Tapes, Four Tapes More . . .*

> *"Well, I am not a crook!"*
> *—Richard Nixon, November 11, 1973*

1973 May 19: Henry Petersen, assistant attorney general in the Criminal Division of the Justice Department, a protégé and admirer of Richard Nixon, had, at the request of the president, been put in direct charge of investigating the Watergate burglary, its genesis and after-math. By the time Cox and his team arrived on the scene, Petersen was being criticized for his seeming lack of aggressiveness in pursuing all facets of the case; he was even suspected by some of leaking grand jury testimony to the president.

On the night of May 19, 1973, Petersen was called to the office of the special prosecutor to bring Cox and his executive officer, James Vorenberg, up to date. Petersen was surely aware of another purpose of the meeting: to help Cox determine if the overall responsibility of the various investigations in progress ought to be taken out of the hands of Petersen's superior, Assistant Attorney General Earl J. Silbert, and turned over to the special counsel's team.

During an increasingly testy interview, Petersen recounted to Cox and his team that on the Sunday afternoon when Haldeman and Ehrlichman had resigned and John Dean had been fired, he, Petersen, had been summoned by the president to the Old Executive Office Building across from the White House. The president was under the impression that Petersen had offered Dean immunity from prosecu-tion if he cooperated with the investigation. Nixon demanded to know why Petersen had done that, since the president had expressly ordered that no one in the White House be given immunity. When Petersen denied such immunity was offered, the president, in words so offensive that Petersen could not repeat them verbatim, insisted that he had, that Dean had told the president so, and if Petersen doubted it, "You can listen to the tape." The possibility that a con-versation between the president of the United States and a prosecut-ing attorney in a case where the president had interests, had been recorded, surprised and intrigued Archibald Cox. Certainly it was something to look into later.

June 6: At a meeting attended by White House lawyers Leonard Garment, J. Fred Buzhardt, Charles Alan Wright, Archibald Cox and James Vorenberg, Cox made a formal request for the notes, the memo Petersen had written about it and the tape of the conversation between the president and Petersen of April 16. Additionally, he wanted the White House logs listing all calls and meetings between key White House aides and the president that had taken place between June l972 and May 1973. The president's lawyers were adamant that the special counsel could not have such materials, had no right to them, and that the executive privilege of presidents, past and future, to refuse to surrender documents necessary to the conduct of their office, was sacrosanct. "The president," Mr. Wright wrote in a memorandum the day after the meeting, "could hardly be expected by others to rummage through his papers to see what they could find that could be used against him . . . the meanest defendant in a two-bit criminal case cannot be subjected to the procedures . . . (proposed) to be used against the president of the United States."

After the meeting, Cox scheduled a press conference without mentioning its purpose, which was to introduce new members of his team. When White House lawyer Buzhardt called Vorenberg asking what Cox was going to say at the press conference, Vorenberg, sensing an opportunity to take advantage of the White House's unnecessary concern, reminded Buzhardt that the prosecutor's office had not received the material it had requested. The ruse worked; within an hour a package arrived from the White House. Although it did not include the memorandum, the record of the telephone call or the tape requested, it did contain comprehensive logs of dates and times of telephone conversations and meetings between the president and his advisers.

June 25: While the members of the Ervin committee sat in stunned silence, John W. Dean III, ousted counsel to the president, drew a picture of intrigue and corruption, the availability of hush money and the suborning of perjury by witnesses, which would be shocking enough in its breadth and intensity if committed by a criminal cartel, let alone with the knowledge and complicity of the president of the United States.

July 16: In testimony before the Ervin committee, Alexander Butterfield, a deputy assistant to the president, mentioned, almost casually, that in February 1971, Nixon had ordered the installation of a microphone and recording equipment in his office. Since its installation, every conversation of the president in his White House office, in the cabinet room, and in the Executive Office Building had been recorded. Phones in the White House and at the presidential retreat at Camp David had been monitored.

July 18: Using the logs of dates and times supplied by the White House, Archibald Cox formally requested of the White House through presidential lawyer J. Fred Buzhardt, eight specific tapes.

In response to Cox's request, Charles Alan Wright, acting as the president's constitutional lawyer, issued the following opinion:

"It is for the president, and only the president, to weigh whether the incremental advantage that these tapes would give you in a criminal proceeding justified the serious and lasting hurt that disclosure of them would do to the confidentiality that is imperative to the effective functioning of the Presidency."

To which the president added:

"…accordingly, the tapes, which have been under my sole personal control, will remain so. None has been transcribed or made public and none will be."

July 23: General Alexander M. Haig, who had replaced Haldeman as the president's chief of staff, called Richardson to tell him that the president would refuse to turn over the tapes, adding that Nixon was "uptight" about Cox, that there were to be no further "mistakes, or we will get Cox." At the time, Richardson had been giving some thought to instructing Cox that investigation of any illegal wiretapping on the part of the administration was outside his jurisdiction. At Cox's suggestion, a review of his own notes on the extent of Cox's brief convinced Richardson that it was not.

July 23: At 6:30 P.M. a United States marshal left the White House with a receipt signed by J. Fred Buzhardt. In legal effect, the paper acknowledged service on the president of the United States of a subpoena issued by the office of the Special Prosecutor compelling the production of nine tapes (one more had been added to the previous eight) and several memos. Much thought had gone into the decision to take the extreme action of issuing a subpoena to the president, not the least of which was the question of whether it could be done. And if it could, what if the president refused service? Would the court back the special prosecutor? Could the president of the United States be held in contempt of court?

July 25: In response to the subpoena, Nixon, citing an 1865 opinion from James Speed, attorney general under President Abraham Lincoln, wrote to Judge Sirica:

"It would be inconsistent with the public interest and the constitutional position of the presidency to make available recordings of meetings and telephone conversations in which I was a participant, and I must respectfully decline to do so."

Attorney General Richardson issued a statement opining that the position of both sides had merit and urging a compromise. Over the ensuing weeks, several schemes for the production of edited tapes, summarized tapes and summaries by disinterested third parties, were put forward, but none was adopted. By this time it had become clear to Richardson that he was being systematically excluded from White House discussions and decisions regarding the tapes and related matters. He found himself in conflict between his loyalty to a president who had trusted him with appointments to various high office, his responsibility to exercise the constitutional power of his office and his pledge of independence for the special prosecutor. When asked at a news conference what his position would be in a conflict between the president and Cox, Richardson replied that he would be neutral and that the president would have to seek advice from his own lawyer. It was a response that greatly displeased the White House.

July 26: On the afternoon of the 26th, Cox went to meet with the Watergate grand jury. His purpose was to explain the importance of the desired tapes to a just resolution of the case. What he wanted from the jurors was a request to Judge Sirica not for an order of contempt, but a much milder Rule to Show Cause. In laymen's terms, he wanted them to "tell us why you will not give us what we have asked you for." Having listened to Cox, the grand jury went before Judge Sirica to report that it was their unanimous decision that such an order should be issued. The judge gave the White House a little less than two weeks, until 10:00 A.M., August 7, to deliver the tapes or to justify why they would not.

August 7: The While House lawyers refused Judge Sirica's request to show cause why they would not comply with the subpoena for the tapes.

August 22: In hearings before the District Court, in a showdown between the right of executive privacy constitutionally provided to the president of the United States, and the right of a grand jury to have before it all available evidence in a criminal matter, Charles Alan Wright argued to Judge John J. Sirica both privilege and precedent.

"It was a simple fact of history," Wright intoned, "that in 184 years of this republic no court has undertaken to do the things that the Special Prosecutor contends this court ought to do." Wright pointed out to the judge that although Watergate might be unique, the dispute as to what the president could be compelled to do was not. Wright argued further that grave damage to the presidency would result if his ruling gave any or all of the 400 district courts in the United States the precedent of a free pass at a president's private papers.

Cox replied that this was indeed a unique case. Here there existed a likelihood of criminal conduct in the White House, all the more reason to lift the asserted presidential privilege. The prosecution could not present its best case, as it was their duty to do, nor could the defense mount its best case, as was their duty, unless, as the Constitution provided, they had access to all the pertinent evidence.

August 30: In a 23-page opinion, Judge Sirica directed the president to turn over the nine tapes and other subpoenaed material to him for his, the judge's, private review to determine if they were pertinent. "The grand jury," he wrote, "has a right to every man's evidence and that for the purpose of gathering evidence, process (a subpoena) may be issued to anyone."

August 31: The president announced that he would appeal. Even among those not sympathetic to Nixon's cause, consternation was now rising, of an approaching constitutional crisis, and serious attempts to head it off began.

September 12: Wright and Cox again argued the question, this time before the Court of Appeals for the District of Columbia. Two judges had recused themselves from the hearing because of possible conflicts. Two days after the hearing, the court issued an order requiring the parties to reach an agreement by September 20, or the court would issue a decision binding on both of them.

October 10: Vice President Spiro T. Agnew, in an appearance before the U.S. District Court in Baltimore, pleaded no contest to a single count of failure to report $29,500 in taxable income he had received while governor of the state. An intensive investigation by the U.S. Attorney in Maryland had uncovered a pattern of bribe-taking by Agnew that had continued while he was vice president. There was talk of indicting the vice president, which would have, in all probability, led to his conviction and/or impeachment. Attorney General Richardson was unwilling to go that path while the constitutional question of the president's refusal to surrender the tapes was roiling the nation. As part of an agreement with Agnew to drop the more substantial charges against him, the vice president was required to stand up in court and admit that his plea of no contest constituted admission to a felony.

October 12: As the parties in the dispute over the tapes were unable to reach a compromise, the Court of Appeals, by a vote of 5-2, decided that the rule of privilege that pertained to presidential conversations did not apply in a case where the prosecutor made a "uniquely powerful showing" that the tapes in question were necessary to the grand jury's investigation. It then put into perspective just where, in the American system of justice, the only man elected by the whole of the people to represent the whole of the people, the president, stood:

"He (the president) is not above the law's commands. Sovereignty remains at all times with the people, and they do not forfeit through elections the right to have the law construed against and applied to every citizen."

October 14: Alexander Haig telephoned Elliot Richardson, requesting that he come to the White House early the next morning; he had something important to discuss with the attorney general.

October 15, 9:00 A.M.: When Elliot Richardson was ushered into the chief of staff's office, Haig immediately launched into a recital of the dire international crisis facing America. The Egyptian Army had invaded Israel on Yom Kippur, and Syrian troops had crossed over the Golan Heights into Israeli territory. The president, Haig continued, acting decisively, had ordered an airlift of supplies to the Israelis to counterbalance an airlift by the Russians to the Arabs. When Richardson, in jest, suggested he was ready to go into action, the conversation shifted abruptly to its real purpose—the tapes.

The White House had a plan to resolve the stalemate and it was this:

1. The president would prepare an authenticated version of what was contained in the nine subpoenaed tapes for review by Judge Sirica.

2. The tapes were to remain in the president's possession as his personal property and would not be released.

3. The president would fire independent special counsel Cox, thus "mooting" the case.

To Haig's question as to what the attorney general thought of that, Elliot Richardson replied: "If you do that, Al, I'd have to resign." At that, Haig backed off, telling Richardson that perhaps the firing of Cox would be reexamined and that he would talk to the president again. If the White House wished to file an appeal to the U.S. Supreme Court of the decision of the District Court of Appeals, the deadline for doing so was October 19.

October 15, just past noon: Haig called Richardson with a proposal that Senator John Stennis of Mississippi prepare a summary of the tapes for Sirica and Cox, and added that was all the president would do—"Nothing More!"

There were several calls that day between Richardson and Haig, during one of which Haig told Richardson that if Cox did not go along with the proposal, the president wanted his, Richardson's, support, in the firing of Cox. Richardson replied that he did not think such a drastic step would be necessary; if the plan was reasonable, he thought Cox would agree to it.

6:00 P.M.: Cox met informally with Richardson while the attorney general was dressing for a black-tie dinner at the White House. Richardson outlined the White House proposal briefly. Senator Stennis would be given a preliminary record of the nine tapes; verbatim transcripts omitting nonpertinent conversation would be made and then transposed by a third party. Stennis would be free to paraphrase language that might be embarrassing to the president and delete matters related to national security. Cox returned to his office with considerable misgivings.

October 16: In his summation of the president's proposal, Richardson added a paragraph that the arrangement pertained only to the nine subpoenaed tapes, not to "other tapes and documents." J. Fred Buzhardt persuaded Richardson to remove that clause in the copy he would submit to Cox on the grounds that the proposal on its face dealt only with the nine tapes, and that the added clause was redundant.

October 17: Cox replied to the proposal in a generally conciliatory tone, saying that he did not desire a confrontation with the president and that the use of an impartial outsider was not unacceptable. Nevertheless, he listed 11 objections to the plan, one of which addressed a growing concern about both the White House and the special prosecutor—their credibility before the American people. "Could," Cox asked, "the public be fairly asked to confide so difficult and responsible a task to any one man operating in secrecy consulting with only the White House?" Cox went on to suggest that the scheme be expanded to include three special masters, of which group Stennis could be one.

In a telephone conversation that evening with Richardson, Cox assured him that he was not insisting that he, Cox, must personally see the tapes. The idea of a third party or persons reviewing them and submitting a verified transcript of the pertinent conversations was not being ruled out.

Thursday, October 18: Richardson went to the White House with Cox's reply. The president's lawyers considered it a rejection. Richardson was surprised. Perhaps they were confident that if the matter went to the Supreme Court, the president would prevail. All three of Nixon's lawyers agreed that Cox should be fired and that Richardson should be the man to do it. Richardson said that he would not do it. His agreement with Cox and the Senate was that he could not remove the special prosecutor unless he was guilty of "extraordinary impropriety" which, in Richardson's opinion, Cox was not.

That evening: While relaxing at his brother Louis's house outside Washington, Cox received a call asking him to contact Charles Alan Wright at the White House. When he got on, the president's constitutional lawyer outlined a final proposal, which Cox *"had to accept without reservation."* Cox's reply to what seemed to him more ultimatum than proposal was to tell Wright that the matter was too important to settle over the phone and should be put in writing.

The White House's final proposal, more stringent than some it had considered in the past, was that Senator Stennis would listen to the tapes alone, no actual tapes or portions of them would be turned over to Judge Sirica, and Cox was not to subpoena any further presidential tapes, papers or other documents.

October 19: In his letter to Cox, Wright wrote that "The president was willing to permit this unprecedented intrusion into the confidentiality of his office in order that the country might be spared the anguish of further months of litigation and indecision about private presidential papers and meetings."

In Cox's reply, he emphasized that the fourth requirement of the latest proposal—that he give blanket assurance that he would not subpoena tapes or papers in the future—would amount to a refutation of his pledge to the Senate Judiciary Committee that he would challenge such demands as far as the law permitted. "The attorney general was (and I was) confirmed on the strength of that assurance. I cannot break my promise."

The time limit for the White House to file an appeal to the Supreme Court was now only hours away.

It was at a meeting in the White House at approximately 10 o'clock that morning where Elliot Richardson was handed a copy of Wright's letter to Cox. To Richardson the implication of the text was clear and ominous. The use of Senator Stennis to review and select tapes would leave their control in the hands of the White House, and the prohibition against any demand by Cox for other tapes and papers would indeed "moot" the investigation. Richardson protested that in toto it was a proposal never set before Cox, certainly not by Richardson. Richardson also let Wright know of his displeasure that he was neither informed of nor involved in the process. Wright was more interested in Richardson's estimation of what Cox would do if the Stennis plan was forced on him. Would he resign? Richardson's reply, after some thought, was yes, he probably would.

7:00 P.M., approximately: Richardson received a phone call from Alexander Haig informing him that a letter was being drafted directing him to inform Cox that the president would not file an appeal to the Supreme Court, that Cox would be required to accept the Stennis compromise and to seek no further tapes or papers. If he did not, he would be fired. Richardson received the draft 20 minutes after the call from Haig, reached Cox at his unlisted number in Virginia, and read portions of the draft to Cox. Richardson told Cox that he would try to see the president and persuade him to reconsider. He had time to do that, he thought. But he didn't.

The question now in Cox's mind was whether the Nixon White House would, in a preemptive strike, announce the implementation of the Stennis plan. James Doyle, Cox's press secretary, found the answer from a contact at the *Los Angeles Times* Washington bureau. At 8:18 P.M. EST, the White House issued a statement from the president that

Stennis had accepted his role, that the special prosecutor would no longer attempt by judicial process to obtain tapes, notes, etc., and that he, the president, did not wish to intrude on the independence of the special prosecutor.

Cox's reaction was to issue his own statement in which he said that the proposed compromise was not a compromise at all since it would deprive the special prosecutor of admissible evidence of a criminal act. All of that, he added, he would bring to the attention of Judge Sirica.

Meanwhile, Attorney General Richardson sent a message to Alexander Haig that, although he believed the Stennis plan overall a reasonable concept, he could not, without violating their agreement, tell Cox he could not subpoena the tapes. He would, Richardson concluded, seek an early meeting with the president to discuss the matter further.

A Dark and Stormy Night
All men have in themselves that which is truly honorable.
Only they do not think of it.
— Mencius, 372 - 301 B.C.

Saturday, October 20, 1973: By the dawn of the fateful day that would set in motion events that would bring an end to the presidency of Richard Milhous Nixon, Elliot Lee Richardson had made up his mind as to what he must do. While believing that Archibald Cox had missed an opportunity at one time in the negotiations to accept a reasonable compromise, he could not find any instance in which his old law professor had done anything that would warrant his dismissal as independent special prosecutor. If Richardson was directed by the president to fire Cox, he would refuse to do so and would resign—a course of action, he must have known, that would forever end any chance he might have had to one day stand for the office himself.

Cox was conflicted. On the one hand, he had been raised to honor and respect the president of the United States, and had no stomach to fight him. On the other, he had credible evidence that the sitting president had involved himself in a host of illegal activities, and it was Cox's sworn duty to pursue that evidence to whatever conclusion it might lead.

Noon: The special prosecutor scheduled a news conference at the National Press Club at approximately 12:30 P.M. (NBC and CBS would carry it live; ABC was committed to an NCAA football game). Just before stepping in front of the cameras and microphones, Cox received a phone call from Richardson in which the attorney general assured him that his conduct had been far from the "extraordinary impropriety" necessary for his removal.

For the better part of an hour, the tall, thin lawyer, in the professorial tones of an academic confident in his subject, explained his position to those Americans who might be watching. How many would be watching a football game on a Saturday in October was problematical. Cox stated his case and took a barrage of questions from the press. If anybody was looking for a scapegoat, they would not find it in Elliot Richardson, who at all times had acted honorably. The White House ultimatum was simply not something he could live with. "I am going to go about my duties under the terms of which I assumed them." The news conference ended at 2:00 P.M.

A few minutes later: Leonard Garment called from the White House to tell Richardson that Haig was really "pissed off," and that Richardson's letter proved he was not aboard.

A few minutes later: Haig called Richardson to point out that the special prosecutor was now in defiance of an order from the president of the United States, and there was no alternative but to fire him. "The president," General Haig intoned, "now orders you to fire Cox." "I can't do that," Richardson said. "Well, I guess you'd better come over and resign" was Haig's response.

Some time later—the White House: Richardson hurried to the White House, only to be left waiting in Haig's office in the company of a silent Garment, Buzhardt and Wright. Nor did the president speak to the attorney general when he was first escorted into the Oval Office. Richardson told Nixon that he had come to offer his resignation. Nixon's reply was that the situation in the Middle East was so dangerous, it would be better if he fired Cox and deferred his own resignation until things there cooled down. Richardson responded that he could not fire Cox, and once again cited their agreement. Nixon then argued that Richardson should view the matter as one in the national interest, not as his personal commitment to Cox.

Richardson's response was that, in his mind, he was acting in what he believed to be the national interest.

Richardson returned to his office and told Deputy Attorney General William D. Ruckelshaus, "The deed is done."

Some time later the same day: Haig called William Ruckelshaus, now the acting attorney general: "Your commander-in-chief is giving you an order. You do not have any alternative under your oath of office. Fire Cox," Haig said, "and then if you have qualms, wait a week until things cool down, and then resign." Ruckelshaus had been anticipating the possibility of things coming to where they now were and had concluded that for him, at that time, there was a convergence of personal morality and the public good. He refused to fire Cox and resigned.

October 20, 1973—evening, a letter delivered by hand:

> Dear Mr Cox:
> As provided by Title 28, section 505 (b) of the United States Code and Title 18, section 0.132 of the Code of Federal Regulations, I have today assumed the duties of acting Attorney General. In that capacity I am, as instructed by the president, discharging you, effective at once, from your position as Special Prosecutor, Watergate Special Prosecution Force.
> Very truly yours,
> Robert Bork
> Solicitor General of the United States

8:30 P.M., White House Press Room: White House Press Secretary Ron Ziegler announced that "President Nixon has tonight discharged Archibald Cox, the Special Prosecutor in the Watergate case. The office of the Watergate Special Prosecution Force has been abolished as of approximately 8 o'clock tonight."

"May none but honest and wise men ever rule under this roof," said John Adams, the first president to occupy the White House.

You know the king is dead when the princes leave his chamber and the rabble raise their voices. The special prosecutor's dignified and reasonable defense of his actions, followed by his summary dismissal and the dissolution of the Office of the Special Prosecutor, raised a tumult throughout the land. Powerful men who had, out of party or personal loyalty, stoutly defended Richard Nixon now turned on him. From the people came an unprecedented howl of indignation. The White House was deluged with more than 450,000 telegrams of protest and its telephones were inundated with angry reaction. From the editorial pages of newspapers over the entire political spectrum, calls for Nixon's resignation or impeachment rang, and denunciation thundered from many pulpits. It was a reaction in its size and intensity no one, not even Richardson or Cox, the Senate or the House, and least of all the president and his advisers, had anticipated.

It seemed apparent to rational men, who by now included the men on his staff, that the president could not survive in office. Yet he soldiered on, ever more isolated with whatever demons were driving him.

On the morning of October 23, 1973, three days after what by that time was referred to as "The Saturday Night Massacre," Charles Alan Wright defended on national television, the now-defunct Stennis plan, and in the afternoon announced in Judge Sirica's court that the president would not defy the law; he would comply with Judge Sirica's orders.

On their return from a long Columbus Day weekend, members of the House of Representatives filed 22 separate bills for impeachment of the president, and a number of other bills to create a new office of Special Prosecutor truly independent of the executive.

On the 26th, in an attempt at a preemptive strike, the president announced he would set up his own special prosecutor office and then, to his disadvantage, he blurted out that he had no intention of turning over any more tapes: "The tougher it gets, the cooler I get." It now seemed permissible in some quarters to speculate on the condition of the president's mental health.

On November 1, the president's lawyers reported that two of the subpoenaed tapes were missing. That revelation was later expanded to include 18 minutes of the much-desired June 20 conversation between Nixon and Haldeman. The tape of March 21, 1973, however, did expose a conversation between Nixon, Haldeman and Dean over the amount needed and mechanics of raising and delivering hush money to the Watergate defendants.

In May, Leon Jaworski, who had replaced Cox as special prosecutor, demanded an additional 64 tapes. The White House refused. Sirica ordered compliance. The White House went to the Appellate Court. Jaworski took the case directly to the Supreme Court.

The White House released 46 tapes to the public. Although edited to put Nixon in the best possible light, the vulgarity and cursing emanating from the mouth of the president horrified many.

On July 24, 1974, Warren Burger, chief justice of the Supreme Court, announced that it was the unanimous decision of the Court in the case of *United States v. Nixon* that the president (who had appointed Burger chief justice) must comply with the order and turn over all requested tapes.

Over a three-day period, July 27 to 30, the House Judiciary Committee, including several former Nixon defenders from the Republican side, convinced that a recently revealed tape of June 23, 1973, in which the president was heard conspiring to enlist both the FBI and CIA in the Watergate coverup, warranted his removal from office. The panel voted three Articles of Impeachment.

On August 8, 1974, Richard Milhous Nixon, 37th president of the United States, announced his resignation from office, the first president to do so.

Epilogue

In the aftermath of their respective firings and resignations, Archibald Cox and Elliot Richardson found themselves in a situation rare in America—there were two political heroes at one time.

Richardson took to the lecture circuit, the Chubb Fellowship at Yale and the Godkin lectureship at Harvard. In December of 1974, President Ford appointed him to that most prestigious of American ambassadorships, the one where so many Massachusetts men had served, the Court of St. James. Before the year was out, Ambassador Richardson let President Ford know of the ambassador's discontent with the lack of attention to himself and his assignment on the part of Secretary of State Henry Kissinger. Unwilling to sever political ties to the more liberal wing of the party that Richardson exemplified, President Ford appointed him Secretary of Commerce. Richardson retained that position, his fourth cabinet post, throughout the Ford administration, and was for three years of the following presidency of

Jimmy Carter, American ambassador to the United Nations' Law of the Sea Conference.

Professor Cox resumed his distinguished tenure at the law school at Harvard University.

Had men and history played different roles, Archibald Cox might well have been a justice of the Supreme Court, and Elliot Richardson a serious candidate for president of the United States. The irony of the self-destruction, personal and political, of Richard Milhous Nixon, was that encouraging his operatives to break the law to gain political advantage over his opposition was unnecessary. Nixon had the 1972 election won well before the men of Watergate broke the law in a nod to one man's electoral paranoia.

CHAPTER VI

The O'Neill

In many ways the public career of Thomas P. "Tip" O'Neill was shaped by transitions. When he came of age in the working class neighborhood of his home in Cambridge, second- and third-generation sons of Irish immigrants were turning away from the pattern of graduation from high school to lifetime employment on the police or fire department or with a public utility or with the state or city to seek advancement through higher education. In local politics, the influence of aging Irish ward bosses was waning, and in the Commonwealth, Republican control of the Massachusetts government was slowly eroding. During O'Neill's service in the leadership of the U.S. House, that body was in transition from one controlled by entrenched committee chairmen to a more participatory body and a stronger Speaker. Nationally, the appetite for social legislation seem sated, as the pendulum of American politics was moving, if slowly, from the liberal left to the conservative right.

Thomas Phillip O'Neill Jr. was born on December 9, 1912, in Cambridge, in the top-floor flat of a tri-level apartment building the locals referred to as a "three-decker." The O'Neills had been politically active from the days of his Irish-born grandfather. Tom's father had been elected to the Cambridge Common Council at age 28, and later, having topped the Civil Service examination for the job, was appointed the city's superintendent of sewers. Young Tom's education was

THE O'NEILL • 359

exclusively Catholic: parochial grammar school, St. John's High School, and under the Jesuits at Boston College. "Tip," as he came to be almost universally called, was elected to the Massachusetts House in 1936.

In 1948, three rival slates for delegates to the Democratic National Convention appeared on the Massachusetts ballot. One, which included the name of majority leader of the U.S. House, John W. McCormack, was headed by James Michael Curley, recently released from the federal penitentiary at Danbury. Another was put together by the Democratic State Committee, and the third by members of the legislature. The Curley delegation won, O'Neill maintained, because of Curley's manipulation of the ballots in Boston. Political chicanery aside, John McCormack was so impressed by O'Neill's work during the campaign that he urged the five-term legislator to attempt to take Democratic control of the state House of Representatives.

O'Neill, enlisting a cadre of young enthusiasts, many of them veterans of World War II and some with and some without political experience, targeted the nearby suburbs, where a migration from the Democrat-voting cities of the Commonwealth had swelled the ranks of the party. When the results were in, the seemingly unassailable 144 to 96 Republican majority of 1946-1947 had turned to a narrow 122 to 118 Democratic majority. On January 5, 1949, Thomas P. O'Neill Jr. was (save for the exception of Henry Wilson's maneuvering for the election of Nathaniel Banks Jr. in 1851), elected the first Democratic Speaker of the 319 year-old Massachusetts House of Representatives, and the first of his faith and heritage. It would be ten years before his party would solidify majority control of the body, but if any Yankee Republican puffing his Cuban at the Union or the Tavern Club had the prescience to realize it, that January day in 1949 was the beginning of the end to the century-old dominance of the Republican Party in Massachusetts.

Unlike some of the Republican Speakers he had served under—one of whom would not even let a Democratic Representative enter his office—O'Neill was not vindictive toward the new minority. He showed both respect for their persons and magnanimity in such things as the assignment of office space to the minority leadership. The slim majority his party held taught O'Neill important lessons in successful legislative leadership. The skills in accommodation and compromises, understanding of differing personalities, and attention to detail that O'Neill learned in the

Massachusetts House would serve him well in the U.S. Congress, a body he joined in January of 1953, having won the House seat vacated by John F. Kennedy in his successful candidacy for the U.S. Senate.

The Practicing Professional

In *The American Speakership*, Ronald A. Peters Jr. traces the evolution of the Speakership of U.S. House through four periods: the parliamentary, the partisan, the feudal and the democratic. When Tip O'Neill arrived in the House in January 1953, the chairmen of powerful committees with long incumbency, most Southern and conservative, still held sway, as they had in Speaker McCormack's day, over the House. It was, however, like the Massachusetts legislature when O'Neill assumed the Speakership of the House there, a body in transition. The majority leader, John W. McCormack, found in O'Neill a man who, while retaining an undiminished commitment to the social policies of his party, could deal with both the new members who demanded more meaningful participation in the process, and the often crusty and more conservative committee chairmen. In the 92nd Congress (1971-1973) under the Speakership of Carl Albert, O'Neill was elected majority whip, and in the 94th, majority leader. It was in that 94th Congress that the dominance of the old powerful chairman was finally broken. The House O'Neill was to preside over when he was chosen Speaker in January 1977, was more democratic, participatory, and younger. The Speaker's Democratic Party had comfortable control of the House, 292 to143, the Democrats also held sway in the Senate, 61 seats to the Republicans' 38. The newly elected president, Jimmy Carter, was also a Democrat. Speaker O'Neill, skilled politician, experienced leader that he was, could not have asked for anything more on which to build a substantial legislative legacy.

The Speakership of Tip O'Neill in Two Parts
The Carter Years

If there was ever a "self-made" president, it was James Earl Carter, the former governor of Georgia. In his campaign he studiously ignored the party and its leaders, and in turn they abhorred him. He arrived in

Washington having run on an anti-Washington platform. A religious man of deep convictions, he thought of himself more than an occupant, but as a trustee of the presidency. He brought with him a staff of equally pure and politically unsullied young men. To get elected is one thing, to govern successfully another. The new administration was soon enough confronted with the reality that when the Founding Father's established three separate and ostensibly equal branches of government, they created the same number of institutional egos. That truism, with its resulting powers and privileges, perks and personalities, needs to be scrupulously observed by anyone who wishes to succeed in the nation's capital. It was almost as if, having won the presidency with little help from and much disdain for the "political establishment," Carter and his people believed they could govern without it.

The initial relationship of Jimmy Carter with Speaker O'Neill was marked by indifference, even disdain, for the Speaker and his House, and a near total lack of consultation before legislation, too much of it, was sent up to the House. O'Neill faced other difficulties in enacting Carter's programs beyond the attitude of the president and his staff. The pendulum of American politics was swinging to the right; the long years of social legislation that had begun with Franklin Roosevelt's New Deal so many years ago was coming to an end. To top it off, O'Neill was more liberal than the president and a significant number of the House majority.

For the four years of his Speakership under Carter, O'Neill used all his accumulated powers and skills—choice committee assignments, friendly persuasion, toughness when needed, tit vote for tat vote, referrals to committees, delay, compromise when necessary, uncanny knowledge of the needs of each member, and appeals to the better instincts of each—to pass most of Carter's legislation. Much of what the president wanted he got, albeit in some water-downed version. Both the president and the Speaker suffered major defeats. Yet through all of those troubled years, Thomas P. O'Neill managed to preserve what others would abandon, if he could not enrich the large array of federal law and programs designed by the Democratic Party to raise up those Americans in the lowest of circumstance, he would preserve them.

The Reagan Years

There he stood, a bulbous-nosed, overweight, aging, cigar-smoking, liberal Boston Irish pol; a caricaturist's dream. And he stood alone, the Speaker of the House did. Carter had been chased from office by inflation, high unemployment, a stagnant economy, and the national trauma of the unrescued American hostages in Iran. In the House, O'Neill's 119-vote majority had been reduced to 51, and a goodly number of them were more comfortable with the new president's political philosophy than with that of the Speaker's. News was worse in the Senate, where the Democrats' previous majority of 17 was now a minority of 7. O'Neill's opponent was the spell-binding leader of conservative Republican reconstructionism—Hollywood star and former governor of California Ronald Wilson Reagan. Their ensuing political battles—the stuff of wandering storytellers had the combatants resided in the land of their ancestors—would thrust the Speaker into a role few of his predecessors ever played, that of the nationally recognized leader of his party. The Reaganites were correct in characterizing Tip O'Neill as "a liberal Boston Irish Pol." Their mistake lay in thinking they could make an ogre out of a man who had spent a lifetime practicing two of the better instincts of that genre: compassion and political astuteness.

Donnybrook

Reagan began his presidency by slam-dunking O'Neill, quickly acquiring House passage of his "supply-side" economic program, which included massive tax cuts and substantially increased military spending. O'Neill's majority in the House was too small, and the tide of conservatism running too strong, for the Speaker to do much about it. O'Neill bided his time as the "Reagan Revolution" rolled on during the first seven months of the president's term. O'Neill's major legislative concern was the preservation of the array of social policies he held so dear to his heart. It was one thing for the Carter administration to stop the adoption of new social initiatives; the Reagan administration wanted to turn them back or scale them down. In September 1981, Reagan, heady with the quick success of his tax and budget plans, took a misstep, the proposed cutback in what had come to be the corner-stone of liberal social legislation—Social Security. Taking advantage of the national recognition that the Republican attacks had foisted on him, the Speaker went on a vigorous and sustained attack against the president and his policies. The heartless Reagan, O'Neill thundered, was enriching the already wealthy on the backs of the middle class, the working man, and the widow. The only thing that stood between greed and compassion was the Democratic Party and its only standing general, Tip O'Neill.

In Reagan's case, the legislative honeymoon most new presidents enjoy was short-lived, as O'Neill expected it would be. The massive cuts achieved in his first year, coupled with a substantial rise in military spending and insufficient cuts in other programs, resulted in the largest deficit in U.S. history. In 1982, the Speaker saw the abandonment of Reagan's beloved supply-side economics as he presided over the passage of the president's proposed $98 billion tax increase. In the 99th Congress, the Speaker's last, he witnessed the Democratic majority in the House grow by 10 more votes than he had at the beginning of the Reagan presidency.

When Thomas P. O'Neill Jr., Democrat, Cambridge, relinquished the gavel on January 2, 1987, he retired from 52 years in elective office, the last ten as Speaker of the House of Representatives, the longest continuous service in that exalted office in the history of the United States. All in all, with Speakers Frederick Huntington Gillett, Joseph William Martin Jr., John William McCormack, and Thomas P. O'Neill, Jr. Massachusetts men held the office of Speaker of the national House for a total of twenty-nine years of the 20th century.

Author's Note

It was my thought in writing *Extraordinary Tenure* to put to paper the widely held belief that in the Commonwealth of Massachusetts there exists a particular political culture of long standing, and to present a chronicle of that culture in an orderly, interesting, and readable way. The reader will find little new material in my chronicling of the public lives and times of those men and women who have personified that culture. I am therefore most grateful to the researchers and writers who have in various fashions provided the material necessary for the book.

Massachusetts Men and Women
and their
Extraordinary Tenure
in elected and appointed positions
in the government of the United States

from John Adams,
Vice President of the United States
1789 - 1797
to Thomas P. O'Neill, Jr.
Speaker of the United States House of Representatives
1977 - 1987

While the author has made every attempt to present a complete and accurate listing of those Massachusetts men and women who are the subject of this book, he would appreciate any corrections the reader feels he/she can comfortably make citing the source.

Corrected as of November 19, 2003.

Sources:
Principal Officers of the Department of State and United States Chiefs of Missions 1788-1990 Washington, DC: U.S. Government Printing Office.
Encyclopedia of Congress
The Oxford Companion to the Supreme Court of the United States. Oxford University Press 1992.
Members of the Supreme Court of the United States Published by the Curator's Office, Supreme Court of the United States (Revised September, 1994.)

Chronological List

Eighteenth Century

Under the Articles of Confederation:

Year:	Name:	Office:
1780-1783	Dana, Francis	Minister - Russia
1781-1788	Adams, John	Minister - Netherlands
1785-1788	Adams, John	Minister - United Kingdom
1785-1789	Knox, Henry	Secretary of War

Under the Constitution:

Year:	Name:	Office:
1789-1814	Otis, Samuel A.	Secretary of the Senate
1789-1797	Adams, John	Vice President
1789-1810	Cushing, William	Justice Supreme Court
1789-1795	Knox, Henry	Secretary of War
1789-1791	Osgood, Samuel	Postmaster General
1791-1795	Pickering, Timothy	Postmaster General
1794-1797	Adams, John Q.	Minister - Netherlands
1795-1795	Pickering, Timothy	Secretary of War
1795-1800	Pickering, Timothy	Secretary of War
1797-1799	Sedgwick, Theodore	President Pro-tem Senate
1796	Adams, John Q.	Minister - Portugal
1796-1803	King, Rufus	Minister - United Kingdom
1797-1801	Adams, John Q.	Minister - Germany
1797-1801	Adams, John	President
1799-1801	Sedgwick, Theodore	Speaker of the House

Nineteenth Century

Year:	Name:	Office:
1800-1800	Dexter, Samuel	Secretary of War
1801-1801	Dexter, Samuel	Secretary of Treasury
1801-1801	Lincoln, Levi	Secretary of State
1801-1809	Dearborn, Henry	Secretary of War

YEAR:	NAME:	OFFICE:
1801-1804	Lincoln, Levi	Attorney General
1804-1808	Bowdoin, James	Minister - Spain
1807-1811	Varnum, Joseph .	Speaker of the House
1809-1814	Adams, John Q.	Envoy/Minister - Russia
1809-1812	Eustis, William	Secretary of War
1811-1845	Story, Joseph	Justice Supreme Court
1813-1815	Varnum, Joseph B.	President Pro-tem Senate
1813-1814	Gerry, Elbridge	Vice President
1814-1818	Crownshield, Benjamin	Secretary of Navy
1814-1819	Erving, George W.	Minister - Spain
1814-1818	Eustis, William	CdA - Netherlands
1815-1817	Adams, John Q.	Minister - United Kingdom
1817-1825	Adams, John Q.	Secretary of State
1818-1824	Everett, Alexander H.	CdA - Netherlands
1822-1824	Dearborn, Henry A. Sr.	Minister - Portugal
1825-1826	King, Rufus	Minister - United Kingdom
1825-1829	Adams, John Q.	President
1825-1829	Everett, Alexander H.	Minister - Spain
1825-1831	Forbes, John M.	CdA - Argentina
1826-1830	Appleton, John James	CdA - Sweden
1832-1832	Baylies, Francis	CdA - Argentina
1835-1837	Wheaton, Henry	Minister - Germany
1841-1843	Webster, Daniel	Secretary of State
1841-1845	Everett, Edward	Minister - United Kingdom
1841-1843	Webster, Daniel Fletcher	Chief Clerk - State Dept.
1843-1844	Henshaw, David	Secretary of Navy
1843	Everett, Edward	Commissioner - China
1843-1847	Everett, Alexander H.	Commissioner - China
1843-1844	Cushing, Caleb	Minister - China
1845-1846	Bancroft, George	Secretary of Navy
1846-1849	Bancroft, George	Minister - United Kingdom
1847-1849	Winthrop, Robert Charles	Speaker of the House
1849-1852	Lawrence, Abbott	Minister - United Kingdom
1850-1852	Webster, Daniel	Secretary of State
1851-1857	Curtis, Benjamin R.	Justice Supreme Court
1852-1853	Everett, Edward	Secretary of State
1853-1857	Cushing, Caleb	Attorney General
1845-1857	Parker, Peter	Commissioner - China

Year:	Name:	Office:
1856-1857	Banks, Nathaniel	Speaker of the House
1861-1867	Motley, J. Lothrop	Minister - Austria
1861-1867	Burlingame, Anson	Minister - China
1861-1868	Adams, Charles F.	Minister - United Kingdom
1864-1870	Hale, Charles	Counsul-General - Egypt
1867-1874	Bancroft, George	Minister - Germany
1869-1873	Boutwell, George S.	Secretary of Treasury
1869-1870	Hoar, Ebenezer	Attorney General
1869-1870	Motley, J. Lothrop	Minister - United Kingdom
1869-1877	Peirce, Henry A.	Minister - Hawaii
1873-1874	Richardson, William A.	Secretary of Treasury
1873-1875	Wilson, Henry	Vice President
1874-1877	Russell, Thomas	Minister - Venezula
1874-1877	Cushing, Caleb	Minister - Spain
1877-1880	Lowell, James Russell	Minister - Spain
1877-1881	Devens, Charles	Attorney General
1880-1885	Lowell, James Russell	Minister - United Kingdom
1881-1882	Payson, Charles	CdA - Denmark
1881-1881	French, Henry A.	Secretary of Treasury
1882-1902	Gray, Horace	Justice Supreme Court
1885-	Williams, George W.	Minister - Haiti
1885-1889	Endicott, William C.	Secretary of War
1889-1890	Loring, George B.	Minister - Portugal
1889-1892	Washburn, John D.	Minister - Switzerland
1890-1893	Heard, Augustine	Minister - Korea
1892-1893	Wharton, William F.	Secretary of State
1892-1893	Coolidge, T. Jefferson	Minister - France
1893-1897	Collins, Patrick A.	Counsel General - Great Britian
1893-1895	Olney, Richard	Attorney General
1895-1897	Olney, Richard	Secretary of State
1897-1902	Long, John Davis	Secretary of Navy
1897-1900	Draper, William F.	Ambassador - Italy

TWENTIETH CENTURY

Year:	Name:	Office:
1900-1905	Meyer, George von L.	Ambassador - Italy
1902-1932	Holmes, Oliver Wendell Jr.	Justice Supreme Court

Year:	Name:	Office:
1902-1904	Moody, William Henry	Secretary of Navy
1904-1906	Moody, William Henry	Attorney General
1905-1907	Meyer, George von L.	Ambassador - Russia
1906-1910	Moody, William Henry	Justice Supreme Court
1906-1911	Peirce, Herbert H.D.	Minister - Norway
1907-1909	Meyer, George von L.	Postmaster General
1907	Lodge, Henry Cabot	President Pro-tem Senate
1907-1909	Dodge, H. Percival	Minister - Hounduras
1907-1909	Dodge, H. Percival	Minister - El Salvador
1908-1908	Coolidge, John Gardner	Minister - Nicaragua
1908-1910	Brown, Phillip M.	Minister - Hounduras
1909-1910	Dodge, H. Percival	Minister - Morocco
1909-1913	Meyer, George von L.	Secretary of the Navy
1909-1913	Hitchcock, Frank H.	Postmaster General
1911-1913	Dodge, H. Percival	Minister - Panama
1911-1913	Guild, Curtis	Ambassador - Russia
1912-1913	Anderson, Larz	Ambassador - Japan
1913-1914	Williams, George Fred	Minister - Greece
1913-1914	Williams, George Fred	Minister - Montenegro
1914-1921	Stimson, Frederic J.	Ambassador - Argentina
1916-1939	Brandeis, Louis	Justice Supreme Court
1919-1926	Dodge, H. Percival	Minister - Yugoslavia
1919-1924	Gillett, Frederick H.	Speaker of the House
1920-1921	Grew, Joseph C.	Minister - Denmark
1920-1922	Phillips, William	Ambassador - Netherlands
1920-1922	Phillips, William	Ambassador - Luxembourg
1921-1922	Dresel, Ellis Loring	CdA - Germany
1921-1923	Coolidge, Calvin	Vice President
1921-1924	Grew, Joseph C.	Minister - Switzerland
1921-1924	Child, Richard Washburn	Ambassador - Italy
1921-1929	Weeks, John W.	Secretary of War
1922-1930	Washburn, Albert H.	Minister - Austria
1924-1927	Phillips, William	Minister - Luxembourg
1924-1927	Phillips, William	Ambassador - Belgium
1926-1930	Dodge, H. Percival	Minister - Denmark
1923-1929	Coolidge, Calvin	President
1927-1929	Phillips, William	Minister - Canada
1927-1932	Grew, Joseph C.	Ambassador - Turkey

YEAR:	NAME:	OFFICE:
1928-1929	Whiting, William F.	Secretary of Commerce
1929-1933	Adams, Charles F.	Secretary of the Navy
1930-1932	Forbes, William Cameron	Ambassador - Japan
1930-1932	Ratshesky, Abraham C.	Minister - Czechoslovakia
1932-1941	Grew, Joseph C.	Ambassador - Japan
1933-1945	Perkins, Frances	Secretary of Labor
1936-1941	Phillips, William	Ambassador - Italy
1938-1940	Kennedy, Joseph P.	Ambassador - Great Britain
1939-1962	Frankfurter, Felix	Justice Supreme Court
1945-1967	Saltonstall, Leverett	U.S. Senator
1947-1949	Martin, Joseph W. Jr.	Speaker of the House
1947-1949	Bohlen, Charles E.	Counsellor - State Department
1948-1952	Crocker, Edward S. 2nd	Ambassador - Iraq
1948-1953	Tobin, Maurice J.	Secretary of Labor
1953-1954	Cabot, John M.	Assist. Secretary of State
1954-1957	Cabot, John M.	Ambassador - Sweden
1957-1959	Cabot, John M.	Ambassador - Columbia
1959-1961	Cabot, John M.	Ambassador - Brazil
1953-1955	Martin, Joseph W. Jr.	Speaker of the House
1953-1958	Weeks, Sinclair	Secretary of Commerce
1954-1958	Willauer, Whiting	Ambassador - Honduras
1955-1957	Conant, James B.	Ambassador - Germany
1955-1960	Harrington, Julian F.	Ambassador - Panama
1957-1957	Rutter, Peter	CdA - Ghana
1958-1960	Wiggleworth, Richard B.	Ambassador - Canada
1958-1961	Willauer, Whiting	Ambassador - Costa Rica
1959-1961	Herter, Christian A.	Secretary of State
1959-1961	Stimpson, Harry F. Jr.	Ambassador - Paraguay
1959-1966	Stebbins, Henry E.	Ambassador - Nepal
1960	Bohlen, Charles E.	Career Ambassador
1961-1971	McCormack, John W.	Speaker of the House
1961-1963	Kennedy, John F.	President
1961-1964	Kennedy, Robert F.	Attorney General
1961-1963	Galbraith, J. Kenneth	Ambassador - India
1961-1965	Cox, Archibald	Solicitor General
1961-1966	Reischauer, Edwin O.	Ambassador - Japan
1962-1965	Torbet, Horace G. Jr.	Ambassador - Somalia
1962-1970	Bohlen, Charles	Ambassador - France

YEAR:	NAME:	OFFICE:
1963-1964	Lodge, Henry Cabot Jr.	Ambassador - Viet Nam
1963-1968	Henderson, Douglas	Ambassdor - Bolivia
1964-1968	Ryan, Robert J.	Ambassador - Niger
1965-1967	Lodge, Henry Cabot Jr.	Ambassador - Viet Nam
1965-1968	O'Brien, Lawrence F.	Postmaster General
1966-1969	Stebbins, Henry E.	Ambassador - Uganda
1967-1973	Griswold, Erwin N.	Solicitor General
1967-1979	Brooke, Edward W.	U.S. Senator
1967-1968	Lodge, Henry Cabot Jr.	Ambassador at Large
1968-1969	Lodge, Henry Cabot Jr.	Ambassador - Germany
1969-1973	Volpe, John A.	Secretary of Transportation
1969-1974	Donovan, Eileen	Ambassador - Barbados
1970-1973	Richardson, Elliot L.	Secretary of HEW
1973-1973	Richardson, Elliot L.	Secretary of Defense
1973-1973	Richardson, Elliot L.	Attorney General
1973-1973	Cox, Archibald	Special Prosecutor
1973-1977	Volpe, John A.	Ambassador - Italy
1974-1975	Porier, William J.	Ambassador - Canada
1975-1976	Richardson, Elliot L.	Ambassador - United Kingdom
1975-1977	Richardson, Elliot L.	Secretary of Commerce
1975-1976	McAuliffe, Eugene V.	Minister - Hungary
1976-1979	Stearns, Monteagle	Ambassador - Ivory Coast
1977-1980	Richardson, Elliot L.	Ambassador at Large
1977-1980	White, Robert E.	Ambassador - Paraguay
1977-1987	O'Neill, Thomas P. Jr.	Speaker of the House
1980-1981	White, Robert E.	Ambassador - El Salvador
1980-1984	Thayer, Harry E. T.	Ambassador - Singapore
1983-1985	Heckler, Margaret	Secretary - Health & Human Services
1985-1989	Heckler, Margaret	Ambassador - Ireland
1985-1989	Fried, Charles	Solicitor General
1986-1989	Moore, Jonathan	Ambassador at Large

CONSTITUTIONAL OFFICES

PRESIDENTS OF THE UNITED STATES

PRESIDENT:	TERM
Adams, John	03/04/1797 - 03/03/1801
Adams, John Quincy	03/04/1825 - 03/03/1829
Coolidge, Calvin	08/03/1923 - 03/03/1925 03/04/1925 - 03/03/1929
Kennedy, John Fitzgerald	01/20/1961 - 11/22/1963

VICE PRESIDENTS OF THE UNITED STATES

VICE PRESIDENT:	TERM:	PRESIDENT:
Adams, John	04/30/1789 - 03/03/1797	George Washington
Gerry, Elbridge	03/04/1813 - 11/23/1814	James Madison
Wilson, Henry	03/04/1873 - 11/22/1875	U.S. Grant
Coolidge, Calvin	03/04/1921 - 08/02/1923	Warren G. Harding

UNITED STATES SENATORS

NAME:	TERM:
Sedgwick, Theodore	06/11/1796 - 03/03/1799 *President Pro-Tempore 5th Congress*
Pickering, Timothy	03/04/1803 - 03/03/1811

NAME:	TERM:
Varnum, Joseph B.	06/29/1811 - 03/03/1817 *President Pro-Tempore 13th Congress*
Webster, Daniel	03/04/1827 - 02/22/1841 03/04/1845 - 07/22/1850
Sumner, Charles	04/24/1851 - 03/11/1874
Boutwell, George Sewall	03/17/1873 - 03/03/1877
Crane, Murray Winthrop	10/12/1904 - 03/03/1913
Lodge, Henry Cabot	03/04/1893 - 11/09/1924 *President Pro-Tempore 62nd Congress*
Walsh, David Ignatius	03/04/1919 - 03/03/1925 12/06/1926 - 01/03/1947
Saltonstall, Leverett	01/04/1945 - 01/03/1967
Brooke, Edward W. III	01/03/1967 - 01/03/1979

SPEAKERS OF THE HOUSE

NAME	CONGRESSES	YEARS	SPEAKER
Theodore Sedgwick	1st - 4th 6th	03/04/1789 - 06/11/1796 03/04/1799 - 03/03/1801	 6th
Joseph Varnum	4th - 12th	03/04/1795 - 06/19/1811	10th,11th
Robert C. Winthrop	26th - 31st	11/09/1840 - 05/25/1842 11/29/1842 - 07/30/1850	 30th
Nathaniel Banks	33rd - 35th 39th - 42nd 44th - 45th 51st	03/04/1853 - 12/24/1857 12/04/1865 - 03/03/1873 03/04/1875 - 03/03/1879 03/04/1889 - 03/03/1891	34th
Frederick H. Gillett	53rd - 68th	03/04/1893 - 03/03/1925	66th - 68th

NAME	CONGRESSES	YEARS	SPEAKER
Joseph W. Martin, Jr.	69th - 89th	03/04/1925 - 01/03/1967	80th, 83rd
John W. McCormack	70th - 91st	11/06/1928 - 01/03/1971	87th - 91st
Thomas P. O'Neill, Jr.	83rd - 99th	01/03/1953 - 01/01/1987	95th - 99th

Note: At three times in the history of the United States, both the sitting President and the Speaker of the House have been Massachusetts men:

    1799:   Speaker Theodore Sedgwick - President John Adams
    1923:   Speaker Frederick Gillett - President Calvin Coolidge
    1961:   Speaker John W. McCormack - President John F. Kennedy

JUSTICES OF THE SUPREME COURT OF THE UNITED STATES

JUSTICE:	POSITION:	TERM:	APPOINTED BY:
Cushing, William	Associate Justice	1790-1810	Washington
Story, Joseph	Associate Justice	1811-1845	Madison
Curtis, Benjamin R.	Associate Justice	1851-1857	Fillmore
Gray, Horace	Associate Justice	1882-1902	Arthur
Holmes, Oliver Wendell	Associate Justice	1902-1932	T. Roosevelt
Moody, William Henry	Associate Justice	1906-1910	T. Roosevelt
Brandeis, Louis	Associate Justice	1916-1939	Wilson
Frankfurter, Felix	Associate Justice	1939-1962	F. Roosevelt

PRESIDENTIAL CABINET MEMBERS

PRESIDENT:	POSITION:	TERM:
George Washington		*04/30/1789 - 03/03/1793*
Henry Knox	War	09/12/1789
Samuel Osgood	Postmaster General	09/26/1789 - 08/12/1791
Timothy Pickering	Postmaster General	08/12/1791
George Washington (second term)		*03/04/1793 - 03/03/1797*
Henry Knox	War	01/02/1795
Timothy Pickering	War	02/02/1795
Timothy Pickering	War (Ad Interim)	12/10/1795-02/05/1795
Timothy Pickering	Postmaster General	02/25/1795
Timothy Pickering	State (Ad Interim)	08/20/1795
Timothy Pickering	State	12/10/1795
John Adams		*03/04/1797 - 03/03/1801*
Samuel Dexter	Treasury (Ad Interim)	01/01/1801
Timothy Pickering	State	05/12/1800
Samuel Dexter	War	05/13/1800 - 06/12/1800
Thomas Jefferson		*03/04/1801 - 03/05/1805*
Levi Lincoln	State	03/05/1801 (one day)
Samuel Dexter	Treasury	05/06/1801
Henry Dearborn	War	03/05/1801
Levi Lincoln	Attorney General	03/05/1801 - 12/31/1804
Henry Dearborn	Navy (Ad Interim)	04/01/1801
Thomas Jefferson (second term)		*03/04/1805 - 03/03/1809*
Henry Dearborn	War	02/17/1809
James Madison		*03/04/1809 - 03/03/1813*
William Eustis	War	03/07/1809-12/31/1812
James Madison (second term)		*03/04/1813 - 03/03/1817*
Benjamin Crowninshield	Navy	12/19/1814
James Monroe		*03/04/1817 - 03/03/1821*
Benjamin Crowninshield	Navy	10/01/1818
John Quincy Adams	State	03/05/1817

PRESIDENT:	POSITION:	TERM:
James Monroe (second term)		*04/04/1821 - 03/03/1825*
John Quincy Adams	State	03/03/1825
John Quincy Adams		*03/04/1825 - 03/03/1829*
None		
Andrew Jackson		*03/04/1829 - 03/03/1837*
None (first and second term)		
Martin Van Buren		*03/04/1837 - 03/03/1841*
None		
William Henry Harrison		*03/04/1841 - 04/04/1841*
Daniel Webster	State	03/05/1841
John Tyler		*04/06/1841 - 03/03/1845*
Daniel Webster	State	05/09/1843
David Henshaw	Navy	*07/24/1843 - 02/15/1844*
James K. Polk		*03/04/1845 - 03/03/1849*
George Bancroft	Navy	03/10/1845 - 09/09/1846
Zachary Taylor		*03/04/1849 - 07/09/1850*
None		
Millard Fillmore		*07/10/1850 - 03/03/1853*
Daniel Webster	State	07/22/1850 - 10/24/1852
Edward Everett	State	11/06/1852 - 03/03/1853
Franklin Pierce		*03/04/1853 - 03/03/1857*
Caleb Cushing	Attorney General	03/07/1853
James Buchanan		*03/04/1857-03/03/1861*
Caleb Cushing	Attorney General	03/06/1857
Abraham Lincoln (first and second term)		*03/04/1861 - 04/15/1865*
None		
Andrew Johnson		*04/15/1865 - 03/03/1869*
None		

PRESIDENT:	POSITION:	TERM:
U. S. Grant:		*03/04/1869 - 03/03/1873*
George S. Boutwell	Treasury	03/11/1869
Ebenezer R. Hoar	Attorney General	03/05/1869 - 06/23/1870
U. S. Grant (second term)		*03/04/1873 - 03/03/1877*
George S. Boutwell	Treasury	03/17/1873
William M. Richardson	Treasury	03/17/1873 - 06/02/1874
Rutherford B. Hayes		*03/04/1877 - 03/03/1881*
Charles Devens	Attorney General	03/12/1877
James A. Garfield		*03/04/1881 - 09/19/1881*
Charles Devens	Attorney General	03/05/1881
Henry A. French	Treasury (Asst. Sect)	03/04/1881 (interim)
Chester A. Arthur		*09/20/1881 - 03/03/1885*
Henry A. French	Treasury (Ad Interim)	09/08/1884
		10/28/1884
Grover Cleveland		*03/04/1885 - 03/03/1889*
William C. Endicott	War	03/06/1885
Benjamin Harrison		*03/04/1889 - 03/03/1893*
William F. Wharton	State (Asst. Sect)	06/04/1892 - 06/29/1892
	(Ad Interim)	02/23/1893
William G. Endicott	War	03/05/1893
Grover Cleveland (second term)		*03/04/1893 - 03/03/1897*
William F. Wharton	State (Asst. Sect).	03/06/1893 (interim)
Richard Olney	Attorney General	03/06/1893 - 06/08/1895
Richard Olney	State	06/08/1895
William McKinley		*03/04/1897 - 03/03/1901*
Richard Olney	State	03/05/1897
John D. Long	Navy	03/05/1897
William McKinley (second term)		*03/04/1901 - 09/14/1901*
John D. Long	Navy	03/05/1901
Theodore Roosevelt		*09/14/1901 - 03/03/1905*
John D. Long	Navy	04/29/1902

PRESIDENT:	POSITION:	TERM:
Theodore Roosevelt (first term continued)		*09/14/1901 - 03/03/1905*
William H. Moody	Navy	04/29/1902-07/01/1904
William H. Moody	Attorney General	07/01/1904
Theodore Roosevelt (second term)		*03/04/1905 - 03/03/1909*
William H. Moody	Attorney General	03/06/1905 - 12/12/1906
George von L. Meyer	Postmaster General	03/04/1907
William Howard Taft		*03/04/1909 - 03/03/1913*
George von L. Meyer	Postmaster General	03/05/1909
Frank H. Hitchcock	Postmaster General	03/05/1909 - 03/05/1913
George von L. Meyer	Navy	03/05/1909 - 03/05/1913
Woodrow Wilson (first and second term)		*03/04/1913 - 03/03/1921*
None		
Warren G. Harding		*03/04/1921 - 08/02/1923*
John W. Weeks	War	03/05/1921
Calvin Coolidge		*08/03/1923 - 03/03/1925*
John W. Weeks	War	Retained
Calvin Coolidge (second term)		*03/04/1925 - 03/03/1929*
John W. Weeks	War	10/13/1925 - 03/03/1929
William F. Whiting	Commerce	08/21/1928 - 12/11/1928
Herbert C. Hoover		*03/04/1929 - 03/03/1933*
Charles F. Adams	Navy	03/05/1929 - 03/04/1933
William F. Whiting	Commerce	03/05/1929
Franklin D. Roosevelt (first - fourth terms)		*03/04/1933 - 04/12/1945*
Frances Perkins	Labor	03/04/1933 - 06/01/1945
Harry S. Truman		*04/12/1945 - 01/20/1949*
Maurice J. Tobin	Labor (Ad Interm)	08/13/48
Harry S. Truman (second terms)		*01/20/1949 - 01/20/1953*
Maurice J. Tobin	Labor	02/01/1949 - 01/20/1953
Dwight D. Eisenhower		*01/20/1953 - 01/20/1957*
Sinclair Weeks	Commerce	01/21/1953

PRESIDENT:	POSITION:	TERM:
Dwight D Eisenhower (second term)		*01/20/1957 - 01/20/1961*
Sinclair Weeks	Commerce	11/13/1958
Christian A. Herter	State	04/21/1959 - 01/20/1961
John F. Kennedy		*01/21/1961 - 11/22/1963*
Robert F. Kennedy	Attorney General	01/21/1961
Lyndon B. Johnson		*11/22/1963 - 01/20/1965*
Robert F. Kennedy	Attorney General	10/04/1964
Lyndon B. Johnson (second term)		*01/20/1965 - 01/20/1969*
Lawrence F. O'Brien	Postmaster General	09/01/1965 - 04/23/1968
Richard M. Nixon		*01/20/1969 - 01/20/1973*
John A. Volpe	Transportation	01/20/1969 - 01/18/1973
Elliot L. Richardson	HEW	06/15/1970
Richard M. Nixon (second term)		*01/20/1973 - 08/09/1974*
Elliot L. Richardson	HEW	02/02/1973
Elliot L. Richardson	Defense	01/29/1973 - 05/26/1973
Elliot L. Richardson	Attorney General	05/23/1973 - 10/20/1973
Gerald L. Ford		*08/09/1974 - 01/20/1977*
Elliot L. Richardson	Commerce	12/11/1975 - 01/20/1977
James Earl Carter		*01/20/1977 - 01/20/1981*
None		
Ronald Reagan		*01/20/1981 - 01/20/1985*
Margaret Heckler	Health & Human Services	03/03/1983
Ronald Reagan (second term)		*01/20/1985 - 01/20/1989*
Margaret Heckler	Health & Human Services	12/12/1985

UNITED STATES DEPARTMENT OF STATE

SECRETARIES OF STATE:	TERM:	PRESIDENT:
Pickering, Timothy	08/20/1795 - 05/12/1800	Washington
Adams, John Quincy	03/05/1817 - 03/03/1825	Monroe
Webster, Daniel	03/05/1841 05/08/1843 07/22/1850 - 10/24/1852	Harrison Tyler Fillmore
Everett, Edward	11/06/1852 - 03/03/1853	Fillmore
Olney, Richard	06/08/1895 - 03/05/1897	Cleveland
Herter, Christian A.	04/21/1959 - 01/20/1961	Eisenhower

*Note: Lincoln Levi was interim Secretary of State for one day: 03/05/1801.
William Wharton served as interim Secretary of State on two occasions: June 04 to
June 29, 1892 and February 24 to March 06, 1893.*

UNITED STATES DEPARTMENT OF STATE OFFICIALS

OFFICIAL:	POSITION:	TERM:
Abramowitz, Morton L.	Ass. Sec. Intelligence/Research	1985-1989
Barbour, Walworth	Career Ambassador	08/11/1969
Bell, David Elliott	Administrator/ International Development	1961-1966
Benson, Lucy Wilson	Under Sec International Security Affairs	1977-1980
Bohlen, Charles E.	Counselor	1947-1949
		1951-1953
	Career Ambassador	06/24/1960
Bundy, Harvey H.	Assistant Secretary	1931-1933
Cabot, John M.	Asst. Sec. Inter-American Affairs	1953-1954
Chayes, Abram	Assistant Secretary/Legal Advisor	1961-1964
Doebelle, Edith H. J.	Chief of Protocol	1978-1979
Doebelle, Evan S.	Chief of Protocol	1977-1978
Faunce, Anthony Dep.	Inspector Genl/Foreign Assistance	1969-1973

OFFICIAL:	POSITION:	TERM:
Gilbert, Carl J.	U.S. Trade Representative	1969-1971
Grew, Joseph	Under Secretary of State	1924-1927
		1933-1936
		1944-1945
Hale, Charles	Assistant Secretary	1872-1873
Hawkins, Harry C.	Dir. Foreign Service Institute	1950-1952
Herter, Christian A.	Under Secretary of State	1957-1959
	U. S. Trade Representative	1962-1966
Hughes, Robert John	Assistant Sect. Public Affairs	1982-1985
Ilchman, Alice Stone	Asst. Sec. Educational & Cultural Affairs	1978
Lodge, Henry Cabot	Ambassador at Large	1967-1968
Moore, Jonathan	Ambassador at Large	1986-1989
	Dir. Bureau/Refugee Programs	1987-1989
Newell, Barbara W.	U.N. Ed./Scientific/ Cultural Organization	1979-1981
Phillips, William	3rd Asst. Secretary	1909
		1914-1917
	Assistant Secretary	1917-1920
	Under Secretary	1922-1924
		1933-1936
Peirce, Herbert H.D.	3rd Asst. Secretary	1901-1906
Porter, William J.	Under Sect. Political Affairs	1973-1974
Quincy, Josiah	Assistant Secretary	1893
Richardson, Elliot	Under Secretary	1969-1970
	Ambassador at Large	1977-1980
Sayre, Francis Bowes	Assistant Secretary	1933-1939
Shaw, G. Howland	Assistant Secretary	1941-1944
Springsteen, George S. J.	Executive Secretary	1974-1976
Webster, Daniel Fletcher	Chief Clerk	1841-1843
Wharton, William F.	Assistant Secretary	1889-1893

DIPLOMATS

Symbols & Abbreviations:

AE/P	Ambassador Extraordinary & Plenipotentiary	EE	Envoy Extraordinary
		Comm	Commissioner
Amb	Ambassador	MP	Minister Plenipotentiary
C	Career Foreign Service Officer	MR	Minister Resident
CdA	Charge d'Affaires	NC	Non Career

OFFICIAL	COUNTRY	TITLE	TERM
Adams, Charles Francis	United Kingdom	EE/MP	03/1861 - 05/1868
Adams, John	Netherlands	MP	01/1781 - 03/1788
	United Kingdom	MP	02/1785 - 02/1788
Adams, John Quincy	Netherlands	MP	05/1794-06/1797
	Portugal	MP	05/1796
			Did not serve
	Germany	MP	06/1797 - 05/1801
	Russia	MP	06/1809 - 04/1814
	United Kingdom	EE/MP	06/1815 - 05/1817
Anderson, Larz	Belgium	EE/MP	08/1911 - 12/1912
	Japan	AE/P	11/1912 - 03/1913
Appleton, John James	Sweden	CdA	05/1826 - 08/1830
	Portugal	*Nomination rejected by Senate*	
Bancroft, George	United Kingdom	EE/MP	09/1846 - 08/1849
	Germany	EE/MP	06/1867 - 06/1874
Barbour, Walworth	Israel	C AE/P	05/1961 - 01/1973
Baylies, Francis	Argentina	CdA	01/1832 - 09/1832
Bohlen, Charles	Soviet Union	C AE/P	03/1953 - 04/1957
	Philippines	C AE/P	05/1957 - 10/1959
	France	C AE/P	09/1962 - 02/1968
Bowdoin, James	Spain	MP	11/1804 *did not go*
Brown, Phillip M.	Honduras	EE/MP	11/1908 - 02/1910
Brown, William Andreas	Israel	C AE/P	11/1988
Burlingame, Anson	Austria	EE/MP	03/1861
			Did not serve
	China	EE/MP	06/1861 - 11/1867
Cabot, John M.	Finland	C EE/MP	02/1950 - 09/1952
	Pakistan	*Took oath, did not go to post.*	

OFFICIAL	COUNTRY	TITLE	TERM
Cabot, John M	Poland	C AE/P	01/1962 - 09/1965
Capps, Edward	Greece	EE/MP	06/1920
	Montenegro	EE/MP	06/1920
Child, Richard Washburn	Italy	AE/P	05/1921 - 01/1924
Collins, Patrick Andrew	United Kingdom	NC/CG	05/1893 - 05/1897
Coolidge, John Gardner	Nicaragua	EE/MP	06/1908 - 11/1908
Coolidge, T. Jefferson	France	EE/MP	05/1892 - 05/1893
Conant, James B.	Germany	AE/P	05/1955 - 02/1957
Crocker, Edward S. 2nd	Iraq	C AE/P	09/1948 - 06/1952
Curley, James M.	Poland	*1933 Nomination withdrawn.*	
Cushing, Caleb	China	EE/MP/	
		COM	05/1843 - 08/1844
	Spain	EE/MP	01/1874 - 04/1877
Dana, Francis	Russia	Minister	12/1780 - 09/1783
Dana, Richard Henry Jr.	United Kingdom	*1876 Rejected by Senate*	
Dearborn, Henry A. Sr.	Portugal	EE/MP	05/1822 - 06/1824
Dodge, H. Percival	El Salvador	C EE/MP	07/1907 - 02/1909
	Honduras	C EE/MP	07/1907 - 02/1909
	Morocco	C EE/MP	05/1909 -0 7/1910
	Panama	C EE/MP	07/1911-06/1913
	Yugoslavia	C EE/MP	07/1919 - 03/1926
	Denmark	C EE/MP	02/1926 - 03/1930
Donovan, Eileen	Barbardos	C AE/P	07/1969 - 08/1974
Draper, William F.	Italy	AE/P	04/1897 - 06/1900
Dresel, Ellis Loring	Germany	CdA	11/1921 - 04/1922
Erving, George W.	Spain	MP	08/1814 - 05/1819
	Turkey	Cd/A	*Not commissioned*
Eustis, William	Netherlands	EE/MP	12/1814 - 05/1818
Everett, Alexander H.	Netherlands	CdA	06/1818 - 04/1824
	Spain	EE/MP	03/1825 - 08/1829
	China	Comm	03/1845 - 06/1847
Everett, Edward	United Kingdom	EE/MP	09/1841 - 08/1845
	China	Comm	03/1843
			declined appointment
Fay, Theodore S.	Switzerland	MR	06/1853 - 07/1861
Forbes, John M.	Argentina	CdA	03/1825 - 06/1831
Forbes, W. Cameron	Japan	AE/P	06/1930 - 03/1932

Official	Country	Title	Term
Galbraith, J. Kenneth	India	AE/P	03/1961 - 07/1963
Grew, Joseph C.	Denmark	C EE/MP	04/1920 - 10/1921
	Switzerland	C EE/MP	09/1921 - 03/1924
	Turkey	Amb	05/1927 - 03/1932
	Japan	C AE/P	02/1932 - 08/1941
Guild, Curtis	Russia	AE/P	04/1911 - 04/1913
Hale, Charles	Egypt	Agt/CG	05/1864 - 05/1870
Harrington, Julian F.	Panama	C AE/P	07/1955 - 07/1960
Heard, Augustine	Korea	MR/CG	01/1890 - 06/1893
Heckler, Margaret	Ireland	AE/P	12/1985 - 08/1989
Henderson, Douglas	Bolivia	C AE/P	11/1963-08/1968
Kennedy, Joseph P.	United Kingdom	AE/P	01/1938-10/1940
King, Rufus	United Kingdom	MP	05/1796-05/1803
			05/1825-06/1826
Lawrence, Abbott	United Kingdom	EE/MP	08/1849-10/1852
Lodge, Henry Cabot	Vietnam	AE/P	08/1963-06/1964
			07/1965-04/1967
	Germany	AE/P	04/1968-01/1969
	United Nation	AE/P Rep	01/1953-09/1960
Loring, George B.	Portugal	MR/CG	03/1889-05/1890
Lowell, James Russell	Spain	EE/MP	06/1877-05/1880
	United Kingdom	EE/MP	01/1880-05/1885
McAuliffe, Eugene V.	Hungary	C AE/P	03/1975-03/1978
Meyer, George Von L.	Italy	AE/P	12/1900-04/1905
	Russia	AE/P	03/1905-01/1907
Motley, J. Lothrop	Austria	EE/MP	08/1861-06/1867
	United Kingdom	EE/MP	04/1869-12/1870
Parker, Peter	China	Comm	08/1845-08/1857
Payson, Charles	Denmark	CdA	06/1881-02/1882
Phillips, William	Netherlands	C EE/MP	03/1920-04/1922
	Luxembourg	C EE/MP	05/1920-04/1922
	Belgium	C AE/P	02/1924-03/1927
	Luxembourg	C AE/P	02/1924-03/1927
	Canada	C EE/MP	02/1927-12/1929
	Italy	C AE/P	08/1936-10/1941
Peirce, Henry A.	Hawaii	MR	05/1869-09/1877
Peirce, Herbert H. D.	Norway	EE/MP	06/1906-05/1911

Official	Country	Title	Term
Porter, William J.	Algeria		11/1961-07/1965
	Korea	C AE/P	06/1967-08/1971
	Saudi Arabia	C AE/P	12/1975-05/1977
	Canada	C AE/P	02/1974-12/1975
Ratshesky, Abraham C.	Czechoslovakia	EE/MP	01/1930-05/1932
Reischauer, Edwin O.	Japan	AE/P	03/1961-08/1966
Richardson, Elliot	United Kingdom	AE/P	02/1975-01/1976
Russell, Thomas	Venezuela	MR	04/1874-01/1877
Rutter, Peter	Ghana	C CdA	04/1957-06/1957
			Not commissioned
Ryan, Robert J.	Niger	C AE/P	07/1964-08/1968
Stearns, Monteagle	Cote D'Ivoire	C AE/P	10/1976-07/1979
Stebbins, Henry E.	Nepal	C AE/P	09/1959-06/1966
	Uganda	C AE/P	06/1966-09/1969
Stimpson, Harry F. Jr.	Paraguay	C AE/P	09/1959-03/1961
Stimson, Frederic J.	Argentina	AE/P	10/1914-04/1921
Thayer, Harry E. T.	Singapore	C AE/P	10/1980-06/1984
Torbet, Horace G. Jr.	Somalia	C AE/P	02/1962-08/1965
	Bulgaria	AE/P	10/1970-10/1973
Tudor, William	Brazil	CdA	06/1827-03/1830
Volpe, John A.	Italy	AE/P	02/1973-01/1977
Washburn, Albert H.	Austria	EE/MP	10/1922-04/1930
Washburn, John D.	Switzerland	MR/CG	
		(EE/MP)	03/1889-08/1892
Wheaton, Henry	Germany	EE/MP	03/1835-07/1837
White, Robert E.	Paraguay	C AE/P	10/1977-01/1980
	El Salvador	C AE/P	03/1980-02/1981
Wigglesworth, Richard B.	Canada	AE/P	10/1958-10/1960
Willauer, Whiting	Honduras	AE/P	02/1954-03/1958
	Costa Rica	AE/P	04/1958-04/1961
Williams, George Fred	Greece	EE/MP	12/1913-09/1914
	Montenegro	EE/MP	12/1913-09/1914
Williams, George W.	Haiti	MR/CG	1885 *Did not serve*
Wolcott, Roger	Italy	AE/P	07/1900
			Declined
Woodbury, Charles L.	Bolivia	CdA	1853 *Did not serve*

LIST OF WORKS CONSULTED

The Adams Family:

Nagel, Paul C. *Descent From Glory–Four Generations of the Adams Family.* Oxford University Press, 1983.

Ferling, John. *John Adams Life.* Knoxville: University of Tennessee Press, 1992.

MCullough, David. *John Adams.* New York: Simon & Schuster, 2001.

Hargreaves, Mary W. M. *The Presidency of John Quincy Adams.* University of Kansas Press, 1985.

Nagel, Paul C. *John Quincy Adams, A Public Life, A Private Life.* New York: Alfred A. Knopf, 1997.

Bancroft, George:

Handlin, Lillian. *The Intellectual as Democrat.* New York: Harper & Row, 1984.

Banks, Nathaniel Prentice:

Harrington, Fred Harvey. *Fighting Political Major General N. P. Banks.* Philadelphia: University of Pennsylvania Press, 1948.

Hollandsworth, James G. Pretense of Glory *The Life of General Nathaniel P. Banks.* Baton Rouge, Louisiana: Louisiana State University Press, 1998.

Collins, Patrick:

Curran, Michael Philip. *Life of Patrick Collins.* Norwood, Massachusetts: Norwood Press, 1906.

Coolidge, Calvin:

Fuess, Claude M. *Calvin Coolidge, the Man from Vermont.* Boston: Little, Brown, 1940.

Cox, Archibald:

Gormley, Ken. *Archibald Cox: Conscience of a Nation.* New York: Da Capo Press, 1999.

Cushing, Caleb:

Fuess, Claude M. *The Life of Caleb Cushing*. New York: Harcourt, Brace & Co. New York, 1923.

Everett, Edward:

Frothingham, Paul Revere. *Edward Everett, Orator and Statesman*. Boston, New York: Houghton Mifflin Co., 1925.

Gerry, Elbridge:

Billias, George Athan. *Elbridge Gerry, Founding Father and Republican Statesman*. New York: McGraw-Hill, 1976.

Grew, Joseph C.:

Henrichs, Waldo C., Jr. *American Ambassador Joseph W. Grew and the Development of the United States Diplomatic Tradition*. Boston: Little, Brown, 1966.

Kennedy, Joseph P.:

Smith, Amanda ed. *Hostage to Fortune: The Letters of Joseph P Kennedy*. New York: Viking Press, 2001.

Koskoff, David E. *Joseph P. Kennedy: A Life and Times*. Englewood Cliffs, New Jersey: Prentice-Hall, 1974.

Kennedy, John F.:

O'Donnell, Kenneth P., Powers, David F., with Joe McCarthy. *"Johnny, We Hardly Knew Ye" Memories of John Fitzgerald Kennedy*. Boston-Toronto: Little, Brown, 1970.

Burner, David, edited by Oscar Handlin. *John F. Kennedy and a New Generation*. New York. Harper Collins, 1988.

Knox, Henry:

Brooks, Noah. *A Soldier of the Revolution*. Noah Books: 1990. Reprint of the 1990 ed. published by Putnam, New York.

Lodge, Henry Cabot (1850-1924):

Garraty, John Arthur. *Henry Cabot Lodge, a Biography*. New York: Knopf, 1953.

Lodge, Henry Cabot (1902-1985):

Miller, William J. (William Johnson). *Henry Cabot Lodge, a Biography.* New York: Heineman, 1967.

O'Neill, Thomas P., Jr.:

O'Neill, Thomas P., Jr. *Man of the House: The Life and Political Memoirs of Speaker Tip O'Neill (with William Novak).* New York: Random House, 1987.

Farrell, John Aloysius. *Tip O'Neill, A Biography.* Boston, Little, Brown and Company, 2001.

Pickering, Timothy:

Clarfield, Gerard H. *Timothy Pickering: American Diplomat.* University of Pittsburgh Press, 1980.

Sedgwick, Theodore:

Welch, Richard F. *Theodore Segwick, Federalist.* Middletown, Connecticut: Wesleyan University Press, 1965.

Story, Joseph:

Dunne, Gerald T. *Justice Story and the Rise of the Supreme Court.* New York: Simon and Schuster, 1970.

Sumner, Charles:

David, Herbert Donald. *Charles Sumner and the Coming of the Civil War.* New York: Fawcett Columbine, 1960.

Webster, Daniel:

Baxter, Maurice G. *Daniel Webster and the Union.* Cambridge, Massachusetts: Belknap Press of Harvard University Press, 1984.

Baxter, Maurice G. *One and Inseparable Daniel Webster and the Union.* Cambridge, Massachusetts: Belknap Press of Harvard University Press, 1984

Wilson, Henry:

Abbott, Richard H. *Cobbler in Congress: The Life of Henry Wilson 1812-1875.* University of Kansas Press, 1972.

The Presidency:

The Presidents. Funk & Wagner Special Edition. Indianapolis, Indiana: The Curtis Publishing Company, 1989.

Martin, Fenton S., Goehlert U. *American Presidents: A Bibliography.* Washington, D.C.: Congressional Quarterly, 1987.

Nelson, Michael ed. *The Presidency and the Political System.* Washington, D.C.: Congressional Quarterly Press, 1984.

Vice Presidency:

Healy, Diana Dixon. *American Vice Presidents: Our First Forty-Three.* New York: Athenaeum, 1984.

Barzman, Sol. *Madmen and Geniuses: The Vice Presidents of the United States.* Chicago: Follett, 1974.

The Supreme Court of the United States:

Hall, Kermit L., editor in chief. *The Oxford Companion to the Supreme Court of the United States.* New York: Oxford, 1992.

Abraham, Henry J. *Justices and Presidents.* Cambridge: Oxford University Press, 1985.

The Senate of the United States:

Swanson, Roy. *The United States Senate 1787-1801.* Washington, D.C.: U.S. Government Printing Office, 1989.

Baker, Richard A. *The Senate of the United States; A Biographical History.* Malabar, Florida: R. E. Krieger, 1988.

The House of Representatives of the United States:

Parker, Glen R. *Studies of Congress.* Washington, D.C.: Congressional Quarterly Press, 1985.

Currie, James T. *The United States House of Representatives.* Malabar, Florida: R. E. Krieger, 1988.

Speakership:

Peters, Ronald M. Jr. *The American Speakership: The Office in Historical Perspective.* Baltimore: The Johns Hopkins University Press. 2nd edition, 1997.

Kennon, Donald R. *The Speakers of the U.S. House of Representatives: A Bibliography, 1789-1984.* Baltimore: Johns Hopkins University Press, 1986.

Congress:

A Bicentennial Directory of the United States Congress 1774-1989. Washington, D.C.: U.S. Printing Office, 1989.

The Department of State:

Principle Officers of the Department of State and the United States Chief of Missions, 1778-1990. Washington, D.C.: U.S. Government Printing Office.

Plischke, Elmer. *Diplomats and Their Mission, A Profile of American Diplomatic Emissaries since 1776.* Washington, D.C.: American Enterprise Institute of Public Policy, 1975.

Bending, Andrew H. *The Making of Foreign Policy.* Washington. D.C.: Potomac Books Inc, 1966.

Presidential Cabinets:

Cohen, Jeffrey E. *The Politics of the U.S. Cabinet.* Pittsburgh: The University of Pittsburgh Press, 1988.

Political Parties:

Kayden, Xandra, Mahe, Eddie, Jr. *The Party Goes On: The Persistence of the Two-Party System in the United States.* New York: Basic Books, 1985.

Massachusetts History:

Records of the Governor and Company of the Massachusetts Bay in New England. 5 volumes 1628-1686. Ed. by Nathaniel Bradstreet Shurtleff, M.D. Boston: The Press of William White, Printer to the Commonwealth, 1853-1854.

Morison, Samuel Eliot. *Builders of the Bay Colony.* Boston: Houghton Mifflin Co, 1958.

American History:

Ratner, Sidney; Soltow, James H.; and Sylla, Richard. *The Evolution of the American Economy.* New York. Basic Books, 1979.

Morison, Samuel Eliot. *The Oxford History of the American People.* New York: New American Library, 1972.

Norton, Katzman, Escott, Chaudaoff, Paterson and Tuttle. *A People and a Nation.* Boston: Houghton Mifflin Company. 4th ed, 1996.

North, Douglas C. *The Economic Growth of the United States 1790-1860.* W. W. Norton & Co., 1966.

Freidel, Frank & Pencak, Williams eds. *The White House. The First Hundred Years.* Boston: Northeastern University Press, 1994.

McCormick, Richard P. *The Presidential Game.* New York: Oxford University Press, 1982.

Wright, Conrad Edick ed. *Massachusetts and the New Nation.* Boston: Massachusetts Historical Society, 1992.

Blum, Morgan, Rose, Schlesinger, Jr., Stampp and Woodward. *The American Experience. A History of the United States since 1865.* New York: Harcourt Brace Jovanovich, 1978.

Ehrenhalt, Alan. *The United States of Ambition.* New York: Times Books, 1991.

Of Particular Note:

Baltzell, E. Digby. *Puritan Boston & Quaker Philadelphia.* New Brunswick, New Jersey: Transaction Publishers, 1966.

General References:

The Encyclopedia of American Facts and Dates. 8th edition. New York: Harper and Row, 1987.

The New York Public Library Desk Reference. 2nd edition. New York: Prentice Hall General Reference, 1993.

Encyclopedia Britannica. 2004 Ultimate Reference Suite DVD.

Index